GOREN'S EASY STEPS TO WINNING BRIDGE

This TMI-Watts self-tutoring course presents the fundamental concepts of contract bridge, **IN ACCORDANCE WITH THE 1963 RULES**, for the student who is completely unacquainted with the game.

It is not intended that this course should teach the more advanced aspects of contract bridge; consequently, there is no assertion of completeness. However, after completing this programed course, the student should have gained sufficient knowledge of the game to enjoy participating in rubber contract bridge. He should also have the necessary foundation to begin a more advanced study of the game.

Specific topics include: the card deck, the cut and deal, number and rank of suits, trick-taking, trumping, bidding, responses to openers, rebids, opening leads to suit and No Trump contracts, the finesse, playing for a drop, scoring, and proprieties.

The course includes reference material, exercises, tests, a glossary, and an index. Unit 12 contains a set of specially designed charts directing the step-by-step operations of bidding, responding, and play of the hand under any condition that may arise. They are arranged in convenient form for use at the bridge table.

The course consists of 1438 frames and takes from 15 to 20 hours to complete.

IN ACCORDANCE WITH THE 1963 RULES

PROGRAMED TEXTBOOK

Self-Tutoring Course by TMI-WATTS

FIRST EDITION

FRANKLIN WATTS, INC.

575 Lexington Avenue • New York 22

221 SAN PEDRO DR., N.E.
ALBUQUERQUE, NEW MEXICO

FIRST PRINTING OF FIRST EDITION

PATENT PENDING

Library of Congress Catalog Card Number 63-21364

Printed in the U.S.A. by the Polygraphic Company of America

ACKNOWLEDGEMENTS

CHARLES H. GOREN *is one of the most successful bridge players in the United States and a recognized authority wherever the game is played. TMI gratefully acknowledges the assistance of Mr. Goren in the preparation of this course and for his review of the final manuscript. Mr. Goren's fame in bridge circles lies in his invention of the bidding system called the point count method, which carries his name. In the years following World War II, this method of determining the strength of a bridge hand grew rapidly in popularity because of its simplicity and greater accuracy over other methods. It was soon credited with having standardized the game of bridge throughout the world. This TMI-Watts course is based on the Goren point count method. In 1936 Mr. Goren became the 13th Life Master of the American Contract Bridge League, and by 1957 he had won every honor and trophy that bridge has to offer, including 37 national championships. In 1958 he and his partner were winners of the Masters Pairs Championship. Mr. Goren received his education at McGill University in Montreal, Canada, and, prior to devoting himself completely to the field of contract bridge, he was a practicing lawyer in Philadelphia. He is the author of numerous books on bridge, including the best-selling Goren's New Contract Bridge Complete. His syndicated column appears in more than 200 publications.*

W. L. Graves served as TMI subject matter expert during the preparation of the course. Mr. Graves has played and studied bridge for the past 35 years. From 1953 until 1956 he directed the Taos Duplicate Bridge Club at Taos, New Mexico. During this same period, he taught bridge to several different groups of players ranging from beginners to advanced players. Mr. Graves has won trophies in duplicate bridge tournaments in both New Mexico and Washington, D. C. He has a Master's rating in the American Contract Bridge League and is an enthusiastic student of the Goren method.

D. E. Cornell, III, Executive Vice-President of TMI, performed an initial edit of the program and, with the assistance of Edward Rickert, developed the charts for the opening bid, responses, and opening leads. Mr. Cornell and Dr. James L. Evans developed the charts for the play of the hand, rebids, and ruffing.

Donald Tosti, TMI Program Editor, had supervisory and editorial responsibility for the technical aspects of programing this material.

Special acknowledgement is due the following TMI staff members: Edward Rickert and Norma Law, who were principally involved in the construction, development, and validation of this course; Paul C. Thomas, who contributed during the initial stage of the course; Marge McMinn and Sharon Dixon, artists; Jane Angell, Rita Dickey, Sheila Fisher, Thomas Harshbarger, and Jack Malm, editors.

This TMI-Watts self-tutoring course was prepared under the general programing direction of Lloyd E. Homme, Ph. D., President of TMI, and James L. Evans, Ph. D., Vice-President of TMI.

CONTENTS

PROGRAMED LEARNING

Learning should be fun. However, in the early stages of learning a subject, students make many mistakes. As a result, they often conclude that they do not like the subject. They would be more correct to conclude that they do not like to make errors.

For a long time, educators, psychologists, and people in general thought that it was impossible to learn without errors. Many teachers felt that making errors was, in some mysterious way, "good for you." This idea is now outdated. Recent developments in psychology and education have demonstrated that students can proceed to mastery of a subject with a negligible number of errors along the route. For this to happen, however, the material from which the student learns must be carefully prepared, or "programed," in a special way. The basic idea is that the most efficient, pleasant, and permanent learning occurs when the student proceeds through a course by a large number of small, easy-to-take steps. This is precisely what your self-tutoring course has been designed to do.

This course has been constructed on the basis of learning principles of recognized soundness. It benefits both the student and the instructor. It provides the student with the advantages of a private tutor; at the same time, it frees the instructor from routine lecturing, testing, scoring, and grading duties. This permits a much more efficient use of classroom time than has been possible previously. Students can come to class with a firm grasp of the fundamental concepts and operations in a topic. This permits the instructor to devote more time to laboratory work, enlightened class discussion, and implications and relationships with other areas. New developments in the field or topics of special interest may also be explored.

An examination of the learning situation within this course reveals fundamental differences from conventional study procedures.

First, the student goes through a carefully graded sequence of material which has been demonstrated to produce learning. With conventional textbook and lecture procedures, it is impossible for the writer or teacher to assess accurately at what point the student makes errors or "loses the point." Programed presentations, however, have been evaluated experimentally. This course has been through a series of thorough revisions on the basis of responses actually made by students. In this way, ambiguous statements and instructions have been removed and additional examples have been added to difficult portions. Such a step-by-step analysis and revision of the learning sequence is not possible in the case of textbooks and lectures.

Second, the use of the self-tutoring course insures active participation in the learning process by the student. Since each step in a course requires one or more specific written responses, the instructor can be confident at the end of a course that the student has been responding actively to the material. No comparable assurance is possible when a student has merely attended a lecture or read a textbook.

Third, the self-tutoring course provides the student with immediate confirmation of the correctness of his answers. In this way, the confidence of the student grows, since he can see that he is correct on almost every response. Such rapid confirmation is not possible in the nonprogramed situation, unless the student has a private tutor. Homework problems and test results simply cannot be scored by the teacher and returned in time to be really effective in helping the student master a topic.

Fourth, the student is provided with a method of proceeding at a rate of his own choosing. The quicker student need no longer be held back. On the other hand, the more methodical student can take as much time as he needs without being embarrassed by the fact that others are proceeding at a more rapid rate. When occasional mistakes are made, the student can correct them in private.

In summary, this course provides the student with a carefully prepared, experimentally tested sequence to proceed through as he gains competence in the topic he is studying. During the learning, he will be responding actively and receiving immediate confirmation of the correctness of his responses. He can proceed as slowly or as rapidly as he wishes. The instructor can be relieved of the more routine aspects of teaching, and be freed to review and elaborate upon the basic understanding of the topic which the self-tutoring course will provide.

Of particular interest to the staff of TMI-Watts are the reactions from students and instructors to this method of learning. Comments, particularly those of a critical nature, are invited. The heart of the programed approach to learning is the modification of the learning sequence on the basis of the responses of the students using the sequence. We are especially interested in the response errors made by the students.

Programed learning is an ongoing experiment in education. The TMI-Watts staff invites both instructors and students to participate in, and contribute to, this experiment. Any techniques, suggestions, or findings of methods for using the course more effectively, both in its initial presentation and on the review of the concepts presented, will be gratefully received and acknowledged.

TECHNICAL CONSIDERATIONS

TMI-Watts' self-tutoring course Goren's Easy Steps To Winning Bridge was comprehensively validated in TMI's Learning Laboratory. Results indicated that the material presented in this course is sufficient for reasonably adequate performance at the bridge table. An overall mean score of 18 per cent on the pre-test was raised to an end achievement of 86 per cent correct on the final post-test.

After completion of this introductory course, students were able to play an acceptable game with hands of bridge as monitored from their first hand by a Life Master and bridge teacher. However, in order that the student may increase his proficiency in specific subjects, he is referred to Charles H. Goren's Goren's New Contract Bridge Complete, New York: Doubleday, 1957.

It will be noted that emphasis has been given to proper bridge terminology, so that the reader may discuss the game in conventionally accepted language. To this end, a glossary has been supplied.

NOTE

Some of the units contain reference material and exercises. As you proceed through the course, you will be instructed from time to time to refer to these pages. As an aid to proper table usage, a glossary and an index are also provided. This supplementary material may be used as a refresher after completion of the course.

Pre- and Post-Tests are also included in Units 1 through 11. You should take the Pre-Test on a separate sheet of paper before you begin each unit and the Post-Test after you have completed the unit. A comparison of the results of the two tests will show the progress made in that unit. Although the number of questions varies from test to test, in computing your per cent score give equal weight to each question. If your score is above 90 per cent on any unit Pre-Test, you may skip that unit.

Also included with the course are a series of eight charts in Unit 12. These charts are to be used with Units 5, 6, 7, 8, 9, and 10. Proper use of these charts will help you master the essentials of the opening bid, responses, rebids, opening leads against suit and No Trump contracts, play of the hand, and ruffing. Instructions for the use of the charts are contained in Unit 12. Experimental validation of the course revealed that the charts may be used successfully during play.

TO THE READER

The contents of this book are arranged in a special question-and-answer sequence known as "Programed Instruction." When you turn to page 3, you will note that the small red numbers in the right-hand margin give the key to the correct answers located along the bottom margin of each page.

UNIT 1

preliminaries

This unit describes the bridge deck - the number of cards in each deck, suits, rank of the cards in a suit, and suit ranks. It also discusses partnerships and the rules of dealing, cutting, and making the deck.

PRE- AND POST-TEST

1. How many decks of cards are used at a bridge table?

2. How many cards are in a bridge deck?

3. Name the suits in the order of lowest to highest rank.

4. The players have drawn the following cards.

   ♦8 ♦J ♠K ♥5

   Do the arrows show the partnerships correctly?

5. The players have drawn the following cards.

   ♠K ♦10 ♠6 ♥10

   Indicate the partnerships.

6. The players have drawn the following cards.

   ♣J ♥5 ♠10 ♦J

   Who is the dealer?

7.  N W E S — For the figure shown, W's partner is (   ).

8.  N W E S — Players N and S are W's __________.

9.  N W E S — Who cuts for S?

10. Which shows the correct way for W to cut? a.  N W E S b.  N W E S

11.  N W E S — If E is the dealer, he deals the first card to (   ). He deals the last card to (   ).

12.  N W E S — What does E do while W is dealing?

13.  N W E S — If E was the last dealer, then (   ) is the next dealer.

14. The dealer finds the shuffled deck to his (right/left).

1 (Before you begin, take the Pre-Test for Unit 1 on page 2.)

If the answer to a question is a single word, you will see a single line like this: ________.

Washington, D. C., is the capital of the United __________. 1

2 If the answer is two or more specific words, you will see two or more lines like this: __________ __________.

Washington, D. C., is the capital of the __________ __________. 7

3 Parentheses are used when your answer should be a number, symbol, or letter.

The number coming before 10 is (   ). 3

4 You may see two or more pairs of parentheses.

The symbol for A(ce) is A.
The symbol for K(ing) is (   ).
The symbol for Q(ueen) is (   ). 2

5 This means the answer is a symbol and a word: (   ) __________.

Here are (   ) __________ out of the deck. 5

6 In some multiple choice questions, the possible answers are separated by slash marks.

You are asked which answer is correct. (There *may* be more than one.)

This course is about (hearts/bridge/rummy/poker). 6

7 Some frames will list the answers as [A/B/(both)/(neither)].

You will learn the fundamentals of [poker/hearts/(both)/(neither)].

Since neither poker nor hearts is correct, the correct answer is __________. 8

8 Some questions require that you answer in your own words.

What is the name of this course? 4

1	2	3	4	5	6	7	8
States	K Q	9	Goren's Easy Steps To Winning Bridge	3 cards	bridge	United States	(neither)

9 Occasionally you will see a multiple-choice frame like this. A chicken has: The correct answer will appear in the confirmation area like this ☐☑. The check mark in the box on the right means "two legs" is correct.	four legs.	two legs.	6
10 In some multiple-choice frames both choices may be correct. People have: If the answer is "both," the word BOTH will appear in the confirmation area.	eyes.	arms.	7
11 When neither choice in a multiple-choice frame is correct, the word NEITHER will appear in the confirmation area. Dogs have:	two legs.	six legs.	3
12 In order to get a BOTH answer correct, it is necessary to:	mark the first correct answer you read.	read both choices that are presented.	5
13 The subject of the course you are studying is ________			4
14 A table of bridge is played with four players. Which of the following represents a table of bridge players?	a. b.	c.	8
15 How many players are needed for a table of bridge?	two	three	1
16 Bridge is *ordinarily* played with two decks of cards whose backs are easily told apart. Which of the following pairs of decks would be appropriate at a bridge table?			2

1	2	3	4	5	6	7	8
NEITHER Four is correct.	BOTH	NEITHER	bridge	☐☑	☐☑	BOTH	c.

17 How many decks of cards, with backs easily told apart, are ordinarily used at a bridge table?	one	two	1

18 The two decks of cards used at a bridge table must have:	the same backs.	backs which in some way are easy to tell apart.	8

19 Here are some questions you may or may not know. If you get them all correct, you may go directly to frame 26. If you miss any, you will be taught the correct answer.
A bridge deck is an ordinary 52-card deck. 2

a. There are ( ) suits.
b. Each suit has ( ) cards.
c. The names of the suits are ______, ______, ______, and ______.

20 There are four suits in a bridge deck.

Each suit has 13 cards.

What is the total number of cards in a single bridge deck? 7

21 How many suits are there in a bridge deck?	four	three	3

22 Match the names of the suits with the figures. 5

a. Diamonds c. Spades
b. Clubs d. Hearts

1) Spades 2) 3) 4) Clubs

23 Name the suits. 4

a. b. c. d.

24 Each suit has 13 cards.

How many Spades are there in the deck? 6

1	2	3	4	5	6	7	8
[ ] [✓]	a. 4 b. 13 c. Clubs, Diamonds, Hearts, Spades	[✓] [ ]	a. Hearts b. Diamonds c. Spades d. Clubs	a. 3) b. 4) c. 1) d. 2)	13	52	[ ] [✓]

25 In a bridge deck there are 13

(Hearts/Jacks).

3

26 The 13 cards in a suit are: 2, 3, 4, 5, 6, 7, 8, 9, 10, J(ack), Q(ueen), K(ing), and A(ce).

Which of the following cards belongs in a bridge deck?

4

27  This card is called the five of Hearts.

Which of these cards is the four of Spades?

8

28 a.  This is the Queen of ___________.

b.  This is the ___________ of Hearts.

7

29 There are ( ) suits and ( ) cards in each suit.

The names of the suits are ___________, ___________, ___________, and ___________.

6

30  This is the ___________ of ___________.

2

31 *Ranking* means arranging objects in order.

If we ranked the letters of the alphabet, B would rank higher than C.

Which would rank higher than E?

A	Z

5

32 Which of these does not belong in a bridge deck?

Ace	Joker

1

1	2	3	4	5	6	7	8
☐☑	Jack of Diamonds	Hearts	NEITHER	☑☐	4 13 Clubs Diamonds Hearts Spades	a. Clubs b. Ace	☐☑

33	The cards in a suit are ranked in this way. lowest 2 3 4 5 6 7 8 9 10 J Q K A highest. J(ack) ranks higher than:	K(ing).	5.	4
34	The highest ranking card in a suit is the: 2 3 4 5 6 7 8 9 10 J Q K A	K(ing).	2.	2
35	What is the lowest ranking card in a suit?			8
36	Which of these is a higher RANKING card than ♥5?	♥J	♥A	1
37	The suits in a bridge deck are also ranked. Spades - highest Hearts - next-to-highest Diamonds - next-to-lowest Clubs - lowest Diamonds rank (higher/lower) than Hearts.			6
38	Suit ranking from lowest to highest is: ♣ ♦ ♥ ♠ . a. The lowest ranking suit is ___________. b. The highest ranking suit is ___________.			5
39	Which of the following is ranked properly from lowest to highest?	♣ ♦ ♠ ♥	♦ ♣ ♥ ♠	3
40	Bridge is a partnership game. This means that of the four players:	each plays to win over the other players.	there are two sets of partners and each partnership plays to win.	7

1	2	3	4	5	6	7	8
BOTH	NEITHER A(ce).	NEITHER ♣ ♦ ♥ ♠	☐ ☑	a. Clubs b. Spades	lower	☐ ☑	2

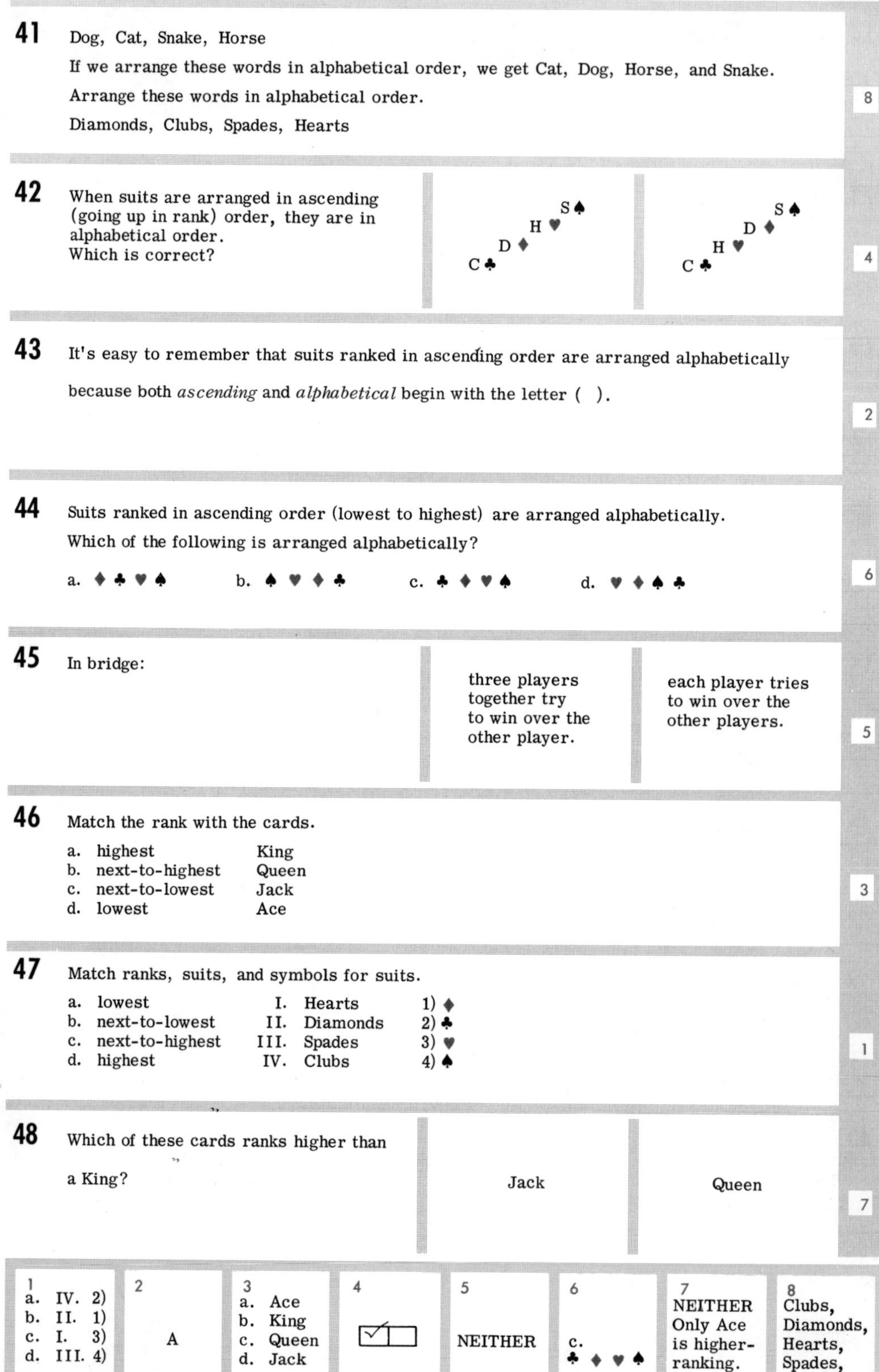

41 Dog, Cat, Snake, Horse

If we arrange these words in alphabetical order, we get Cat, Dog, Horse, and Snake.

Arrange these words in alphabetical order. 8

Diamonds, Clubs, Spades, Hearts

---

42 When suits are arranged in ascending (going up in rank) order, they are in alphabetical order.
Which is correct? 4

C ♣ D ♦ H ♥ S ♠	C ♣ H ♥ D ♦ S ♠

---

43 It's easy to remember that suits ranked in ascending order are arranged alphabetically

because both *ascending* and *alphabetical* begin with the letter ( ). 2

---

44 Suits ranked in ascending order (lowest to highest) are arranged alphabetically.

Which of the following is arranged alphabetically?

a. ♦ ♣ ♥ ♠ b. ♠ ♥ ♦ ♣ c. ♣ ♦ ♥ ♠ d. ♥ ♦ ♠ ♣ 6

---

45 In bridge: 5

three players together try to win over the other player.	each player tries to win over the other players.

---

46 Match the rank with the cards.

a. highest King
b. next-to-highest Queen
c. next-to-lowest Jack 3
d. lowest Ace

---

47 Match ranks, suits, and symbols for suits.

a. lowest I. Hearts 1) ♦
b. next-to-lowest II. Diamonds 2) ♣
c. next-to-highest III. Spades 3) ♥ 1
d. highest IV. Clubs 4) ♠

---

48 Which of these cards ranks higher than

a King? 7

Jack	Queen

1	2	3	4	5	6	7	8
a. IV. 2) b. II. 1) c. I. 3) d. III. 4)	A	a. Ace b. King c. Queen d. Jack	☑☐	NEITHER	c. ♣ ♦ ♥ ♠	NEITHER Only Ace is higher-ranking.	Clubs, Diamonds, Hearts, Spades,

49 To draw a card from a deck means to pick a card at RANDOM from a deck which is face down.

Which picture shows a card being drawn correctly? 6

50 Which of the following is ranked properly in ascending (going up in rank) order?

Spades, Hearts, Diamonds, Clubs	Clubs, Diamonds Hearts, Spades

4

51 Which is a lower RANKING suit than ♦ ?

♥	♣

3

52 Arrange the four suits in order of ascending (going up) rank. 5

53 To draw a card from a deck means to pick a card at random from a deck which is face down.
When you draw:

you can't see what card you are picking.	you can see what card you are picking.

8

54 Which of the following is RANKED properly?

♠ ♥ ♦ ♣	♣ ♦ ♠ ♥

7

55 You draw from a deck which looks like: 1

56 Suits are arranged alphabetically when they are RANKED in (ascending/descending) order.

Spades
Hearts
Diamonds
Clubs

2

1	2	3	4	5	6	7	8
☐ ☑	ascending	☐ ☑	☐ ☑	Spades, Hearts, Diamonds, Clubs	☑ ☐	☑ ☐	☑ ☐

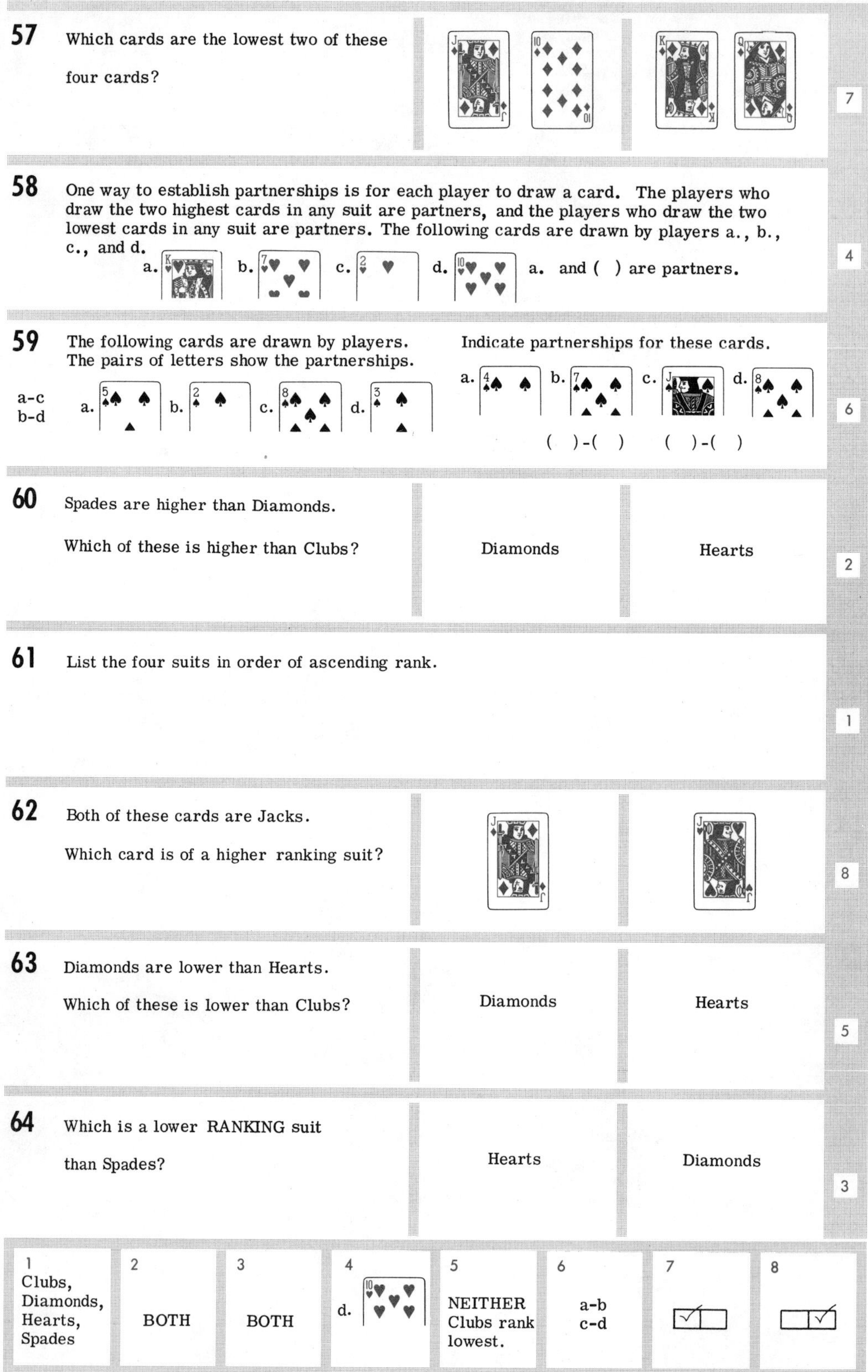

57 Which cards are the lowest two of these four cards? — 7

58 One way to establish partnerships is for each player to draw a card. The players who draw the two highest cards in any suit are partners, and the players who draw the two lowest cards in any suit are partners. The following cards are drawn by players a., b., c., and d.

a. b. c. d. a. and ( ) are partners. — 4

59 The following cards are drawn by players. The pairs of letters show the partnerships.

a-c
b-d

a. b. c. d.

Indicate partnerships for these cards.

a. b. c. d.

( )-( ) ( )-( ) — 6

60 Spades are higher than Diamonds.

Which of these is higher than Clubs?

Diamonds	Hearts

2

61 List the four suits in order of ascending rank. — 1

62 Both of these cards are Jacks.

Which card is of a higher ranking suit? — 8

63 Diamonds are lower than Hearts.

Which of these is lower than Clubs?

Diamonds	Hearts

5

64 Which is a lower RANKING suit than Spades?

Hearts	Diamonds

3

1	2	3	4	5	6	7	8
Clubs, Diamonds, Hearts, Spades	BOTH	BOTH	d.	NEITHER Clubs rank lowest.	a-b c-d		

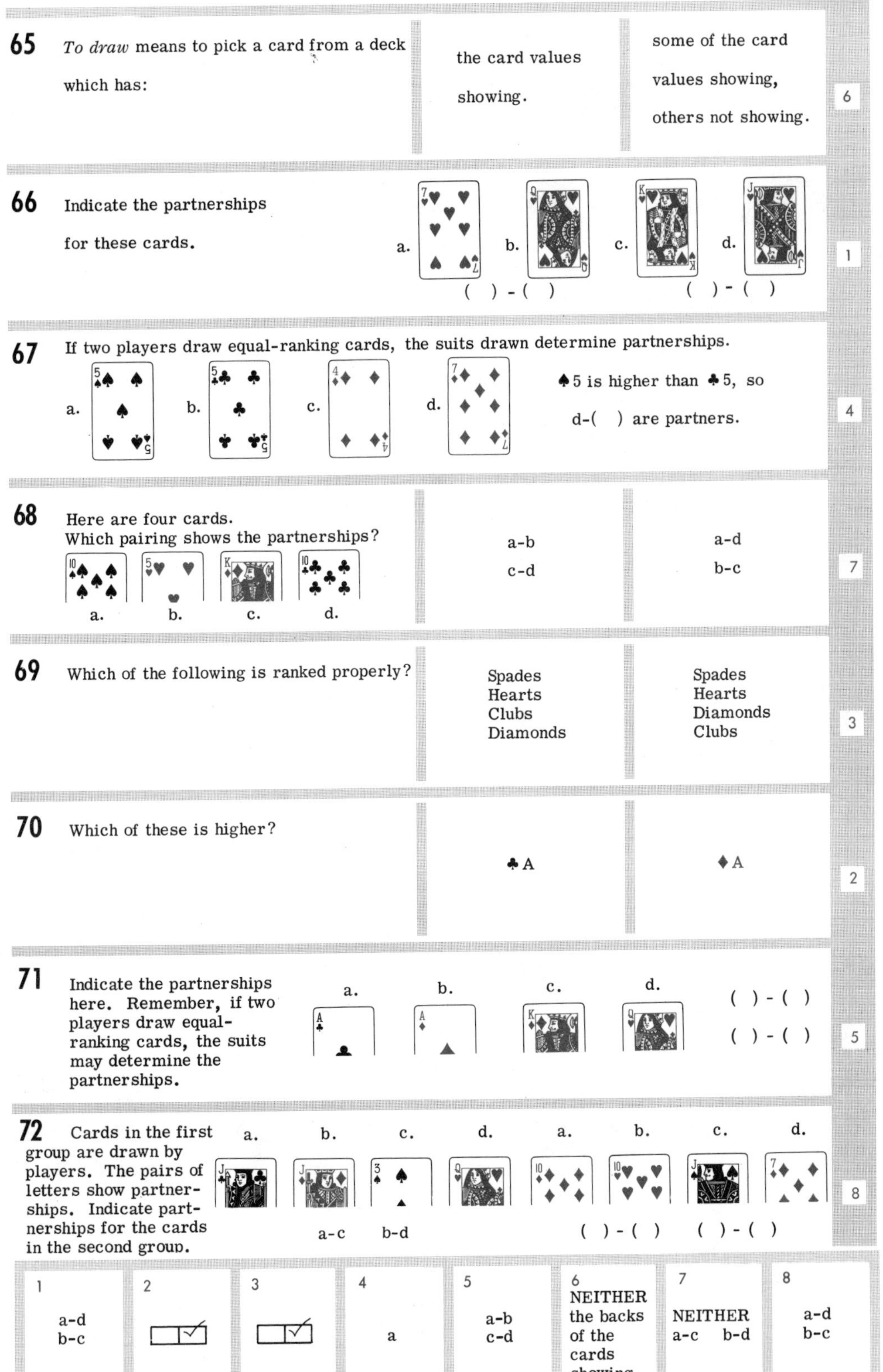

65 *To draw* means to pick a card from a deck which has:

the card values showing.	some of the card values showing, others not showing.	6

66 Indicate the partnerships for these cards.

a. b. c. d.

( ) - ( ) ( ) - ( ) 1

67 If two players draw equal-ranking cards, the suits drawn determine partnerships.

a. b. c. d.

♠5 is higher than ♣5, so d-( ) are partners. 4

68 Here are four cards.
Which pairing shows the partnerships?

a. b. c. d.

a-b c-d	a-d b-c	7

69 Which of the following is ranked properly?

Spades Hearts Clubs Diamonds	Spades Hearts Diamonds Clubs	3

70 Which of these is higher?

♣A	♦A	2

71 Indicate the partnerships here. Remember, if two players draw equal-ranking cards, the suits may determine the partnerships.

a. b. c. d.

( ) - ( )
( ) - ( ) 5

72 Cards in the first group are drawn by players. The pairs of letters show partnerships. Indicate partnerships for the cards in the second group.

a. b. c. d. a. b. c. d.

a-c b-d ( ) - ( ) ( ) - ( ) 8

1	2	3	4	5	6	7	8
a-d b-c	☐☑	☐☑	a	a-b c-d	NEITHER the backs of the cards showing.	NEITHER a-c b-d	a-d b-c

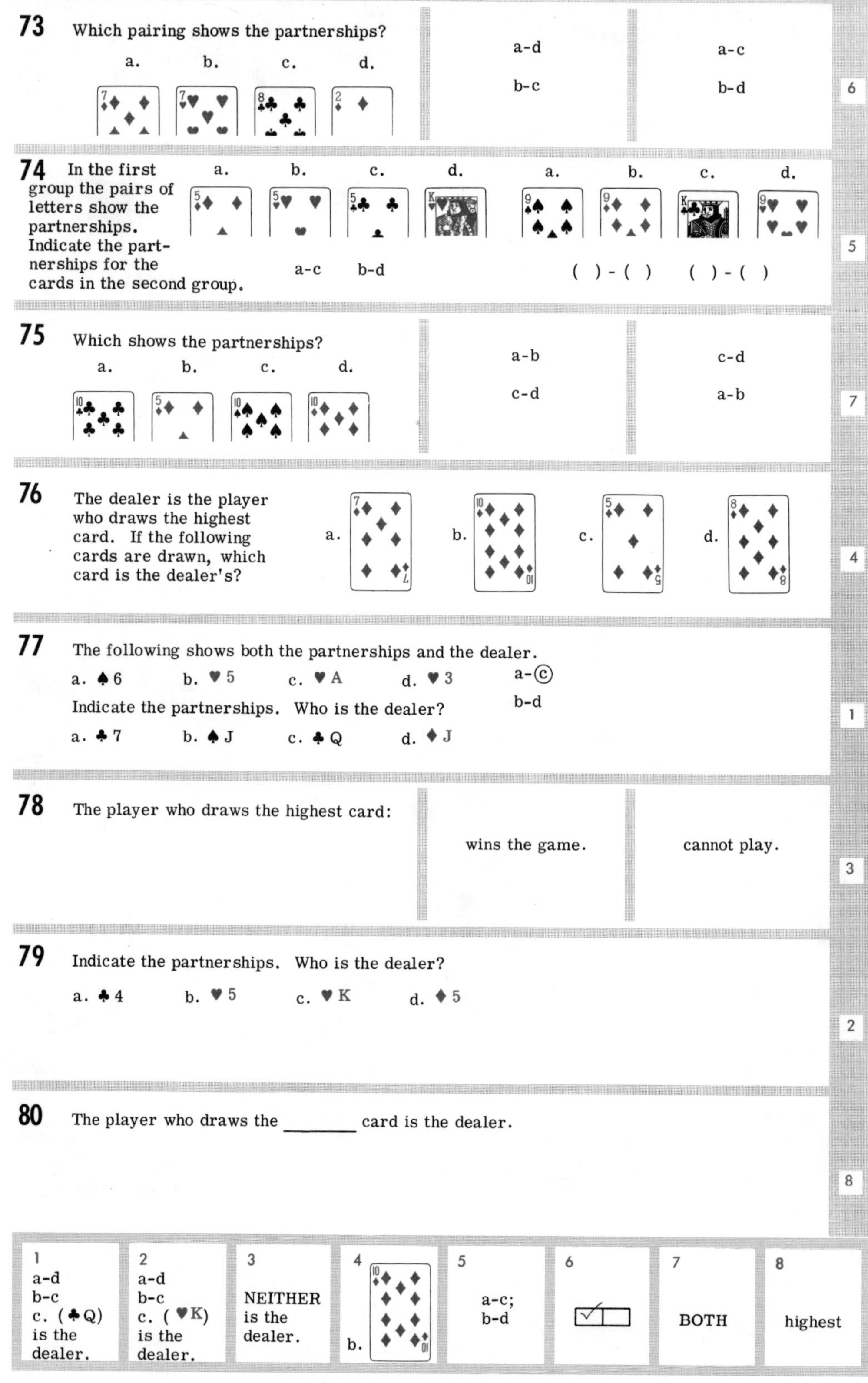

73 Which pairing shows the partnerships?

a. 7♦ b. 7♥ c. 8♣ d. 2♦

a-d	a-c
b-c	b-d

6

74 In the first group the pairs of letters show the partnerships. Indicate the partnerships for the cards in the second group.

a. 5♦ b. 5♥ c. 5♣ d. K♥ a-c b-d

a. 9♠ b. 9♦ c. K♣ d. 9♥ ( ) - ( ) ( ) - ( )

5

75 Which shows the partnerships?

a. 10♣ b. 5♦ c. 10♠ d. 10♦

a-b	c-d
c-d	a-b

7

76 The dealer is the player who draws the highest card. If the following cards are drawn, which card is the dealer's?

a. 7♦ b. 10♦ c. 5♦ d. 8♦

4

77 The following shows both the partnerships and the dealer.

a. ♠ 6 b. ♥ 5 c. ♥ A d. ♥ 3 a-ⓒ b-d

Indicate the partnerships. Who is the dealer?

a. ♣ 7 b. ♠ J c. ♣ Q d. ♦ J

1

78 The player who draws the highest card:

wins the game.	cannot play.

3

79 Indicate the partnerships. Who is the dealer?

a. ♣ 4 b. ♥ 5 c. ♥ K d. ♦ 5

2

80 The player who draws the ________ card is the dealer.

8

1	2	3	4	5	6	7	8
a-d b-c c. (♣Q) is the dealer.	a-d b-c c. (♥K) is the dealer.	NEITHER is the dealer.	b. 10♦	a-c; b-d	☑☐	BOTH	highest

81 Positions at a bridge table are laid out just like the points on the compass. N stands for North, E stands for East, S stands for South, and W stands for _____.

5

---

82 Positions at a bridge table are laid out just like the points on a compass. If this is a picture of a compass, which is the correct positioning at the table?

3

---

83 *Cutting the cards* means lifting a part of the deck (from 4 to 48 cards) and placing it to the left of the deck toward the dealer. Which shows the correct cut of cards?

Dealer

You

6

---

84 Who is the dealer here?

N  E  S  W 

7

---

85 Indicate partnerships. Who is the dealer?

a. ♠ 2 b. ♦ K c. ♠ 10 d. ♣ 5

1

---

86 The dealer gives a shuffled deck to his right-hand opponent to cut.

If W is the dealer, S cuts the deck.

If S is the dealer, ( ) cuts the deck.

8

---

87 The dealer gives a shuffled deck to his:

left-hand opponent.	right-hand opponent.

2

---

88 Who cuts the deck for E?

4

1	2	3	4	5	6	7	8
a-d b-c b. (♦K) is the dealer.	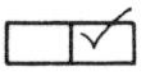		N	West	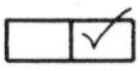	E 	E

89 Who cuts the deck?

the dealer's right-hand opponent	the dealer's left-hand opponent.

8

90 The dealer deals the cards one at a time. Which picture illustrates this principle?

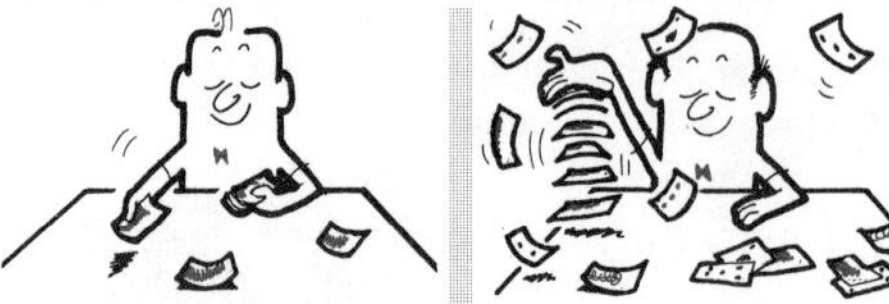

1

91

	N	
W		E
	S	

The dealer deals the cards one at a time, giving the first card to his left-hand opponent. If E is the dealer, who receives the first card?

3

92

	N	
W		E
	S	

Dealer

S is the dealer. The first person to receive a card is W, the next is N, then E. The dealer deals in (clockwise/counterclockwise) rotation.

6

93 The dealer gives the first card to:

himself.	his partner.

2

94 The dealer deals the cards:

a. two at a time.
b. one at a time.
c. four at a time.

5

95 Which shows the correct way to deal?

4

96 Arrange the symbols of the suits in ascending order.

a. ♦ b. ♣ c. ♠ d. ♥

7

1	2	3	4	5	6	7	8
☑☐	NEITHER his left-hand opponent.	S	☑☐	b. one at a time.	clockwise	c. ♠ d. ♥ a. ♦ b. ♣	☑☐

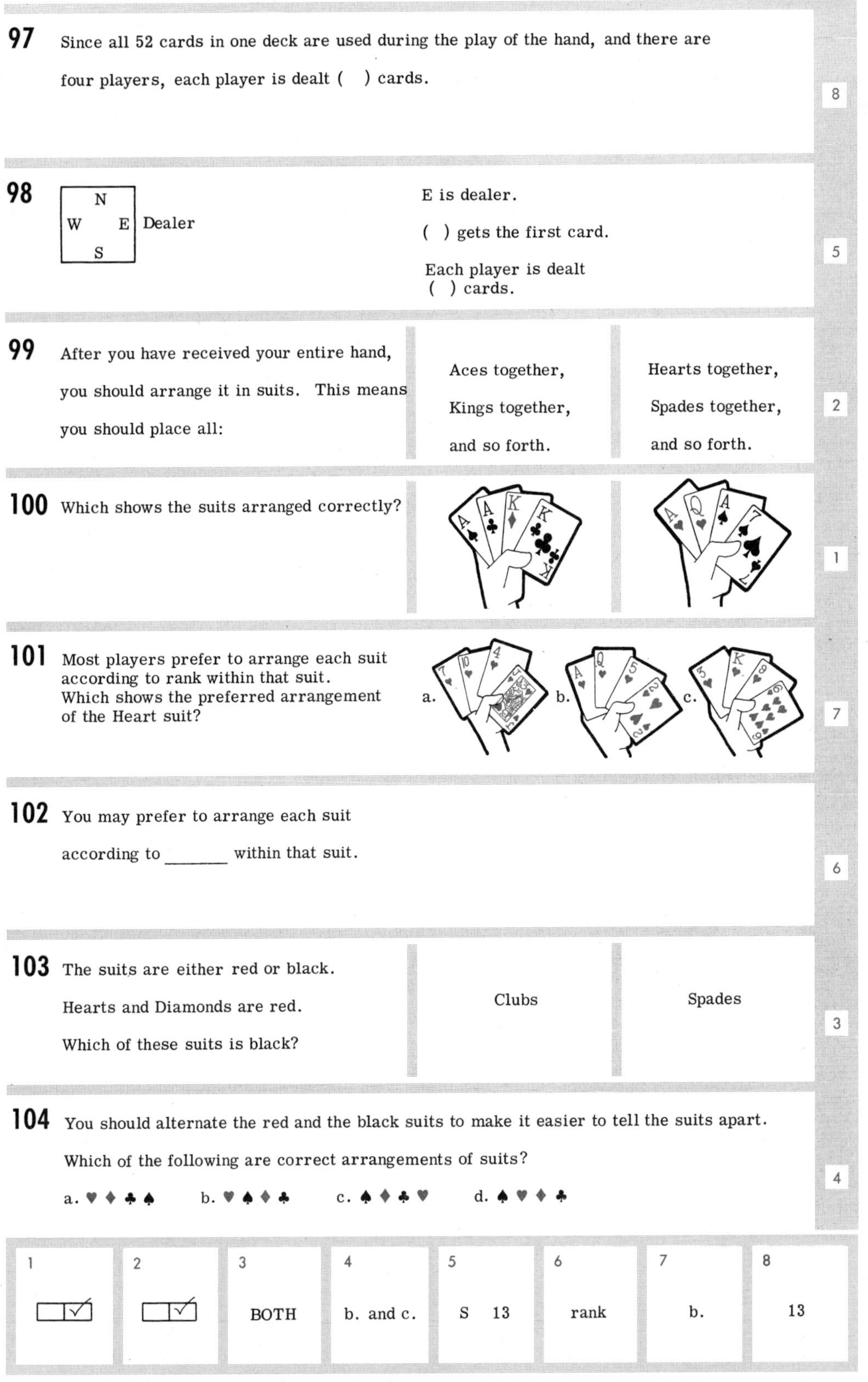

97 Since all 52 cards in one deck are used during the play of the hand, and there are four players, each player is dealt ( ) cards. 8

98

	N	
W		E Dealer
	S	

E is dealer.

( ) gets the first card.

Each player is dealt ( ) cards. 5

99 After you have received your entire hand, you should arrange it in suits. This means you should place all:

Aces together, Kings together, and so forth.	Hearts together, Spades together, and so forth.

2

100 Which shows the suits arranged correctly? 1

101 Most players prefer to arrange each suit according to rank within that suit. Which shows the preferred arrangement of the Heart suit?

a. b. c. 7

102 You may prefer to arrange each suit according to _______ within that suit. 6

103 The suits are either red or black.

Hearts and Diamonds are red.

Which of these suits is black?

Clubs	Spades

3

104 You should alternate the red and the black suits to make it easier to tell the suits apart.

Which of the following are correct arrangements of suits?

a. ♥ ♦ ♣ ♠ b. ♥ ♠ ♦ ♣ c. ♠ ♦ ♣ ♥ d. ♠ ♥ ♦ ♣ 4

1	2	3	4	5	6	7	8
☐☑	☐☑	BOTH	b. and c.	S 13	rank	b.	13

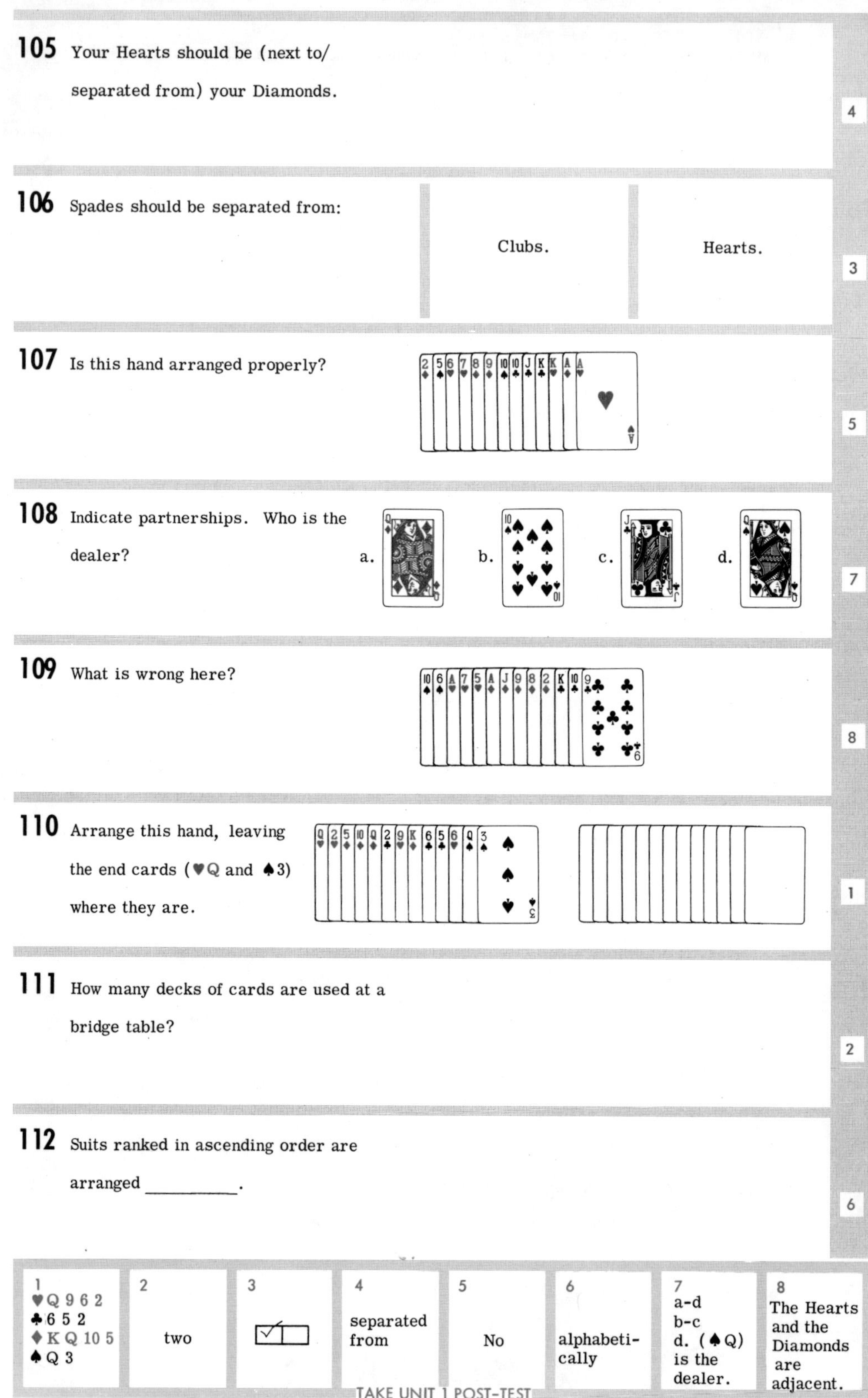

105 Your Hearts should be (next to/ separated from) your Diamonds. 4

106 Spades should be separated from:

Clubs.	Hearts.

3

107 Is this hand arranged properly? 5

108 Indicate partnerships. Who is the dealer? a. b. c. d. 7

109 What is wrong here? 8

110 Arrange this hand, leaving the end cards (♥Q and ♠3) where they are. 1

111 How many decks of cards are used at a bridge table? 2

112 Suits ranked in ascending order are arranged __________. 6

1	2	3	4	5	6	7	8
♥Q 9 6 2 ♣6 5 2 ♦K Q 10 5 ♠Q 3	two	☑☐	separated from	No	alphabetically	a-d b-c d. (♠Q) is the dealer.	The Hearts and the Diamonds are adjacent.

TAKE UNIT 1 POST-TEST

SHUFFLING AND DEALING

While the dealer is dealing one deck of cards for play, his partner is shuffling the other deck. After the partner finishes shuffling, he places the cards to his right.

After a hand is played, the person to the left of the last dealer becomes the new dealer. Dealerships move in a clockwise direction. The new dealer takes the shuffled deck which he finds to his left and gives it to his right-hand opponent (the old dealer) to cut. A simple way to remember this procedure is to remember that when you move the whole deck, you move it to the right. To help you remember this, notice that the words *wHole* and *rigHt* both have the letter *H* in them.

UNIT 2

who takes the trick?

This unit discusses the rules of trick-taking. It defines trump and teaches which card wins a trick.

PRE- AND POST-TEST

1. | | N | |
|---|---|---|
| W | | E |
| | S | |

N leads. Who plays next?

2. | | N | |
|---|---|---|
| W | | E |
| | S | |

S played last. Who led?

3. | | N | |
|---|---|---|
| W | | E |
| | S | |

E leads. Who plays next?

4. A Spade is led and Diamonds are trumps. You have: ♠K ♥none ♦3 ♣none
You (must play ♠K/may play ♠K/may play ♦3).
5. A Diamond is led and Hearts are trumps. You have: ♠none ♥2 ♦none ♣3
You (must play ♥2/must play ♣3/may play either the ♥2 or the ♣3).
6. The ♦7 is led and you have the ♦3 and ♦A. You (must play the ♦A/must play the ♦3/may play either the ♦A or the ♦3).
7. Spades are trumps and N leads. Who takes this trick?

	N ♠5	
W ♠9		♥A E
	♥5 S	

8. Diamonds are trumps and S leads. Who takes this trick?

	N ♦2	
W ♣A		♣2 E
	♣K S	

9. Hearts are trumps and E leads. Who takes this trick?

	N ♣A	
W ♦2		♦Q E
	♦3 S	

10. Spades are trumps and N leads. Who takes this trick?

	N ♥2	
W ♣J		♦K E
	♦3 S	

11. The bid is at No Trump and W leads. Who takes this trick?

	N ♠A	
W ♣2		♣10 E
	♠5 S	

12. How many cards in a trick?
13. Following suit with a lower card is called __________.
14. To play first to a trick means __________ __________.
15. If N gathers the first trick won by N-S, then (   ) gathers all the other tricks won by N-S.

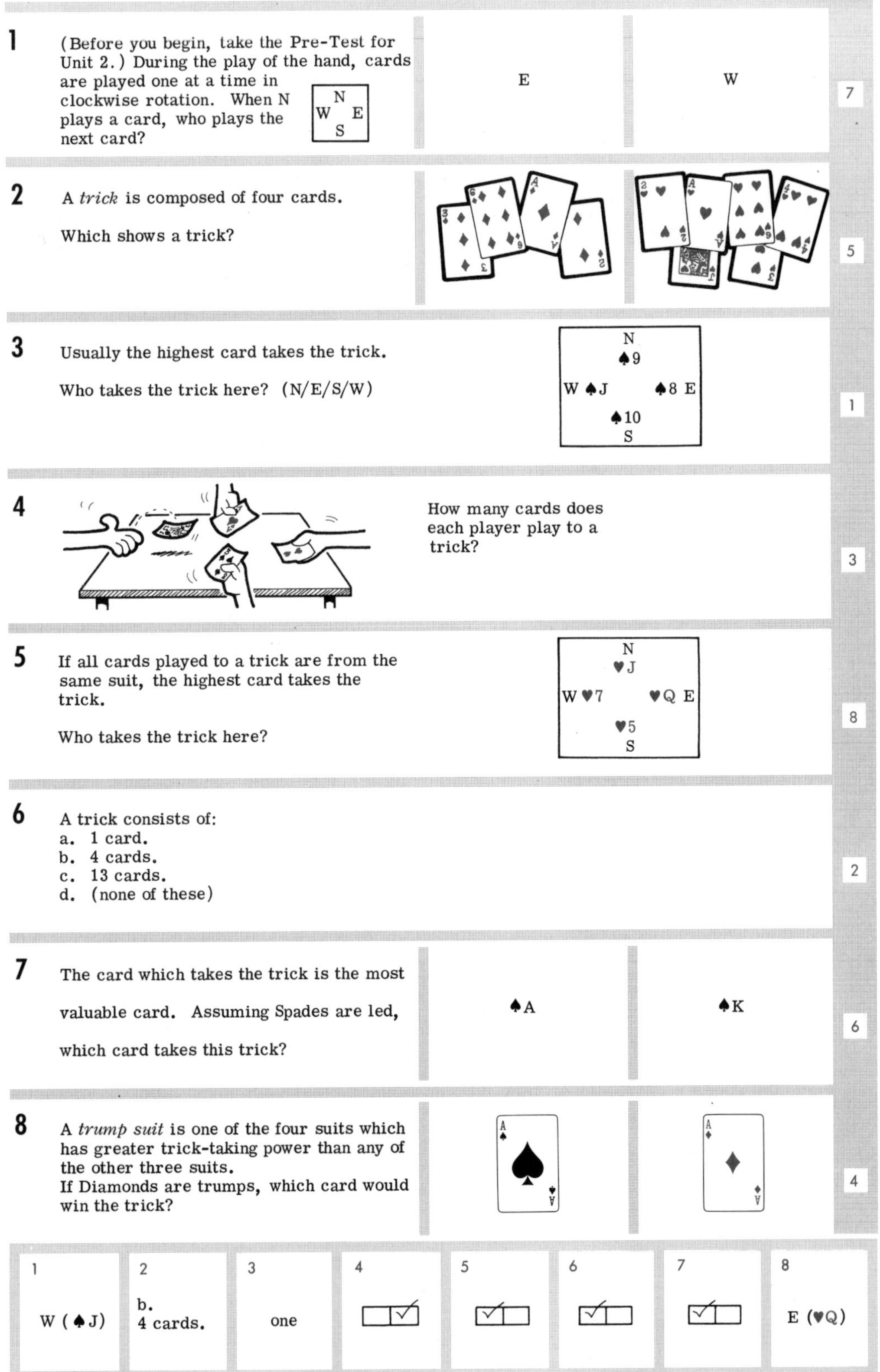

1 (Before you begin, take the Pre-Test for Unit 2.) During the play of the hand, cards are played one at a time in clockwise rotation. When N plays a card, who plays the next card?

E | W 7

2 A *trick* is composed of four cards.

Which shows a trick? 5

3 Usually the highest card takes the trick.

Who takes the trick here? (N/E/S/W)

1

4 How many cards does each player play to a trick? 3

5 If all cards played to a trick are from the same suit, the highest card takes the trick.

Who takes the trick here?

8

6 A trick consists of:

a. 1 card.
b. 4 cards.
c. 13 cards.
d. (none of these)

2

7 The card which takes the trick is the most valuable card. Assuming Spades are led, which card takes this trick?

♠A | ♠K 6

8 A *trump suit* is one of the four suits which has greater trick-taking power than any of the other three suits.
If Diamonds are trumps, which card would win the trick? 4

1	2	3	4	5	6	7	8
W (♠J)	b. 4 cards.	one	☐☑	☑☐	☑☐	☑☐	E (♥Q)

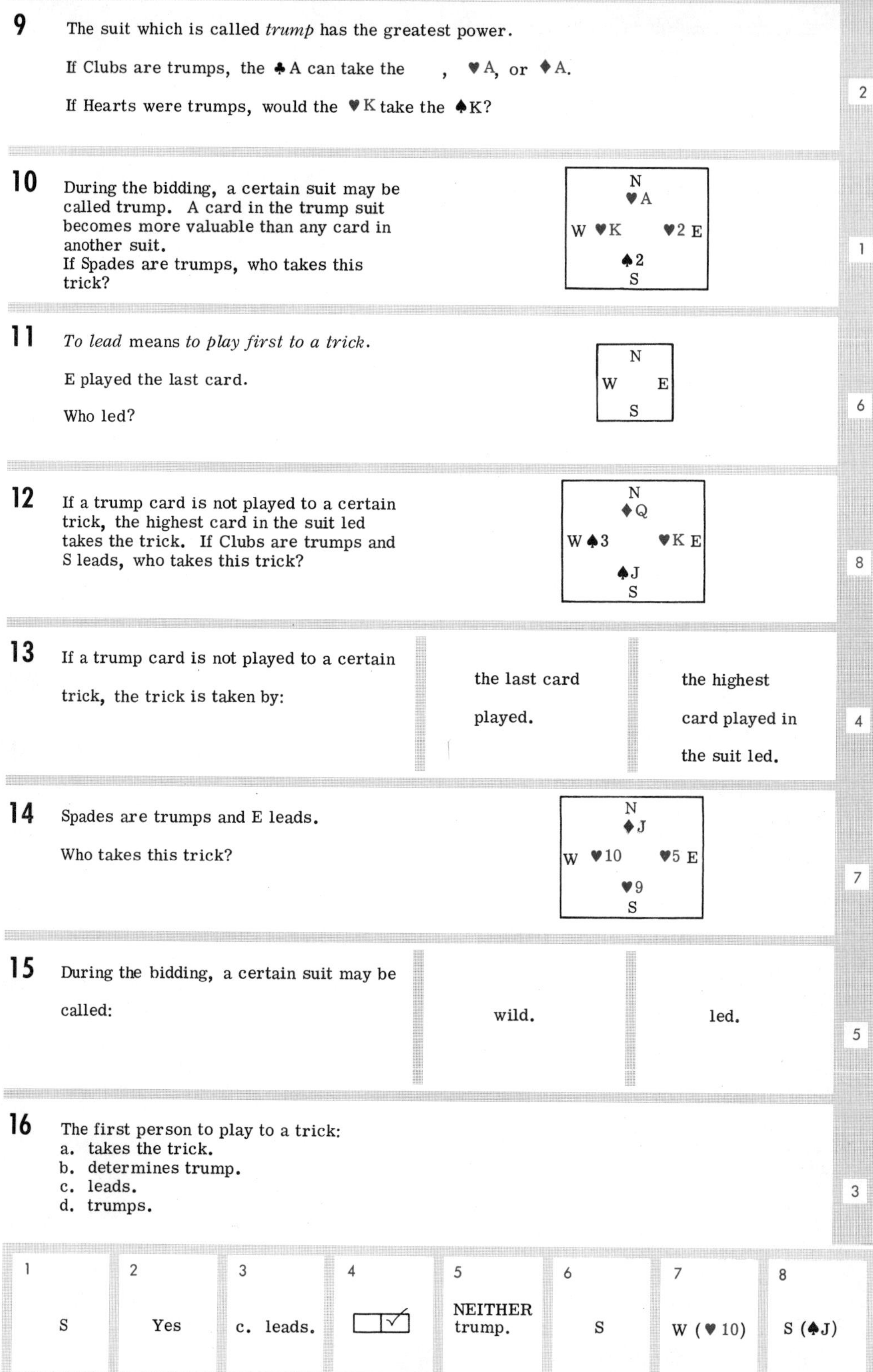

9 The suit which is called *trump* has the greatest power.

If Clubs are trumps, the ♣A can take the ____, ♥A, or ♦A.

If Hearts were trumps, would the ♥K take the ♠K? 2

10 During the bidding, a certain suit may be called trump. A card in the trump suit becomes more valuable than any card in another suit.
If Spades are trumps, who takes this trick? 1

11 *To lead* means *to play first to a trick.*

E played the last card.

Who led? 6

12 If a trump card is not played to a certain trick, the highest card in the suit led takes the trick. If Clubs are trumps and S leads, who takes this trick? 8

13 If a trump card is not played to a certain trick, the trick is taken by: 4

the last card played.	the highest card played in the suit led.

14 Spades are trumps and E leads.

Who takes this trick? 7

15 During the bidding, a certain suit may be called: 5

wild.	led.

16 The first person to play to a trick:
a. takes the trick.
b. determines trump.
c. leads.
d. trumps. 3

1	2	3	4	5	6	7	8
S	Yes	c. leads.	☐ ☑	NEITHER trump.	S	W (♥10)	S (♠J)

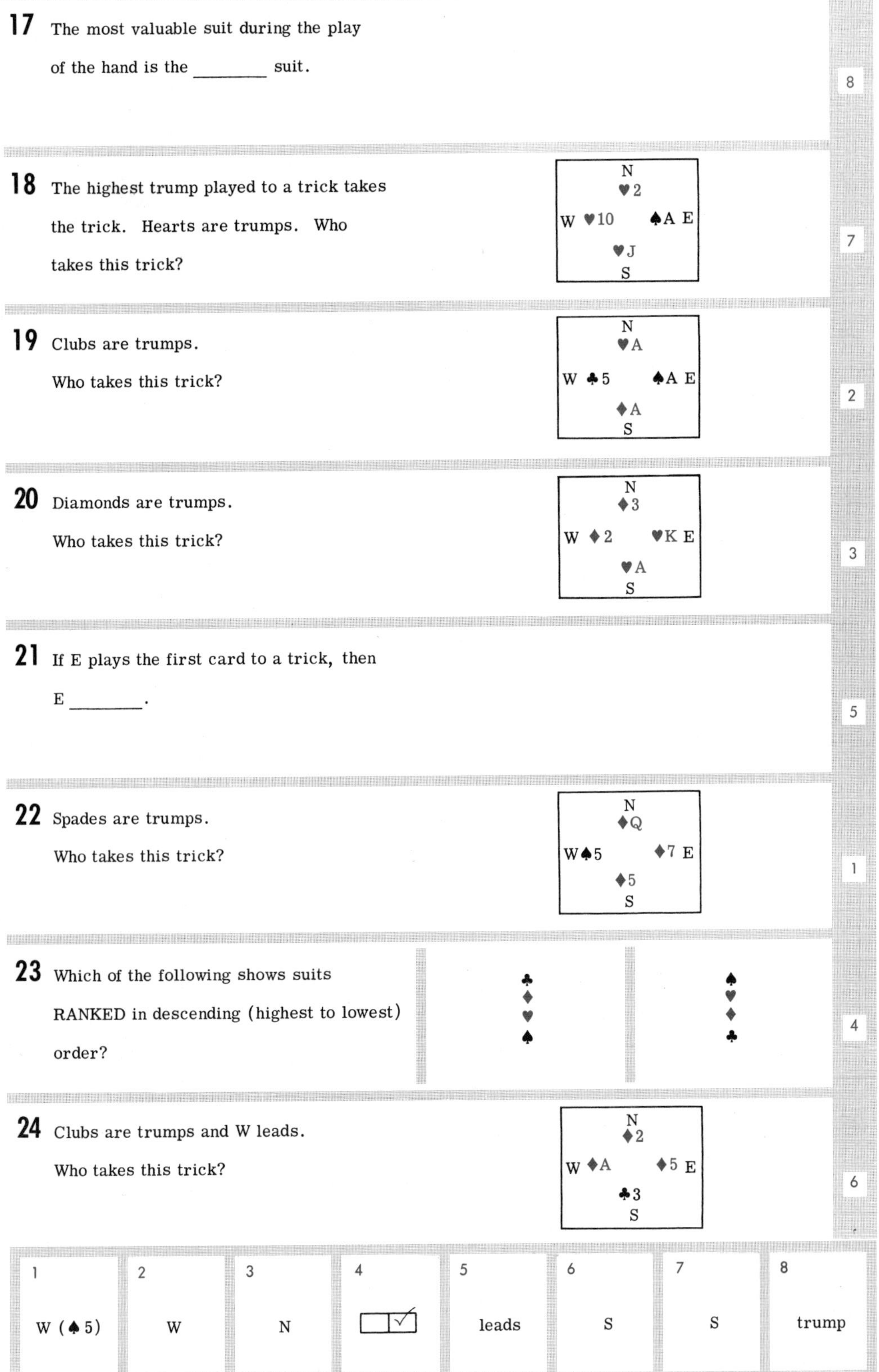

17 The most valuable suit during the play of the hand is the ________ suit. 8

18 The highest trump played to a trick takes the trick. Hearts are trumps. Who takes this trick? 7

	N ♥2	
W ♥10		♠A E
	♥J S	

19 Clubs are trumps. Who takes this trick? 2

	N ♥A	
W ♣5		♠A E
	♦A S	

20 Diamonds are trumps. Who takes this trick? 3

	N ♦3	
W ♦2		♥K E
	♥A S	

21 If E plays the first card to a trick, then E ________. 5

22 Spades are trumps. Who takes this trick? 1

	N ♦Q	
W♠5		♦7 E
	♦5 S	

23 Which of the following shows suits RANKED in descending (highest to lowest) order? 4

♣ ♦ ♥ ♠	♠ ♥ ♦ ♣

24 Clubs are trumps and W leads. Who takes this trick? 6

	N ♦2	
W ♦A		♦5 E
	♣3 S	

1	2	3	4	5	6	7	8
W (♠5)	W	N	☐ ☑	leads	S	S	trump

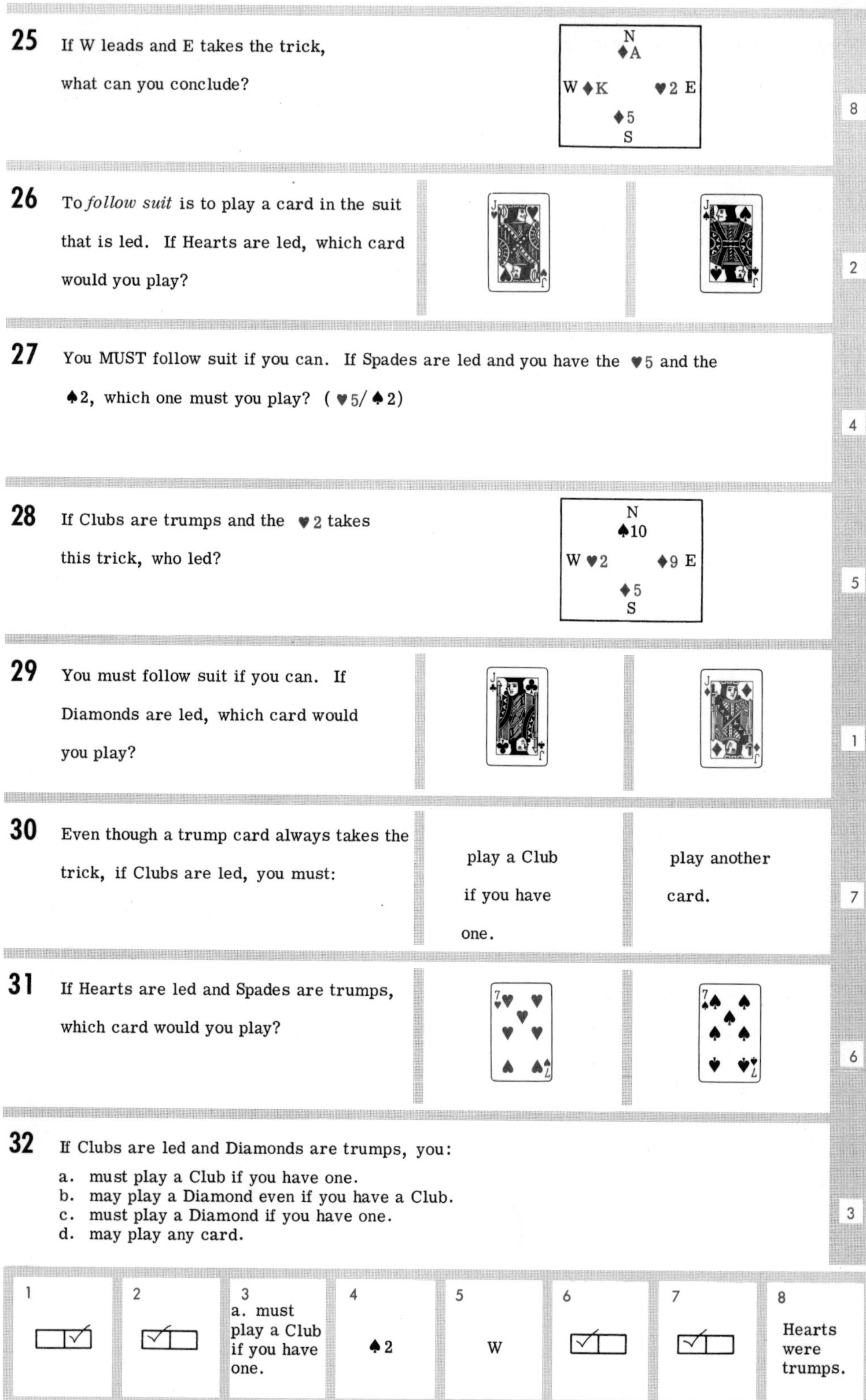

25 If W leads and E takes the trick, what can you conclude?

N ♦A
W ♦K — ♥2 E
♦5 S

8

26 To *follow suit* is to play a card in the suit that is led. If Hearts are led, which card would you play?

[J♥] [J♠]

2

27 You MUST follow suit if you can. If Spades are led and you have the ♥5 and the ♠2, which one must you play? (♥5/♠2)

4

28 If Clubs are trumps and the ♥2 takes this trick, who led?

N ♠10
W ♥2 — ♦9 E
♦5 S

5

29 You must follow suit if you can. If Diamonds are led, which card would you play?

[J♣] [J♦]

1

30 Even though a trump card always takes the trick, if Clubs are led, you must:

play a Club if you have one.	play another card.

7

31 If Hearts are led and Spades are trumps, which card would you play?

[7♥] [7♠]

6

32 If Clubs are led and Diamonds are trumps, you:

a. must play a Club if you have one.
b. may play a Diamond even if you have a Club.
c. must play a Diamond if you have one.
d. may play any card.

3

1	2	3	4	5	6	7	8
[ ][✓]	[✓][ ]	a. must play a Club if you have one.	♠2	W	[✓][ ]	[✓][ ]	Hearts were trumps.

33 Four players are getting ready to play and draw these four cards. Which are the partnerships and who is the dealer?

a. b. c. d.

7

---

34 You may play either a higher card or a lower card in the suit which is led. If N plays ♣10 and you are E holding ♣J and ♣2, you:

a. must play ♣J.
b. must play ♣2.
c. may play either the ♣J or ♣2.

1

35

	N ♦J	
W ♦2		♦K E
	S	

Playing a higher card than has already been played in the suit that is led is called *covering.*

Here W led the ♦2, N played the ♦J, and E played the ♦K. N has covered the ♦2 Has E covered the ♦J?

4

---

36 Playing a higher card in the suit that is led is called:

covering.	covering.

6

---

37 To play the first card to a trick is to:

trump.	cover.

2

38

W played the ♥7, then N played the ♥2

Did N cover?

8

---

39 If you choose to play a lower card than has already been played in the suit that is led, you are *ducking.* If S leads with the ♣J, and W holds the ♣Q and ♣9, which card should W play to duck?

5

40

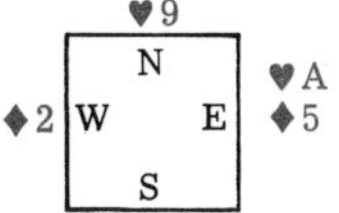

W leads the ♦2 and N plays the ♥9. You have the ♦5 and ♥A. (These are the only cards you have left.) You must play the (♥A/♦5).

3

1	2	3	4	5	6	7	8
c. may play either the ♣J or ♣2.	NEITHER lead.	♦5	Yes	☐☑	BOTH	a-b c-d d is the dealer.	No

41 

	cover	duck

7

42 You have the ♦7 and ♦A. Your left-hand opponent leads the ♦J. In this sense, *to duck* means to play the:

♦7.	♦A.

4

43 To follow suit means:
a. to play the same suit which your right-hand opponent has played.
b. to play the same suit which was led.

2

44 You have the ♣9 and ♣J. Your partner leads the ♣10. If you play the ♣J, you have:

ducked.	covered.

8

45 Hearts are trumps. W leads.
Who takes this trick?

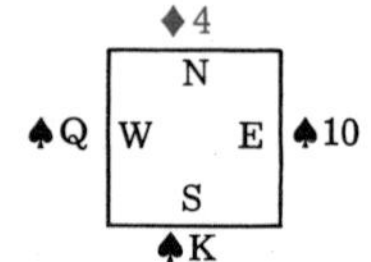

5

46 You have the ♠8 and ♠K. Your opponent leads the ♠10. If you play the ♠8, you have:

covered.	ducked.

1

47

	♠2 ♥7 ♦K	
	N	
♠6 ♥5 4	W E	♥10 8 ♣3
	S	
	♠5 ♣7 2	

Each player has three cards. N has the ♠2, ♥7, and ♦K. What cards does E have?

6

48 You have the ♥4 and ♥K. Your right-hand opponent plays the ♥9.

a. If you play the ♥K, you have ____________.

b. If you play the ♥4, you have ____________.

3

1	2	3	4	5	6	7	8
☐☑	b. to play the same suit which was led.	a. covered b. ducked	☑☐	S (♠K)	♥10 8 ♣3	☑☐	☐☑

49 You are E and you have the three cards shown in your hand. Which card must you play?

	♣8			
Lead ♥7	N W E S	♣9 ♥10 5		

♣9	♥7

4

50 If you cannot follow suit, you may play any card in your hand.

Diamonds are led and you have ♣7 6, ♥7 2, and ♠J 10.

Which of these may you play? 6

51 Playing a higher card than has already been played in the suit which is led is called:

ducking.	ruffing.

7

52 If you cannot follow suit, you:

a. may play any card in your hand.

b. must play a trump card if you have one. 1

53 If you cannot follow suit, you may play a trump card if you have one.

Spades are trumps and you are N. S leads the ♥5. You have only the ♦7 and ♠5. If you play the (♠5/ ♦7), you have trumped. 5

	♠5 ♦7	
♥A	N W E S	
	♥5	

54 Which is ducking?

(The King was led.) 8

55 Playing a trump card when you cannot follow suit is called *ruffing*. If Hearts are trumps, E has ruffed if he plays the ( ). 3

	♦A	
♦K Lead	N W E S	♠5 ♥10 ♣4
	♦10	

56 Match these.

a. playing a trump card when you cannot follow suit — 1) ducking

b. playing a lower card than was played in the suit led — 2) covering

c. playing a higher card than was played in the suit led — 3) ruffing

2

1	2	3	4	5	6	7	8
a. may play any card in your hand.	a. 3) b. 1) c. 2)	♥10	NEITHER	♠5	any of them	NEITHER covering.	☐☑

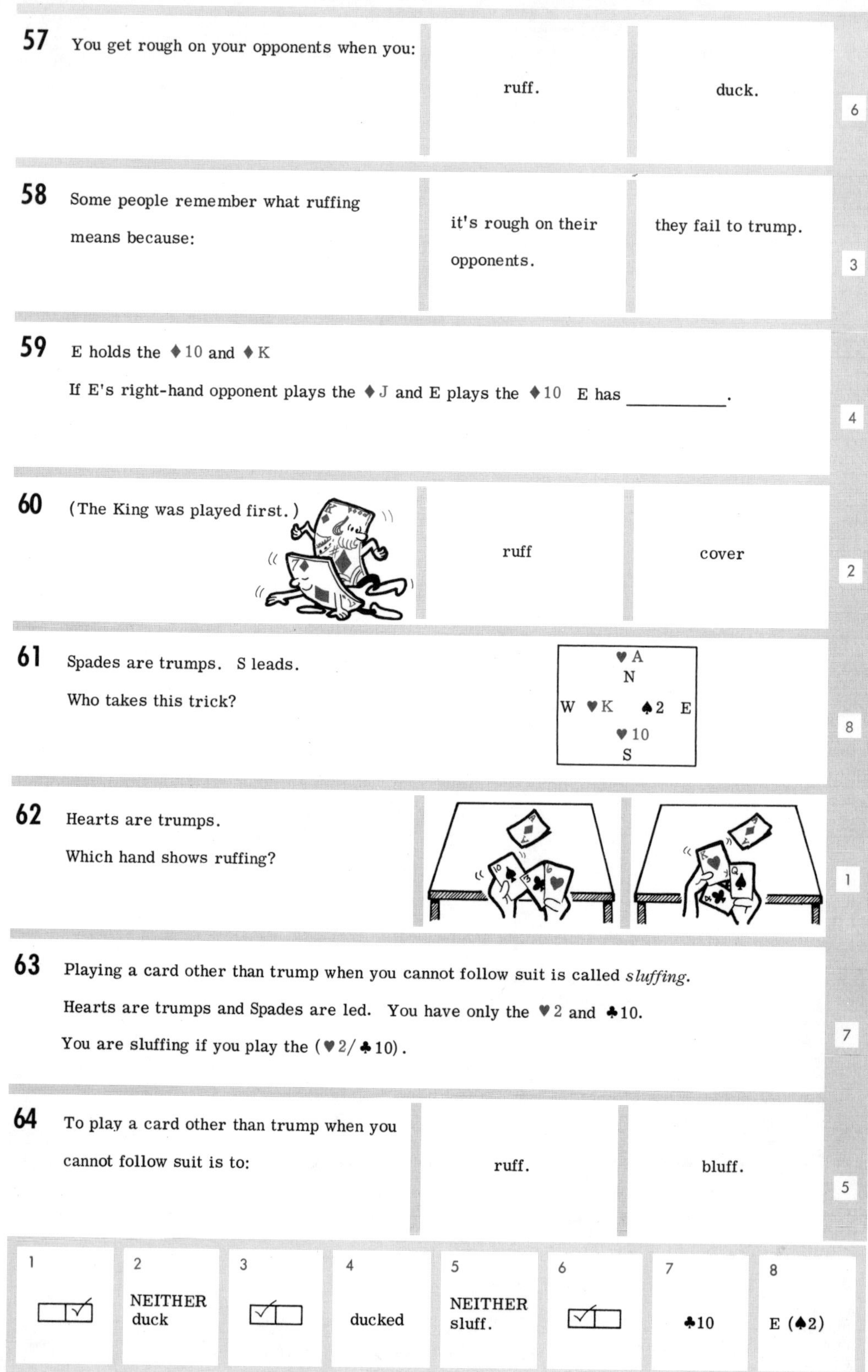

57 You get rough on your opponents when you:

ruff.	duck.

6

58 Some people remember what ruffing means because:

it's rough on their opponents.	they fail to trump.

3

59 E holds the ♦10 and ♦K

If E's right-hand opponent plays the ♦J and E plays the ♦10 E has __________. 4

60 (The King was played first.)

ruff	cover

2

61 Spades are trumps. S leads.

Who takes this trick?

	N: ♥A	
W: ♥K		E: ♠2
	S: ♥10	

8

62 Hearts are trumps.

Which hand shows ruffing? 1

63 Playing a card other than trump when you cannot follow suit is called *sluffing*.

Hearts are trumps and Spades are led. You have only the ♥2 and ♣10.

You are sluffing if you play the (♥2/♣10). 7

64 To play a card other than trump when you cannot follow suit is to:

ruff.	bluff.

5

1	2	3	4	5	6	7	8
☐☑	NEITHER duck	☑☐	ducked	NEITHER sluff.	☑☐	♣10	E (♠2)

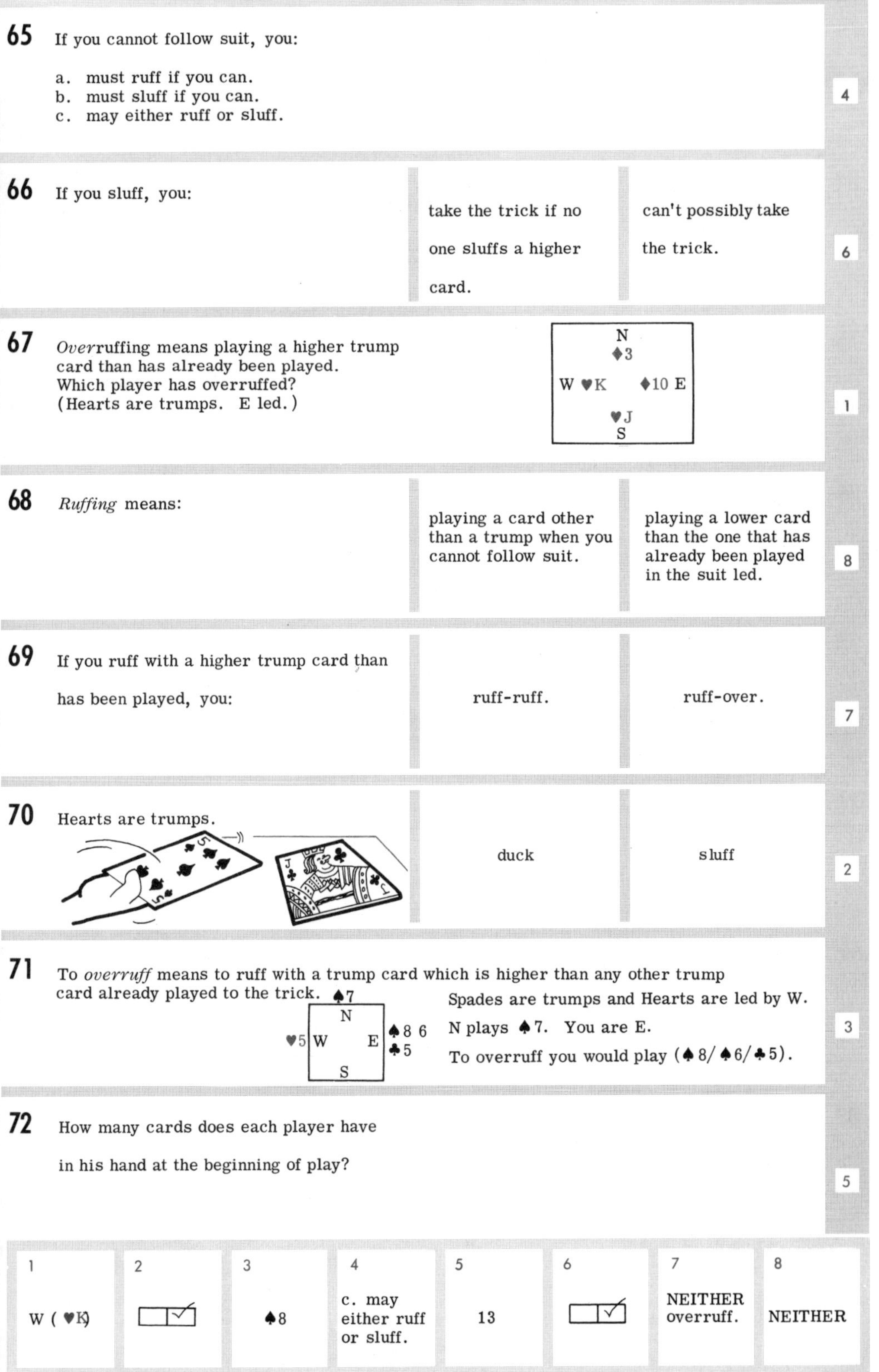

65 If you cannot follow suit, you:

a. must ruff if you can.
b. must sluff if you can.
c. may either ruff or sluff. 4

66 If you sluff, you:

take the trick if no one sluffs a higher card.	can't possibly take the trick.	6

67 *Over*ruffing means playing a higher trump card than has already been played.
Which player has overruffed?
(Hearts are trumps. E led.)

N
♦3
W ♥K ♦10 E
♥J
S

1

68 *Ruffing* means:

playing a card other than a trump when you cannot follow suit.	playing a lower card than the one that has already been played in the suit led.	8

69 If you ruff with a higher trump card than has been played, you:

ruff-ruff.	ruff-over.	7

70 Hearts are trumps.

duck	sluff	2

71 To *overruff* means to ruff with a trump card which is higher than any other trump card already played to the trick.

♠7
N
♥5 W E ♠8 6 ♣5
S

Spades are trumps and Hearts are led by W.
N plays ♠7. You are E.
To overruff you would play (♠8/♠6/♣5). 3

72 How many cards does each player have in his hand at the beginning of play? 5

1	2	3	4	5	6	7	8
W (♥K)	☐ ☑	♠8	c. may either ruff or sluff.	13	☐ ☑	NEITHER overruff.	NEITHER

73 This picture shows that:

Spades are trumps.	Hearts are trumps.

5

74 Spades are trumps and N leads.

Who takes this trick?

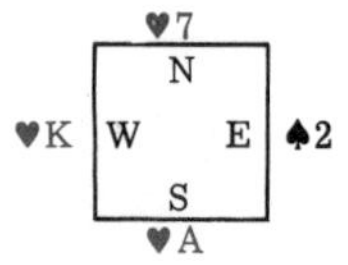

2

75 What is it called when you play a card other than trump when you cannot follow suit?

1

76 Diamonds are trumps and W leads.

Which card takes this trick?

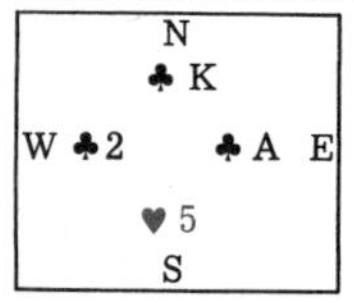

7

77 Which is ducking?

3

78 Hearts are trumps and S leads.

Who takes this trick?

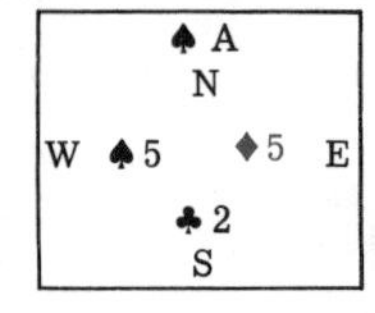

4

79 To play a higher trump card than has already been played when you cannot follow suit in a trick is to:

ruff.	overruff.

8

80 Which shows the correct rotation for the order of playing to a trick?

a. 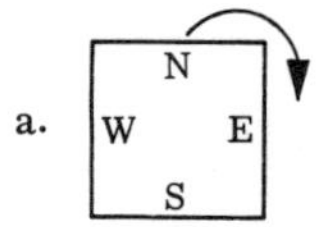

b.

N
W E
S

6

1	2	3	4	5	6	7	8
sluffing	E (♠2)		S (♣2)	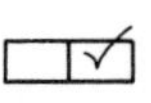	a.	♣A (E)	☐☑

81 Hearts are led and Diamonds are trumps.

You have the ♠2, ♥7, ♦9, and ♣5.

You would play the (♠2/ ♥7/ ♦9/ ♣5).

5

82 What does *covering* mean?

3

83 The ♦J led and Clubs are trumps. You have the ♦A, ♦5, and ♣3.

You may play:
- a. ♦A.
- b. ♦5.
- c. either ♦A or ♦5.
- d. neither ♦A or ♦5.

4

84 What is it called when you play a trump when you cannot follow suit?

6

85 Clubs are trumps and a Spade is led. You have: ♠ none, ♥5, ♦7, ♣2.

You:
- a. must play the ♣2.
- b. may play the ♥5, ♦7, or ♣2.
- c. must play either the ♥5 or ♦7.
- d. (None of these is correct.)

7

86 What is it called when you play anything other than trump when you cannot follow suit?

1

87 Match these.

- a. playing a card other than trump when you cannot follow suit
- b. playing a higher trump than has already been played when you cannot follow suit
- c. playing a higher card than has been played in the suit led

1) covering
2) sluffing
3) overruffing
4) ruff

8

88 Indicate partnerships. Who is the dealer?

a. ♠3 b. ♥8 c. ♦8 d. ♣9

2

1	2	3	4	5	6	7	8
sluffing	a-c b-(d)	playing a higher card than one in suit led	c) either ♦A or ♦5.	♥7	ruffing	b. may play the ♥5, ♦7, or ♣2.	a. 2) b. 3) c. 1)

89 What is it called when you play a higher trump than has already been played when you cannot follow suit in a trick?

1

90 Which is ruffing?

Clubs are trumps.

3

91 If a trump card is not played to a certain trick, then the highest card played in the suit which is ___________ takes the trick.

7

92 What is it called when you follow suit with a lower card?

8

93 Clubs are trumps.

If N leads, who wins this trick?

	N ♠5	
W ♠J		♠7 E
	♦K S	

2

94 Whenever a hand is played without trumps, it is called a *No Trump* hand. When hands are played without trumps, you cannot:

cover.	ruff.

6

95 Must there always be a trump suit?

5

96 Spades are trumps. E leads with the ♣J. S ruffs with the ♠8. Since W has no Clubs, he can ________ with the ♠10.

4

1	2	3	4	5	6	7	8
overruffing	W (♠J)	NEITHER	overruff	No	☐☑	led	ducking

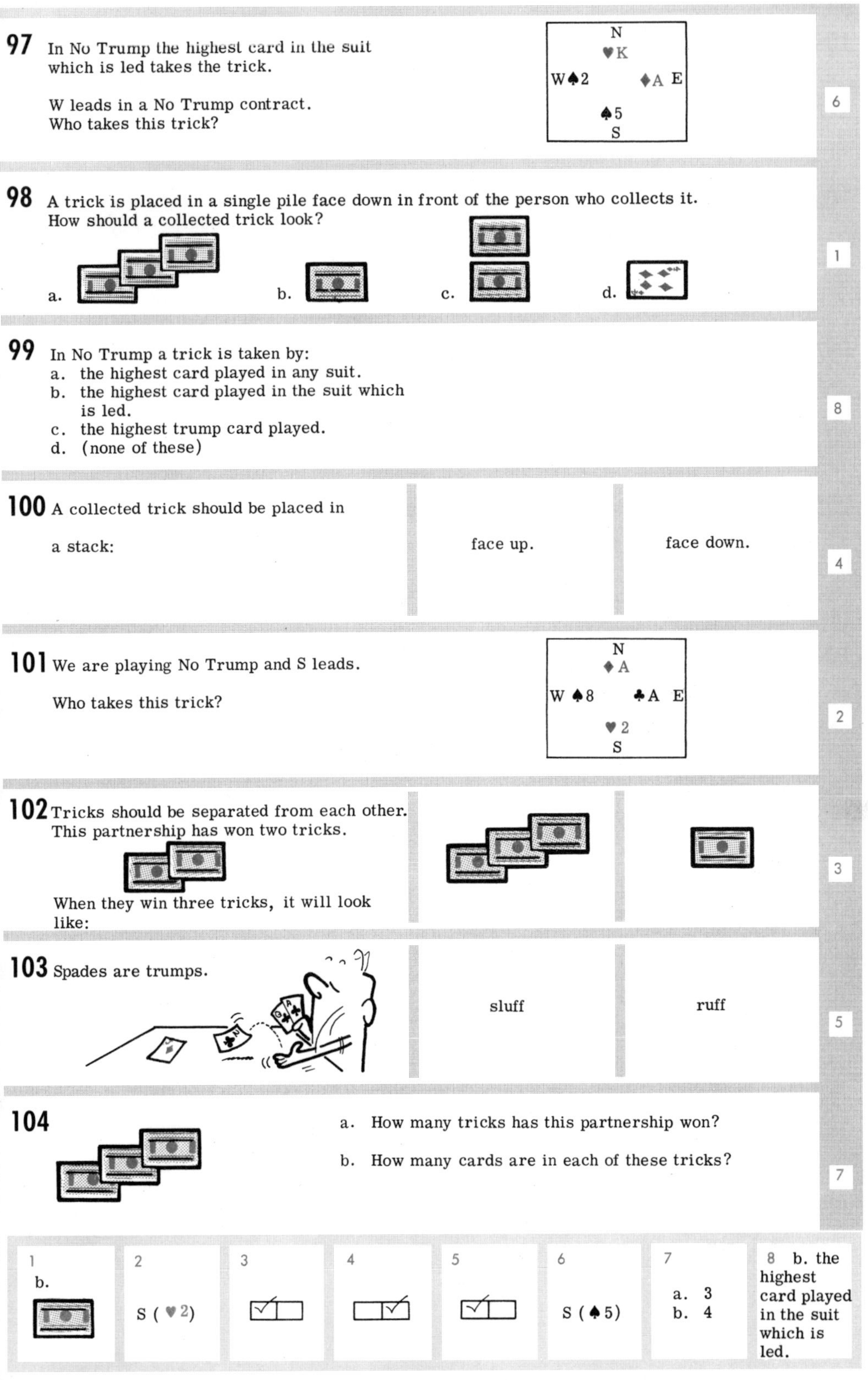

97 In No Trump the highest card in the suit which is led takes the trick. 6

W leads in a No Trump contract.
Who takes this trick?

98 A trick is placed in a single pile face down in front of the person who collects it.
How should a collected trick look? 1

a. b. c. d.

99 In No Trump a trick is taken by: 8

a. the highest card played in any suit.
b. the highest card played in the suit which is led.
c. the highest trump card played.
d. (none of these)

100 A collected trick should be placed in a stack: 4

	face up.	face down.

101 We are playing No Trump and S leads. 2

Who takes this trick?

102 Tricks should be separated from each other.
This partnership has won two tricks. 3

When they win three tricks, it will look like:

103 Spades are trumps. 5

	sluff	ruff

104 7

a. How many tricks has this partnership won?

b. How many cards are in each of these tricks?

1	2	3	4	5	6	7	8
b.	S (♥2)	☑☐	☐☑	☑☐	S (♠5)	a. 3 b. 4	b. the highest card played in the suit which is led.

105 One member of a partnership gathers in all the tricks taken by that partnership.

	N	
W		E
	S	

If E gathers the first trick won by E-W, then ( ) gathers all the other tricks won by E-W. 1

106 The tricks won by a partnership are gathered:

by the partner who wins the trick.	alternately by the partners.

8

107 What does the term *ruff* mean?

7

108

	N ♦A	
W ♦2		♦3 E
	♦5 S	

After a trick is won, the person who won it leads the next card.

a. Who wins this trick?

b. Who leads after this trick is taken? 4

109 ______ ______

duck	sluff

5

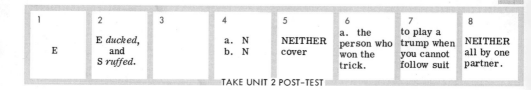

110 After a trick is won, the next card is led by:

a. the person who won the trick.
b. the person to the left of the winner.
c. the winner's partner.
d. the person to the left of the last leader. 6

111 Clubs are trumps.

The play: W leads with the ♥J, N plays the ♦8, E plays the ♥9, and S plays the ♣3.

W led, N sluffed, E __________, and S __________. 2

1	2	3	4	5	6	7	8
E	E *ducked*, and S *ruffed*.		a. N b. N	NEITHER cover	a. the person who won the trick.	to play a trump when you cannot follow suit	NEITHER all by one partner.

TAKE UNIT 2 POST-TEST

UNIT 3

who takes the bid?

The rules of bidding are discussed - the opening bid, passing, insufficient bids, the final bid, the declarer, the dummy, and who makes the opening leads.

PRE- AND POST-TEST

1. Your partnership takes the bid at 4 Spades. This means you hope to take at least:
   a. 4 Spade tricks.
   b. 4 tricks.
   c. 10 Spade tricks.
   d. 10 tricks.

2. Your opponents take the bid at 3 No Trump. To set them, you must take at least:
   a. 4 tricks.
   b. 5 tricks.
   c. 11 tricks.

3.

	N	
W		E
	S	

E is the dealer.
Who makes the initial call?

4. What is wrong with the following bidding?

	N	
W		E
	S	

First bid: S bids 1 Club.
Second bid: E bids 1 Spade.

5. What is wrong with the following bidding?

	N	
W		E
	S	

First bid: W bids 1 Heart.
Second bid: N bids 1 Club.

6. What is wrong with this bidding?

S	W	N	E
pass	1 Heart	pass	1 No Trump
pass	pass	pass	2 Hearts

7. The bidding has gone as follows.

S	W	N	E
1 Heart	pass	pass	1 Spade
2 Diamonds	pass	↑	

May N bid at this point? ——↑

8. The bidding of a certain deal is shown here.

W	N	E	S
pass	1 Diamond	1 Heart	1 Spade
2 Hearts	2 Spades	3 Hearts	4 Spades
pass	pass	pass	

a. This hand is played at ( ) ___________.

b. Who is the declarer?

c. Who plays the hand?

d. Who is the dummy?

9. The bidding of a certain deal is shown here.

N	E	S	W
1 Heart	pass	1 No Trump	pass
2 Clubs	pass	2 Hearts	pass
pass	pass		

a. This hand is played at ( ) ___________.

b. ( ) is the declarer.

c. ( ) makes the opening lead.

10. The bidding of a certain deal is shown here.

E	S	W	N
1 Diamond	1 Heart	1 No Trump	2 Diamonds
pass	2 No Trump	pass	3 No Trump
pass	pass	pass	

a. ( ) is the declarer.

b. ( ) makes the opening lead.

11. If the opening caller passes, ( ) more consecutive passes are required to close the auction.

1 (Before you begin, take the Pre-Test for Unit 3.)
When a bridge player says a number between 1 and 7 followed by the name of a suit, it is called a *bid*.

Which is a bid?
a. 8 Spades b. 3 c. Hearts d. 4 Diamonds

1

---

2 A *bid* is made up of a number between 1

and ( ) followed by the name of a _______.

8

---

3 Each of the two parts of a bid has its own meaning.

The *suit* part of the bid tells what suit will be trumps.

In "3 Spades" the player is bidding for *Spades* to be trumps.

In "7 Hearts" the player is bidding for ___________ to be trumps.

6

---

4 What is a bid? Use your own words.

2

---

5 If a player bids "3 Clubs," what does the

Club part of the bid mean?

Use your own words.

5

---

6 In bridge it is possible to play hands with *no* suit as trump.

You can guess that a player who wishes to play without *any* trump suit might bid

[1 Heart/1 No Trump/(both)/(neither)].

7

---

7 When a player says a number from 1 to 7 followed by the *name of a suit* or *No Trump*,

he is making a ___________.

4

---

8 Which is a bid?

1 Spade	2 No Trump

3

1	2	3	4	5	6	7	8
d. 4 Diamonds	a number between 1 and 7 followed by the name of a suit	BOTH	bid	The player is bidding for Clubs to be trumps.	Hearts	1 No Trump	7 suit

9	Which suit is trump if you bid 2 No Trump?	Clubs	Spades	5
10	A bid consists of a number followed by the name of a suit or *No Trump*. Which is a bid?	Pass	1 Heart	2
11	Since there are four cards to a trick and 52 cards in a deck, the total number of tricks in the play of the hand is ( ).			1
12	An offer to win a specified number of tricks in play is called a bid. Which might represent a bid?	pass	1 Spade	8
13	The first 6 tricks a team takes are called *book*. There are 13 tricks in all. How many tricks above book (more than 6) are there left?	7	0	4
14	Which is a bid?	an offer to win a specified number of tricks in some suit or No Trump	4 Hearts	3
15	The first 6 tricks are called *book*. The side taking the bid must make its book plus bid. A contract of 5 means that the side bidding must make book plus ( ) more tricks.			6
16	Which is the higher bid?	2 Diamonds	1 Heart	7

1	2	3	4	5	6	7	8
13	☐☑	BOTH	☑☐	NEITHER	5	☑☐	☐☑

17 The first 6 tricks are called a book. The side taking the bid must make a book plus its bid. A contract of 3 means that the side bidding must make 6 + 3, or 9 tricks. A contract of 5 means that the side bidding must make ( ) tricks. 5

18 How many tricks are in a book?

4	13

4

19

1 Spade (opening bid)

	N	
pass W		E pass
	S	
	pass	

The contract is the last bid which is made.

The contract is 1 ___________.

8

20 The final bid which determines the number of tricks to be made is the __________.

2

21 A book is 6 tricks.
There are 13 tricks in all.
The most tricks over book you could take would be:

8.	9.

6

22 A bid is an offer to win a specified number of tricks in play.

A contract of 4 means that the required total of tricks to be made is 6 + 4, or 10 tricks.

What is the required total of tricks to be made with a contract of 2?

1

23 A book is:

the first 6 tricks.	the tricks taken after the first 6.

7

24 The suit which is trump is determined by the contract.

When the contract is 4 Spades, which are trumps?

Diamonds	Clubs

3

1	2	3	4	5	6	7	8
8 (6 + 2)	contract	NEITHER Spades	NEITHER 6	11 (6 + 5)	NEITHER 7.	☑☐	Spade

25 What is the contract in when Hearts are trumps? 5

26 What is an offer to win a certain number of tricks in play called? 6

27 Match these. 1

a. an offer to win a specified number of tricks in play
b. the final bid which determines the number of tricks to be made

1) contract
2) bid
3) trump

28 A contract of 5 Hearts means that the side bidding hopes to take 11 tricks (book + 5) with Hearts as trumps.
A contract of 3 Clubs means that the side bidding hopes to take ( ) tricks with ________ as trumps. 8

29 What are the first 6 tricks taken by one side called? 7

30 Example of a contract. 5 Clubs 3

required total tricks = 5 + book ← → trump suit

Match these.

a. trump suit
b. required total tricks = 6 + book

1) 6
2) Spades

31 Which shows Clubs are trumps and that 7 tricks must be made? 2

1 Club	2 Clubs

32 Which shows the suits ranked properly? 4

Spades Hearts Diamonds Clubs	Spades Diamonds Hearts Clubs

1	2	3	4	5	6	7	8
a. 2) b. 1)	☑☐	a. 2) Spades b. 1) 6	☑☐	Hearts	a bid	book	9 Clubs

33 Which player would have a required total of 10 tricks to make his bid?

4♠'s	4♥'s

1

34 A *call* may be either a bid or a pass.

The dealer always makes the initial call.

If N is dealer, ( ) bids next.

	N	
W		E
	S	

5

35 Since the dealer makes the initial call, is he always opening bidder?

2

36 The period during which the bidding takes place is called the *auction.*

The auction takes place:

after the hand is dealt.	before the hand is played.

4

37 The first person to bid is called the opening bidder.
If N bid 1 Club, who is the opening bidder?

	N	
W		E
	S	

6

38 The period during which the bidding takes place is called the:
a. bidding time.
b. action.
c. auction.
d. deal.

3

39 The contract is 2 Hearts.

W led.

Who takes the trick?

	N ♥4	
W ♦3		♦A E
	♥8 S	

8

40 The opening bidder is:

a. the dealer.
b. to the left of the dealer.
c. to the right of the dealer.
d. the dealer's partner.
e. the first player to make a bid.

7

1	2	3	4	5	6	7	8
BOTH	No (He may pass.)	c. auction.	BOTH	E	N	e. the first player to make a bid.	S

41 Which shows that Diamonds are trumps and 9 tricks must be made?

2 Diamonds	4 Diamonds

6

42 Bidding, like playing, proceeds in a clockwise direction. If S is the opening bidder, who bids next?

4

43 Which correctly shows ducking?

(The card standing was led first.)

7

44 The contract is 4 Spades.

S leads.

Who takes this trick?

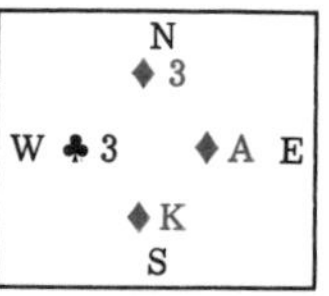

2

45

N
W E
S

E is dealer.

List in proper order the next three bidders after E.

1

46

1 Spade (opening bid)
pass W N E pass S
2 Spades

A *pass* means that the player does not wish to enter the auction at this time.

Which 2 players passed in this bidding sequence?

3

47 A pass by a player means that the player does not want to:
a. play.
b. bid at all.
c. enter the auction at this time.
d. have his partner bid.

5

48 After the first bid or pass, three passes in sequence mean that the auction is over. In which of these is the auction over? S is dealer.

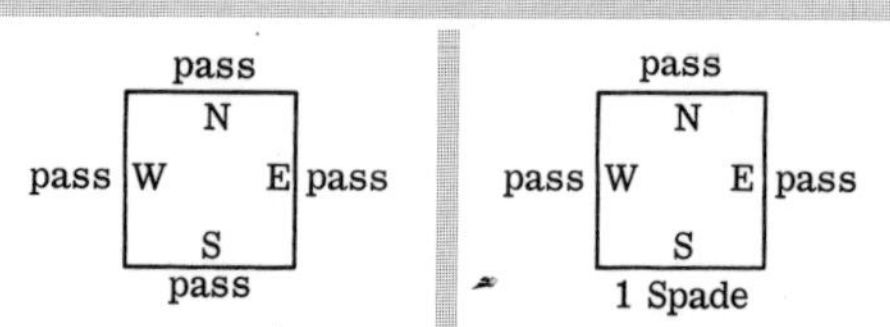

8

1	2	3	4	5	6	7	8
S W N	E (♦A)	E W	W	c. enter the auction at this time.	NEITHER 3 Diamonds	☑☐	BOTH

49 How many more passes in sequence finish the auction after the opening (first) bid?

3	4

8

50

S	W	N	E
1 Heart	pass	2 No Trump	pass
3 Hearts	pass	4 Hearts	pass
pass	pass		

Which of the following describes S?

bid 2 No Trump	opening bidder

4

51 Which shows Diamonds as trumps and 13 as the required total tricks to be taken?

13 Diamonds	7 Diamonds

6

52 Match these.

a. the final bid where the bidder names the trump suit and the number of tricks he must make
b. any offer to win a certain number of tricks
c. the period during which the bidding takes place

1) bid
2) auction
3) contract
4) trump

5

53 The dealer makes the first call, but this may or may not be the opening bid.
a. If West deals, who makes the first call?
b. Who *may* make the first bid?

1

54 The contract can be in any of the suits. It can also be in No Trump. You can guess that No Trump means:
a. no suit is trump.
b. only trump cards can take a trick.

3

55 The contract is 5 Hearts. W leads. Match these.

a. N
b. E
c. S

1) ruffed
2) overruffed
3) covered
4) ducked

N ♣Q
W ♣J
♥8 E
♥10 S

2

56 A contract of 1 in any suit or No Trump means that the side bidding hopes to take 6 + 1 tricks. In this case the E-W team hopes to take:
a. 1 trick.
b. 7 tricks.
c. 1 Club trick.
d. (none of these)

N: pass
W: pass
E: 1 Club (opening bid)
S: pass

7

1	2	3	4	5	6	7	8
a. W b. any of the four players	a. 3) b. 1) c. 2)	a. no suit is trump.	☐ ☑	a. 3) b. 1) c. 2)	☐ ☑	b. 7 tricks.	☑ ☐

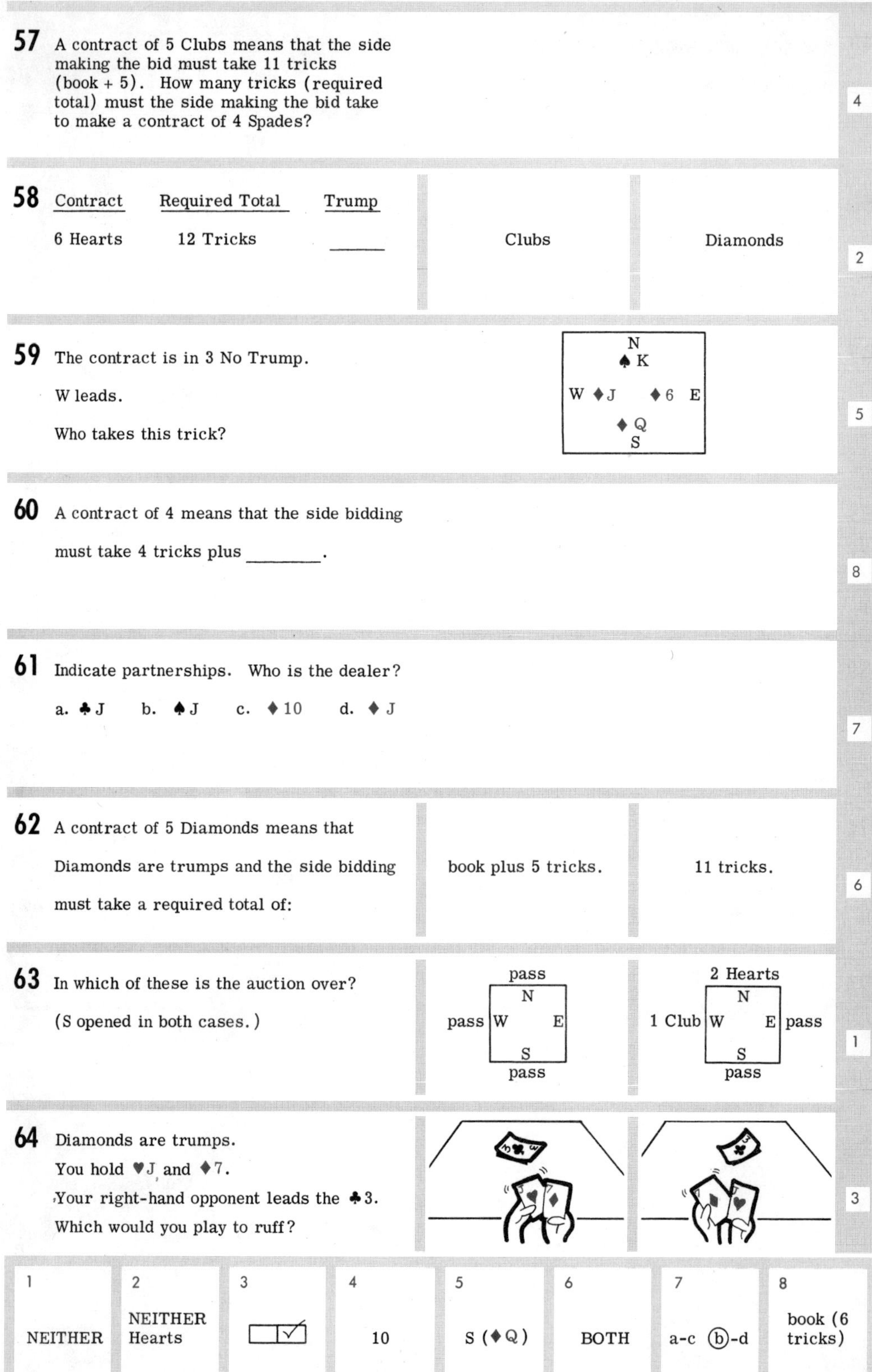

57 A contract of 5 Clubs means that the side making the bid must take 11 tricks (book + 5). How many tricks (required total) must the side making the bid take to make a contract of 4 Spades? 4

58

Contract	Required Total	Trump		
6 Hearts	12 Tricks	______	Clubs	Diamonds

2

59 The contract is in 3 No Trump.

W leads.

Who takes this trick?

N: ♠ K
W: ♦ J
E: ♦ 6
S: ♦ Q

5

60 A contract of 4 means that the side bidding must take 4 tricks plus ________. 8

61 Indicate partnerships. Who is the dealer?

a. ♣ J b. ♠ J c. ♦ 10 d. ♦ J

7

62 A contract of 5 Diamonds means that Diamonds are trumps and the side bidding must take a required total of:

book plus 5 tricks.	11 tricks.

6

63 In which of these is the auction over?

(S opened in both cases.)

N: pass, W: pass, S: pass, E: —	N: 2 Hearts, W: 1 Club, E: pass, S: pass

1

64 Diamonds are trumps.
You hold ♥J and ♦7.
Your right-hand opponent leads the ♣3.
Which would you play to ruff?

3

1	2	3	4	5	6	7	8
NEITHER	NEITHER Hearts	☐☑	10	S (♦Q)	BOTH	a-c (b)-d	book (6 tricks)

65 A contract of 6 Diamonds means that the side bidding must take a required total of ( ) tricks with Diamonds as _________. 7

66

N	E	S	W
1 Club	pass	pass	1 Heart
2 Clubs	pass	pass	pass

In the bidding sequence shown, the contract is ( ) ___________ and is taken by the (N-S/E-W) team. 6

67 Remember that the suits are RANKED:

highest - ________,
next-to-highest - ________,
next-to-lowest - ________, 5
lowest - ________.

68 A book refers to the first ( ) tricks. 8

69 The contract is 3 No Trump.

What is the required total of tricks needed to make the contract?

8 tricks	2 tricks plus book

4

70 The lowest bid possible is 1 Club.

You can guess that 1 (Diamond/Spade) is the next possible lowest bid. 1

71 The sequence of permissible bids is:
1♣, 1 ♦, 1 ♥, 1♠, 1 NT,
2♣, 2 ♦, 2 ♥, 2♠, 2 NT,
3♣, and so on through 6 NT,
7♣, 7 ♦, 7 ♥, 7♠, 7 NT.
1♣ is the lowest possible bid.

(NT = No Trump)

__________ is the highest possible bid. 3

72 A 1 Club bid is lower than a 1 Heart bid.

A 1 Diamond bid is (higher/lower) than a 1 Spade bid. 2

1	2	3	4	5	6	7	8
Diamond	lower	7 NT	NEITHER 9 tricks	Spades Hearts Diamonds Clubs	2 Clubs N-S	12 trumps	6

73 The dealer is always the (contractor/ declarer/initial caller/opening bidder). 8

74 A 1 No Trump bid is (higher/lower) than a 1 bid in any of the suits. 5

75 Any 2 bid is higher than any 1 bid. 1 Spade is a (HIGHER / LOWER) bid than 2 Clubs. 6

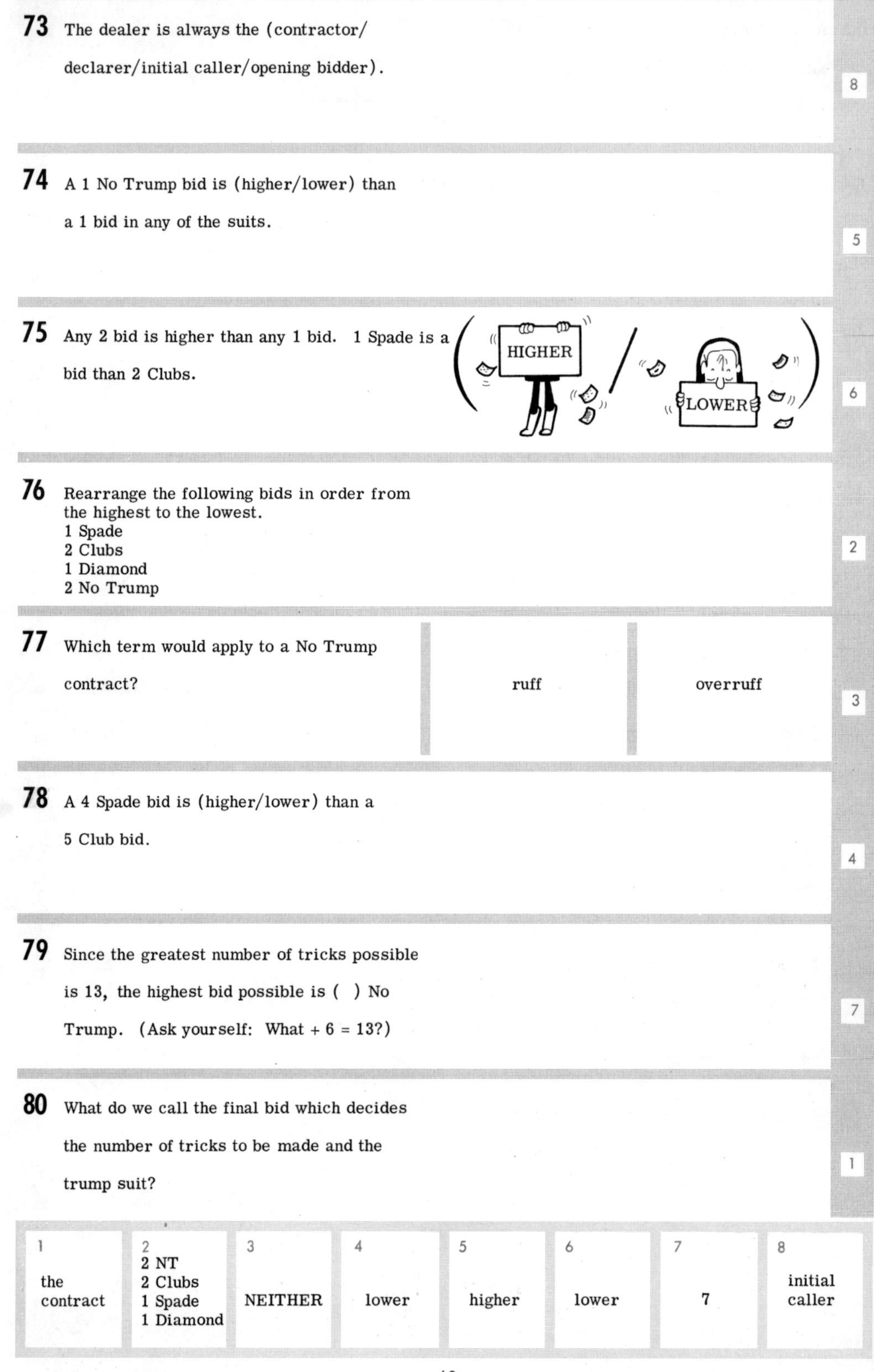

76 Rearrange the following bids in order from the highest to the lowest.
1 Spade
2 Clubs
1 Diamond
2 No Trump 2

77 Which term would apply to a No Trump contract?

ruff	overruff

3

78 A 4 Spade bid is (higher/lower) than a 5 Club bid. 4

79 Since the greatest number of tricks possible is 13, the highest bid possible is ( ) No Trump. (Ask yourself: What + 6 = 13?) 7

80 What do we call the final bid which decides the number of tricks to be made and the trump suit? 1

1	2	3	4	5	6	7	8
the contract	2 NT 2 Clubs 1 Spade 1 Diamond	NEITHER	lower	higher	lower	7	initial caller

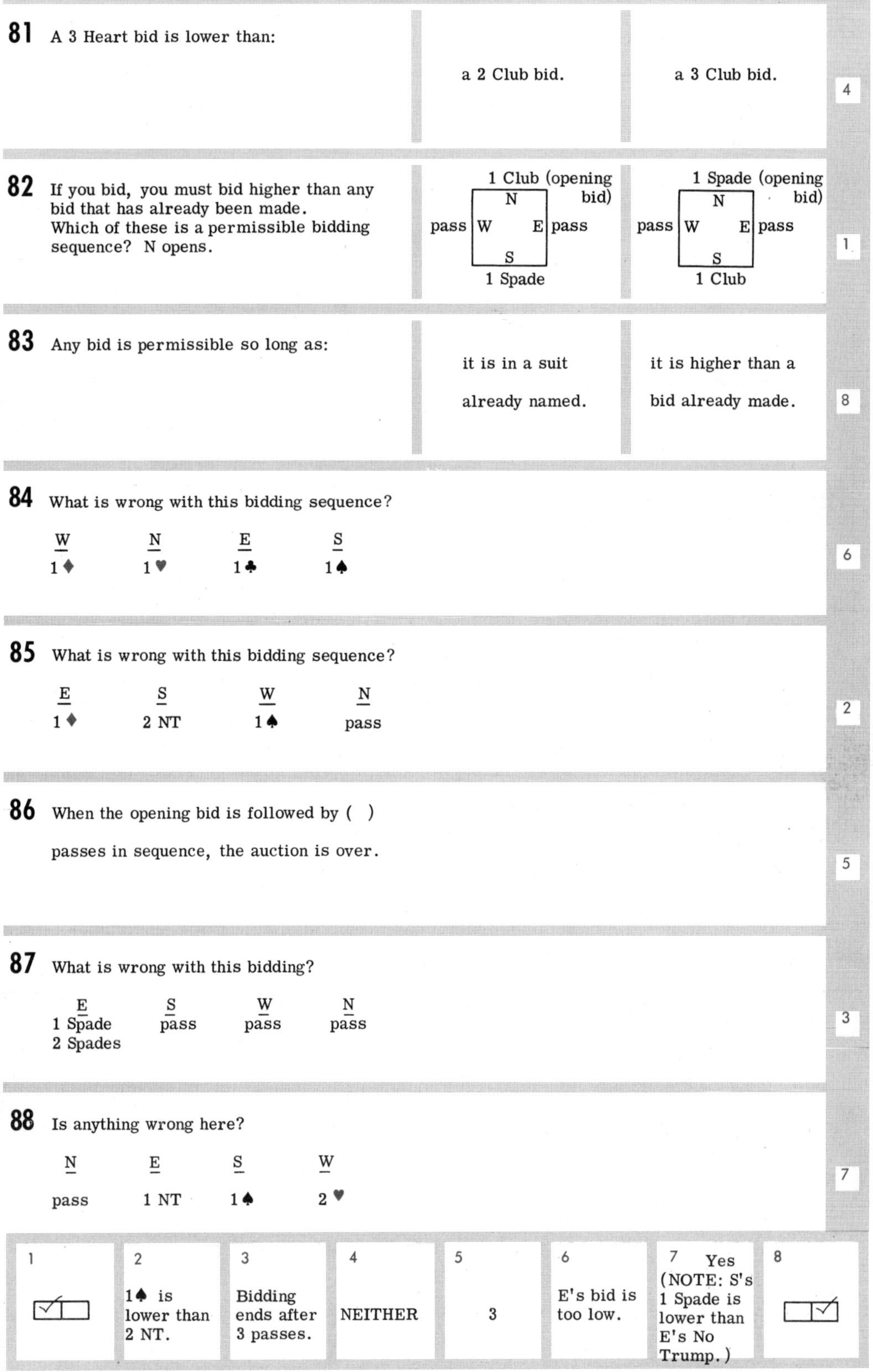

81 A 3 Heart bid is lower than:

a 2 Club bid.	a 3 Club bid.

4

82 If you bid, you must bid higher than any bid that has already been made. Which of these is a permissible bidding sequence? N opens.

N: 1 Club (opening bid); E: pass; S: 1 Spade; W: pass	N: 1 Spade (opening bid); E: pass; S: 1 Club; W: pass

1

83 Any bid is permissible so long as:

it is in a suit already named.	it is higher than a bid already made.

8

84 What is wrong with this bidding sequence?

W	N	E	S
1 ♦	1 ♥	1 ♣	1 ♠

6

85 What is wrong with this bidding sequence?

E	S	W	N
1 ♦	2 NT	1 ♠	pass

2

86 When the opening bid is followed by ( ) passes in sequence, the auction is over.

5

87 What is wrong with this bidding?

E	S	W	N
1 Spade	pass	pass	pass
2 Spades			

3

88 Is anything wrong here?

N	E	S	W
pass	1 NT	1 ♠	2 ♥

7

1	2	3	4	5	6	7	8
☑☐	1♠ is lower than 2 NT.	Bidding ends after 3 passes.	NEITHER	3	E's bid is too low.	Yes (NOTE: S's 1 Spade is lower than E's No Trump.)	☐☑

89 The period during which the bidding takes place is called the: 4

a. contract.
b. deal.
c. overruff.
d. auction.

90 You may bid when it is your turn even though you have previously passed. 2

E	S	W	N
1 Spade	2 Clubs	pass	pass
2 Spades	pass		

May W bid at this point?

91 Which shows Clubs as trumps and 8 as the required total of tricks to be taken? 5

1 Club	8 Clubs

92 The last bid made during the auction is called the __________. 8

3 If you have passed once and one of the other players has bid: 7

a. you must always pass when it is your turn to bid again.
b. you must throw in your hand.
c. you may bid when it is your turn to bid again.
d. you may bid out of turn.

94 Which of the following shows an *improper* bidding sequence? 6

N
W E
S

N W E S	N E W S

95 What is wrong with the following sequence? 1

E	S	N
1 Club	pass	1 Diamond

N
W E
S

96 3

E	S	W	N
pass	pass	pass	pass

May E bid at this point?

1	2	3	4	5	6	7	8
N has bid out of turn.	Yes	No	d) auction.	NEITHER 2 Clubs	BOTH	c. you may bid when it is your turn to bid again.	contract

97 What is wrong with the following bidding?

First bid: E - 1 Spade

Second bid: S - 1 Diamond

	N	
W		E
	S	

7

98 The contract is 7 No Trump.

a. What is the required total of tricks the side must take?

b. What is trump?

6

99 The auction is over when the last bid is followed by three passes in sequence. However, if the dealer passes, how many consecutive passes in all must occur to close the auction?

2	4

5

100 What is wrong here?

N	E	S	W
pass	1 Club	1 Spade	pass
pass	pass	1 No Trump	

8

101 The bid is taken by the team which makes the final bid. Who takes the bid here?

N	E	S	W
1 Club	1 Spade	2 Clubs	2 Diamonds
3 Clubs	pass	pass	pass

N-S	E-W

4

102 In which of these may W bid at point X?

N	E
pass	pass
S	**W**
pass	X

N	E
1 Club	1 Spade
2 Clubs	pass
S	**W**
pass	pass
pass	X

1

103 The bid is taken by the team which:

a. makes the first bid.
b. first names the final suit.
c. makes the final bid.

3

104 Which is true?

1 Diamond is lower than 1 No Trump.	1 No Trump is higher than 1 Diamond.

2

1	2	3	4	5	6	7	8
BOTH	BOTH	c. makes the final bid.	☑☐	☐☑	a. 13 b. No suit is trump.	S bid too low. 1 Diamond is less than 1 Spade.	S may not bid again after 3 consecutive passes.

105

E	S	W	N
pass	1 Club	1 Spade	pass
2 Spades	pass	pass	pass

a. What is the contract?

b. Which team took it? 8

106 A contract in Hearts means that Hearts are (low/trumps/valentines). 5

107

E	S	W	N
1 Club	pass	pass	2 Clubs
pass	pass	pass	

a. What is the contract?
b. Who took it? 6

108 A contract of 3 Clubs means that Clubs are trumps and the team which takes the bid hopes to take a required total of ( ) tricks. 2

109 The players who make the final bid (the contract) are called the *contractors*. Here the contractors are (N-S/E-W). 3

N	E	S	W
1 Club	pass	pass	pass

110 A No Trump bid is higher than a suit bid.

Which is higher than 1 Spade?

2 Clubs	1 No Trump

4

111

S	W	N	E
pass	pass	pass	1 Spade
2 Clubs	2 Spades	pass	pass
pass			

a. What is the contract?

b. Who are the contractors?

c. What is the required total of tricks? 7

112 A contract of 4 Hearts means that Hearts are ________ and a required total of 10 tricks must be made by the contractors. 1

1	2	3	4	5	6	7	8
trumps	9	N-S	BOTH	trumps	a. 2 Clubs b. N-S	a. 2 Spades b. E-W c. 8	a. 2 Spades b. E-W

113

W	N	E	S
1 Spade	pass	1 No Trump	2 Clubs
2 No Trump	pass	pass	pass

Here the contractors (E-W) hope to take 8 tricks in:
a. No Trump.
b. Spades.
c. Clubs.
d. (none of these)

4

114

W	N	E	S
1♦	2♣	2♦	3♣
pass	pass	pass	

a. Which suit is trump?

b. Who are the contractors?

c. What is the required total of tricks?

1

115 What is the lowest permissible bid?

8

116

N	E	S	W
pass	pass	1♠	pass
3♠	pass	4♠	pass
pass	pass		

a. Here N-S are the ________.

b. The contract is ( ) ________.

6

117 The first member of the contractors to name the trump suit is called the *declarer*.

N	E	S	W
1♣	pass	2♣	pass
pass			

The declarer here is ( ).

2

118 A contract of 6 Diamonds means that Diamonds are trumps and the contractors hope to take a required total of:

6 tricks. | 6 Diamond tricks.

3

119 The contractors bid 4 Spades but took only a total of 9 tricks. Is this less than their required total?

5

120 The first member of the contractors to name the trump suit is called the:
a. caller.
b. trumper.
c. decaller.
d. declarer.

7

1	2	3	4	5	6	7	8
a. Clubs b. N-S c. 9	N	NEITHER 12 tricks.	a. No Trump	Yes (NOTE: The required total was 10.)	a. contractors b. 4 Spades	d. declarer	1 Club

121 The bid is 5 No Trump. In which case do the contractors make *less* than the required total?

if they take a total of 9 tricks	if they take a total of 13 tricks

4

122

N	E	S	W
1 ♦	2 ♣	pass	3 ♣
pass	pass	pass	

a. Who are the contractors?

b. Who is the declarer?

1

123 The declarer is the:
a. person who makes the final bid.
b. person who first bids the trump suit.
c. first member of the contractors to bid the trump suit.

3

124 Which contract shows that 7 is the required total of tricks to be made?

5

125

E	S	W	N
pass	1 Spade	2 Clubs	2 No Trump
3 Clubs	3 No Trump	pass	pass
pass			

N is the ________.

2

126 The dealer is always the:

opening bidder.	declarer.

7

127

E	S	W	N
1 ♣	pass	3 ♣	pass
5 ♣	pass	pass	pass

a. Who is the declarer?

b. Who is the dealer?

6

128 The players who make the final bid are the contractors.
The first member of the contractors to name the trump suit is the ________.

8

1	2	3	4	5	6	7	8
a. E-W b. E	declarer	c. first member of the contractors to bid the trump suit.	☑☐	BOTH	a. E b. E	NEITHER person who makes the first call.	declarer

129

E	S	W	N
1♣	1♥	1♠	2♣
2♠	3♣	pass	5♣
pass	pass	pass	

a. What are trumps?
b. Who is the declarer?
c. What is the required total of tricks?
d. Who dealt?

7

130 The declarer's partner is called the *dummy*.

S	W	N	E
1♣	pass	2♣	pass
pass	pass		

Who is the dummy here?

4

131 The contract is 5 Diamonds. S leads.

Who takes this trick?

N: ♦6
W: ♠J
E: ♦8
S: ♠10

3

132

W	N	E	S
pass	1♣	pass	2♥
pass	3♥	pass	4♥
pass	pass	pass	

a. Who is opening bidder?
b. Who is declarer?
c. Who is dummy?

5

133 Who is dummy?

the player who makes the opening bid	the player who passes first

1

134

S	W	N	E
1♦	pass	1♥	1♠
2♥	2♠	3♥	3♠
pass	4♠	pass	pass
pass			

In this bidding sequence, ( ) is the declarer.

2

135

S	W	N	E
1♥	1♠	2♦	2♥
3♥	3 NT	pass	4♥
pass	pass	pass	

Who is the declarer?

8

136

N	E	S	W
1♥	pass	1 NT	pass
pass	pass		

What is the contract here?

1 Heart	1 No Trump

6

1	2	3	4	5	6	7	8
NEITHER declarer's partner	E	E (♦8)	N	a. N b. S c. N	☐☑	a. Clubs b. N c. 11 d. E	E

137

W	N	E	S
pass	1♠	pass	2♠
pass	pass	pass	

In this bidding sequence, S is the:

dummy.	declarer.

6

138

N	E	S	W
1♣	pass	1♥	2♣
2♦	pass	2♠	3♣
3♥	pass	3 NT	pass
4♥	pass	pass	pass

a. Who is the declarer?

b. What is the contract?

7

139 The opponents of the contractors are called the *defenders*.

E	S	W	N
1♣	pass	1 NT	pass
pass	pass		

Here (E-W/N-S) are the defenders.

3

140 Contractors Defenders

Declarer Dummy

N S E W

Contractors are called declarer and dummy. Do the defenders have different titles too?

1

141 The declarer is:

a. the first to mention the trump suit.
b. the first member of the contractors to mention the trump suit.
c. the first to bid.
d. the last to bid.

4

142 What are the opponents of the contractors called?

5

143

N
♣3
W ♦J ♦7 E
♥5
S

Clubs are trumps. E leads. Match these.

a.	sluff	1)	S
b.	ruff	2)	W
c.	cover	3)	N
		4)	E

2

144

S	W	N	E
1♣	pass	2♣	pass
pass	pass		

Which is true?

Here E-W are the defenders.	S is the declarer.

8

1	2	3	4	5	6	7	8
No	a. 1) S b. 3) N c. 2) W	N-S	b.	defenders	☑☐	a. S b. 4 Hearts	BOTH

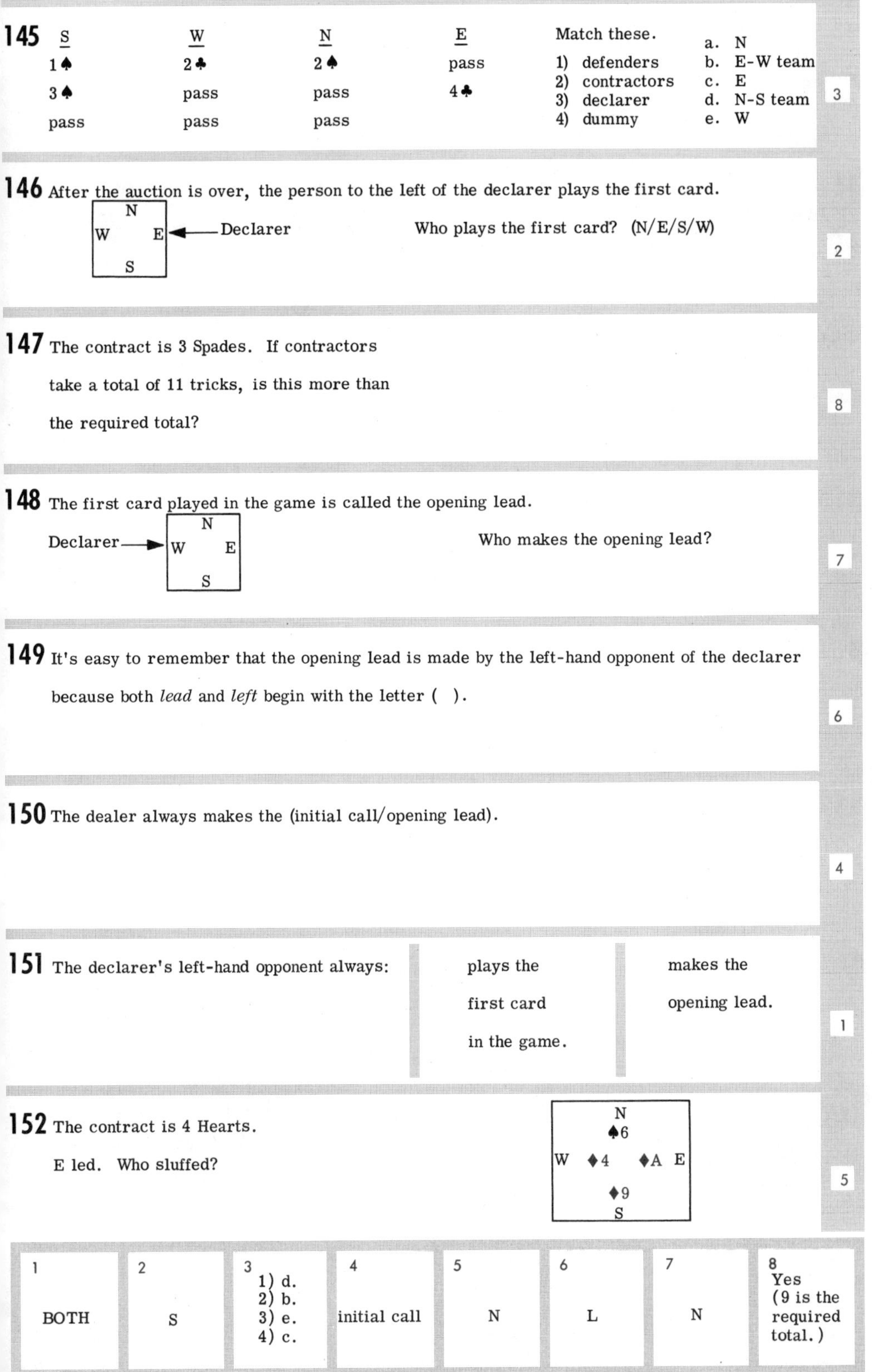

145

S	W	N	E
1♠	2♣	2♠	pass
3♠	pass	pass	4♣
pass	pass	pass	

Match these.

1) defenders	a. N
2) contractors	b. E-W team
3) declarer	c. E
4) dummy	d. N-S team
	e. W

3

146 After the auction is over, the person to the left of the declarer plays the first card.

Who plays the first card? (N/E/S/W) 2

147 The contract is 3 Spades. If contractors take a total of 11 tricks, is this more than the required total? 8

148 The first card played in the game is called the opening lead.

Who makes the opening lead? 7

149 It's easy to remember that the opening lead is made by the left-hand opponent of the declarer because both *lead* and *left* begin with the letter ( ). 6

150 The dealer always makes the (initial call/opening lead). 4

151 The declarer's left-hand opponent always:

plays the first card in the game.	makes the opening lead.

1

152 The contract is 4 Hearts.

E led. Who sluffed?

5

1	2	3	4	5	6	7	8
BOTH	S	1) d. 2) b. 3) e. 4) c.	initial call	N	L	N	Yes (9 is the required total.)

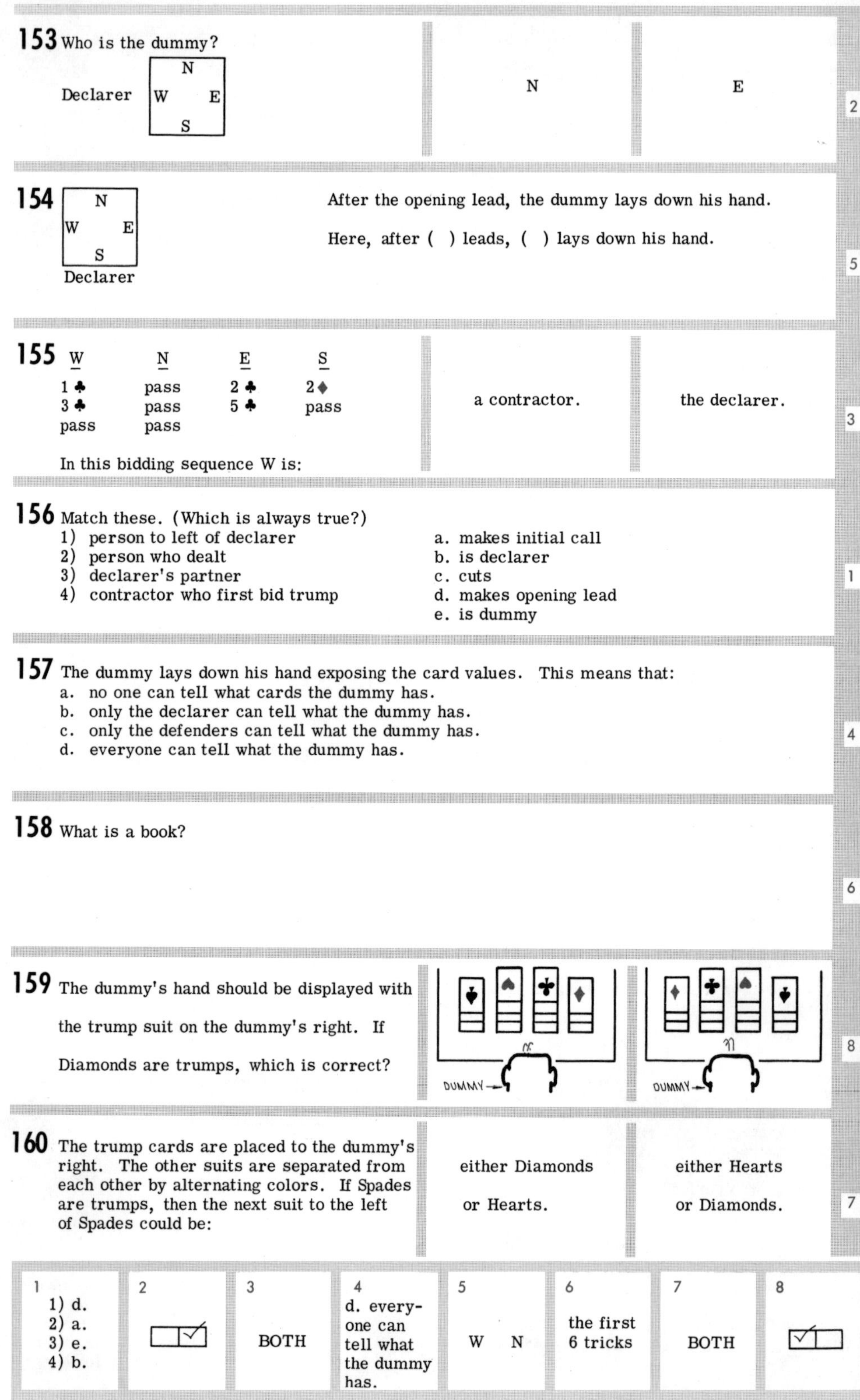

153 Who is the dummy?

Declarer [box: N / W E / S]

	N	E	2

154 [box: N / W E / S] Declarer

After the opening lead, the dummy lays down his hand.

Here, after ( ) leads, ( ) lays down his hand. 5

155

W	N	E	S
1 ♣	pass	2 ♣	2 ♦
3 ♣	pass	5 ♣	pass
pass	pass		

In this bidding sequence W is:

a contractor.	the declarer.	3

156 Match these. (Which is always true?)

1) person to left of declarer
2) person who dealt
3) declarer's partner
4) contractor who first bid trump

a. makes initial call
b. is declarer
c. cuts
d. makes opening lead
e. is dummy

1

157 The dummy lays down his hand exposing the card values. This means that:

a. no one can tell what cards the dummy has.
b. only the declarer can tell what the dummy has.
c. only the defenders can tell what the dummy has.
d. everyone can tell what the dummy has.

4

158 What is a book?

6

159 The dummy's hand should be displayed with the trump suit on the dummy's right. If Diamonds are trumps, which is correct?

8

160 The trump cards are placed to the dummy's right. The other suits are separated from each other by alternating colors. If Spades are trumps, then the next suit to the left of Spades could be:

either Diamonds or Hearts.	either Hearts or Diamonds.	7

1	2	3	4	5	6	7	8
1) d. 2) a. 3) e. 4) b.	[second box checked]	BOTH	d. everyone can tell what the dummy has.	W N	the first 6 tricks	BOTH	[first box checked]

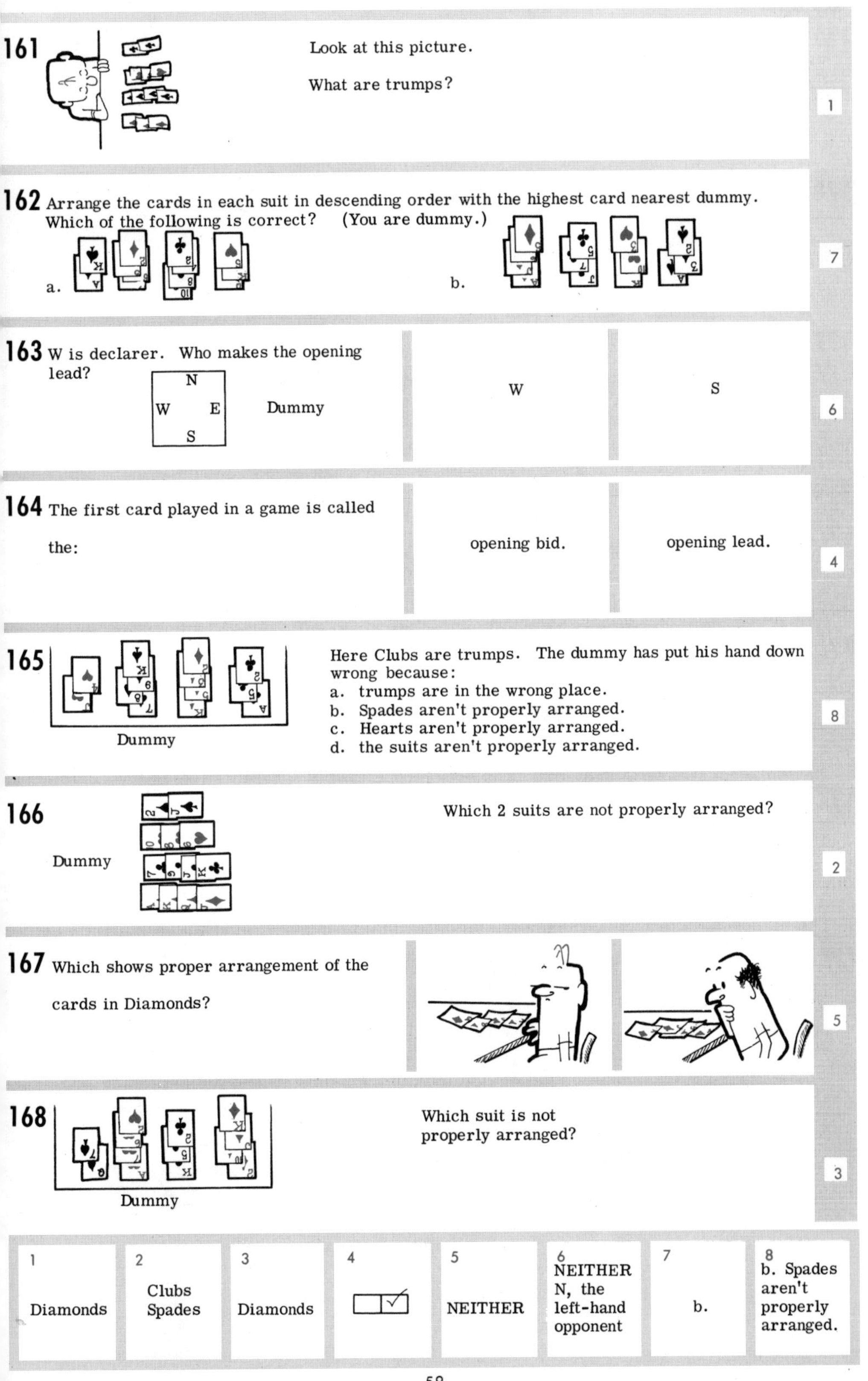

161 Look at this picture.

What are trumps? 1

162 Arrange the cards in each suit in descending order with the highest card nearest dummy. Which of the following is correct? (You are dummy.)

a. b. 7

163 W is declarer. Who makes the opening lead?

	N	
W		E
	S	

Dummy

W | S 6

164 The first card played in a game is called the:

opening bid. | opening lead. 4

165 Dummy

Here Clubs are trumps. The dummy has put his hand down wrong because:

a. trumps are in the wrong place.
b. Spades aren't properly arranged.
c. Hearts aren't properly arranged.
d. the suits aren't properly arranged. 8

166 Dummy

Which 2 suits are not properly arranged? 2

167 Which shows proper arrangement of the cards in Diamonds? 5

168 Dummy

Which suit is not properly arranged? 3

1	2	3	4	5	6	7	8
Diamonds	Clubs Spades	Diamonds	☐☑	NEITHER	NEITHER N, the left-hand opponent	b.	b. Spades aren't properly arranged.

169 The declarer plays both his hand and the dummy's. This means that the dummy (does/does not) play. 7

---

170 Which is the opening lead?

the first bid	the lead to the last trick

5

---

171 The dummy's hand is played by:

his partner.	the declarer.

6

---

172 The opening lead is made by the person to the left of the declarer. The next card is played:

a. by the declarer from the dummy's hand.
b. by the declarer from his own hand.
c. (both)
d. (neither)

Dummy
opening lead ⟶
Declarer

4

---

173 Remember that a hand is played in (clockwise/counterclockwise) rotation. 2

174

N	E	S	W
pass	1 ♥	pass	2 ♣
pass	2 ♥	pass	3 ♣
pass	pass	pass	

1) Who is dealer?
2) Who is declarer?
3) Who is dummy?
4) Who makes the opening lead?

1

---

175 After a trick is taken, the next lead is made:

a. from the dummy.
b. by the declarer.
c. by the person to the left of the last leader.
d. by the winner of the trick.

8

---

176 Does this picture show the declarer playing a card from the dummy's hand? 3

1	2	3	4	5	6	7	8
1) N 2) W 3) E 4) N	clockwise	Yes	a. by the declarer from the dummy's hand.	NEITHER the lead to the first trick	BOTH	does not	d. by the winner of the trick.

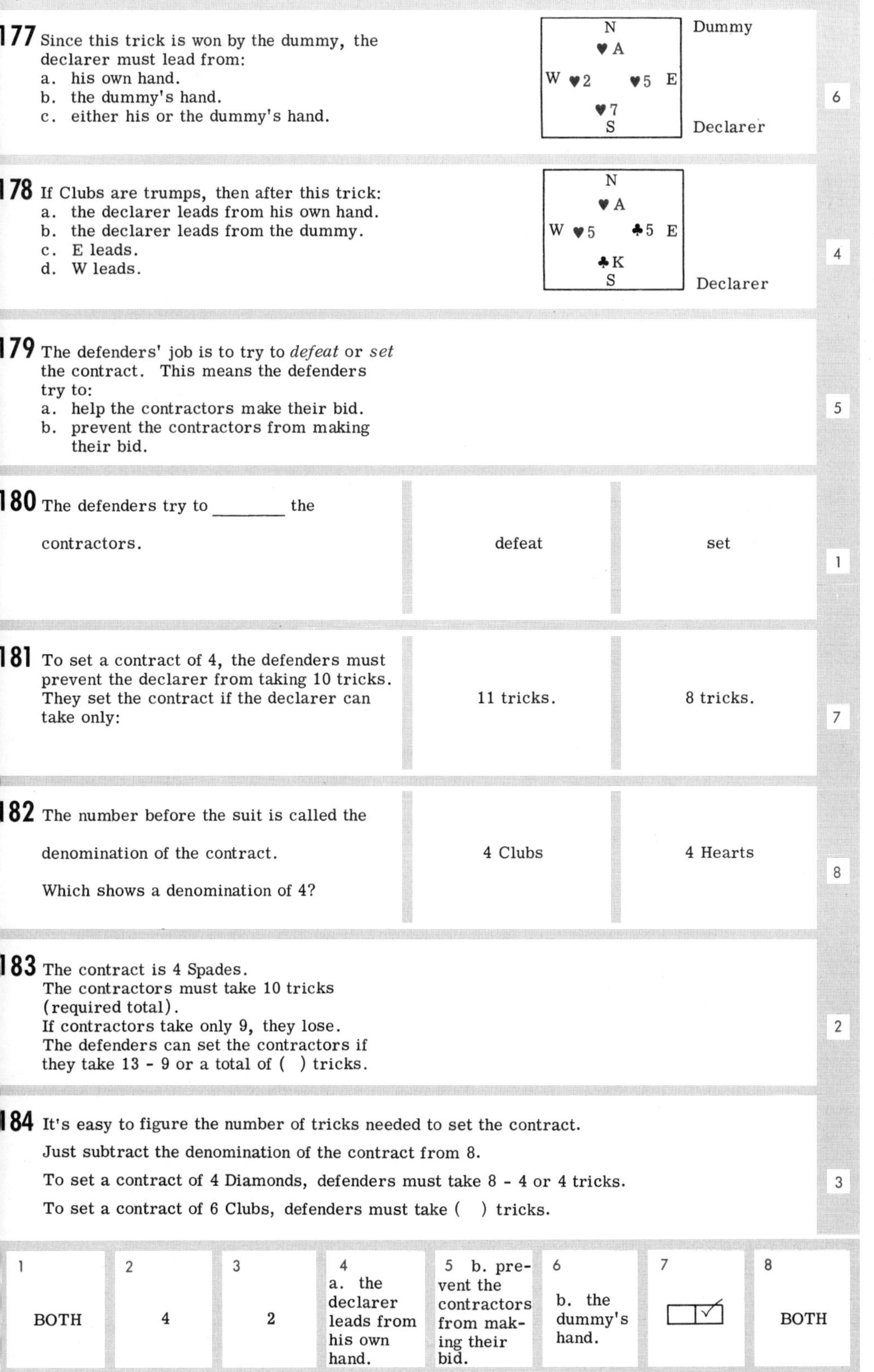

177 Since this trick is won by the dummy, the declarer must lead from:
a. his own hand.
b. the dummy's hand.
c. either his or the dummy's hand.

6

178 If Clubs are trumps, then after this trick:
a. the declarer leads from his own hand.
b. the declarer leads from the dummy.
c. E leads.
d. W leads.

4

179 The defenders' job is to try to *defeat* or *set* the contract. This means the defenders try to:
a. help the contractors make their bid.
b. prevent the contractors from making their bid.

5

180 The defenders try to ________ the contractors.

defeat	set

1

181 To set a contract of 4, the defenders must prevent the declarer from taking 10 tricks. They set the contract if the declarer can take only:

11 tricks.	8 tricks.

7

182 The number before the suit is called the denomination of the contract.

Which shows a denomination of 4?

4 Clubs	4 Hearts

8

183 The contract is 4 Spades.
The contractors must take 10 tricks (required total).
If contractors take only 9, they lose.
The defenders can set the contractors if they take 13 - 9 or a total of ( ) tricks.

2

184 It's easy to figure the number of tricks needed to set the contract.

Just subtract the denomination of the contract from 8.

To set a contract of 4 Diamonds, defenders must take 8 - 4 or 4 tricks.

To set a contract of 6 Clubs, defenders must take ( ) tricks.

3

1	2	3	4	5	6	7	8
BOTH	4	2	a. the declarer leads from his own hand.	b. prevent the contractors from making their bid.	b. the dummy's hand.	☐☑	BOTH

185 A contract of 4 is set if the contractors take:	9 or less tricks.	10 or more tricks.	1
186 A contract of 5 is made if the declarer takes:	10 tricks.	9 tricks.	8

187 A contract of 5 is set if the declarer takes 10 or less tricks. This means the defenders must take (3/2/4) tricks. 7

188 To determine the number of tricks needed to set the contract, subtract the denomination of the contract from:	8.	eight.	5

189 The contract is 2 Spades.

a. To make the contract, the contractors must take at least ( ) tricks.

b. To set the contract, the defenders must take at least ( ) tricks. 2

190 To set a given contract, defenders need to take at least 8 - (amount of contract) tricks. For example, to set a contract of 6, defenders must take (8 - 6) tricks. What would defenders need to set a 3♠ contract? 6

191 To set a contract of 1, how many tricks must defenders take?	1	8	4
192 N ♥Q; W ♥5; ♥J E; ♣5 S. Spades are trumps. E leads.	N covered.	S ducked.	3

1	2	3	4	5	6	7	8
☑ ☐	a. 8 b. 6	☑ ☐	NEITHER 8 - 1 = 7	BOTH	5 tricks	3	NEITHER 11 tricks.

193 To set a contract of 5, defenders must take at least ( ) tricks.

3

1	2	3	4	5	6	7	8
		3					

TAKE UNIT 3 POST-TEST

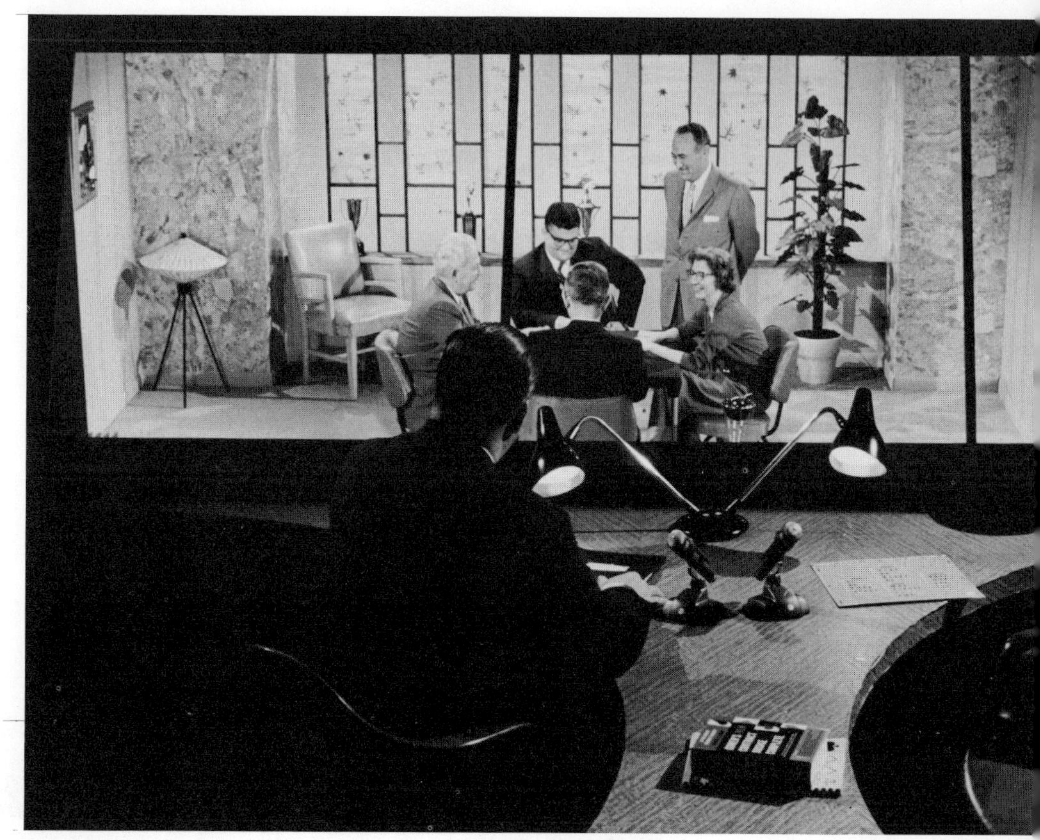

FROM THE TV SHOW "CHAMPIONSHIP BRIDGE"

Mr. Goren tells four masters (Mrs. Sobel, Mr. Hodge, Mr. Lazard, and Mr. Hazen) what they did right.

FROM THE TV SHOW "CHAMPIONSHIP BRIDGE"

Mr. Goren in a friendly get-together with the Italian World Championship Team.

UNIT 4

scoring

Sufficient scoring information is discussed to guide the beginning player in his bidding. He is shown a scoring table and taught how to use it. A brief discussion of the penalty double, premiums, sacrifice bidding, and penalties is included.

PRE- AND POST-TEST

1. When two games are made by a partnership before their opponents make two games, it is called a __________.

2. A score for tricks bid and made which is less than game is called a __________ - __________.

3. For each of the suits, list what is game.
   a. __________Clubs
   b. __________No Trump
   c. __________Hearts
   d. __________Diamonds
   e. __________Spades

4. Is it possible to win a rubber, having less points than your opponents?

5. If you make two games while your opponents make only game, you win (300/500/700/100) points above the line.

6. ( ) scoring points are needed for game.

7. If you bid and make 7 of any suit, you have made a __________ __________.

8. Your part-score does not count toward game if your opponents make game. (True/False)

9. Write *above* or *below* after each of the following to indicate whether the points received are scored above or below the line.
   a. points for overtricks
   b. penalty points collected from opponents
   c. points for tricks bid and made
   d. points for part-score
   e. bonus for honors
   f. points for winning a rubber
   g. slam bonuses

10. If you bid and make 6 of any suit or No Trump, you have made a small __________.

11. If you have a part-score of 60 points, in order to make game:
    a. you must make 30 points before your opponents get a part-score.
    b. you must make 40 points before your opponents get a part-score.
    c. you must make 40 points before your opponents make game.
    d. you must make 30 points before your opponents make game.

12. After your side has made game, your side is __________.

13. If you make two games before your opponents have made game, you win (300/500/700/100) points above the line.

14. Score these hands on a scoring sheet similar to the one below.

1st Hand - WE bid 3 Clubs and take 10 tricks.

2nd Hand - WE bid and make 1 No Trump.

3rd Hand - THEY bid and make 2 Diamonds doubled.
(Don't forget premium for making doubled contracts.)

4th Hand - WE bid 2 No Trump and take 8 tricks.

5th Hand - THEY bid 4 Spades and make it.

6th Hand - WE bid 2 Hearts and make 7 tricks.

7th Hand - WE bid 4 Hearts and make 11 tricks.

WE	THEY

15. Who won rubber game?

16. Who are the winners? How many points did the winning team score over the opponents?

BRIDGE POINTS SUMMARY

When doubled contracts are made, each trick is worth double value below the line. That is:

Minors doubled:	Each trick (over 6) is worth 40 points.
Majors doubled:	Each trick (over 6) is worth 60 points.
No Trump doubled:	First trick (over 6) is worth 80 points, and each additional trick is worth 60 points.

PENALTIES

If declarer fails to make his contract, opponents score as follows.

	Not Vulnerable		Vulnerable	
	Not Doubled	Doubled	Not Doubled	Doubled
1 Down	50	100	100	200
2 Down	100	300	200	500
3 Down	150	500	300	800

PREMIUMS

	Not Vulnerable	Vulnerable
For bidding and making Small Slam (12 tricks) –	500	750
For bidding and making Grand Slam (13 tricks) –	1000	1500
For holding four trump honors in one hand –	100	100
For holding five trump honors in one hand –	150	150
For holding four Aces in one hand at No Trump –	150	150
For making any doubled or redoubled contract –	50	50

POINTS FOR GAME

Major – 30 points per trick
Minor – 20 points per trick
No Trump – 30 points per trick plus 10 extra for first trick.
Reach rubber before opponents score game – 700
Reach rubber after opponents score game – 500

GAME VALUES

At the beginning of a rubber, the side that wins a game scores 100 points or more below the line. This is not, however, the true value of that game, because if you and your partner make the second game of a rubber, you will receive 700 points. Therefore, the value of a game is roughly 300 points outside what is written down on the scorepad.

In order to know whether or not it is more advantageous to set your opponents double or to bid and make game, you should keep the value of game in mind.

For example, if you are vulnerable but your opponents are not, and you wish to determine whether or not it is better to 1) set your opponents 2 tricks at 4 Clubs doubled, or 2) to bid and make 4 Hearts, you would choose the second alternative. You would stand to gain 700 points for making rubber if you make your contract of 4 Hearts. This is much better than the 300 points you would receive for setting your opponents. On the other hand, if your opponents are not vulnerable and you are, and you wish to know whether or not to allow opponents to bid and make 5 Diamonds, or be set 1 trick doubled, your correct choice would be the second alternative. Opponents would be awarded only 200 points if you are set 1 trick; whereas, if you allowed them to make game, they would receive approximately 300 points.

EXERCISE SCORE SHEETS

WE	THEY

Frame 60

WE	THEY

Frame 63

WE	THEY

Frame 64

WE	THEY

Frame 94

WE	THEY

Frame 96

WE	THEY

Frame 107

WE	THEY

Frame 109

WE	THEY

Frame 119

WE	THEY

Frame 124

WE	THEY

Frame 127

WE	THEY

Frame 150

WE	THEY

Frame 162

WE	THEY

Frame 173

WE	THEY

Frame 175

WE	THEY

Extra

WE	THEY

Extra

1 (Before you begin, take the Pre-Test for Unit 4.)
Some knowledge of scoring should be learned even by the beginner, since it should guide both his bidding and his playing. 1

GO TO NEXT FRAME

2 One way to score points is for your team to make your contract. This means that:

a. you must take the bid.

b. you must take the bid and make at least the number of tricks you contracted for. 8

c. you must prevent your opponents from making their contract.

3 As contractor, you do not score any points unless you take at least the number of tricks you have contracted for. 5

Do you get points if you are set?

4 To make a 3 bid is the same as taking at least 6 + 3 or 9 tricks.

To make a 5 bid you must take ( ) tricks (required total). 4

5 Here are the suits ranked.
Spades
Hearts
Diamonds
Clubs
Which two suits are the highest? 3

Spades Hearts	Diamonds Clubs

6 Clubs and Diamonds are called the *minor* suits. Which cards are in the *major* suits? 2

A ♥	5 ♠

7 Each trick over book (6 tricks) that is bid for and taken in the minor suits is worth 20 points.

If you bid 3 Clubs and make 9 tricks, you get 3 times 20 or 60 points. 7

If you bid 5 Diamonds and take 11 tricks, you get ( ) points.

8 To *make 4 tricks* means that you take 10 tricks.

To *make* 6 tricks you take: 6

10 tricks.	12 tricks.

1	2	3	4	5	6	7	8
	BOTH	☑☐	11 (6 + 5)	No	☐☑	100	b.

9 You bid 4. You need a required total of 10. You make 3. You took an actual total of 9. You:	made your contract.	were set.	8
10 Each trick *over* book that is bid for and taken in the minor suits is worth ( ) points.			2
11 If the contract is not made, no points are given to the contractor. a. If you bid 6 Clubs and make 5, you get ( ) points. b. If you bid 2 Diamonds and make 2, you get ( ) points.			4
12 Label each of the following suits *major* or *minor*. a. b. c. d.			5
13 If you bid 3 Clubs and take 9 tricks, you get:	60 points.	90 points.	1
14 How many tricks over book must be made to fulfill a contract of 5 Clubs?	6	4	7
15 If you bid 2 Clubs and make 2, you get ( ) points.			6
16 Each trick over 6 that is bid for and taken in the major suits is worth 30 points. If you bid 4 Hearts and just make it, you get ( ) points.			3

1	2	3	4	5	6	7	8
[✓][ ]	20	120	a. 0 b. 40	a. minor b. major c. minor d. major	40	NEITHER 5	[ ][✓]

17 a. Each trick bid for and made in the major suits is worth ( ) points.

b. Each trick bid for and made in the minor suits is worth ( ) points.

7

18 To bid and make 3 Diamonds, you must take a required total of:

	8 tricks.	3 tricks.

1

19 A contract is in a minor suit and the required total tricks is 11. How many points will the contractors receive?

	100	220

4

20 If you bid 3 Diamonds and take 8 tricks, you get ( ) points.

6

21 In No Trump the first trick counts 40 points. Each trick above the first trick counts 30 points. If you bid and make 3 No Trump, you get ( ) points.

2

22 Bid and made 3 NT = 3 times 30 + 10 = 100.

Bid and made 6 NT =

	6 times 30 + 10.	190.

8

23 Each trick taken in a No Trump contract after the first trick is worth:

	the same as the first trick.	10 points less than the first trick.

5

24 Points in No Trump have the same value as the major suits except that you add 10 points at the end. If you bid and make 2 No Trump, you get 2 times 30 + 10 = ( ) points.

3

1	2	3	4	5	6	7	8
NEITHER 9 tricks.	100	70	[✓][ ]	[ ][✓]	0 (NOTE: You are set if you took only 8 tricks.)	a. 30 b. 20	BOTH

25 Match.

1) made a 3-Club bid
2) made a 3-Spade bid
3) made a 3-No Trump bid

a. 90
b. 70
c. 60
d. 100

7

26 If you bid and make 7 No Trump, how many points do you make?

220 | 210

4

27 Match these.

1) made a bid of 1 in a major suit
2) made a bid of 1 in a minor suit
3) made a bid of 1 in No Trump

a. 40
b. 30
c. 20
d. 10

2

28 Clubs are trumps. S leads.

N has: a. sluffed.
b. overruffed.
c. ruffed.
d. covered.

N
♥ 3
W ♦K ♦7 E
♦ 10
S

8

29 How does scoring for No Trump differ from the major suits?

5

30 Eleven tricks is the required total for this hand. Which of the following contracts represents the required total?

a. 4 Spades
b. 3 No Trump
c. 5 Clubs
d. 2 Diamonds

1

31 If you bid and make 1 No Trump, you get ( ) points.

3

32 A contract of 4 Diamonds means that you must make a required total of ( ) tricks.

6

1	2	3	4	5	6	7	8
c. 5 Clubs	1) b. 2) c. 3) a.	40	☑☐	You add 10 points at the end.	10	1) c. 2) a. 3) d.	a. sluffed.

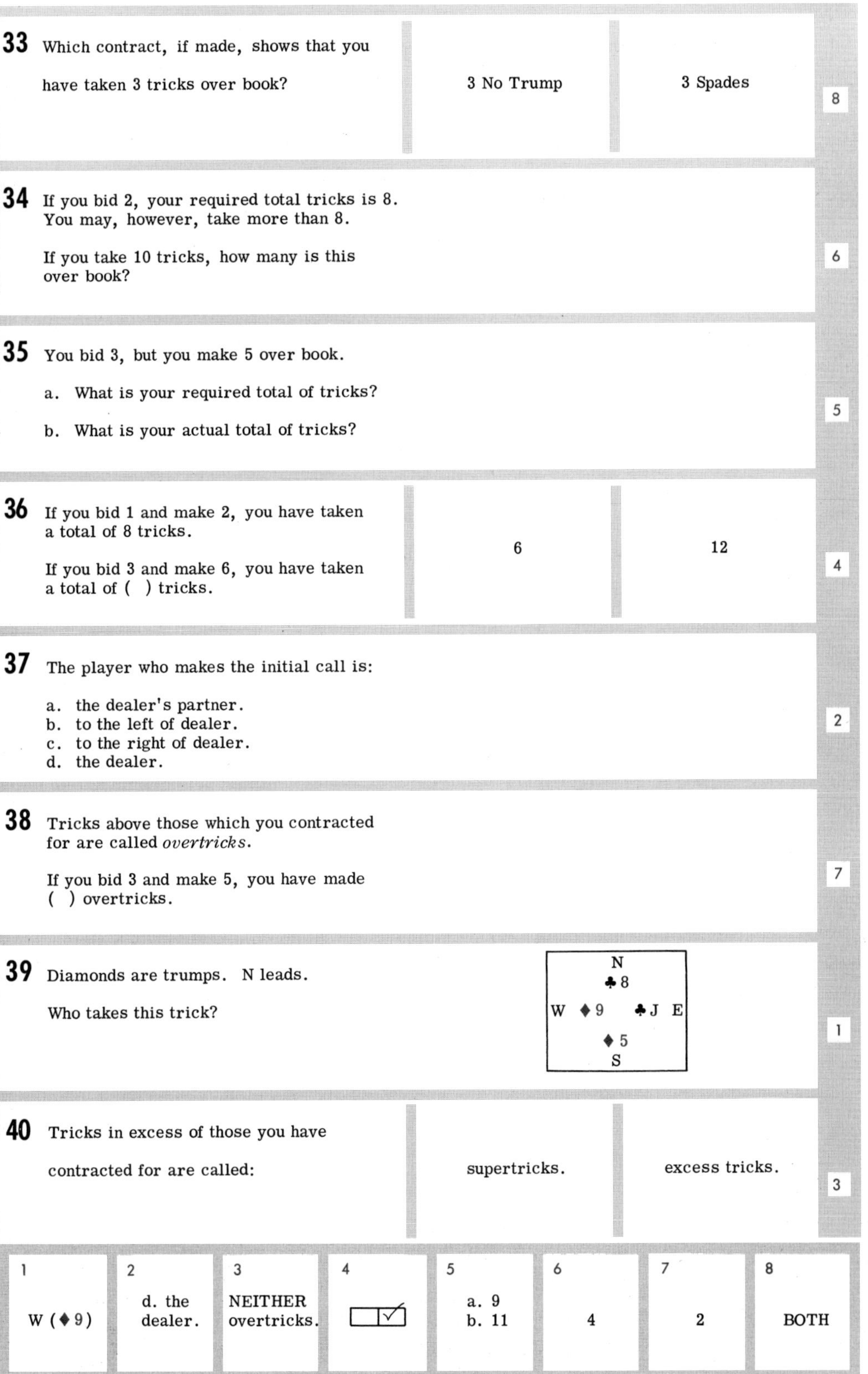

33 Which contract, if made, shows that you have taken 3 tricks over book?

3 No Trump	3 Spades

8

34 If you bid 2, your required total tricks is 8. You may, however, take more than 8.

If you take 10 tricks, how many is this over book?

6

35 You bid 3, but you make 5 over book.

a. What is your required total of tricks?

b. What is your actual total of tricks?

5

36 If you bid 1 and make 2, you have taken a total of 8 tricks.

If you bid 3 and make 6, you have taken a total of ( ) tricks.

6	12

4

37 The player who makes the initial call is:

a. the dealer's partner.
b. to the left of dealer.
c. to the right of dealer.
d. the dealer.

2

38 Tricks above those which you contracted for are called *overtricks*.

If you bid 3 and make 5, you have made ( ) overtricks.

7

39 Diamonds are trumps. N leads.

Who takes this trick?

N
♣8
W ♦9 ♣J E
♦5
S

1

40 Tricks in excess of those you have contracted for are called:

supertricks.	excess tricks.

3

1	2	3	4	5	6	7	8
W (♦9)	d. the dealer.	NEITHER overtricks.	☐☑	a. 9 b. 11	4	2	BOTH

41 Who makes the opening lead?

	N	
W		E
	S	

Declarer

N | S

6

42 Tricks bid for and made are called *game tricks*.

You bid 2 and make 5.
You have 2 game tricks.
You have 3 overtricks.

You bid 3 and make 4.
a. How many game tricks?
b. How many overtricks?

7

43 Overtricks are scored just like game points.

One overtrick in a minor suit is 20 overtrick points.

Four overtricks in a major suit are ( ) overtrick points.

5

44 The contract is 2 Clubs. You make 5.

a. How many overtrick points do you make?

b. How many game points do you make?

1

45 You bid 4 Spades and make 5.

a. You make ( ) points for overtricks.

b. You make ( ) game points.

3

46 Score Card

WE	THEY
50	

The person keeping score always refers to his team as *WE* and the opponents as *THEY*. Who has a score here?

WE | THEY

4

47 Score Card

WE	THEY	
B		← above line
		← Line
A		← below line

Points toward game are scored below the line.

If WE bid and make 2 No Trump, WE would score 70 points in position (A/B).

2

48

WE	THEY	
30		
		← Line
90		

Points for overtricks are scored above the line. (They are over the top of game tricks.)

If WE bid 3 Spades and make 4, WE score ( ) points below the line and ( ) points above the line.

8

1	2	3	4	5	6	7	8
a. 60 b. 40	A	a. 30 b. 120	[✓][ ]	120	[ ][✓]	a. 3 b. 1	90 30

49

WE	THEY

Points for overtricks are scored

(above/below) the line.

1

50

WE	THEY
A	C
B	D

If your opponents (THEY) bid 2 Clubs and make 5, they score 40 points in position ( ) and 60 points in position ( ).

8

51 You bid and make 6 No Trump.

(NOTE: This means you bid 6 and made 6.)

How many game points do you have?

5

52 You bid 3 Spades and make 6.

a. How many points do you score above the line?

b. How many points below the line?

3

53 To win a game you have to bid for and make at least 100 points. In order to make game, you have to:

a. bid and make ( ) No Trump (100 points),
b. bid and make ( ) in the major suits (120 points), or
c. bid and make ( ) in the minor suits (100 points).

2

54 How many points are needed to make game?

7

55 WE bid and make 6 Spades.

How many points are scored below the line?

4

56 When you make a contract which is worth at least 100 points, you have won a:

match.	round.

6

1	2	3	4	5	6	7	8
above	a. 3 b. 4 c. 5	a. 90 b. 90	180	190 (or 6 times 30 + 10)	NEITHER game.	100	D C

57 WE bid 2 Hearts and made 5.

Which shows this score?

WE	THEY
90	
60	

WE	THEY
60	
40	

3

58 THEY bid 3 Clubs and made 2.

How many game points are scored below the line?

1

59 a. For game in the minor suits you need to bid and make (2/3/4/5).

b. For game in No Trump you need to bid and make (2/3/4/5).

c. For game in the major suits you need to bid and make (2/3/4/5).

5

60 WE bid 4 Spades and made 5.

Score this on a sample score sheet on page 71.

4

61 Only those tricks bid for count toward game.
For example, if you bid 2 No Trump and make 3, you (do/do not) make game.

2

62 Which are overtricks?

tricks in excess of those you have contracted for

all tricks over book

6

63 Overtricks in No Trump are worth 30 points.

We bid 3 No Trump and make 4.

Score this on a sample score sheet on page 71.

(NOTE: Add the extra 10 points to game tricks, not to overtricks.)

7

64 THEY bid 1 No Trump and made 3.

Score this on a sample score sheet on page 71.

8

1

0 (NOTE: WE set opponents.)

2

do not

3

☑☐

4

WE	THEY
30	
120	

5

a. 5
b. 3
c. 4

6

☑☐

7

WE	THEY
30	
100	

8

WE	THEY
	60
	40

65 Overtricks count the same number of points as other tricks.
However, they do not count toward game.
If you bid 3 Spades and make 4, you get 120 points; however, only ( ) points count toward game. 8

66

WE	THEY
	30
	120

Have THEY made game here? 7

67 Which shows WE made game?

WE	THEY
100	50
80	40

WE	THEY
40	0
60	100

5

68

WE	THEY
30	70
60	120

Part-score, because it is less than 100.

Part-score is a score for tricks bid and made which is less than game. Which shows a part-score?

WE	THEY
	20
	100

WE	THEY
30	
70	

1

69

WE	THEY
A	B
C	D

← Line

If your opponents bid and make 2 Clubs, they would score 40 points in position (A/B/C/D). 6

70 Points below the line but less than game are called part-score.
Which of the following shows a part-score?

a.

WE	THEY
	60
	120

b.

WE	THEY
40	
60	

c.

WE	THEY
40	

d.

WE	THEY
100	

4

71

WE	THEY
30	
90	60

Part-score is so called because it is only part of game score (less than 100 points).

Have WE made game here? 2

72

WE	THEY
	60
	90

This shows a part-score of ( ) points made by THEY. 3

1	2	3	4	5	6	7	8
☐☑	No	90	b. WE 40, 60 / THEY (blank)	NEITHER	D	Yes	90

73 Which of these would give enough game points for game?

Bid and made 3 Hearts.	Bid and made 4 Clubs.

7

74 Which shows that WE have a part-score of 40?

WE	THEY
40	
20	

WE	THEY
	20
	40

8

75 What are overtricks?

5

76 Which of these would give enough game points for game?

Bid and made 4 Spades.	Bid and made 5 Diamonds.

6

77

WE	THEY
30	

To complete your part-score you need to bid and make enough additional points for game.
If you have a part-score of 30 points, you need (   ) points for game.

1

78

WE	THEY
30	
20	

a. How many points do WE need to make game?

b. How many points do THEY need?

3

79 Which shows WE bid 3 No Trump and made 5?

WE	THEY
70	
90	

WE	THEY
70	
100	

2

80

WE	THEY
20	

Two ways for WE to make game here are to bid and make:

a. 3 Clubs. c. 2 Spades.

b. 4 Clubs. d. 3 Spades.

4

1	2	3	4	5	6	7	8
70	NEITHER Overtricks in No Trump are 30 points.	a. 80 b. 100	b. 4 Clubs (80 points) d. 3 Spades (90 points)	tricks in excess of those you have contracted for	BOTH (4 Spades = 120, 5 Diamonds = 100)	NEITHER	NEITHER

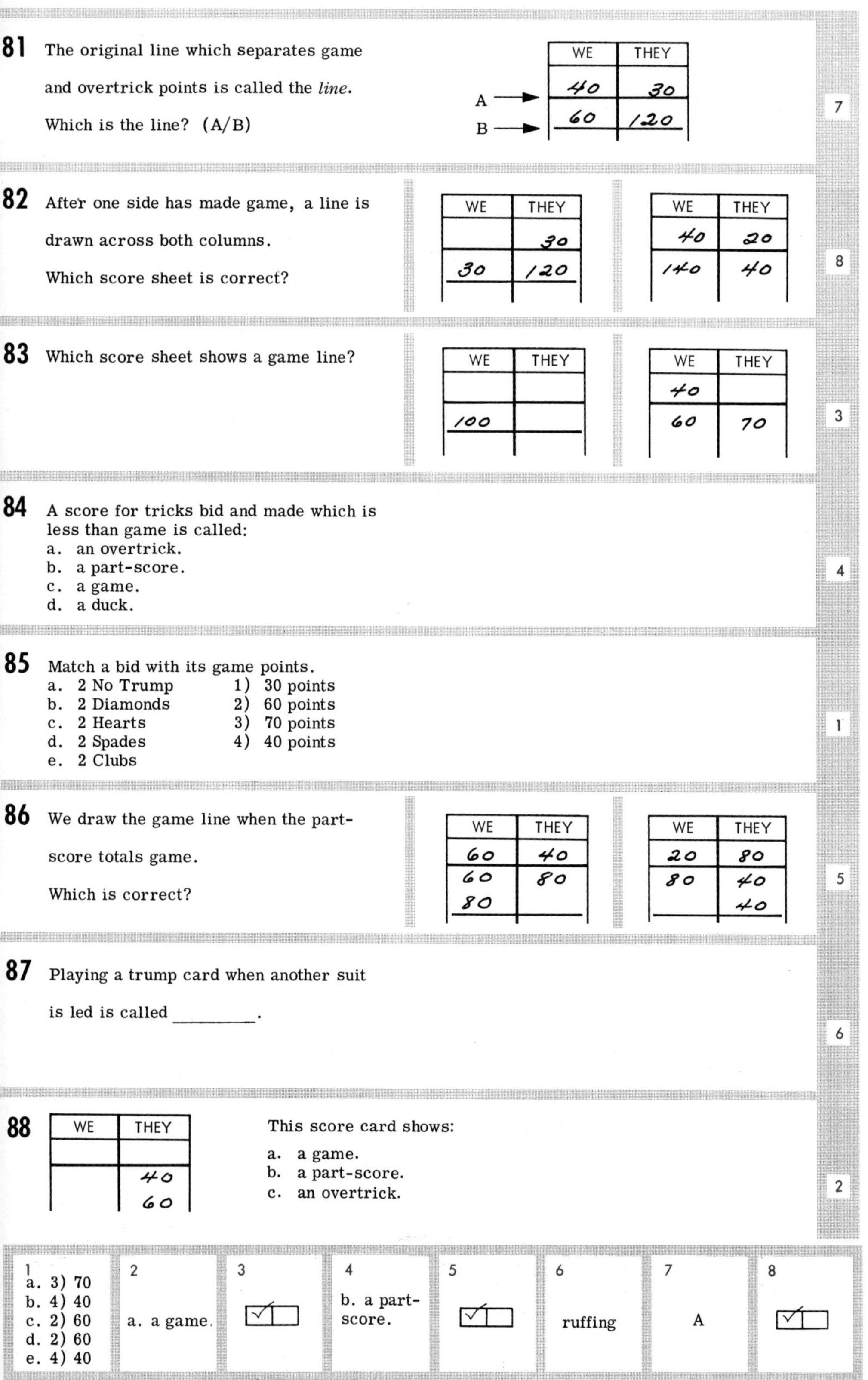

81 The original line which separates game and overtrick points is called the *line*. Which is the line? (A/B) 7

WE	THEY
40	30
60	120

A → (line below 40/30) B → (line below 60/120)

82 After one side has made game, a line is drawn across both columns. Which score sheet is correct? 8

WE	THEY
	30
30	120

WE	THEY
40	20
140	40

83 Which score sheet shows a game line? 3

WE	THEY
100	

WE	THEY
40	
60	70

84 A score for tricks bid and made which is less than game is called: 4

a. an overtrick.
b. a part-score.
c. a game.
d. a duck.

85 Match a bid with its game points. 1

a. 2 No Trump	1) 30 points
b. 2 Diamonds	2) 60 points
c. 2 Hearts	3) 70 points
d. 2 Spades	4) 40 points
e. 2 Clubs	

86 We draw the game line when the part-score totals game. Which is correct? 5

WE	THEY
60	40
60	80
80	

WE	THEY
20	80
80	40
	40

87 Playing a trump card when another suit is led is called ________. 6

88 This score card shows: 2

WE	THEY
	40
	60

a. a game.
b. a part-score.
c. an overtrick.

1	2	3	4	5	6	7	8
a. 3) 70 b. 4) 40 c. 2) 60 d. 2) 60 e. 4) 40	a. a game.	☑☐	b. a part-score.	☑☐	ruffing	A	☑☐

89

WE	THEY
40	20
40	60
20	40

When one side has made game, the opponents' previous part-scores no longer count toward game.

In the score card shown, a. (WE/THEY) have made game, so 7

b. (WE/THEY) no longer have a part-score.

90

Declarer

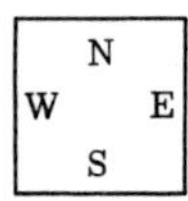

Match these.

a. dummy
b. person who makes opening lead
c. contractors
d. defenders

1) N-S team
2) W
3) N
4) E
5) E-W team

3

91 In which of the following score cards do the points scored by WE below the line not count toward game?

WE	THEY
	40
40	60

WE	THEY
40	100

2

92

W	N	E	S
pass	1♦	1♥	1♠
pass	2♠	3♥	3♠
pass	4♠	pass	pass
pass			

a. ( ) is the declarer.

b. The dummy is ( ). 6

c. What is the required total tricks?

93 Which shows the following scored correctly?
1st hand - WE bid 2 Diamonds and made 3.
2nd hand - THEY bid 3 Spades and made 4.
3rd hand - THEY bid 1 No Trump and made 2.

WE	THEY
	30
20	30
40	90
	40

WE	THEY
	40
20	30
40	90
	30

1

94 Score the following and draw a line in the appropriate place to show game.

1st hand - WE bid 3 Clubs and made 4.

2nd hand - THEY bid 2 No Trump and made 3. 4

3rd hand - WE bid 2 Spades and made 2.

(Use a sample score sheet on page 71.)

95 A bid of 4 Spades means the contractors will try to take a required total of ( ) tricks. 5

96 Score this. 1st hand - WE bid 1 Club and made 2. (Use a sample score sheet on page 71.)

2nd hand - THEY bid 2 Spades and made 3.

3rd hand - WE bid 3 Diamonds and made 3. 8

4th hand - THEY bid 1 No Trump and made 3.

1

☑ ☐

2

☐ ☑

3

a. 4)
b. 3)
c. 5)
d. 1)

4

WE	THEY
20	30
60	70
60	

5

10

6

a. S
b. N
c. 10

7

a. THEY
b. WE

8

WE	THEY
	60
20	30
20	60
60	40

97 The game line does *not* extend to the edges of the score sheet.

Which shows the game line drawn correctly?

WE	THEY
	40
120	60

WE	THEY
30	30
40	90
40	60

7

98 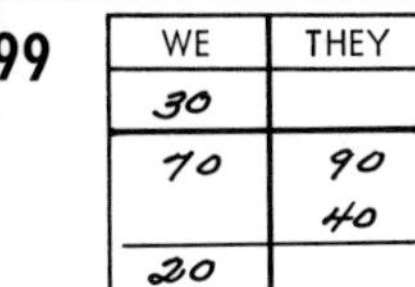

Line

Game

After game has been made by one side, the players begin again on a new game, and all points toward this new game are scored below the game line.

The score card shows that WE made game, and after this (WE/THEY) made a part-score of ( ). 6

99

WE	THEY
30	
70	90
	40
20	

Line

Overtrick points made after game are still scored above the line.

In the score shown, you (can/cannot) tell if the 30 overtrick points made by WE were made before or after the first game. 4

100 Points scored for the previous game do not count toward the new game.

Do THEY have 130 points toward the next game?

WE	THEY
70	90
	40

2

101 The first side to win two games wins a *rubber*.

Which of the following shows that a rubber has been won?

WE	THEY
100	
	120
130	

WE	THEY
100	
120	

1

102

N
♦5
W ♦Q ♣8 E
♥3
S

Hearts are trumps. W leads. N ducks.
a. Who sluffed?
b. Who ruffed?
c. Who took the trick?

3

103 The first side to win two games wins a:
a. rummy.
b. bridge.
c. rubber.
d. game.

5

104 Which shows WE winning a rubber?

WE	THEY
100	
	120
130	

WE	THEY
	100
120	
	130

8

1	2	3	4	5	6	7	8
BOTH	No	a. E b. S c. S	cannot	c. rubber.	THEY 60	BOTH	☑☐

105 Two lines are drawn under the score which ends the rubber. 8

Which of these is correct?

WE	THEY
100	
	120
130	

WE	THEY
100	
	120
130	

106 How many tricks are there in a book? 4

13

7

107 Whenever game is made you must put a line under game score. 6
Copy the scores on this sheet, and draw the game line(s) needed.

Use page 71.

WE	THEY
30	20
100	40
	120

← Line

108 Which shows the lines drawn properly? 5

WE	THEY
	20
	30
120	70
	100
100	

WE	THEY
40	30
60	120
	70
	40

109 Score this. 1
1st hand - THEY bid 2 Clubs and made 3.
2nd hand - WE bid and made 3 No Trump.
3rd hand - WE bid and made 4 Spades.

(Use page 71.)

110 3

WE	THEY
30	
20	

This score card shows:

a. an overtrick.
b. a game.
c. a part-score.

111 You bid 4 Diamonds and make 3. How many points do you receive? 2

112 Must 3 games always be made to reach a rubber? 7
If your answer is no, explain when 3 games are not necessary to reach rubber.

1

WE	THEY
	20
100	40
120	

2 none (0 points)

3 c. a part-score.

4 NEITHER 6

5 BOTH

6

WE	THEY
30	20
100	40
	120

7 No, not when one team wins first 2 games.

8 ☐ ☑

113 If a side wins a rubber before their opponents have scored a game, they get an additional 700 points scored above the line. Which is correct?

WE	THEY
700	
100	
100	

WE	THEY
	700
100	
	100
	100

6

114 If a side wins a rubber after their opponents have scored a game, they get 500 points above the line. Which shows this correctly?

WE	THEY
500	
100	
120	

WE	THEY
	500
100	
	120
	100

5

115 How many points is each trick over book

bid for and made in Spades worth?

4

116 Match these.

If a side wins a rubber:
1) before opponents score a game,
2) after opponents score a game,

a. it gets 500 bonus points.
b. it gets 200 bonus points.
c. it gets 700 bonus points.
d. it gets 1000 bonus points.

8

117 Match these.

In a rubber:
1) WE took 2 games; THEY took 1.
2) WE took 2 games; THEY scored but did not reach game.
3) WE took a game; THEY took 2 games.

a. WE get 500 above the line.
b. WE get 700 above the line.
c. THEY get 500 above the line.
d. THEY get 700 above the line.

1

118 Which of these is correct?

WE	THEY
	700
100	
	120
	100

WE	THEY
500	30
60	40
40	
120	

7

119 Score this, using a sample score sheet on page 71. (Be sure to put a line under game score and give bonuses.)
1st hand - THEY bid 2 Clubs and made 4.
2nd hand - WE bid 3 No Trump and made it.
3rd hand - WE bid 1 No Trump and made 2.
4th hand - THEY bid 4 Spades and made 5.
5th hand - WE bid 5 Clubs and made it. GO TO NEXT FRAME

3

120 This is how your score sheet should look.

Check and then go on to next frame.

	WE	THEY	
	500	30	← 4th hand
3rd hand →	30	40	← 1st hand
2nd hand →	100	40	← 1st hand
3rd hand →	40	120	← 4th hand
5th hand →	100		

2

1	2	3	4	5	6	7	8
1) a. 2) b. 3) c.			30	☐ ☑	☑ ☐	NEITHER	1) c. 2) a.

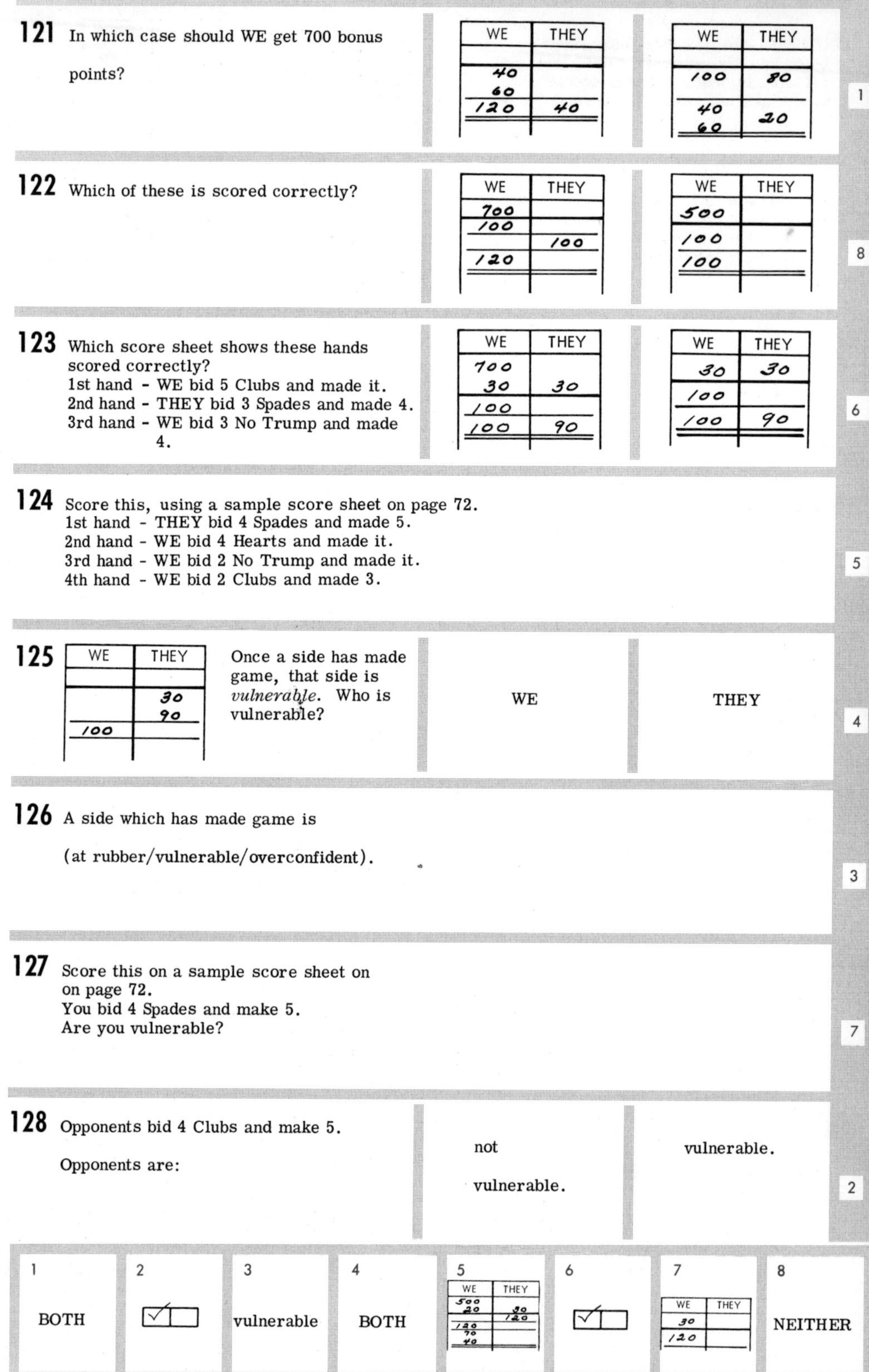

121 In which case should WE get 700 bonus points?

WE	THEY
40	
60	
120	40

WE	THEY
100	80
40	20
60	

1

122 Which of these is scored correctly?

WE	THEY
700	
100	
	100
120	

WE	THEY
500	
100	
100	

8

123 Which score sheet shows these hands scored correctly?
1st hand - WE bid 5 Clubs and made it.
2nd hand - THEY bid 3 Spades and made 4.
3rd hand - WE bid 3 No Trump and made 4.

WE	THEY
700	
30	30
100	
100	90

WE	THEY
30	30
100	
100	90

6

124 Score this, using a sample score sheet on page 72.
1st hand - THEY bid 4 Spades and made 5.
2nd hand - WE bid 4 Hearts and made it.
3rd hand - WE bid 2 No Trump and made it.
4th hand - WE bid 2 Clubs and made 3.

5

125

WE	THEY
	30
	90
100	

Once a side has made game, that side is *vulnerable*. Who is vulnerable?

WE

THEY

4

126 A side which has made game is

(at rubber/vulnerable/overconfident).

3

127 Score this on a sample score sheet on on page 72.
You bid 4 Spades and make 5.
Are you vulnerable?

7

128 Opponents bid 4 Clubs and make 5.

Opponents are:

not vulnerable.

vulnerable.

2

1 BOTH

2 ☑☐

3 vulnerable

4 BOTH

5

WE	THEY
500	30
20	120
120	
70	
40	

6 ☑☐

7

WE	THEY
30	
120	

8 NEITHER

129 The contract is 4 Diamonds.

If 9 tricks are taken, the contract (is/is not) set. 8

---

130 In which of these hands would the contract be set?

Bid 3 Clubs and take a total of 7 tricks.	Bid 6 Hearts and take a total of 11 tricks.

6

---

131 If contractors are set, opponents receive points above the line.
Contractors bid 5 Clubs and take 10 tricks.
Would opponents receive points here? 5

---

132 WE bid 4 and take 9 tricks. Opponents receive points in position (A/B/C/D).

WE	THEY
A	C
B	D

1

---

133 N-S bid 4 Diamonds. They take a total of 10 tricks. Do their opponents score points above the line? 2

---

134 Which is correct?

If a contract is set, contractors subtract points for each trick lost.	If a contract is set, defenders receive points below the line for each trick.

4

---

135 WE bid 4 Hearts and took only 8 tricks. WE are set by 2 tricks. [Required total less actual total (10 - 8) = 2.] If WE bid 6 Spades and took 9 tricks, WE are set by:

2 tricks.	3 tricks.

7

---

136 WE bid 4 and made 2. WE are set by 2 tricks. This is called being "down 2." WE bid 5 and made 1. We are:

down 5.	down 4.

3

1	2	3	4	5	6	7	8
C	No	☐☑	NEITHER Defenders receive points above line.	Yes	BOTH	☐☑	is

137 Turn to *Bridge Points Summary* on page 70.

Under *Penalties*, what value is directly across from 1 Down? 4

---

138 Turn to page 70. Under *Penalties*, the extreme left-hand column (1 Down, 2 Down, 3 Down) refers to the number of tricks you or your opponent are set.

Assuming that you are not vulnerable and go down 2 tricks, your opponents would receive (   ) points. 8

(NOTE: The contract has not been doubled.)

---

139 THEY bid 3 Hearts and take 8 tricks.
THEY are set 1 trick.
WE bid 5 Spades and take 10 tricks.
How many tricks are WE set? 1

---

140 Match these.

a.	THEY bid 5 Diamonds and take 9 tricks.	1)	0 down
b.	WE bid 4 Hearts and take 9 tricks.	2)	2 down
c.	WE bid 3 Spades and take 9 tricks.	3)	3 down
d.	THEY bid 3 No Trump and take 6 tricks.	4)	1 down

7

---

141 If you are vulnerable and set in your contract, you lose twice as many points as you would if you were not vulnerable. If you are down 1 trick, your opponents receive 50 points. If, however, you are vulnerable, not doubled, your opponents receive (   ) points. 2

---

142 Look at page 70.

What are the missing values?

(not doubled)

	Not Vulnerable	Vulnerable
1 Down	______	______
2 Down	______	______
3 Down	______	______

3

---

143 Your contract is 5 Clubs. You take a total of 10 tricks.

You are vulnerable, not doubled.

a. Are you set? 6

b. If your answer to a. is *yes*, how many points do opponents receive above the line?

---

144 THEY are vulnerable, not doubled.
THEY bid 4 Diamonds and take 10 tricks.
How many points do WE receive above the line? 5

1	2	3	4	5	6	7	8
1 trick	100	50 100 100 200 150 300	50	0 (NOTE: THEY bid and made contract.)	a. Yes b. 100	a. 2) b. 4) c. 1) d. 3)	100

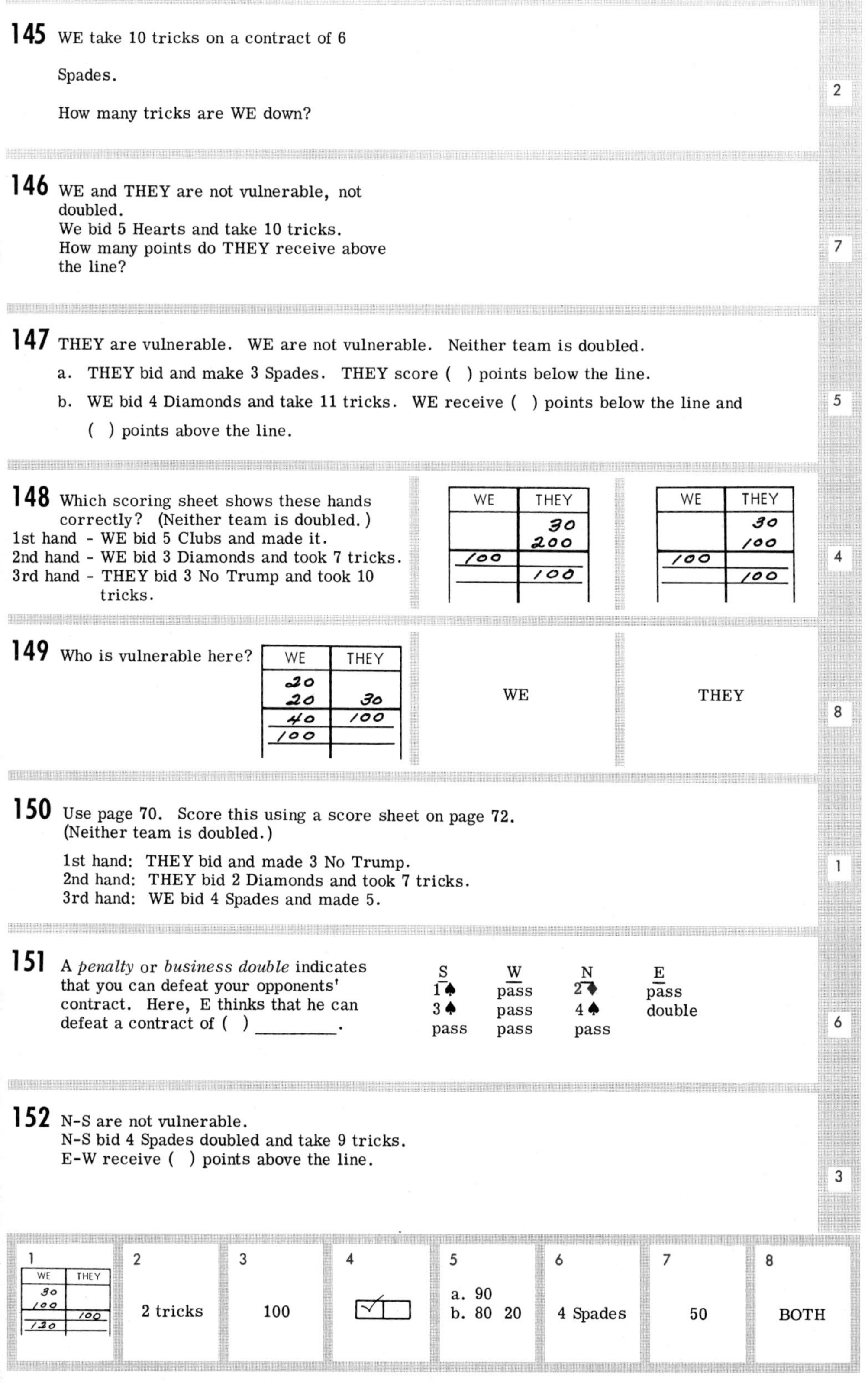

145 WE take 10 tricks on a contract of 6 Spades.

How many tricks are WE down? 2

146 WE and THEY are not vulnerable, not doubled.
We bid 5 Hearts and take 10 tricks.
How many points do THEY receive above the line? 7

147 THEY are vulnerable. WE are not vulnerable. Neither team is doubled.

a. THEY bid and make 3 Spades. THEY score ( ) points below the line.

b. WE bid 4 Diamonds and take 11 tricks. WE receive ( ) points below the line and ( ) points above the line. 5

148 Which scoring sheet shows these hands correctly? (Neither team is doubled.)
1st hand - WE bid 5 Clubs and made it.
2nd hand - WE bid 3 Diamonds and took 7 tricks.
3rd hand - THEY bid 3 No Trump and took 10 tricks. 4

WE	THEY
	30
	200
100	
	100

WE	THEY
	30
	100
100	
	100

149 Who is vulnerable here? 8

WE	THEY
20	
20	30
40	100
100	

WE

THEY

150 Use page 70. Score this using a score sheet on page 72.
(Neither team is doubled.)

1st hand: THEY bid and made 3 No Trump.
2nd hand: THEY bid 2 Diamonds and took 7 tricks.
3rd hand: WE bid 4 Spades and made 5. 1

151 A *penalty* or *business double* indicates that you can defeat your opponents' contract. Here, E thinks that he can defeat a contract of ( ) ________. 6

S	W	N	E
1♠	pass	2♦	pass
3♠	pass	4♠	double
pass	pass	pass	

152 N-S are not vulnerable.
N-S bid 4 Spades doubled and take 9 tricks.
E-W receive ( ) points above the line. 3

1

WE	THEY
30	
100	
	100
120	

2 — 2 tricks

3 — 100

4 — ☑☐

5 — a. 90 b. 80 20

6 — 4 Spades

7 — 50

8 — BOTH

153

S	W	N	E
pass	1♦	1 NT	pass
2 NT	pass	3 NT	pass
pass	pass		

a. N is the ________.
b. Who makes the opening lead?

1

154 Which is a penalty or business double?

doubting the opponents can make their contract	a bid which encourages opponents to make their contract

8

155 Read *Premiums* on page 70.
What is the correct number of points awarded to contractors for the following.
a. bidding and making small slam (12 tricks)
b. bidding and making grand slam (13 tricks)
c. making any doubled or redoubled contract

	Not Vulnerable	Vulnerable
a.		
b.		
c.		

6

156 THEY are vulnerable. THEY bid 6 Hearts doubled and take 10 tricks.
How many points do WE receive above the line?
Look at page 70.

5

157 A bid which indicates that the defenders

think they can set the contract is a:

penalty double.	business double.

4

158 If contractors bid and make a doubled contract, each trick is worth double value below the line.
Will contractors receive double value if they bid 4 Spades doubled and take 10 tricks?

3

159 Turn to page 70.

a. How many points are you awarded for making a doubled contract if you are not vulnerable?
b. Do you receive the same number of points above the line for making a doubled contract when vulnerable?

7

160 If a doubled contract is made, each trick

bid for and made is worth double value

(above/below) the line.

2

1	2	3	4	5	6	7	8
a. declarer b. E	below	Yes	BOTH	500	500 750 1000 1500 50 50	a. 50 b. Yes	☑☐

161 Which is a minor suit?

	Spades	Hearts	8

162 Score this.
THEY bid 2 Spades doubled and made it.
After scoring, find the premium on page 70 for making a doubled contract, and score above the line. Use the sample score sheet on page 72. 6

163 Since doubling doubles the score, you need only half the usual number of tricks for game. You need only 3 in the minors (you can't take $2\frac{1}{2}$ tricks), 2 in the majors, and ( ) in No Trump for game. 5

164 If you make 1 No Trump doubled, do you make game? 1

165 a. How many points do you score below the line for 3 Spades doubled?

b. Is it enough for game? 2

166 Both sides are vulnerable. Look at page 70.
WE bid 6 Hearts and take 9 tricks. WE are not doubled.
How many points do the opponents receive above the line? 4

167 What value would you show below the line for 3 Diamonds doubled and made? 7

168 Points for tricks bid and made (even if doubled) are scored:

	above the line.	below the line.	3

1	2	3	4	5	6	7	8
No (Only 80 points are scored below the line.)	a. 180 points b. Yes	☐ ☑	300	2	WE / THEY: THEY 50, 120	120	NEITHER Clubs or Diamonds

169 Both sides are vulnerable. Look at page 70.
THEY bid 6 Clubs doubled and take 10 tricks.
How many points do WE receive as a premium above the line? 3

170 Look at page 70.
You bid and make a doubled contract.
How many points do you receive above the line? 2

171 Penalties and premiums are entered: 8

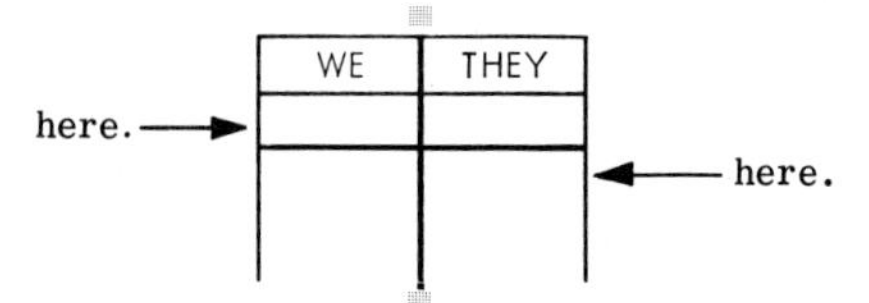

172 For making a doubled contract, the contractors are awarded 50 premium points (above/below) the line. 1

173 Score this, using a score sheet on page 72.
1st hand - WE bid and made 2 Diamonds doubled.
2nd hand - THEY bid and made 3 Hearts doubled.
3rd hand - WE were set 2 tricks at 3 No Trump doubled.
(REMEMBER: Award premiums for each contract doubled and made.) 7

174

WE	THEY
60	90
	40

Here, THEY are (vulnerable/impregnable). 4

175 Score this, using a scoring sheet on page 72.

1st hand - WE made 2 at No Trump doubled.
2nd hand - WE made 3 at 3 Clubs doubled. 5

176 Redoubling doubles the doubled score (or increases the value of each trick four times).
Majors - 120 per trick.
a. Minors - ( ) per trick.
b. No trump - ( ) for first trick.
c. No trump - ( ) for each additional trick. 6

---

1 above

2 50

3 500

4 vulnerable

5

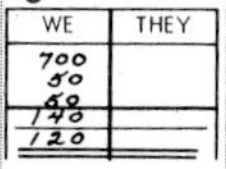

6 a. 80
b. 160
c. 120

7

WE	THEY
	300
50	50
80	180

8 ✓

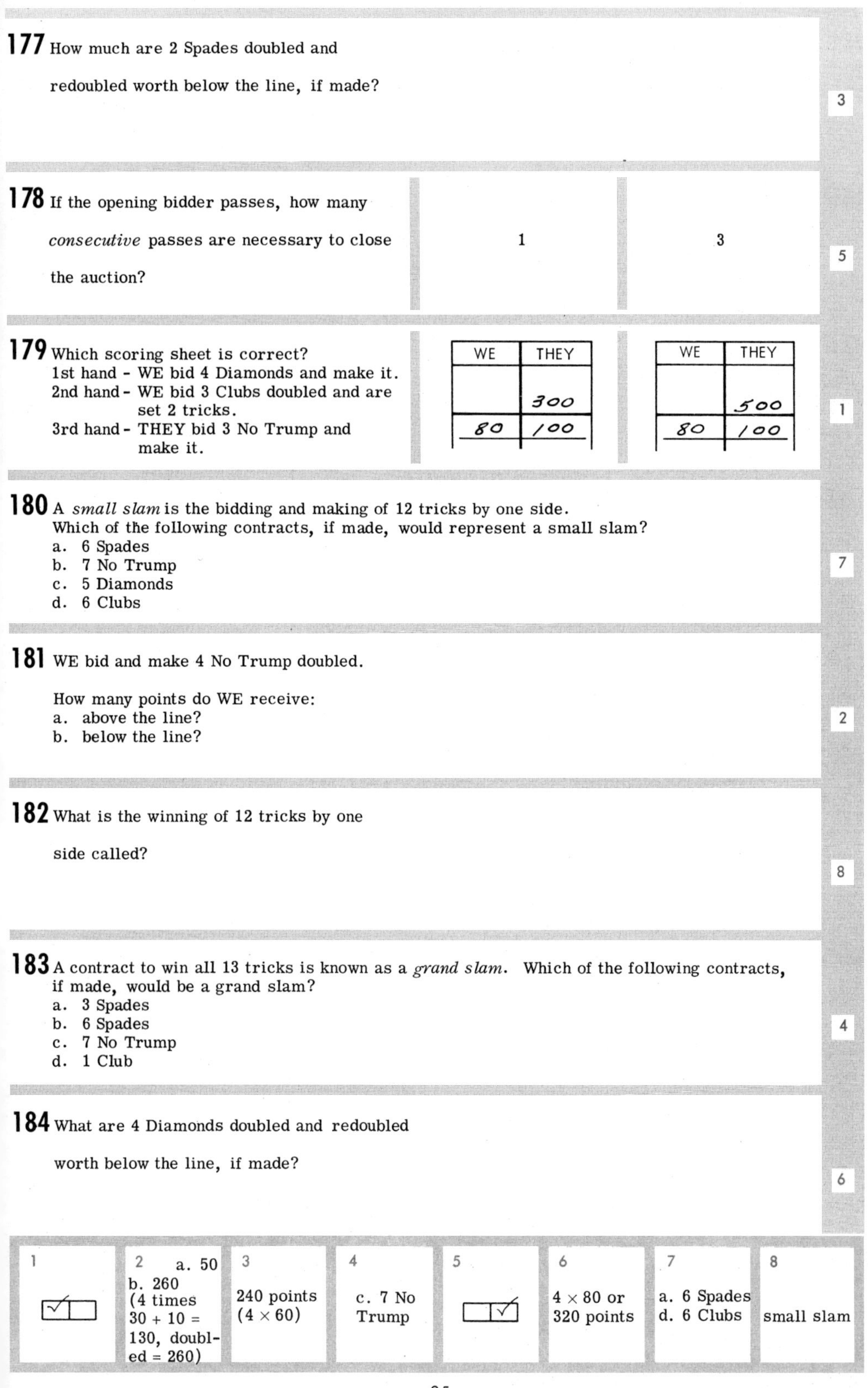

177 How much are 2 Spades doubled and redoubled worth below the line, if made? 3

178 If the opening bidder passes, how many *consecutive* passes are necessary to close the auction?

1	3

5

179 Which scoring sheet is correct?
1st hand - WE bid 4 Diamonds and make it.
2nd hand - WE bid 3 Clubs doubled and are set 2 tricks.
3rd hand - THEY bid 3 No Trump and make it.

WE	THEY
	300
80	100

WE	THEY
	500
80	100

1

180 A *small slam* is the bidding and making of 12 tricks by one side.
Which of the following contracts, if made, would represent a small slam?
a. 6 Spades
b. 7 No Trump
c. 5 Diamonds
d. 6 Clubs

7

181 WE bid and make 4 No Trump doubled.

How many points do WE receive:
a. above the line?
b. below the line?

2

182 What is the winning of 12 tricks by one side called? 8

183 A contract to win all 13 tricks is known as a *grand slam*. Which of the following contracts, if made, would be a grand slam?
a. 3 Spades
b. 6 Spades
c. 7 No Trump
d. 1 Club

4

184 What are 4 Diamonds doubled and redoubled worth below the line, if made? 6

1	2	3	4	5	6	7	8
☑☐	a. 50 b. 260 (4 times 30 + 10 = 130, doubled = 260)	240 points (4×60)	c. 7 No Trump	☐☑	4×80 or 320 points	a. 6 Spades d. 6 Clubs	small slam

185 A side that has won a game toward rubber is ________. 3

186 A grand slam is a contract to win (11/12/13) tricks. 8

187 Use page 70.
E-W have contracted at 4 Diamonds. Assuming that they make contract and are doubled by N-S, they will receive ( ) points above the line. 5

188 If E-W are doubled and set in their contract, then (N-S/E-W) will be assigned points. 2

189 Using page 70, determine the number of points you would receive for setting your opponents 1 trick at 4 Spades doubled. Your opponents are vulnerable. 7

190 A small slam consists of (6/12/18) tricks. 4

191 THEY bid 3 Hearts and were set 1 trick. Since THEY were not vulnerable and were not doubled, the penalty is only ( ) points. 6

192 Points made for premiums or penalties are scored above the line.
If THEY bid and make a small slam and are not vulnerable, they receive 500 points (above/below) the line. 1

1	2	3	4	5	6	7	8
above	N-S	vulnerable	12	50	50	200	13

193 WE bid 5 Spades but succeed in winning

only 9 tricks. 1

How many tricks are we set?

194 Use page 70.

We are vulnerable and not doubled, and 3

are set 2 tricks. What is the penalty?

195 If WE set our opponents, the number of

points is scored in favor of WE 2

(above/below) the line.

196 WE bid and make 5 Diamonds doubled.

WE receive: a. ( ) points above the line.
b. ( ) points below the line. 7

197 If you are vulnerable, how many games are required to reach a rubber?

(NOTE: Remember, when you are vulnerable, you have won a game.) 8

198 It is possible to win the rubber game but lose from the standpoint of points.

Look at this scoring sheet. Who are the winners? (WE/THEY) 4

WE	THEY
500 50 60	800 60 100 30
60 40	70
	120
100	
810	1180 -810 370

199 Which shows that WE won rubber game? 5

WE	THEY
500 50	
240	60 60
100	

WE	THEY
	700
60	100
	120

200 Which shows that WE won both in terms

of points and the rubber game? 6

WE	THEY
500 50 60	800 60 100 30
60 40	70
	120
100	

WE	THEY
500 50 30	20
90	100
240	90
100	40

1	2	3	4	5	6	7	8
2	above	200	THEY	[✓][ ]	[ ][✓]	a. 50 b. 200	one

201 a. If you reach rubber when opponents have not made game, you are awarded ( ) points above the line.

b. If you reach rubber when opponents have made game, you are awarded ( ) points above the line. 4

202 Read *Game Values* on page 70. 3

GO TO NEXT FRAME

203 *Bridge Points Summary*, on page 70, is a review of all points awarded in bridge. Study it now and refer to it any time you are in doubt. 7

GO TO NEXT UNIT

1	2	3	4	5	6	7	8
			a. 700 b. 500				

TAKE UNIT 4 POST-TEST

UNIT 5

trick-taking

The rules of who takes the trick are reviewed. The student learns to count his long-card and honor-card winners. In addition, he discovers when he should play for a drop.

PRE- AND POST-TEST

1. What is the most likely split of Clubs between opponents if you and partner hold the following hand?

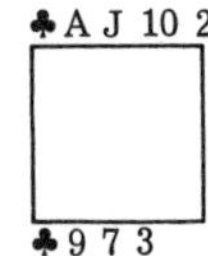

2. What is the maximum number of tricks you can win in the Diamond suit? (Assume the most probable split.)

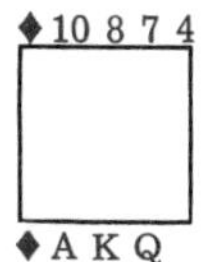

3. Which diagram shows the most probable split of the cards between opponents?

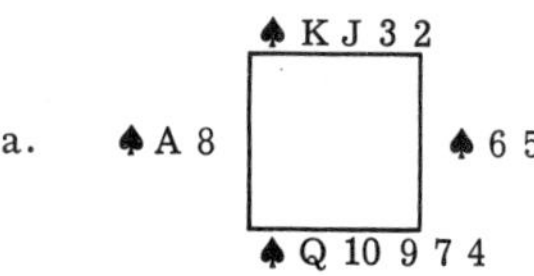

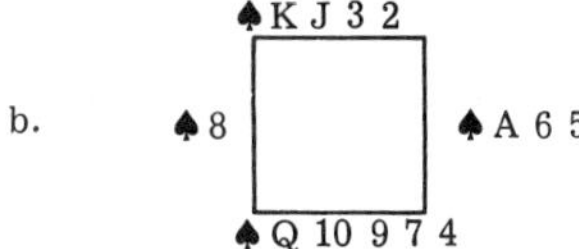

4. Which diagram shows: 1) the most favorable split between opponents and, 2) the most probable split between opponents?

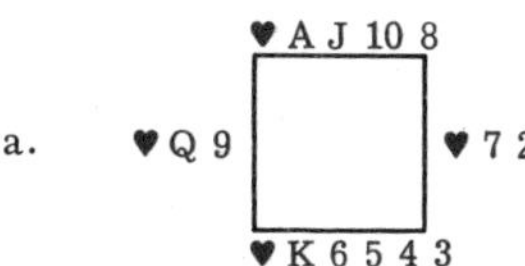

b.

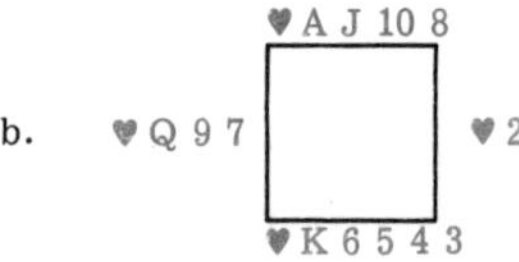

5. How many pairs of touching honors are there in Spades?

♠A K J 10

6. When you count honor tricks in a suit you count [only those in dummy/only those in declarer's hand/(both)/(neither)].

7. If opponents hold 4 cards in a suit, the most probable split is ( ) - ( ) but the most favorable split is ( ) - ( ).

8. How many top tricks are there in Spades?

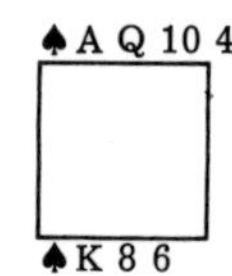

9. The combined holding in both dummy and declarer's hand are counted when you are counting [honor tricks/tricks on top/(both)/(neither)].

10. Which hand shows a sequence?

a.

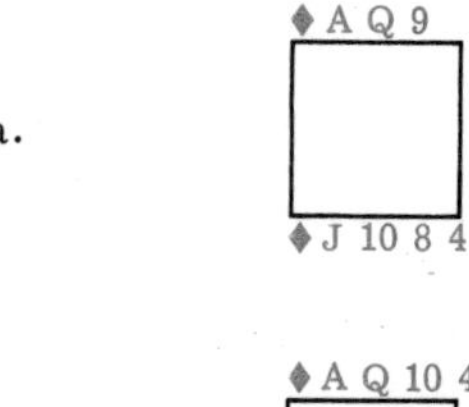

b.

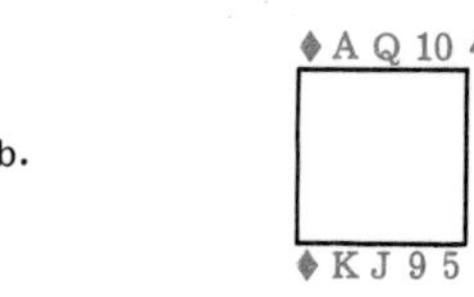

c. both

d. neither

11. a. If you hold the ♥K J 3 2, you have a (sequence/tenace).

    b. If you hold the ♥Q J 3 2, you have a (sequence/tenace).

12. Which hand shows a tenace?

a. 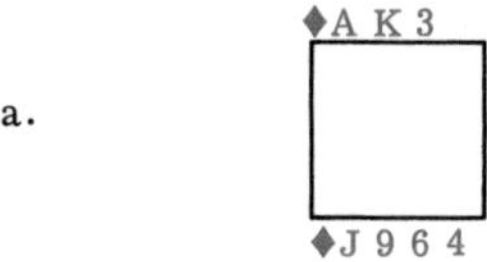

b. 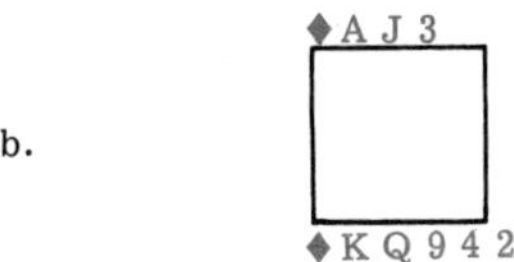

c. both

d. neither

13. A tenace can be in [only one hand/the combined hands of declarer and dummy/(both)/(neither)]. Assume that you do not hold a card of equal rank below the tenace.

14. If your tricks on top doubled is greater than the number of cards out against you, then you would [finesse/play for a drop/(both)/(neither)].

15. 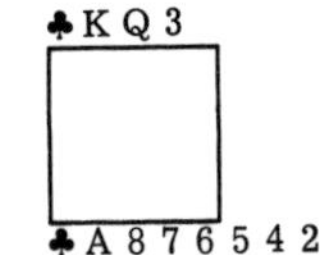

a. How many top tricks?

b. What is the number of top tricks doubled?

c. The number of top tricks doubled is (equal to/less than/greater than) the number of cards out against you.

d. Do you play for a drop?

TABLE OF PROBABILITIES

Opponents hold:	The opponents' cards will be divided:	
7 cards of a suit.	4-3	62 per cent of the time.
	5-2	31 per cent of the time.
	6-1	7 per cent of the time.
	7-0	less than $\frac{1}{2}$ per cent of the time.
6 cards of a suit.	4-2	48 per cent of the time.
	3-3	36 per cent of the time.
	5-1	15 per cent of the time.
	6-0	1 per cent of the time.
5 cards of a suit.	3-2	68 per cent of the time.
	4-1	28 per cent of the time.
	5-0	4 per cent of the time.
4 cards of a suit.	3-1	50 per cent of the time.
	2-2	40 per cent of the time.
	4-0	10 per cent of the time.
3 cards of a suit.	2-1	78 per cent of the time.
	3-0	22 per cent of the time.
2 cards of a suit.	1-1	52 per cent of the time.
	2-0	48 per cent of the time.

SAMPLE FLOW CHART

This sample chart will help you master the more complex procedures found in the charts in Unit 12.

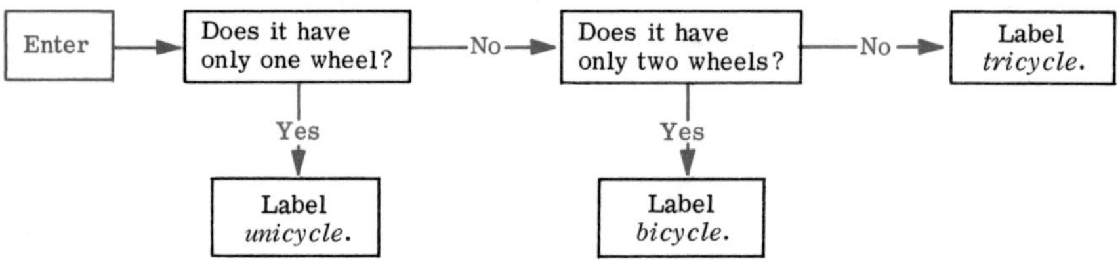

COUNTING HONOR WINNERS FLOW CHART

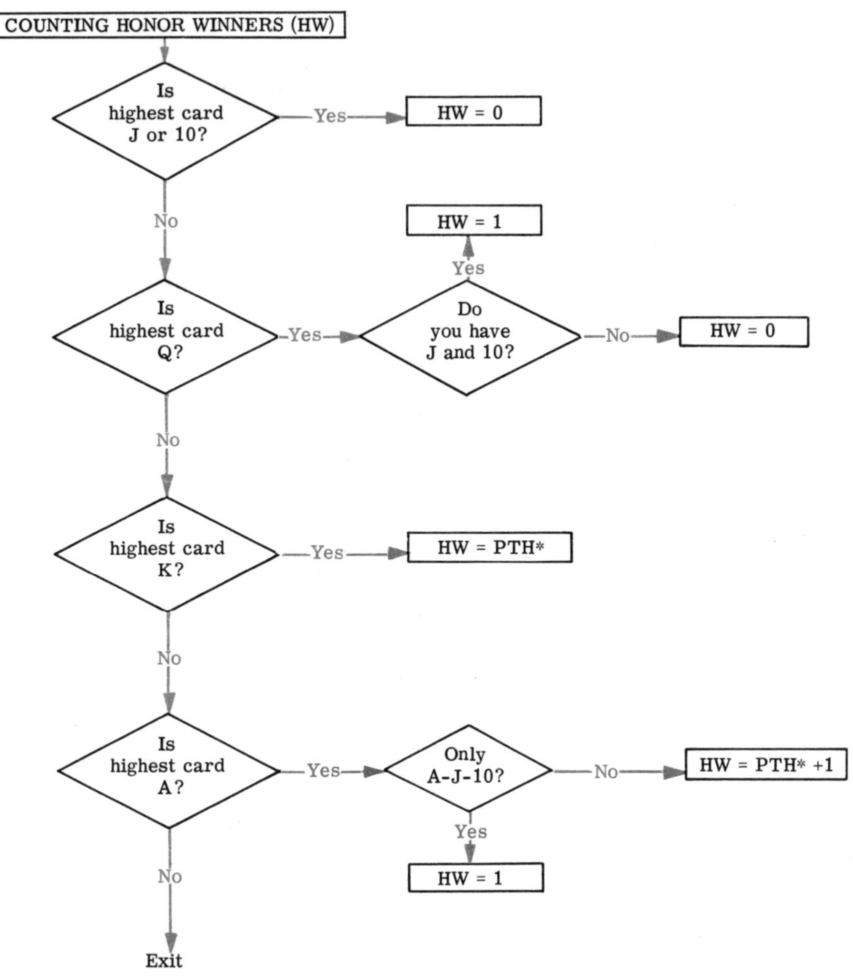

*PTH = Pairs of touching honors (Ace, King, Queen, Jack, and Ten of a suit). For example: Q-J or K-J-10 each have 1 PTH; Q-J-10 has 2 PTH (the Q-J and the J-10); K-Q-J-10 has 3 PTH (the K-Q, the Q-J, and the J-10).

EXERCISES

This exercise consists of several situations that may occur at the bridge table. You are to decide whether to play for a drop or adopt another procedure.

1. Should you play for a drop with your Spades?

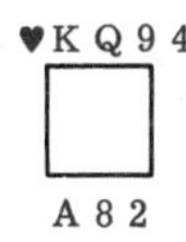

2. Should you play for a drop with Hearts?
   If so, how would you play the hand, *e.g.*, which card would you lead first, what is your play, and so forth?

3. Why shouldn't you play for a drop here?

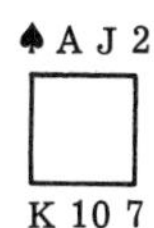

4. With the Spade hand, which would you do? (play for a drop/do not play for a drop)
5. Which of the following diamond suits would you play for a drop?

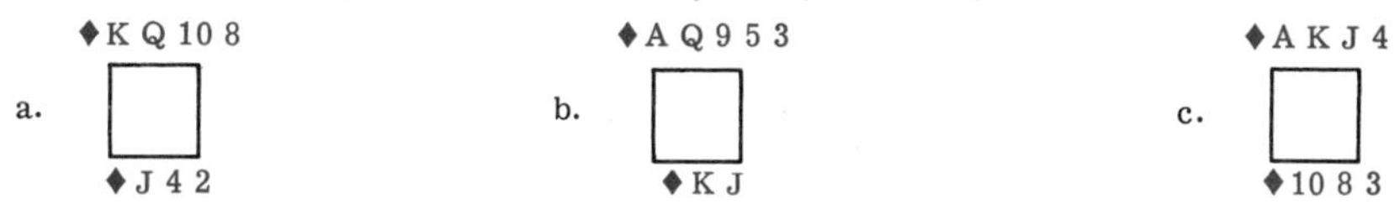

1 (Before you begin, take the Pre-Test for Unit 5.)
Suppose your side wins the auction.
If you play the hand, you are called the (declarer/bidder). 3
The cards your partner lays on the table for you to play are called the
(declarer's/dummy) hand.

2 After declarer's partner lays his cards down, he does not play the rest of the hand.

Declarer's partner may [get a cup of coffee/kibitz/go watch TV/(any of these)]. 5

3 In playing a bridge hand, you will need to count the combined number of cards of each suit in your hand and the dummy hand.
Dummy hand has 3 cards in Spades, and you have 5 cards in Spades. 2
What is the total number of Spades in the combined hands?

4

Total number of cards in a suit = 13. If your hand + dummy hand = 7 in a suit, your opponents have 13 - 7 = 6 in that suit. If you + dummy have 8 Diamonds, your opponents have:	3 Diamonds.	6 Diamonds.	7

5 You and dummy have 9 cards in Diamonds in your combined hands.
How many cards must your opponents have in Diamonds in their combined hands? 1

6

Sometimes both your hand and the dummy will have *exactly* the same number of cards in a given suit. Which of these is an example in which your hand and the dummy have exactly the same number of cards in Clubs?	Dummy has 4 Clubs; you have 4 Clubs.	Dummy has 2 Clubs; you have 3 Clubs.	6

7 Dummy has 6 cards in Clubs and you, as declarer, have only 1 card in Clubs.

This means that your opponents must have ( ) Clubs. 4

8

In which case do both your hand and the dummy have the same number of cards in Hearts?	Dummy: ♥K Q 3 2 You: ♥A J 5	Dummy: ♥5 4 3 You: ♥A K J 7	8

1	2	3	4	5	6	7	8
4	8	declarer dummy	6	(any of these)	[✓] [ ]	NEITHER 5 Diamonds.	NEITHER

9 If both dummy and declarer's hand do not have the same number of cards in a suit, the hand with the most cards in that suit is called the *long hand.*

If dummy has 5 Spades and you, as declarer, have 4 Spades, who has the long hand in Spades? 7

10 The following rule is true except in the case of the trump suit (which we will not deal with in this unit): *The maximum number of tricks you can win in a suit is equal to the number of cards in the long hand of that suit.*

If the dummy has 5 Diamonds and you have 2 Diamonds, what is the maximum number of tricks which you can win in Diamonds? 4

11 Sometimes you, as declarer, and dummy will have the *same* number of cards in a given suit.
For example, suppose dummy has 4 Spades and you have 4 Spades.
If Spades are not trumps, it is easy to see that the maximum number of Spade tricks which you can win is ( ). 3

12 Look at these two holdings.

a. Who has the long hand in Diamonds?

b. What is the maximum number of Diamond tricks you can win?

Dummy: ♦ A 2
Declarer: ♦ K Q 10 7 4 3 5

13 For the remainder of this unit, we no longer will make statements such as, "Spades are not trumps."
So if you are asked, "What is the maximum number of tricks you can take in Spades?" you will know that ____________ are not trumps. 1

14 A bridge player who has 4 Spades in the dummy and 3 Spades in his hand would describe the situation by saying, "My Spades are 4-3." Note that the larger number is usually given first.

If a bridge player has 2 Diamonds in the dummy and 6 Diamonds in his hand, he might describe the situation by saying, "My Diamonds are ( ) - ( )." 2

15 Which of these statements might a bridge player make about the possible distribution in his hand and the dummy?

My Hearts were 4-4.	My Clubs were 3-0.

8

16 Suppose you heard a bridge player say, "My Diamonds are 5-1."
You would know that between himself and the dummy he has a total of ( ) Diamonds.
Since there are 13 cards in Diamonds, the opponents must have ( ) Diamonds. 6

1	2	3	4	5	6	7	8
Spades	6 2	4	5	a. Declarer b. 6	6 7	dummy	BOTH

17 Just as the cards in a suit are distributed or *split* between your hand and the dummy, so are the cards in your opponents' hands split.

If you heard a bridge player say, "I could have made that hand, but the Clubs my opponents held were split 5-1," you would know that one of his opponents held (   ) Clubs and the other opponent held (   ) Club. 6

18 If a bridge player said, "My opponents' Hearts were split 3-2," you would know that the opponents had a total of (   ) Hearts, and the player had a total of (   ) Hearts in his hand and the dummy. 7

19 *My Hearts were split 3-0* means 3 Hearts in one hand and no Hearts in the other. *Opponents' Spades were split 5-0* means:

one opponent had 5 Spades; the other had no Spades.	the opponents had a total of 5 Spades.

3

20 If your opponents have 4 Diamonds, they could be split:

— or

1

21 Opponents have a total of 3 cards. They may be divided:

2-1.	3-0.

4

22 If you and dummy have a total of 8 Spades in your combined hands, the opponents' cards in that suit may be divided:

2-2.	3-1.

5

23 To play bridge well, you must have a good idea of the ways your opponents' cards may be divided. Look at *Table of Probabilities* on page 105. From this table you can tell that if your opponents hold 4 cards of a suit, they will be divided:

a. 3-1 __________% of the time.
b. 4-0 __________% of the time.
c. 2-2 __________% of the time. 2

24 Suppose the opponents hold 6 cards in Clubs. From page 105, you can tell that the most *likely* split is:

3-3.	4-2.

8

1	2	3	4	5	6	7	8
☐ ☑	a. 50 b. 10 c. 40	BOTH	BOTH	NEITHER Opponents must have 5 Spades, not 4.	5 1	5 8	☐ ☑

25 Suppose the opponents hold 4 cards in a suit. The most *even* split is 2-2.

a. Is this also the most likely split?

b. If not, what is? 3

26 The most even split is *not* always the most likely split.

If THEY hold 6 cards: a. What is the even split?
b. What is the most likely split?

If THEY hold 4 cards: c. What is the even split?
d. What is the most likely split? 2

27 There is one case in which an even split is slightly more likely than a noneven split with an even number of cards.

Examine the table on page 105. An even split is slightly more likely when the opponents hold ( ) cards in a suit. 8

28 So far, we have dealt with cases in which the opponents hold 2, 4, or 6 cards in a suit. These are all even numbers.

In these examples, we have seen that if the opponents hold an even number of cards, an even split of the cards (is/is not) always the most likely split. 7

29 If opponents hold an odd number of cards in a suit, the cards must be distributed *unevenly*.

However, some distributions are more *uneven* than others.

Which is a more uneven distribution? (5-2/7-0) 6

30 When opponents hold an odd number of cards in a suit, the cards cannot be split evenly. However, they will usually be split *as evenly as possible*.

Opponents hold 5 cards.

Which is the most likely split? (3-2/4-1/5-0) 4

31 Opponents have 7 Spades.

Which is most probable? 1

32 The 3-2 split can show up either way.

At table 1: a. W has ( ) Diamonds.
b. E has ( ) Diamonds.

At table 2: c. W has ( ) Diamonds.
d. E has ( ) Diamonds. 5

1	2	3	4	5	6	7	8
☑☐	a. 3-3 b. 4-2 c. 2-2 d. 3-1	a. No b. 3-1	3-2	a. 3 b. 2 c. 2 d. 3	7-0	is not	2

33 Suppose that the opponents hold 7 cards in a suit. These can be distributed 4-3, 6-1, 5-2, or 7-0.
Arrange these splits from the most probable to the least probable, and then check with page 105. 2

34 N-S are contractors.

E-W have 7 Clubs.

Which shows the most probable split? 5

35 You (declarer) have 7 Hearts.
Everyone else has exactly 2 Hearts each.
How many times can you lead Hearts
before everyone is out of them? 3

36 Depending upon how their cards are split, one opponent may have more cards in one suit than his partner.
Also, they may possibly have the same number of cards in that suit. In which of these splits does one opponent have more cards in the suit than his partner? (3-1/2-2) 1

37 A very important way to win tricks is to establish *long-card* tricks.
After S leads Diamonds twice, no one else has any left.
How many long-card winners will S have? 4

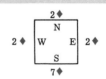

N 2♦
W 2♦ E 2♦
S 7♦

38

N 5♠ Dummy
W 1♠ E 3♠
S You 4♠ Declarer

a. How many cards do you have in your long hand?

b. How many cards in opponents' longest card holding? 6

39 Figuring your number of long-card winners in a suit is simple.
Take the difference between your long-card holding suit and the opponents' longest card holding. Your Spades are 6-3. Your opponents' Spades are 3-1.
Since your longest holding is 6 and the opponents' longest holding is 3, after three leads you will have ( ) long-card winners. 8

40 Suppose your Diamonds are 5-3 and your opponents' Diamonds are 4-1.

How many long-card winners in Diamonds can you establish? 7

1	2	3	4	5	6	7	8
3-1	4-3, 5-2, 6-1, 7-0	twice	5	BOTH	a. 5 b. 3	1	3

41	Your holding is a 4-3 split. What is the most probable split for opponents?	3-3	4-2	1
42	Your Hearts are 6-2. a. How many Hearts do your opponents have between them? b. What is the most probable split? c. Assuming the split to be this way, how many long-card winners will you establish?			7
43	Suppose your Clubs are distributed 4-3. This means your opponents have ( ) Clubs and they will most probably be split ( )-( ). In this case your long-card holding is just as long as the opponents' long-card holding. Will you establish any long-card winners here?			6
44	An *honor* is the Ace, King, Queen, Jack, or Ten of a suit. Which shows at least one honor?			4
45	Suppose we want to classify vehicles into unicycles, bicycles, and tricycles. Turn to *Sample Flow Chart* on page 106. If a vehicle has more than one wheel, which box would you look at?	Does it have only two wheels?	Label *tricycle.*	8
46	Look at page 106. If it has 3 wheels, we label it:	*unicycle.*	*bicycle.*	2
47	Which do you read if it has only two wheels?	Label *bicycle.*	Label *tricycle.*	5
48	Which box must you read to know that this is a unicycle?	Does it have only two wheels?	Does it have only one wheel?	3

1	2	3	4	5	6	7	8
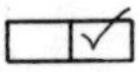 ☐☑	NEITHER tricycle.	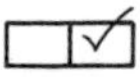 ☐☑	BOTH	 ☑☐	6 4-2 No	a. 5 b. 3-2 c. 3	 ☑☐

49 How many exits are there from a box which contains a question? 7

50 Which of these is a bicycle? 5

51 Here is your holding in Hearts.
Look at *Counting Honor Winners Flow Chart* on page 107.
Find the first diamond-shaped box.
Would you answer *yes* or *no* to that question? 6

52 *HW = 0* means you can't take any *honor winners*. In which case would you be sure you would take no honor winners? 4

53 Suppose your highest card is the Queen. (This means you said *yes* to the second diamond-shaped box on page 107.)
What two other cards do you need for your honor winners to equal 1? 2

54 You have:

Declarer (You) Dummy

Your opponents must have: 1

55 Opponents have A and K.
You have Q, J, and 10.
Which is probably true?

Their A and K will take two tricks.	Their A and K won't take any tricks.

3

56 It is easy to see how honor winners are established.
If you have the Queen, the Jack, and the Ten of Hearts, the first honor will fall on the opponents' Ace, and the second honor will fall on the opponents' King.
Can your third honor fall to any other opponents' honor in that suit? 8

1	2	3	4	5	6	7	8
BOTH	Jack and Ten	☑☐	BOTH	BOTH	Yes	two	No

57	With which of these holdings will your side win a trick?	♥Q J 10 3	♥Q J 9 7	7
58	In counting honor winners in a suit, it is important that you count the combined holdings between yourself and the dummy. Which of these holdings is worth 1 honor winner in Hearts?	Dummy: J 10 2 Declarer: Q 7 5	Dummy: Q 10 3 Declarer: J 4 2	8
59	Read what follows the asterisk at the bottom of page 107. Which of these shows 2 PTH?	A K J 10	K Q J	5
60	If you hold the Q, J, 10, 7, and 3 of Clubs, how many PTH do you have?			2
61	If your highest honor is a King, it is easy to see from page 107 that the number of honor winners is exactly the same as the number of ( ).			3
62	In which case do you have 1 honor winner?	Dummy: K 6 5 Declarer: Q 3 2	Dummy: Q J 10 7 Declarer: 4 3 2	1
63	You hold A, K, Q, and 10. Your A-K and K-Q are equal to 2 pairs of touching honors. But since you hold the Ace, honor winners = PTH + 1, so honor winners = 3. Which shows 2 honor winners?	Q J	A K Q	4
64	It is easy to see why holdings such as K, J, and 10 are worth 1 honor winner. The King will lose to the __________, the Jack or the Ten will lose to the __________, and your third honor will capture the third round in that suit for 1 honor winner.			6

1	2	3	4	5	6	7	8
BOTH	2	PTH (Pairs of Touching Honors)	NEITHER	BOTH (A-K, J-10 and K-Q, Q-J)	Ace Queen	☑☐	BOTH

65 Using page 107, how many honor winners would you give yourself with this holding?

Dummy: ♦A 3 2 7

Your hand: ♦J 10 6 4

66 a. A combined honor holding of only A, J, and 10 is worth ( ) honor winner(s).

b. This is easy to understand since the Ace will capture a trick, but the Jack and the Ten 2

will lose to the opponents' ________ and ________.

67 Use page 107 if necessary.

Which of these combined holdings would you value at 2 honor winners?

Dummy: A J 7	Dummy: K J 10 7
Declarer: 10 3 2	Declarer: Q 3 2

4

68 You have now learned two of the three basic ways of taking tricks in bridge. The first way is based on distribution, in which you establish tricks because you have a holding in a suit which is longer than a holding the opponents have in that suit. These are called ________ - ________ tricks. 5

69 What are tricks called when your cards are higher in RANK than your opponents' cards? 1

70 In most cases, you can find the number of tricks which you can win in a given suit by counting the long-card winners and your honor winners and adding them together. If you figure on 3 long-card winners and 1 honor winner, that suit should produce ( ) winning tricks. 3

71 In counting your long-card winners, first assume the most *probable* split.

If your opponents hold 6 cards, the most *probable* split is ( )-( ). 6

72 The number of long-card winners which you can establish depends on how the opponents' cards are divided. You and dummy have a 5-4 split. How many long-card winners can you establish:

a. if opponents are split 3-1? (most probable split) 8

b. if opponents are split 2-2? (next most probable split)

c. if opponents are split 4-0? (least probable split)

1	2	3	4	5	6	7	8
honor winners	a. 1 b. King Queen	4	NEITHER Right-hand choice has 3 PTH.	long-card	4-2	1	a. 2 b. 3 c. 1

73 Suppose the cards in your hand and the dummy are divided 5-2.
a. What is the opponents' most *likely* split?
b. You will be able to establish ( ) long-card winner(s).
c. However, if the cards happen to be divided 3-3, how many long-card winners can you establish?

6

74 In general, the more evenly the opponents' cards are divided, the more long-card winners you can establish. We can speak of such even splits as *favorable* distributions. If opponents hold 4 cards in a suit, the most probable distribution is ( ) - ( ), but the most *favorable* distribution is ( ) - ( ).

1

75

When 5 cards split 3-2, it is the most even split. When you have a 3-2 split, it is:	most probable.	most favorable.

4

76 Remember that the most *favorable* distribution is when the opponents' cards are split as evenly as possible. Look at *Table of Probabilities* on page 105. Opponents hold 7 cards of a suit.
a. What is the most probable distribution?
b. What is the most favorable distribution for establishing long cards?
c. Are these the same distribution?

5

77 In general, you will be safe in counting the number of winners in a suit by adding the honor winners to your estimated number of long-card winners. Of course, you should use your common sense and not count the same values twice. For example, suppose you have A, K, Q, J, and 10 in your hand and dummy has 4, 3, and 2. Your 5 honors give you ( ) honor winners.

7

78 Dummy: ♥4 3 2
Declarer: ♥A K Q J 10
If the opponents' cards are split 3-2, you should have 2 long-card winners. Five honor winners and 2 long-card winners total 7 tricks. However, since you are counting some of the same cards twice, it is easy to see that you should only count the suit as having ( ) winning tricks.

2

79

Usually, you cannot establish long cards unless you and your partner hold at least 7 cards in your combined hands. (The exceptions to this happen very rarely in bridge.) In which of these hands would you be most likely to try to establish long cards?	Dummy: ♠7 3 2 Declarer: ♠A K 8	Dummy: ♣8 7 6 5 Declarer: ♣J 10 3 2

3

80

N: ♠Q 9 8 6
W: ♠K
S: ♠A J 10 7 5 4 3 2 You

E has no Spades. You and dummy have 12 of the 13 Spades. W has the King. If you play your Ace, what must W do?

8

1	2	3	4	5	6	7	8
3-1 2-2	5	☐ ☑	BOTH	a. 4-3 b. 4-3 c. Yes	a. 4-2 b. 1 c. 2	5	He must play the King.

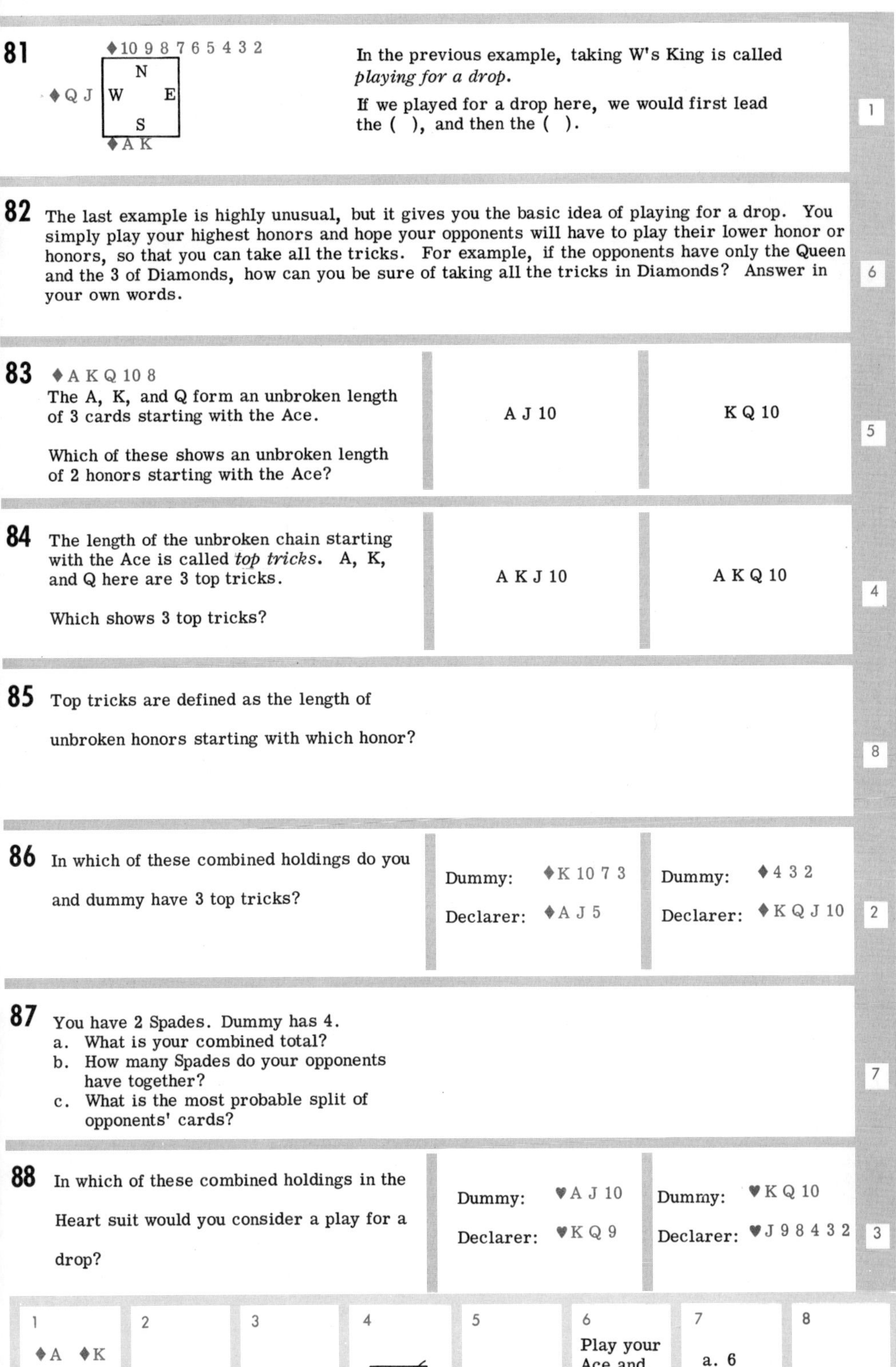

81 ♦10 9 8 7 6 5 4 3 2 (North); ♦Q J (West); ♦A K (South)

In the previous example, taking W's King is called *playing for a drop.*

If we played for a drop here, we would first lead the ( ), and then the ( ). 1

82 The last example is highly unusual, but it gives you the basic idea of playing for a drop. You simply play your highest honors and hope your opponents will have to play their lower honor or honors, so that you can take all the tricks. For example, if the opponents have only the Queen and the 3 of Diamonds, how can you be sure of taking all the tricks in Diamonds? Answer in your own words. 6

83 ♦A K Q 10 8

The A, K, and Q form an unbroken length of 3 cards starting with the Ace.

Which of these shows an unbroken length of 2 honors starting with the Ace?

A J 10	K Q 10

5

84 The length of the unbroken chain starting with the Ace is called *top tricks*. A, K, and Q here are 3 top tricks.

Which shows 3 top tricks?

A K J 10	A K Q 10

4

85 Top tricks are defined as the length of unbroken honors starting with which honor? 8

86 In which of these combined holdings do you and dummy have 3 top tricks?

Dummy: ♦K 10 7 3 Declarer: ♦A J 5	Dummy: ♦4 3 2 Declarer: ♦K Q J 10

2

87 You have 2 Spades. Dummy has 4.

a. What is your combined total?
b. How many Spades do your opponents have together?
c. What is the most probable split of opponents' cards?

7

88 In which of these combined holdings in the Heart suit would you consider a play for a drop?

Dummy: ♥A J 10 Declarer: ♥K Q 9	Dummy: ♥K Q 10 Declarer: ♥J 9 8 4 3 2

3

1	2	3	4	5	6	7	8
♦A ♦K (either order)	NEITHER	NEITHER	☐☑	NEITHER	Play your Ace and then your King.	a. 6 b. 7 c. 4-3	Ace

89 To decide whether or not to play for a drop, you must count your top tricks and also count the number of cards in that suit which the opponents hold. It is easy to count your top tricks by looking at your hand and the dummy. Describe in your own words how you figure out the number of cards which the opponents hold in any suit. 7

90 After you count the number of top tricks which you have in the combined hands of yourself and dummy, you *double* this number. If you have 2 top tricks, you double this number to get 4. If you have A, K, and Q as your top tricks, doubling this number gives you ( ). 4

91 Suppose you have figured that the opponents hold 6 cards and that double your top tricks also equals 6. The number you get by doubling top tricks is (equal to/less than/greater than) the number of cards your opponents hold. 5

92 To play for a drop means you want to take an opponent's card because:	It can wreck your long suit establishment.	It is an honor which may take one of your honors.	3

93 Suppose that double your top tricks is 4. Suppose, also, you have figured that your opponents hold 5 cards. Double your top tricks is (equal to/less than/greater than) the number of cards out against you. 8

94 ♥A K Q J 10 Here is an unbroken sequence from A to 10. ♦A K Q 10 This sequence is broken. What card is missing?	♦Q	♦J	6
95 ♠A K J 10 The Queen is missing; the card right above it in rank is the King. The card right below it in rank is the:	♠Q	♠J	1
96 You Dummy Double your top tricks is:	less than the cards out against you.	greater than the cards out against you.	2

1	2	3	4	5	6	7	8
[ ] [✓]	NEITHER equal to the cards out against you.	[ ] [✓]	6	equal to	[ ] [✓]	Subtract from 13 your total cards in that suit.	less than

97 ♦A Q J 10 Here we have a broken sequence with one honor missing.

a. What card is in rank above the missing honor? 2

b. What card is in rank below the missing honor?

98 If you have the next honor above and the next honor below some honor which the opponents hold, you are said to have a *tenace*, if both your honor cards are in the same hand. For example, if you held K, J, and 3, this would be a tenace, since you have the honor above and the honor below an opponent's honor, which in this case is the ________. 7

99 Remember: In a tenace, you have the honor above and the honor below a missing honor which an opponent holds.

a. If you hold Q, J, 3, and 2, it (is/is not) a tenace. 4
b. If you hold K, J, 3, and 2, it (is/is not) a tenace.

100 Which of these hands has a tenace?

♥Q 10 7 | ♥A Q 8 7 8

101 In Chart 7, page 285, *Play of a Suit Containing At Least One Honor,* find the square which says "Is double the number of top tricks greater than the number of cards out against you?" (It is in the far left-hand column of the chart.)

If you answer *Yes* to this question, what is the next question you ask yourself? 6

102 ♠Q J 4
When you have 2 cards in sequence, they are equal in *rank*. Here you hold the Queen and Jack; therefore, they are equal. Which hand shows 2 cards which are equal?

♥A K 8 4 | ♥K Q 10 5 1

103 A tenace can be divided between you and dummy when an extra card of equal RANK is included in the hands. Which of these has a tenace?

Q 4 ♣
Dummy
A J 10 ♣
You

J 7 2 ♣
Dummy
K 10 4 ♣
You 5

104 Remember that a tenace can be divided between you and dummy when an extra card of equal RANK is included in the hands. Suppose you have only the King as an honor in the dummy and only the Queen as an honor in your hand.
Do you have a tenace in that suit? 3

1	2	3	4	5	6	7	8
BOTH	a. Ace (♦A) b. Queen (♦Q)	No	a. is not b. is	BOTH	Does either hand have a tenace?	Queen	BOTH (Q-10 and A-Q)

105 As soon as you play either of the two cards in the tenace, that tenace is no longer intact. You hold K, J, and 7 in the dummy.
a. Do you still have a tenace if you played the 7?
b. Do you still have a tenace if you played the Jack? 3

106 If your top tricks doubled are greater than or equal to the cards out against you, play for a drop.
In which hand should you play for a drop? 8

Dummy: A 7 6 5 4 ♠	Dummy: Q 9 6 2 ♠
You: K J 10 ♠	You: A K J ♠

107 Suppose you doubled your tricks on top and found that the number was greater than the number of cards out against you.
What does Pocket Chart 7 tell you to do? 6

108 You have decided to play for a drop. What other question should you ask yourself?
(Look at Chart 7.) 7

Do you want to establish suit?	Does either hand have a tenace?

109 Refer to Chart 7.
Yes, you are playing for a drop.
Yes, you have a tenace.
What does the next instruction box tell you to do? 5

Play top tricks to keep tenaces intact as long as possible.	Lead top tricks. Play cards so that suit-establishing trick is taken in long hand.

110 You have decided to play for a drop. You have the King and Jack in the dummy and the Ace in your own hand.
a. Which hand has the tenace?
b. Should you play your Ace or your King first to keep that tenace intact as long as possible? 4

111 Suppose your number of top tricks doubled is greater than the number of cards out against you, and you have 6 cards in that suit. (Look at Chart 7.)
Would you play for a drop? 2

112 When your opponents play their last remaining card (or cards) on any given trick, the cards you have left as long cards are *established*. For example, if the opponents' cards are split 2-2, your long cards will be established after two leads in that suit. If the opponents' cards are split 3-1, your long cards will be established after ( ) leads in that suit. 1

1	2	3	4	5	6	7	8
3	No, you need 7 or more cards.	a. Yes b. No	a. dummy b. You should play the Ace first.	[✓][ ]	Play for drop.	[ ][✓]	[ ][✓]

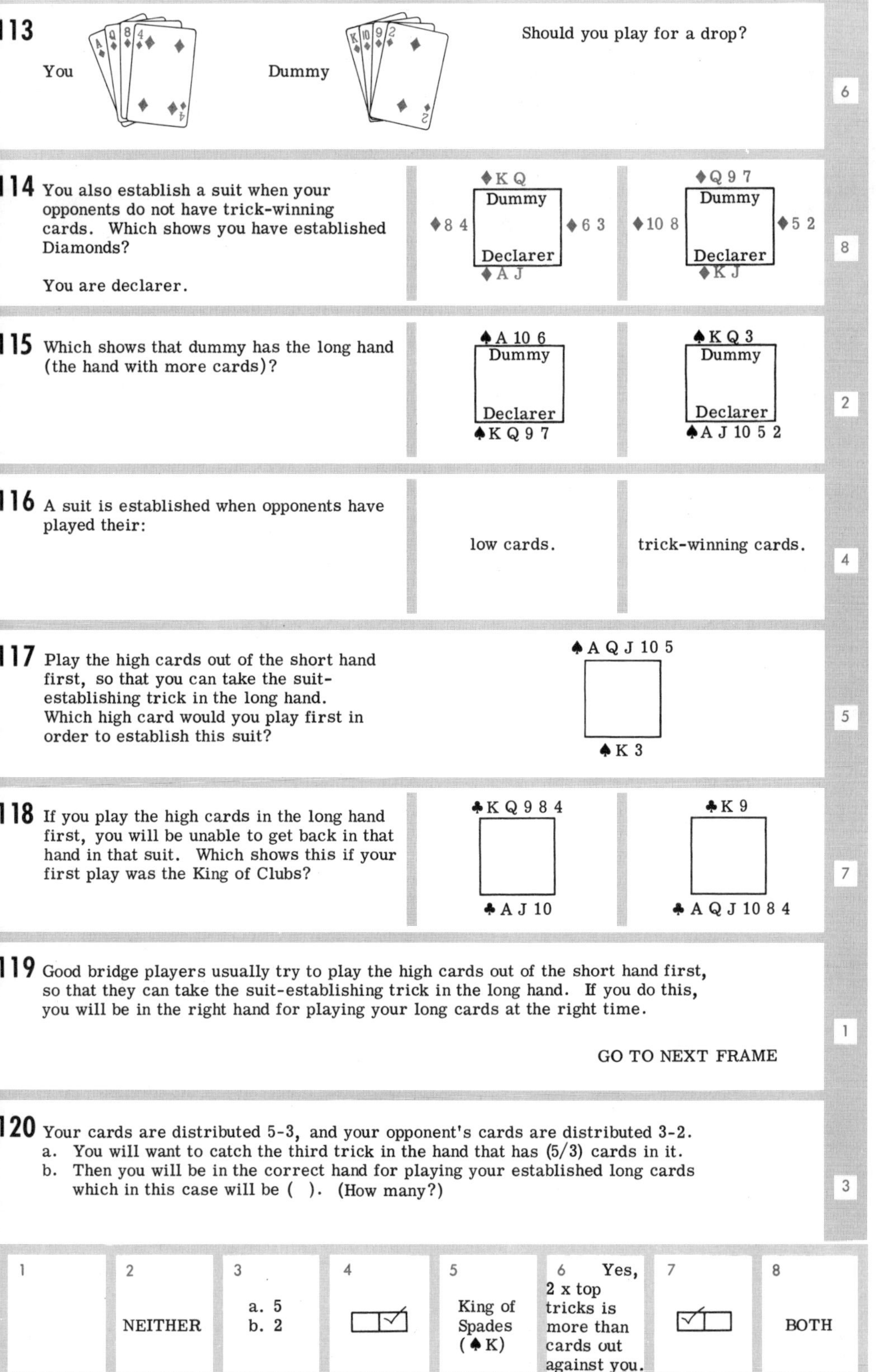

113 You [A Q 8 4 of Diamonds] Dummy [K 10 9 2 of Diamonds]

Should you play for a drop? 6

114 You also establish a suit when your opponents do not have trick-winning cards. Which shows you have established Diamonds?

You are declarer.

♦K Q Dummy / Declarer ♦A J; ♦8 4 / ♦6 3	♦Q 9 7 Dummy / Declarer ♦K J; ♦10 8 / ♦5 2

8

115 Which shows that dummy has the long hand (the hand with more cards)?

♠A 10 6 Dummy / Declarer ♠K Q 9 7	♠K Q 3 Dummy / Declarer ♠A J 10 5 2

2

116 A suit is established when opponents have played their:

low cards.	trick-winning cards.

4

117 Play the high cards out of the short hand first, so that you can take the suit-establishing trick in the long hand. Which high card would you play first in order to establish this suit?

♠A Q J 10 5 / ♠K 3

5

118 If you play the high cards in the long hand first, you will be unable to get back in that hand in that suit. Which shows this if your first play was the King of Clubs?

♣K Q 9 8 4 / ♣A J 10	♣K 9 / ♣A Q J 10 8 4

7

119 Good bridge players usually try to play the high cards out of the short hand first, so that they can take the suit-establishing trick in the long hand. If you do this, you will be in the right hand for playing your long cards at the right time.

GO TO NEXT FRAME

1

120 Your cards are distributed 5-3, and your opponent's cards are distributed 3-2.

a. You will want to catch the third trick in the hand that has (5/3) cards in it.
b. Then you will be in the correct hand for playing your established long cards which in this case will be ( ). (How many?)

3

1	2	3	4	5	6	7	8
	NEITHER	a. 5 b. 2	[ ] [✓]	King of Spades (♠K)	Yes, 2 x top tricks is more than cards out against you.	[✓] [ ]	BOTH

121 Play the high cards out of the (long/short) hand first, so that you can take the suit-establishing trick in the (long/short) hand. 3

122 Suppose you have decided to play for a drop, and you have answered *no* to the question, "Does either hand have a tenace?" What does Chart 7 tell you to do? 5

123 Dummy: ♥K Q 3 Declarer: ♥A 8 7 6 5 4 2

a. In this case you have ( ) top tricks.
b. Doubled, you get ( ).
c. This is (less than/equal to/greater than) the number of cards against you. 4
d. You (do/do not) play for a drop.

124 Dummy: ♥K Q 3 Declarer: ♥A 8 7 6 5 4 2

a. Does either hand have a tenace? You can capture all the tricks in this suit, even if the opponents' cards are divided 3-0. From Chart 7 you have seen that you want to take the suit-establishing trick in the long hand. 2
b. This means that you will play the _________ and _________, and then capture the third round with the _________ in the long hand.

125 By now, you should know *when* to play for a drop and *how* to play for a drop, depending on your holding of top cards. What two things must you have in your hand and the dummy before you consider playing for a drop? 7

126 Describe in your own words how you figure the number of cards which your opponents must hold in a suit. 6

127 Suppose neither you nor dummy has the Ace.

a. Can you make the Ace drop? 1
b. Should you play for any drop?

128 If you doubled your number of top tricks and found that this number was less than the number of cards out against you, does Chart 7 tell you to play for a drop? 8

1	2	3	4	5	6	7	8
a. No (No card can take the Ace.) b. No	a. No b. King Queen Ace	short long	a. 3 b. 6 c. greater than d. do	Lead top tricks. Take suit-establishing trick in long hand.	Subtract from 13 your total cards in that suit.	1) top tricks 2) 7 or more cards	No

129 If you decide to play for a drop, what do you look for next? 7

130 Suppose that you have decided to play for a drop.
One hand has a tenace.
Try to describe how you would play this hand without looking at Chart 7. 4

131 If you are playing for a drop and neither hand has a tenace, you play your top tricks in such manner that the suit-establishing trick is taken in the _______ hand. 2

132 In which case would you play for a drop?

You: K Q J / Dummy: 10 9 8 7	You: A Q J 10 / Dummy: 9 4 2

3

133 Match the following.

a. tenace
b. honor sequence

1) a holding of the card above and the card below an opponent's honor
2) a holding of 2 honors in your hand combined with the dummy hand

5

134 The player who plays first is called the first hand. The player who plays second is the second hand, and so on. If N plays first, who is the fourth hand?

N W E S

E	W

1

135 In which case will both of your opponents have played before you?

N W E S ← You

when W led	when N (dummy) led

8

136 A fundamental principle in winning tricks with your honor cards in bridge is to try to wait until one or both of your opponents have played to that trick. If you lead and then play a card from the third hand, the dummy, one opponent will have played before the dummy. If your left-hand opponent leads, _________ opponent(s) will have played before you play fourth hand. 6

1	2	3	4	5	6	7	8
☐☑	long	NEITHER (on left, no Ace; on right, only 1 top trick)	Play top tricks, keep tenaces intact as long as possible.	a. 1) b. 2)	two (both)	to see whether either hand has a tenace	☑☐

137 E leads, so you are fourth hand. It is easier to make your choice of what to play because:

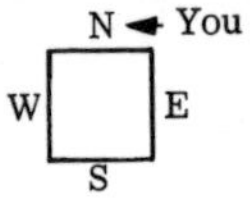

N ← You; W; E; S

you will see only one of your opponents play.	you will see what both your opponents have played.

7

138 W led the 2 of Diamonds. You have the Ace and Queen of Diamonds and play fourth hand.

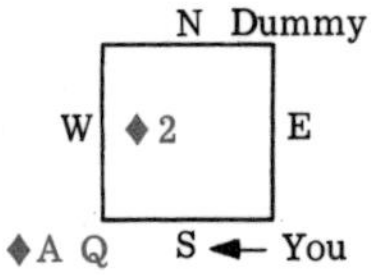

N Dummy; W ♦2; E; ♦A Q S ← You

a. If E plays the King of Diamonds, you can take it with your _______ and your Queen will take a trick too.
b. If E does not play the King of Diamonds, you can take the trick low with your _______, and c. then take the second trick with your ________.

4

139 Now suppose you play first hand.

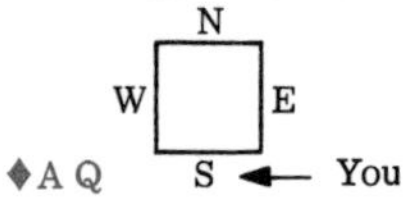

N; W; E; ♦A Q S ← You

If you lead the Ace, opponents will hold their King.
If you lead the Queen, opponents will take it with the King.
The greatest number of tricks you can take in this situation is ( ).

8

140 Consider this point once more, since it is very significant in understanding the importance of *position* of honors in bridge.

a. If your left-hand opponent leads a suit in which you hold A-Q fourth hand, you are certain to take ( ) trick(s).
b. If you have to lead first hand from the hand of the A-Q, you can take only ( ) trick(s).

3

141 Suppose you hold the A-Q and your *right*-hand opponent leads a suit. Your Ace and Queen form a (touching honor/sequence/tenace). They are the cards above and below an opponent's honor, which in this case would be the ________.

2

142 When you hold a tenace, you hope that the opponents' missing honor is just to the right of this tenace. You hope ( ) has the King.

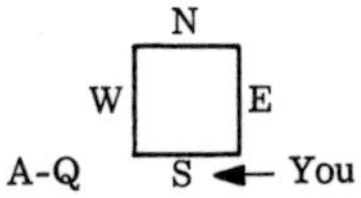

N; W; E; A-Q S ← You

W	E

1

143 If you are lucky, you can still take 2 tricks. If N (dummy) leads and E has the King, E is trapped.

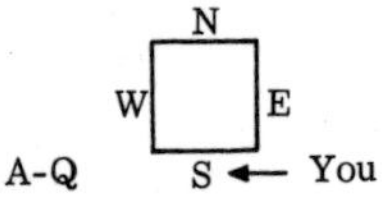

N; W; E; A-Q S ← You

a. If he plays the King, you will take it with your ______ and your ______ will be good for a second trick.
b. If he does not play the King, you can take the trick with the Queen and your _____ will be good for a second trick.

5

144 E has the lead. He can lead the King or a lower card. You have the choice of playing either the Ace or the Queen after E has played. In either case, it is easy to see you can take ( ) tricks.

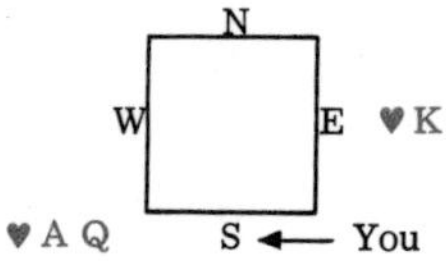

N; W; E ♥K; ♥A Q S ← You

6

1	2	3	4	5	6	7	8
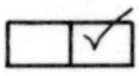 ☐ ☑	tenace King	a. 2 b. 1	a. Ace b. Queen c. Ace	a. Ace Queen b. Ace	2	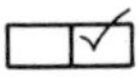 ☐ ☑	1

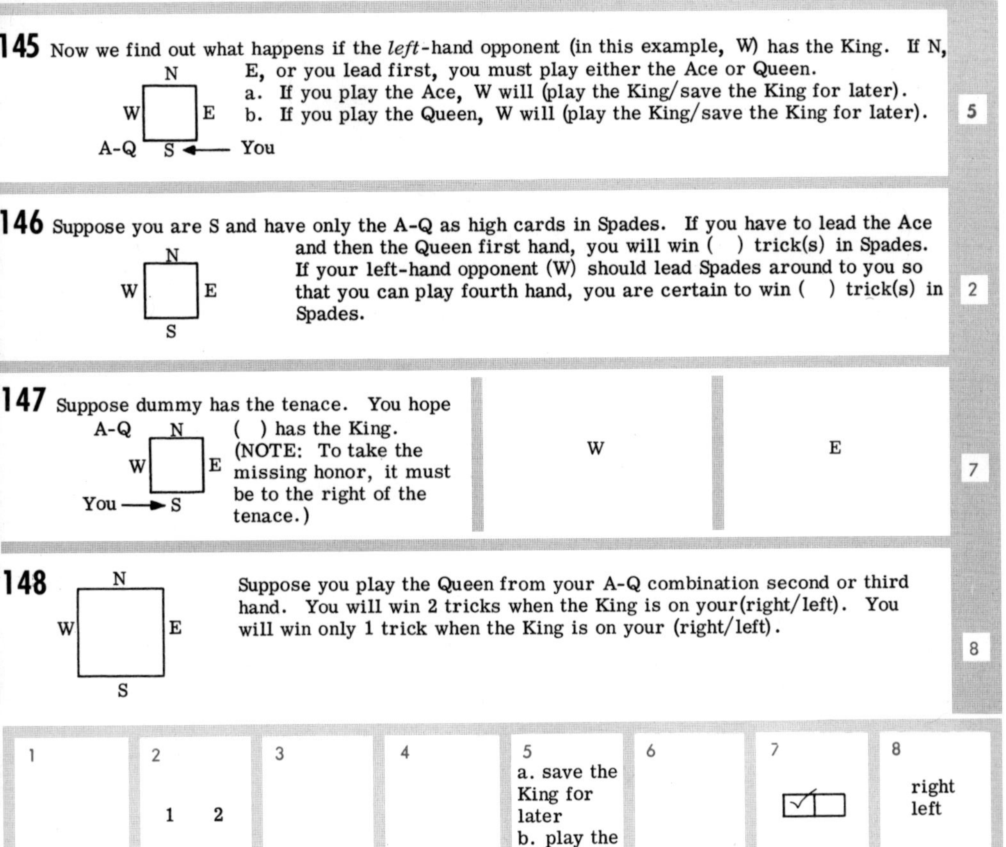

145 Now we find out what happens if the *left*-hand opponent (in this example, W) has the King. If N, E, or you lead first, you must play either the Ace or Queen.

a. If you play the Ace, W will (play the King/save the King for later).

b. If you play the Queen, W will (play the King/save the King for later). 5

146 Suppose you are S and have only the A-Q as high cards in Spades. If you have to lead the Ace and then the Queen first hand, you will win (   ) trick(s) in Spades. If your left-hand opponent (W) should lead Spades around to you so that you can play fourth hand, you are certain to win (   ) trick(s) in Spades. 2

147 Suppose dummy has the tenace. You hope (   ) has the King. (NOTE: To take the missing honor, it must be to the right of the tenace.) 7

W	E

148 Suppose you play the Queen from your A-Q combination second or third hand. You will win 2 tricks when the King is on your(right/left). You will win only 1 trick when the King is on your (right/left). 8

1	2	3	4	5	6	7	8
	1 2			a. save the King for later b. play the King		☑☐	right left

TAKE UNIT 5 POST-TEST

UNIT 6

finessing and ruffing

Further elaboration of Unit 5 occurs here. The student is introduced to the direct and indirect finesse. Hands which are down to the last two cards are discussed to show possible ways to win one or both of these tricks. In the same manner, three- and four-card combinations are discussed. Counting and pulling trump are presented.

PRE- AND POST-TEST

1. If you are the last to play a trick, you are [first hand/third hand/(both)/(neither)].

2. An attempt to win a trick with the lower card of a tenace is a(n) ________.

3. a. Where must the King of Spades be in order to make your Queen good? (W/E)

   b. To make the Queen good, you lead from (N/S).

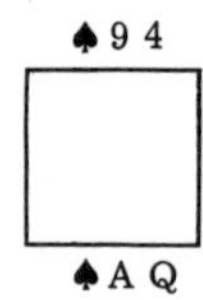

   c. If you answered b. correctly, then you know that you should lead (away from/toward) any honor cards or sequences.

4. Here you are finessing the __________, but finessing against the __________.

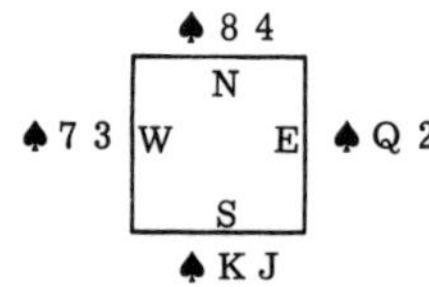

5. In which of these hands might you make an attacking finesse against your opponents' Queen?

a.
♦A K 3
Dummy
Declarer
♦J 10 4

b.
♦A K 3
Dummy
Declarer
♦J 9 4

6. To make an attacking finesse, you [lead toward an honor/lead an honor/lead a small card/(none of these)].

7. You may take tricks with long-card winners, honor tricks, or by __________.

8.
♦3 2
Dummy
Declarer
♦A K 8

Diamonds are trumps. If you lead out this suit, will the opponents capture one or more tricks after the dummy is without cards in Diamonds?

1 (Before you begin, take the Pre-Test for Unit 6.)
In most bridge books, declarer is always S. You might guess that dummy is always ( ). 7

2 In the actual play of the hand, however, is dummy always N? 4

3 In this unit, N will always be the ________,

and S will always be the ________. 8

4 A *finesse* is an attempt to win a trick with the lower card of a tenace. Bridge players also speak of finessing *against* the missing honor which the opponents hold. Therefore, if you lead toward an A-Q tenace and play the Queen, you are: 6

finessing the Queen.	finessing against the King.

5

♠9 4
N
W E
S
♠A K J

Here, if you lead the 9 of Spades, you are leading toward your honors.

If you lead the Ace of Spades, you are leading (away from/toward) your honors. 2

6 When you make a finesse, you have made the (higher/lower) card of a tenace good (enabled it to take a trick). 1

7

♠K J 3

♠10 4

To lead toward the K-J, you may play:
a. ♠10.
b. ♠4.
c. either the ♠10 or the ♠4.
d. neither the ♠10 nor the ♠4. 5

8 To lead away from the K-J, you play the:

♠K J 3

♠10 4

3♠	10♠

3

1	2	3	4	5	6	7	8
lower	away from	[✓][ ]	No	c. either the ♠10 or the ♠4.	BOTH	N	dummy declarer

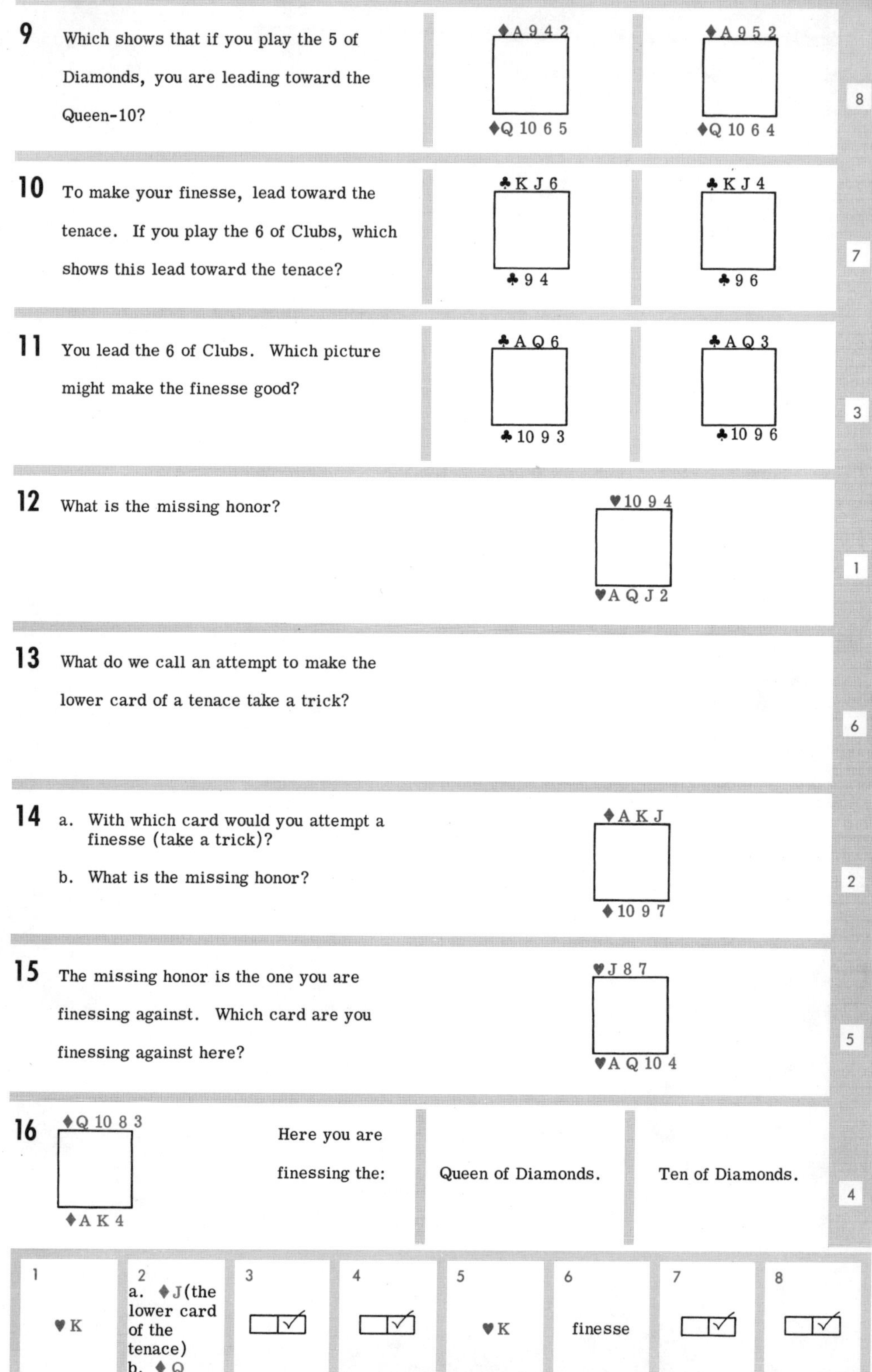

9 Which shows that if you play the 5 of Diamonds, you are leading toward the Queen-10?

♦A 9 4 2 / ♦Q 10 6 5	♦A 9 5 2 / ♦Q 10 6 4

8

10 To make your finesse, lead toward the tenace. If you play the 6 of Clubs, which shows this lead toward the tenace?

♣K J 6 / ♣9 4	♣K J 4 / ♣9 6

7

11 You lead the 6 of Clubs. Which picture might make the finesse good?

♣A Q 6 / ♣10 9 3	♣A Q 3 / ♣10 9 6

3

12 What is the missing honor?

♥10 9 4

♥A Q J 2

1

13 What do we call an attempt to make the lower card of a tenace take a trick?

6

14 a. With which card would you attempt a finesse (take a trick)?

b. What is the missing honor?

♦A K J

♦10 9 7

2

15 The missing honor is the one you are finessing against. Which card are you finessing against here?

♥J 8 7

♥A Q 10 4

5

16 ♦Q 10 8 3

♦A K 4

Here you are finessing the:

Queen of Diamonds.	Ten of Diamonds.

4

1	2	3	4	5	6	7	8
♥K	a. ♦J (the lower card of the tenace) b. ♦Q	☐ ☑	☐ ☑	♥K	finesse	☐ ☑	☐ ☑

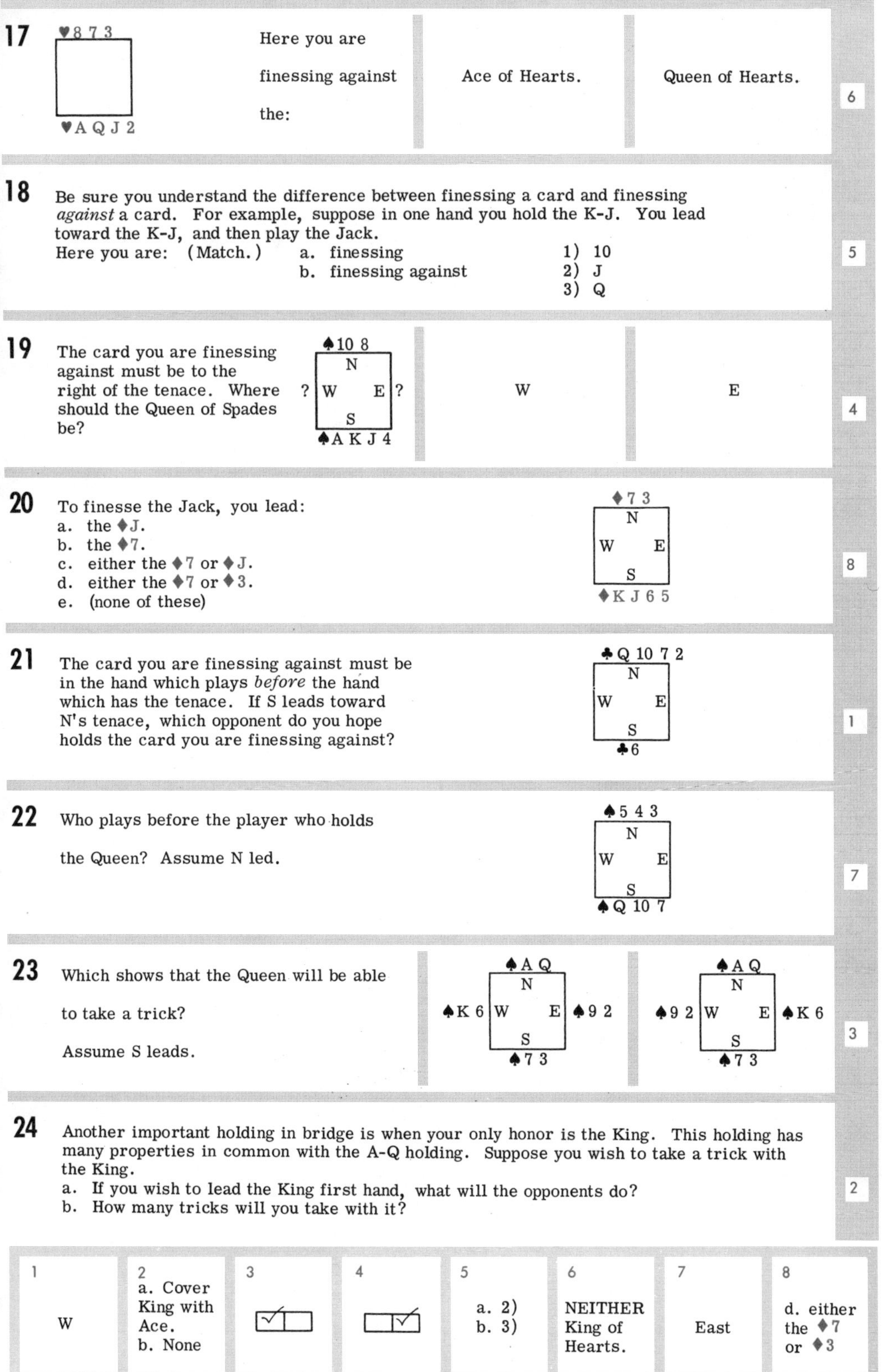

17 ♥8 7 3 / ♥A Q J 2

Here you are finessing against the:

Ace of Hearts.	Queen of Hearts.

6

18 Be sure you understand the difference between finessing a card and finessing *against* a card. For example, suppose in one hand you hold the K-J. You lead toward the K-J, and then play the Jack.

Here you are: (Match.)
a. finessing
b. finessing against

1) 10
2) J
3) Q

5

19 The card you are finessing against must be to the right of the tenace. Where should the Queen of Spades be?

♠10 8 (N); ? W E ?; ♠A K J 4 (S)

W	E

4

20 To finesse the Jack, you lead:
a. the ♦J.
b. the ♦7.
c. either the ♦7 or ♦J.
d. either the ♦7 or ♦3.
e. (none of these)

♦7 3 (N); ♦K J 6 5 (S)

8

21 The card you are finessing against must be in the hand which plays *before* the hand which has the tenace. If S leads toward N's tenace, which opponent do you hope holds the card you are finessing against?

♣Q 10 7 2 (N); ♣6 (S)

1

22 Who plays before the player who holds the Queen? Assume N led.

♠5 4 3 (N); ♠Q 10 7 (S)

7

23 Which shows that the Queen will be able to take a trick?

Assume S leads.

N ♠A Q; W ♠K 6; E ♠9 2; S ♠7 3	N ♠A Q; W ♠9 2; E ♠K 6; S ♠7 3

3

24 Another important holding in bridge is when your only honor is the King. This holding has many properties in common with the A-Q holding. Suppose you wish to take a trick with the King.
a. If you wish to lead the King first hand, what will the opponents do?
b. How many tricks will you take with it?

2

1	2	3	4	5	6	7	8
W	a. Cover King with Ace. b. None	[✓][ ]	[ ][✓]	a. 2) b. 3)	NEITHER King of Hearts.	East	d. either the ♦7 or ♦3

25

W leads Spades.
Since you are playing after both your opponents, you are certain to take a trick with your King.
a. If either of them (W or E) plays the Ace, you play the ( ).
b. Then you take the second round with the ________.

N / W / E / S ← You; ♠K 4

1

26 If the Ace is not played on the first round, you can, of course, take the trick with your ________.

N / W / E / S ← You; ♠K 4

8

27 In which case do you have a tenace?

K 6 4 / Q 9 7 | K 4 / Q 10 9 7

6

28 Which shows that if you play the 3 of Clubs, you are leading toward the Queen and away from the King?

N ♣K 3, S ♣Q 10 7 | N ♣Q J 7, S ♣K 3

5

29 You are S. How many tricks will you take if you keep leading away from the hand which holds the King?

N ♦4 2; W ♦A Q; E ♦7 5; S ♦K 3

4

30 You are S. How many tricks can you take if you play the K-3 combination as fourth hand? Assume W leads the Queen first hand.

N ♦4 2; W ♦A Q; E ♦7 5; S ♦K 3

3

31 Suppose you are S holding the King and a small card. You can attempt to win a trick with the King by leading toward your King from the dummy. If your *right*-hand opponent holds the Ace, you are certain to win a trick with your King. Describe in your own words why this is true.

N ♦6 5; W ♦9 8; E ♦A J; S ♦K 7

7

32 On the other hand, if you have only the King and a small card holding in a suit, and your left-hand opponent holds the Ace, how many tricks do you think you will take with the King?

N ♦6 5; W ♦A J; E ♦9 8; S ♦K 7

2

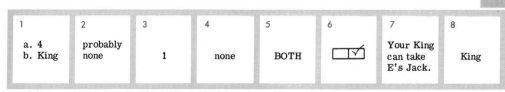

1	2	3	4	5	6	7	8
a. 4 b. King	probably none	1	none	BOTH	☐☑	Your King can take E's Jack.	King

33 You are S holding the King and a small card in Diamonds. If the dummy or your right-hand opponent leads a Diamond, you will take a trick with your King if (E/W) has the Ace. You will not make a trick with the King if (E/W) has the Ace.

♦6 5
N
? W E ?
S
♦K 7

8

34 Sometimes you will be fortunate enough to have your opponents lead around to a tenace fourth hand. Most of the time, however, you will have to develop your honor tricks and tenaces yourself. You can guess that on the basis of what you have learned so far, the best procedure is to lead from dummy or from your own hand (away from/toward) any honor cards or sequences. 6

35 In which case would you play for a drop?

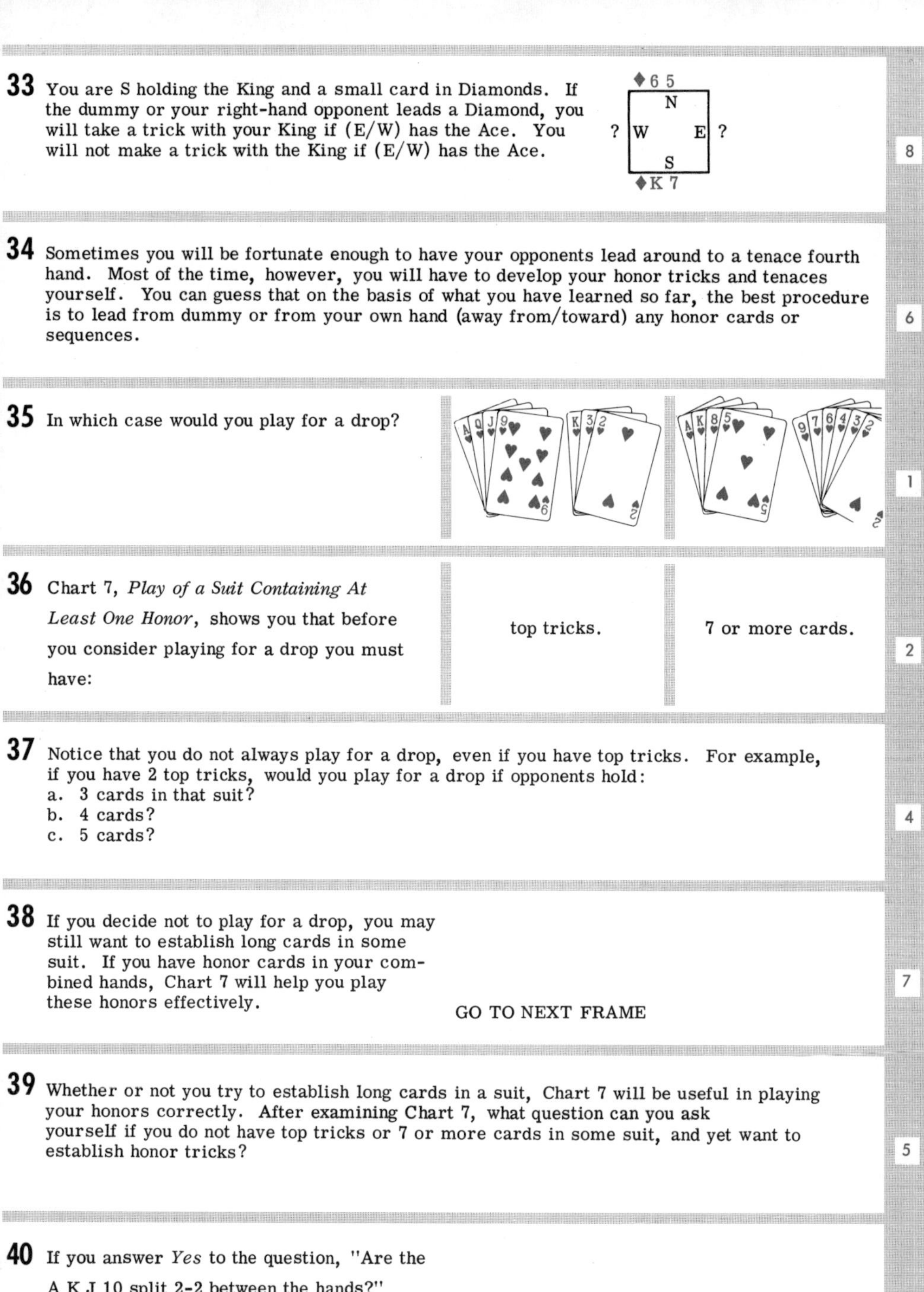

1

36 Chart 7, *Play of a Suit Containing At Least One Honor*, shows you that before you consider playing for a drop you must have:

top tricks.	7 or more cards.

2

37 Notice that you do not always play for a drop, even if you have top tricks. For example, if you have 2 top tricks, would you play for a drop if opponents hold:
a. 3 cards in that suit?
b. 4 cards?
c. 5 cards? 4

38 If you decide not to play for a drop, you may still want to establish long cards in some suit. If you have honor cards in your combined hands, Chart 7 will help you play these honors effectively. 7

GO TO NEXT FRAME

39 Whether or not you try to establish long cards in a suit, Chart 7 will be useful in playing your honors correctly. After examining Chart 7, what question can you ask yourself if you do not have top tricks or 7 or more cards in some suit, and yet want to establish honor tricks? 5

40 If you answer *Yes* to the question, "Are the A K J 10 split 2-2 between the hands?" what question should you ask yourself next? (See Chart 7.) 3

1	2	3	4	5	6	7	8
BOTH	BOTH	A-K in one hand, J-10 in other?	a. Yes b. Yes c. No	A-K-J-10 split 2-2 between the hands?	toward		E (right) W (left)

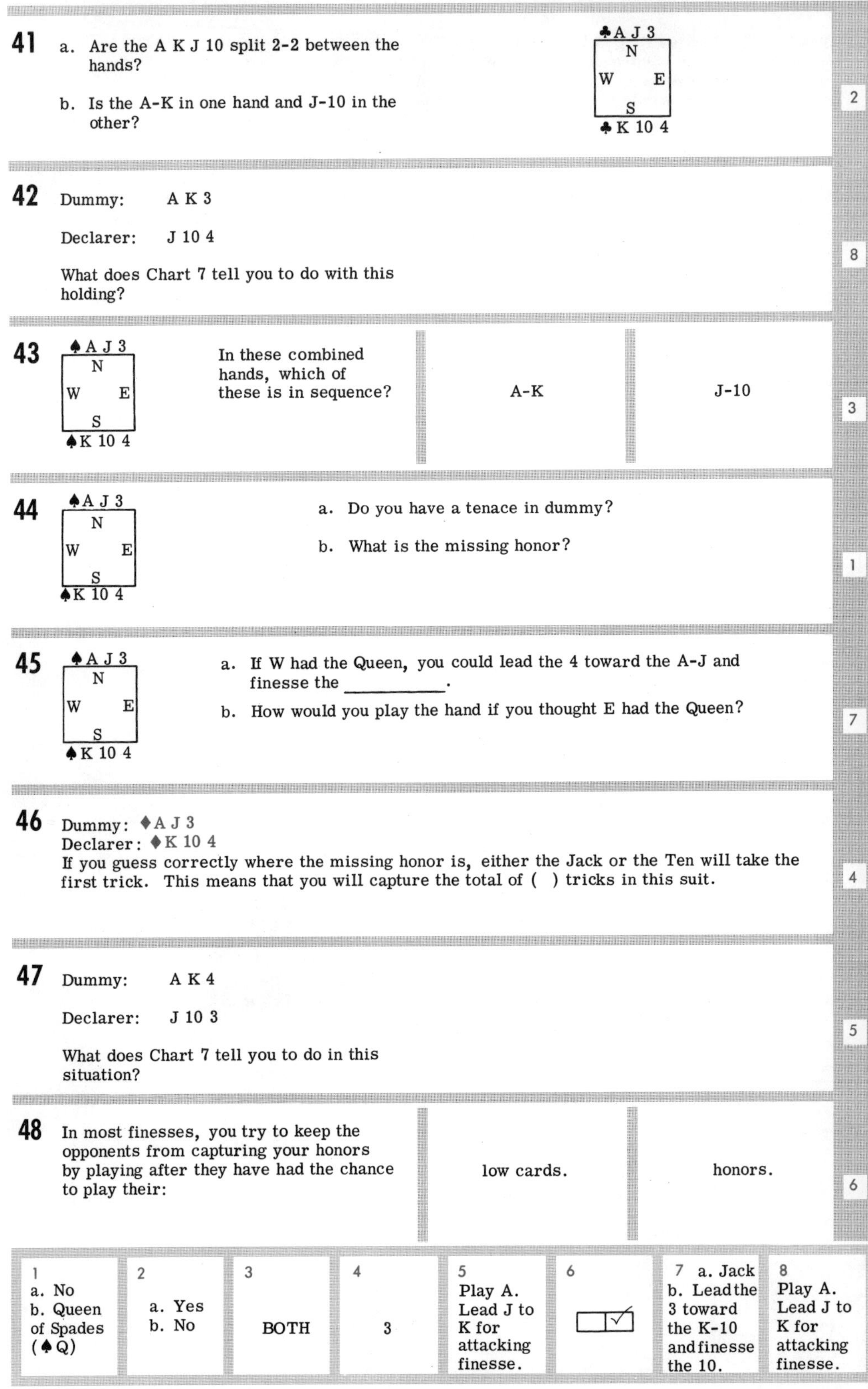

41 a. Are the A K J 10 split 2-2 between the hands?

b. Is the A-K in one hand and J-10 in the other?

♣A J 3
N
W E
S
♣K 10 4

2

---

42 Dummy: A K 3

Declarer: J 10 4

What does Chart 7 tell you to do with this holding?

8

---

43 ♠A J 3
N
W E
S
♠K 10 4

In these combined hands, which of these is in sequence?

A-K	J-10

3

---

44 ♠A J 3
N
W E
S
♠K 10 4

a. Do you have a tenace in dummy?

b. What is the missing honor?

1

---

45 ♠A J 3
N
W E
S
♠K 10 4

a. If W had the Queen, you could lead the 4 toward the A-J and finesse the ___________.

b. How would you play the hand if you thought E had the Queen?

7

---

46 Dummy: ♦A J 3
Declarer: ♦K 10 4
If you guess correctly where the missing honor is, either the Jack or the Ten will take the first trick. This means that you will capture the total of ( ) tricks in this suit.

4

---

47 Dummy: A K 4

Declarer: J 10 3

What does Chart 7 tell you to do in this situation?

5

---

48 In most finesses, you try to keep the opponents from capturing your honors by playing after they have had the chance to play their:

low cards.	honors.

6

1	2	3	4	5	6	7	8
a. No b. Queen of Spades (♠Q)	a. Yes b. No	BOTH	3	Play A. Lead J to K for attacking finesse.	☐ ☑	a. Jack b. Lead the 3 toward the K-10 and finesse the 10.	Play A. Lead J to K for attacking finesse.

49 In *attacking finesse*, you lead an honor, hoping the second hand will cover it, so that the third hand can capture the second honor. If you lead a low card toward an A-Q tenace, and finesse the Queen, are you making an attacking finesse? 3

50 Here is a rule to remember about making attacking finesses:

Never lead an honor first hand unless you hold AT LEAST one in sequence of that honor.

If you hold the J-10 in first hand and the A-K in third hand, you can make an attacking finesse, because the __________ and the __________ are in sequence in first hand. 5

51 Here is the rule:

Never make an __________ finesse unless you have at least __________ in sequence of the honor which you lead from the first hand. 1

52 In which of these hands might you make an attacking finesse against the opponents' Queen?

Dummy: ♣A K 3 Declarer: ♣J 6 4	Dummy: ♣A K 3 Declarer: ♣J 10 4

7

53 Which holding shows a sequence?

N: A 3 2 / S: Q 5 4 (W, E)	N: A K 2 / S: Q 5 4 (W, E)

2

54 N: A 3 2; S: Q 5 4 (W, E)

Leading the Queen toward the Ace shows that:

you have made an incorrect play.	you should *never* lead an honor first hand unless you hold at least one in sequence of that honor.

4

55 Dummy: ♦A K 3 Declarer: ♦J 10 5

Do you play for an attacking finesse with this position? 8

56 N: ♣J 9 7; S: ♣8 3 (W, E)

S leads low toward the J-9. You are:

finessing against the ten.	finessing the nine.

6

1	2	3	4	5	6	7	8
attacking one	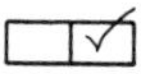 ☐ ☑	No	BOTH	Jack Ten	BOTH	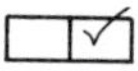 ☐ ☑	Yes

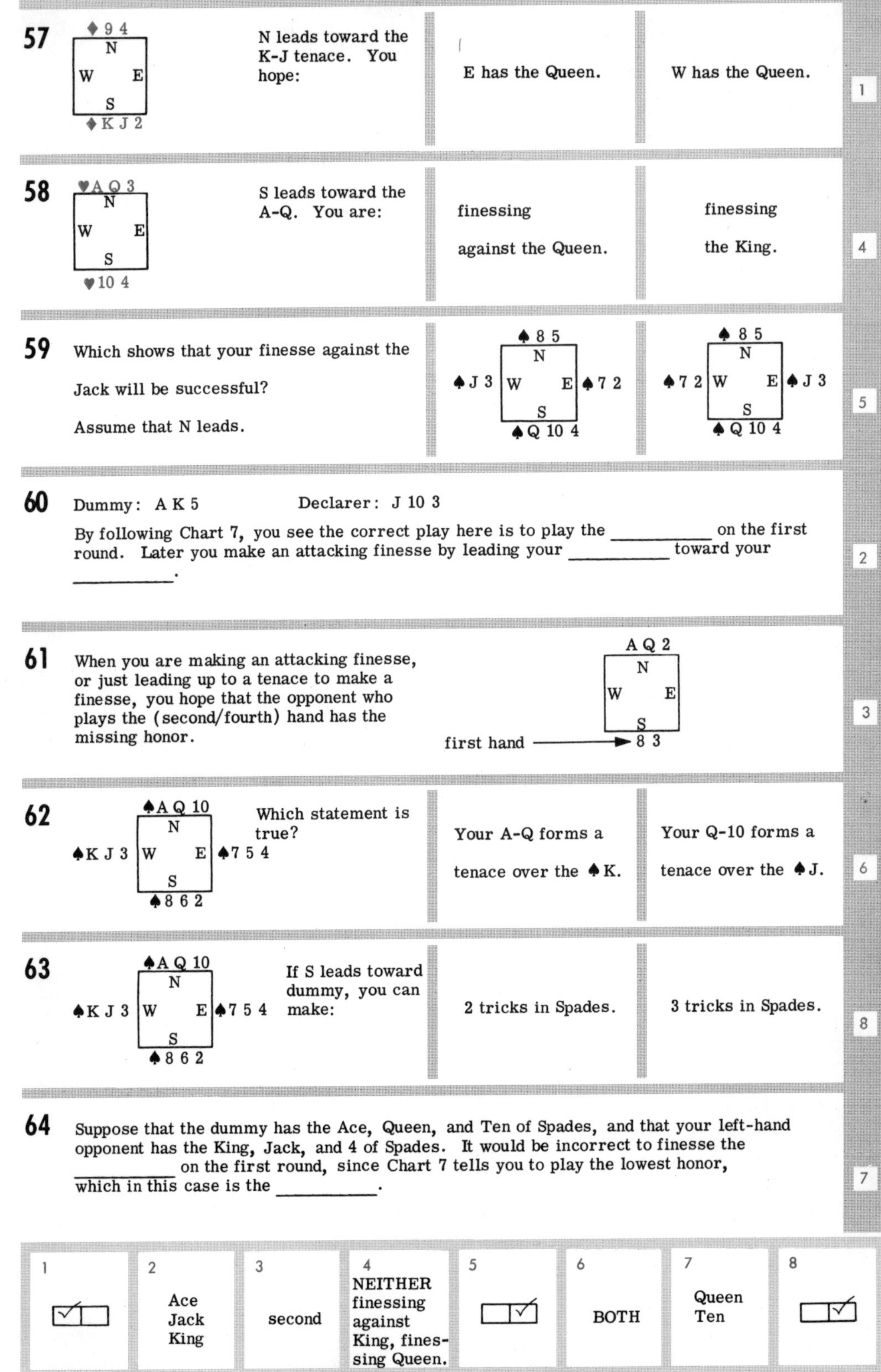

57 ♦ 9 4 (N) / ♦ K J 2 (S)

N leads toward the K-J tenace. You hope:

E has the Queen.	W has the Queen.

1

58 ♥ A Q 3 (N) / ♥ 10 4 (S)

S leads toward the A-Q. You are:

finessing against the Queen.	finessing the King.

4

59 Which shows that your finesse against the Jack will be successful?

Assume that N leads.

N ♠ 8 5; W ♠ J 3; E ♠ 7 2; S ♠ Q 10 4	N ♠ 8 5; W ♠ 7 2; E ♠ J 3; S ♠ Q 10 4

5

60 Dummy: A K 5 Declarer: J 10 3

By following Chart 7, you see the correct play here is to play the ___________ on the first round. Later you make an attacking finesse by leading your ___________ toward your ___________.

2

61 When you are making an attacking finesse, or just leading up to a tenace to make a finesse, you hope that the opponent who plays the (second/fourth) hand has the missing honor.

N: A Q 2; S: 8 3 (first hand ⟶ 8 3)

3

62 N ♠ A Q 10; W ♠ K J 3; E ♠ 7 5 4; S ♠ 8 6 2

Which statement is true?

Your A-Q forms a tenace over the ♠K.	Your Q-10 forms a tenace over the ♠J.

6

63 N ♠ A Q 10; W ♠ K J 3; E ♠ 7 5 4; S ♠ 8 6 2

If S leads toward dummy, you can make:

2 tricks in Spades.	3 tricks in Spades.

8

64 Suppose that the dummy has the Ace, Queen, and Ten of Spades, and that your left-hand opponent has the King, Jack, and 4 of Spades. It would be incorrect to finesse the ___________ on the first round, since Chart 7 tells you to play the lowest honor, which in this case is the ___________.

7

1	2	3	4	5	6	7	8
[✓][ ]	Ace Jack King	second	NEITHER finessing against King, finessing Queen.	[ ][✓]	BOTH	Queen Ten	[ ][✓]

65 Dummy holds A-Q-10, left-hand opponent holds K-J-4, and you finesse the Queen first. Your left-hand opponent will still have the King and the Jack. Even if you lead towards the A-10, either of these honors will force your Ace. This means that instead of taking no tricks in that suit, your opponents will take ( ) trick(s) in that suit. 2

66 Dummy: K 10 3 2 Declarer: Q J 5 4
In yours and dummy's combined hands, you have a ( ) - card honor sequence. The only honor which the opponents hold is the ___________, which will take ( ) trick(s). This means that ( ) of your honors will capture tricks. 7

67 Remember that to make an *attacking* finesse, you lead an honor. You also need another honor which is ___________ in rank with that honor before you consider an attacking finesse. 6

68 An attacking finesse is when you [play for a drop/lead an honor/(both)/(neither)]. 8

69 Dummy: A 4 3 Declarer: Q J 10

With this holding, what is the first question to which you answer *Yes* on Chart 7? 4

70 Dummy: A 3 2 Declarer: Q J 10

Following the instructions in Chart 7, you would lead either the Queen, the Jack, or the Ten (since they are equal in rank it makes no difference) toward the (Ace/Ten). 1
Since you are leading an honor, this is a(n) ___________ finesse against the opponent's ______.

71

♠A 3 2 / N / W E / S / ♠Q J 10	If S leads toward the Ace, he hopes that:	second hand opponent has the King.	W has the King.	3

72

♠A 3 2 / N / W E / S / ♠Q J 10	If S plays the ♠10 first hand and W covers with the ♠K, you know that S can take:	3 tricks in Spades.	0 tricks in Spades.	5

1	2	3	4	5	6	7	8
Ace attacking King	1	BOTH	3-card or better sequence in combined hands?	☑☐	equal	4 Ace 1 3	lead an honor

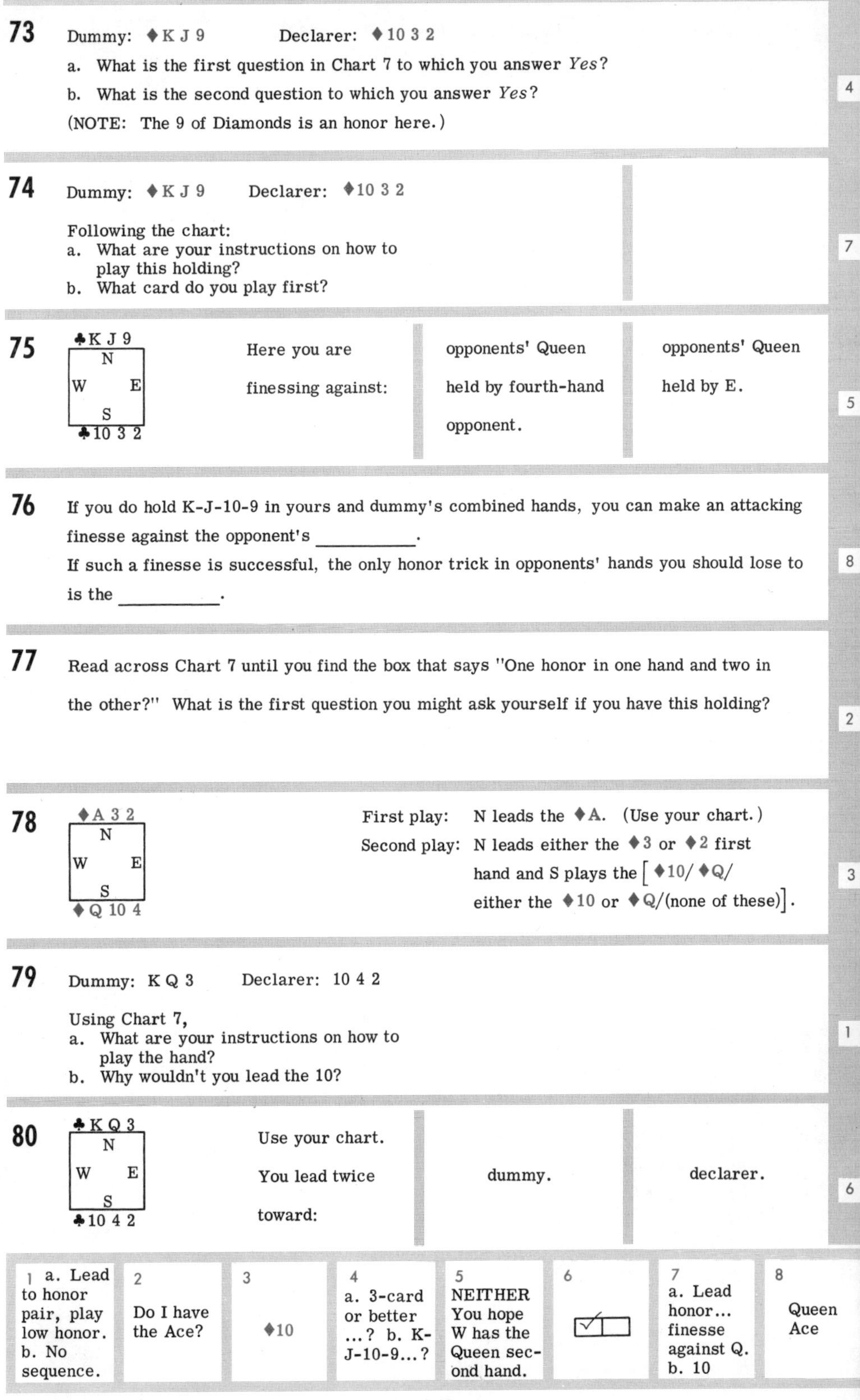

73 Dummy: ♦K J 9 Declarer: ♦10 3 2

a. What is the first question in Chart 7 to which you answer *Yes*?

b. What is the second question to which you answer *Yes*? 4

(NOTE: The 9 of Diamonds is an honor here.)

74 Dummy: ♦K J 9 Declarer: ♦10 3 2

Following the chart:
a. What are your instructions on how to play this holding? 7
b. What card do you play first?

75 ♣K J 9 (N) / ♣10 3 2 (S)

Here you are finessing against:	opponents' Queen held by fourth-hand opponent.	opponents' Queen held by E.

5

76 If you do hold K-J-10-9 in yours and dummy's combined hands, you can make an attacking finesse against the opponent's __________.

If such a finesse is successful, the only honor trick in opponents' hands you should lose to is the __________. 8

77 Read across Chart 7 until you find the box that says "One honor in one hand and two in the other?" What is the first question you might ask yourself if you have this holding? 2

78 ♦A 3 2 (N) / ♦Q 10 4 (S)

First play: N leads the ♦A. (Use your chart.)

Second play: N leads either the ♦3 or ♦2 first hand and S plays the [♦10/♦Q/either the ♦10 or ♦Q/(none of these)]. 3

79 Dummy: K Q 3 Declarer: 10 4 2

Using Chart 7,
a. What are your instructions on how to play the hand? 1
b. Why wouldn't you lead the 10?

80 ♣K Q 3 (N) / ♣10 4 2 (S)

Use your chart. You lead twice toward:	dummy.	declarer.

6

1	2	3	4	5	6	7	8
a. Lead to honor pair, play low honor. b. No sequence.	Do I have the Ace?	♦10	a. 3-card or better ...? b. K-J-10-9...?	NEITHER You hope W has the Queen second hand.	☐☑	a. Lead honor... finesse against Q. b. 10	Queen Ace

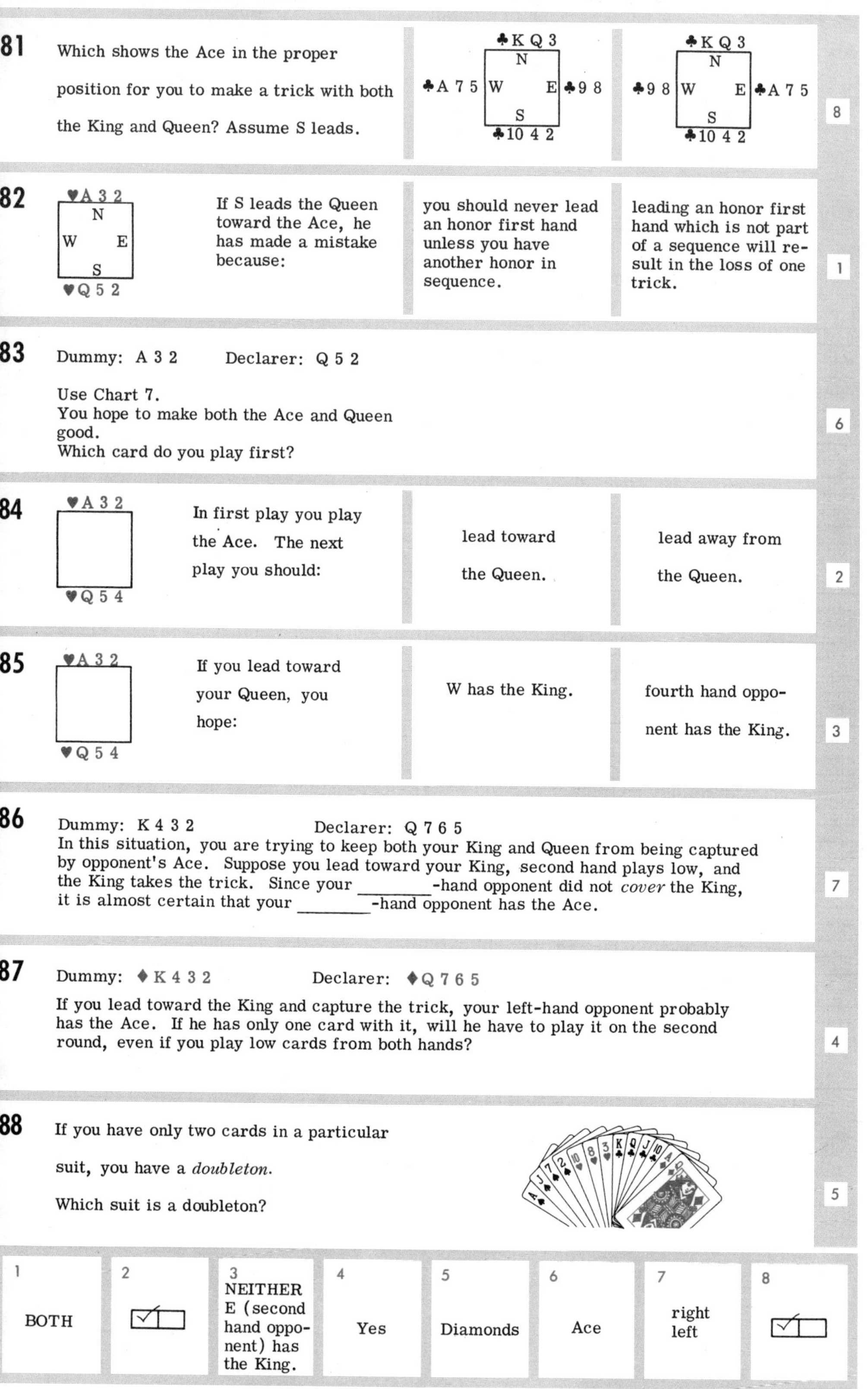

81 Which shows the Ace in the proper position for you to make a trick with both the King and Queen? Assume S leads.

	♣K Q 3	
♣A 7 5	N / W E / S	♣9 8
	♣10 4 2	

	♣K Q 3	
♣9 8	N / W E / S	♣A 7 5
	♣10 4 2	

8

---

82 ♥A 3 2 (N) — ♥Q 5 2 (S)

If S leads the Queen toward the Ace, he has made a mistake because:

you should never lead an honor first hand unless you have another honor in sequence.

leading an honor first hand which is not part of a sequence will result in the loss of one trick.

1

---

83 Dummy: A 3 2 Declarer: Q 5 2

Use Chart 7.
You hope to make both the Ace and Queen good.
Which card do you play first?

6

---

84 ♥A 3 2 — ♥Q 5 4

In first play you play the Ace. The next play you should:

lead toward the Queen.

lead away from the Queen.

2

---

85 ♥A 3 2 — ♥Q 5 4

If you lead toward your Queen, you hope:

W has the King.

fourth hand opponent has the King.

3

---

86 Dummy: K 4 3 2 Declarer: Q 7 6 5
In this situation, you are trying to keep both your King and Queen from being captured by opponent's Ace. Suppose you lead toward your King, second hand plays low, and the King takes the trick. Since your ________-hand opponent did not *cover* the King, it is almost certain that your ________-hand opponent has the Ace.

7

---

87 Dummy: ♦K 4 3 2 Declarer: ♦Q 7 6 5
If you lead toward the King and capture the trick, your left-hand opponent probably has the Ace. If he has only one card with it, will he have to play it on the second round, even if you play low cards from both hands?

4

---

88 If you have only two cards in a particular suit, you have a *doubleton.*

Which suit is a doubleton?

5

1	2	3	4	5	6	7	8
BOTH	(check-box diagram)	NEITHER E (second hand opponent) has the King.	Yes	Diamonds	Ace	right left	(check-box diagram)

89 Having only two cards in a suit is

called a ________. 5

90

♦K 4 3 2

	N	
♦A 8 W		E ♦10 9
	S	

♦Q 7 6 5

Which player has the doubleton Ace?

N	S

8

91

♦K 4 3 2

	N	
♦A 8 W		E ♦10 9
	S	

♦Q 7 6 5

If W leads his Ace on the second round, will he take your King? 4

92 If you are attempting to establish both honor winners and long-card winners in a suit, Chart 7 will be a helpful guide in playing your honors, whether you finesse, play for a drop, or make other plays. However, you will find when actually playing bridge that you cannot always play by following the chart.

GO TO NEXT FRAME 6

93 Even some weak holdings will develop into tricks if you do not lead them. Here, if you lead either the Queen or Jack, you will lose these tricks, because opponents will capture them with their ________ and ________.

♦Q 3 2

	N	
W		E
	S	

♦J 5

3

94 Dummy: Q 5 Declarer: J 3 2
With a holding such as this, if either opponent leads the suit, you will take a trick with either your Queen or Jack. To do this, play low until it is your play on fourth hand. If neither the Ace nor the King have been played, the honor in the ________ hand can then be used to take a trick. 2

95 Dummy: Q 5 Declarer: J 3 2
If either opponent leads, or *plays*, the Ace or King, you will play low both second hand and fourth hand. On the second round, your ________ will force out the opponents' other honor and your ________ will take a trick in that suit. 7

96 Dummy: J 2 Declarer: Q 5 2

a. If your right-hand opponent leads a low card in the suit, what do you play second hand?

b. Are you certain to win a trick if *opponents* lead the first round to this holding? 1

1	2	3	4	5	6	7	8
a. the low card from declarer b. Yes	fourth	Ace King	No	doubleton		Queen (or Jack) Jack (or Queen)	NEITHER W

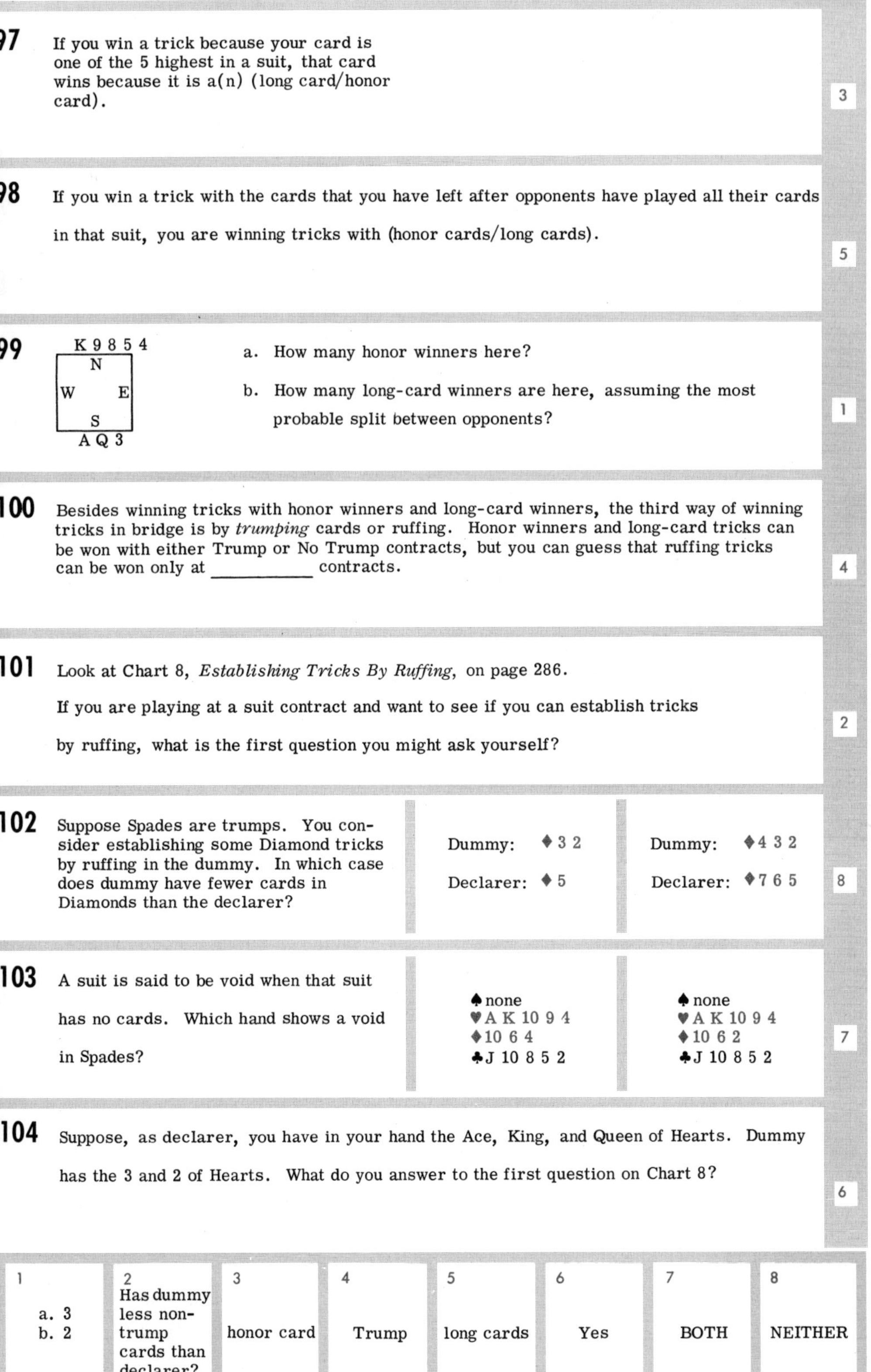

97 If you win a trick because your card is one of the 5 highest in a suit, that card wins because it is a(n) (long card/honor card). 3

98 If you win a trick with the cards that you have left after opponents have played all their cards in that suit, you are winning tricks with (honor cards/long cards). 5

99

	K 9 8 5 4	
W	N S	E
	A Q 3	

a. How many honor winners here?

b. How many long-card winners are here, assuming the most probable split between opponents? 1

100 Besides winning tricks with honor winners and long-card winners, the third way of winning tricks in bridge is by *trumping* cards or ruffing. Honor winners and long-card tricks can be won with either Trump or No Trump contracts, but you can guess that ruffing tricks can be won only at __________ contracts. 4

101 Look at Chart 8, *Establishing Tricks By Ruffing*, on page 286.

If you are playing at a suit contract and want to see if you can establish tricks by ruffing, what is the first question you might ask yourself? 2

102 Suppose Spades are trumps. You consider establishing some Diamond tricks by ruffing in the dummy. In which case does dummy have fewer cards in Diamonds than the declarer?

Dummy:	♦ 3 2	
Declarer:	♦ 5	

Dummy:	♦ 4 3 2	
Declarer:	♦ 7 6 5	8

103 A suit is said to be void when that suit has no cards. Which hand shows a void in Spades?

♠ none
♥ A K 10 9 4
♦ 10 6 4
♣ J 10 8 5 2

♠ none
♥ A K 10 9 4
♦ 10 6 2
♣ J 10 8 5 2 7

104 Suppose, as declarer, you have in your hand the Ace, King, and Queen of Hearts. Dummy has the 3 and 2 of Hearts. What do you answer to the first question on Chart 8? 6

1	2	3	4	5	6	7	8
a. 3 b. 2	Has dummy less non-trump cards than declarer?	honor card	Trump	long cards	Yes	BOTH	NEITHER

105 Dummy: ♣3 2 Declarer: ♣A K Q
Spades are trumps.
a. After ( ) rounds, dummy will be void in the Club suit.
b. At that time, would opponents capture one or more tricks in that suit? 3

106 Dummy: ♦3 2 Declarer: ♦A K 8
a. Does dummy have fewer cards in that suit than declarer?
b. If you lead out this suit, will opponents capture one or more tricks after dummy is void in a suit? 5
c. After what round of that suit will dummy be void?

107 Dummy: ♥4 3 2 Declarer: ♥A K Q J 10
In this case, Hearts are trumps. In drawing trumps, do you need either the 4, the 3, or the 2 to help establish them? If not, why not? Answer in your own words. 4

108 Dummy: ♠A K Q Declarer: ♠6 5 4 3 2
Suppose the opponents' trumps split in the most probable way.
a. This split is ( )-( ).
b. Does dummy have *any* trumps which will not be needed in establishing trumps? 2

109 Dummy: ♥3 ♦4 ♠6 2 Declarer: ♥A K ♦A 5 How would you play these last four cards? Using Chart 8, answer in your own words. 6

(Hearts are trumps.)

110 Except in special cases, you do not gain any tricks by ruffing dummy's tricks in your hand. Suppose dummy has 3 small Hearts and you have the A, K, Q, 3, and 2 of Hearts. If opponents' cards break 3-2, your 3 and 2 will be ____________-____________ winners so you are not gaining anything by ruffing with them. 7

1	2	3	4	5	6	7	8
	a. 3-2 b. No. 3 leads in Spades needed.	a. 2 b. No, because your Queen is a winning honor trick.	No. Honor winners will draw in opponents' trumps.	a. Yes b. Yes c. 2nd	Lead ♦A Ruff ♦5 with ♥3	long-card	

TAKE UNIT 6 POST-TEST

UNIT 7

hand evaluation

The Goren point count system is described in order to show the beginning player the relative worth of his hand. The player learns the appropriate opening bid to each point count in his hand. A large number of examples is presented to provide maximum utilization of the learning process.

PRE- AND POST-TEST

1. How many high-card points are in the deck?

2. Your partner opens with 1 Spade. You hold the following cards.

You know that you should reach at least:

a. game, probably in Spades.

b. small slam, probably in Spades.

c. 3 Spades.

3. Assign the correct number of points for the following terms.

a. void ___________

b. King ___________

c. doubleton ___________

d. Ace ___________

e. singleton ___________

4. Which high card is worth the same number of points as a singleton?

5. What is the least number of points that you must have to make a mandatory opening?

6. From which card would you deduct 1 point if it were the only card in a suit? [King of Diamonds/Jack of Spades/(both)/(neither)]

7. You deduct 1 point from an Aceless hand when you are [opening bidder/second bidder/(both)/(neither)].

8. How many total (high-card plus distribution) points are the following worth?

a. singleton Jack ___________

b. doubleton King ___________

c. doubleton Queen ___________

d. singleton Ace ___________

e. singleton King ___________

9. Which suit has a King as a stopper?

10. How many quick tricks is the King worth?

11. How many quick tricks are in this hand?

12. State how many points you have and what you would open with on each of the following.

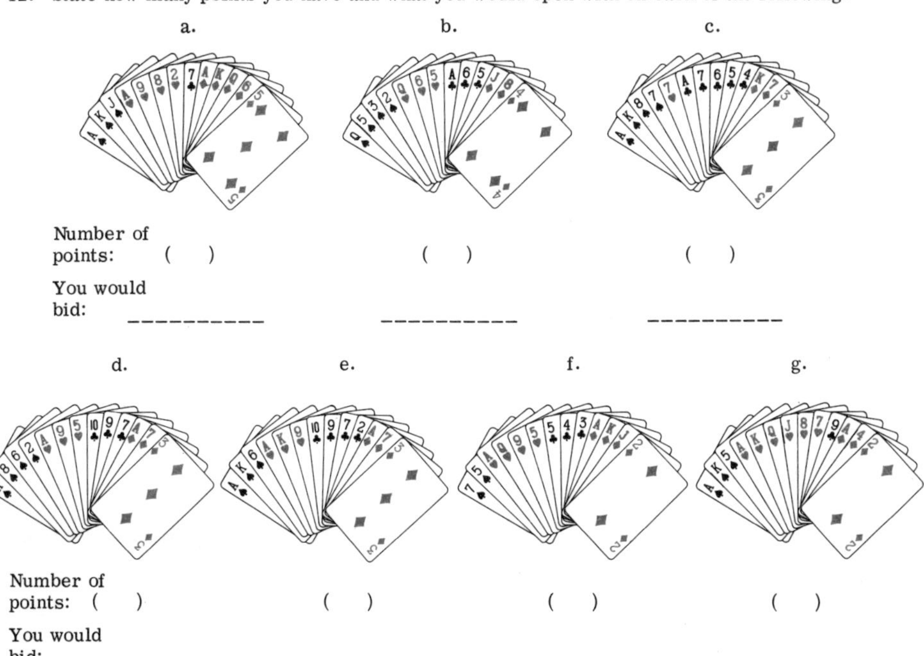

a. b. c.

Number of points: (   ) (   ) (   )

You would bid: __________ __________ __________

d. e. f. g.

Number of points: (   ) (   ) (   ) (   )

You would bid: __________ __________ __________ __________

EXERCISES

1.

This hand is worth (   ) points.
You should bid: (   ) ________.

2.

This hand is worth (   ) points.
You should bid: (   ) ________.

3.

This hand is worth (   ) points.
You should bid: (   ) ________.

4.

This hand is worth (   ) points.
You should bid: (   ) ________.

5.

This hand is worth (   ) points.
You should bid: (   ) ________.

6.

This hand is worth (   ) points.
You should bid: (   ) ________.

7.

This hand is worth (   ) points.
You should bid: (   ) ________.

8.

This hand is worth (   ) points.
You should bid: (   ) ________.

9.

This hand is worth (   ) points.
You should bid: (   ) ________.

10.

This hand is worth (   ) points.
You should bid: (   ) ________.

11.

This hand is worth (   ) points.
You should bid: (   ) ________.

12.

This hand is worth (   ) points.
You should bid: (   ) ________.

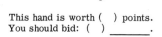

1	(Before you begin, take the Pre-Test for Unit 7.) In the *point count system* of evaluating a hand, face cards are given a numerical value. Which of these shows the point count system?	An Ace is worth 4 points.	An Ace will take a King.	8
2	Here are the four highest cards. K J A Q Arrange them in descending order.	( ) highest ( ) next-to-highest ( ) next-to-lowest ( ) lowest		1
3	In the point count system each Ace equals 4 points and each King equals 3 points. What is the total point count here? ♠K ♣AK ♦A ♥K			6
4	No card below a Jack counts for any points. Which of these has a total of 7 points?	A, 10, 7, 6	K, 8, 5, 3, 2	3
5	Which card has a value of 3 points?	♥A	♠3	2
6	In the point count system the Queen is worth 2 points and the Jack is worth 1 point. Which group totals 9 points?	♠Q 6 4 ♥Q J 9 ♦J 3 2 ♣Q J 7	♠J 8 4 ♥Q 9 7 ♦Q J 5 ♣Q 4 3	4
7	How many points are in this hand? A = 4 K = 3 Q = 2 J = 1			7
8	This hand has: 2 Aces 2 × 4 = 8 3 Kings 3 × 3 = 9 1 Queen 1 × 2 = 2 2 Jacks 2 × 1 = 2 21 points		This hand has: a. 1 Ace = ( ) b. 2 Kings = ( ) c. 4 Queens = ( ) d. 1 Jack = ( ) total points ( )	5

1	2	3	4	5	6	7	8
A K Q J	NEITHER	NEITHER	☑☐	a. 4 b. 6 c. 8 d. 1 total 19 points	17	20	☑☐

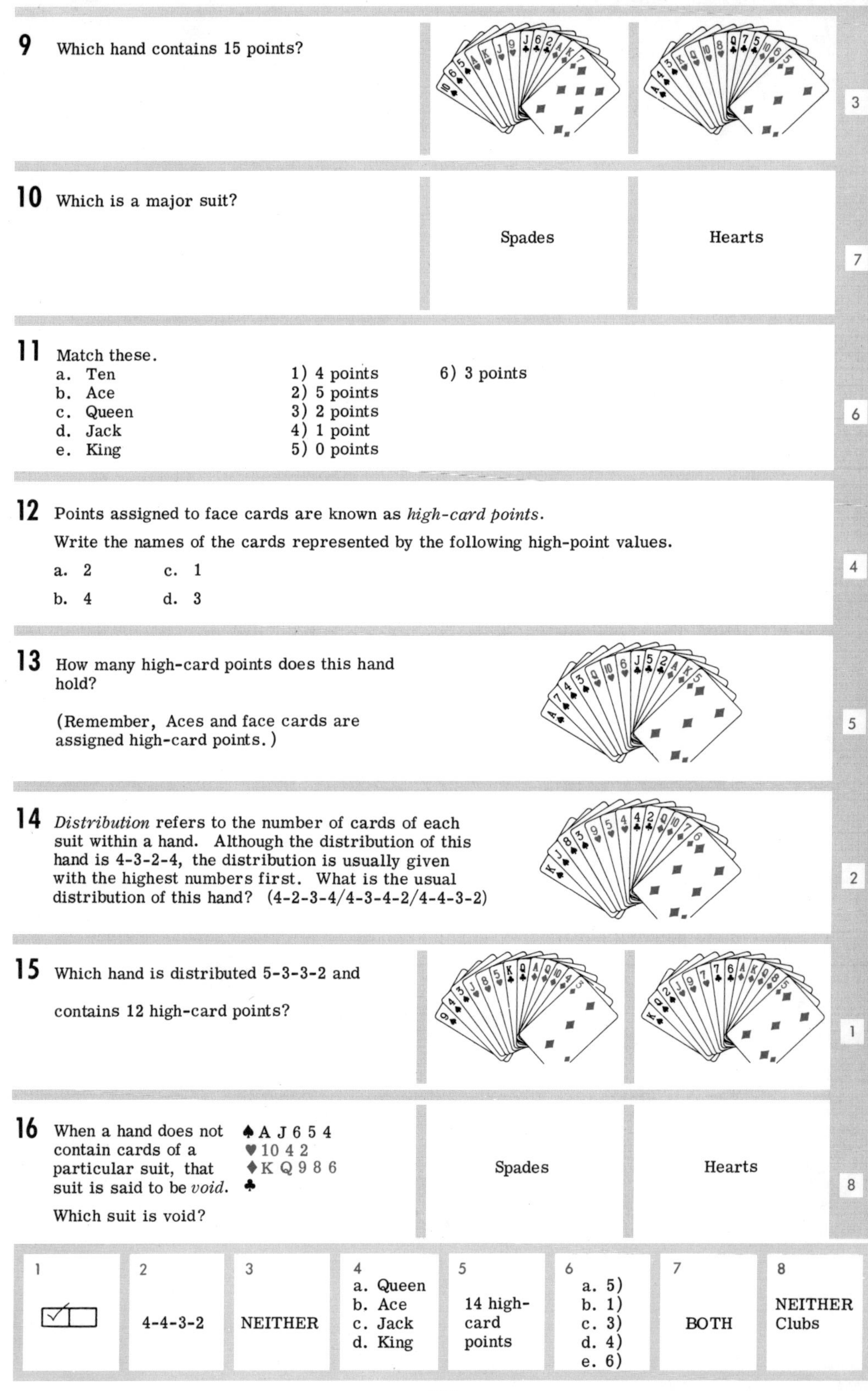

9 Which hand contains 15 points? 3

10 Which is a major suit?

Spades | Hearts 7

11 Match these. 6

a. Ten
b. Ace
c. Queen
d. Jack
e. King

1) 4 points
2) 5 points
3) 2 points
4) 1 point
5) 0 points
6) 3 points

12 Points assigned to face cards are known as *high-card points*.

Write the names of the cards represented by the following high-point values. 4

a. 2 c. 1

b. 4 d. 3

13 How many high-card points does this hand hold?

(Remember, Aces and face cards are assigned high-card points.) 5

14 *Distribution* refers to the number of cards of each suit within a hand. Although the distribution of this hand is 4-3-2-4, the distribution is usually given with the highest numbers first. What is the usual distribution of this hand? (4-2-3-4/4-3-4-2/4-4-3-2) 2

15 Which hand is distributed 5-3-3-2 and

contains 12 high-card points? 1

16 When a hand does not contain cards of a particular suit, that suit is said to be *void*.

Which suit is void?

♠A J 6 5 4
♥10 4 2
♦K Q 9 8 6
♣

Spades | Hearts 8

1	2	3	4	5	6	7	8
☑☐	4-4-3-2	NEITHER	a. Queen b. Ace c. Jack d. King	14 high-card points	a. 5) b. 1) c. 3) d. 4) e. 6)	BOTH	NEITHER Clubs

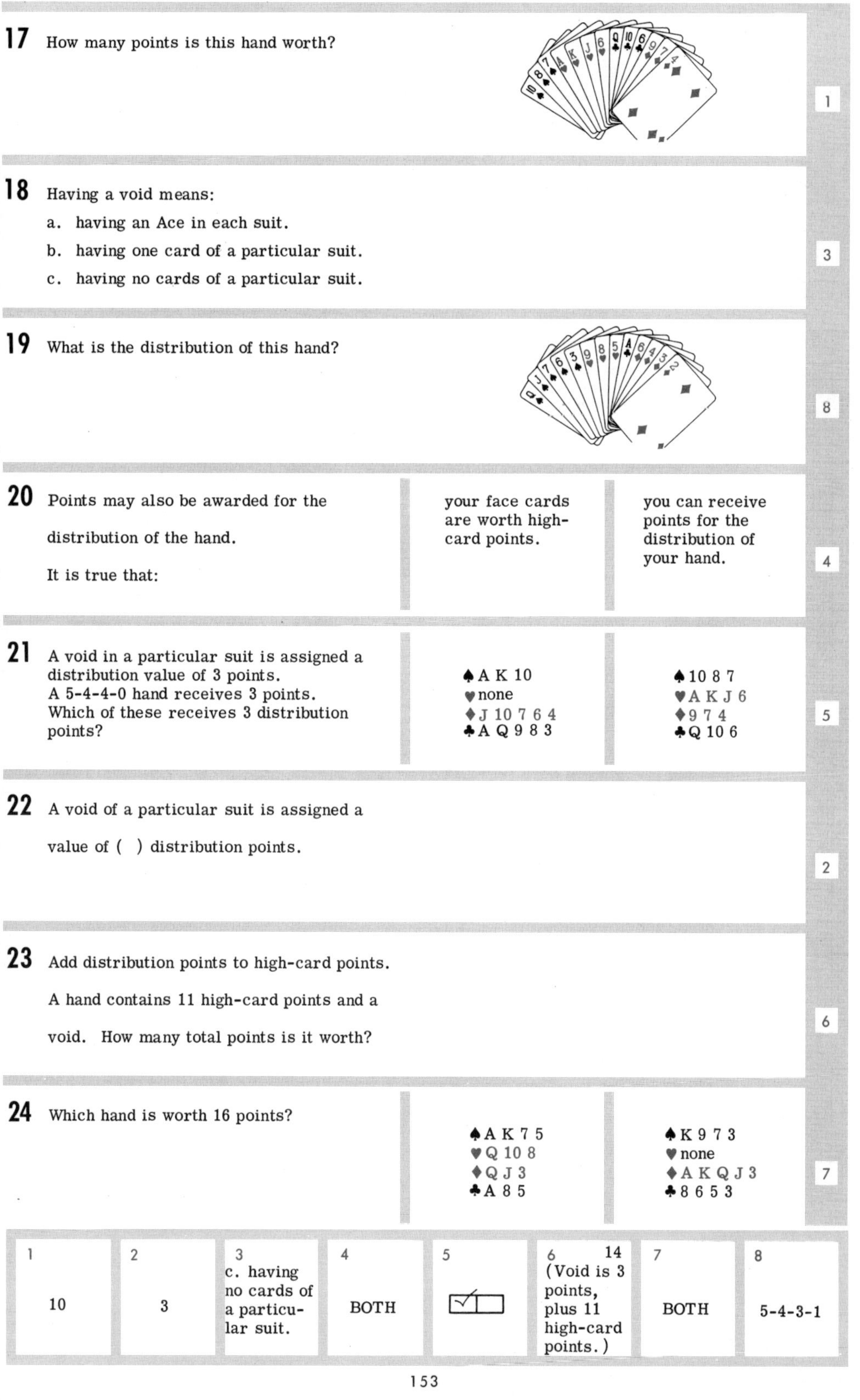

17 How many points is this hand worth? 1

18 Having a void means: 3

a. having an Ace in each suit.

b. having one card of a particular suit.

c. having no cards of a particular suit.

19 What is the distribution of this hand? 8

20 Points may also be awarded for the distribution of the hand.

It is true that:

your face cards are worth high-card points.	you can receive points for the distribution of your hand.	4

21 A void in a particular suit is assigned a distribution value of 3 points.
A 5-4-4-0 hand receives 3 points.
Which of these receives 3 distribution points?

♠A K 10 ♥none ♦J 10 7 6 4 ♣A Q 9 8 3	♠10 8 7 ♥A K J 6 ♦9 7 4 ♣Q 10 6	5

22 A void of a particular suit is assigned a value of ( ) distribution points. 2

23 Add distribution points to high-card points.

A hand contains 11 high-card points and a void. How many total points is it worth? 6

24 Which hand is worth 16 points?

♠A K 7 5 ♥Q 10 8 ♦Q J 3 ♣A 8 5	♠K 9 7 3 ♥none ♦A K Q J 3 ♣8 6 5 3	7

1	2	3	4	5	6	7	8
10	3	c. having no cards of a particular suit.	BOTH	☑☐	14 (Void is 3 points, plus 11 high-card points.)	BOTH	5-4-3-1

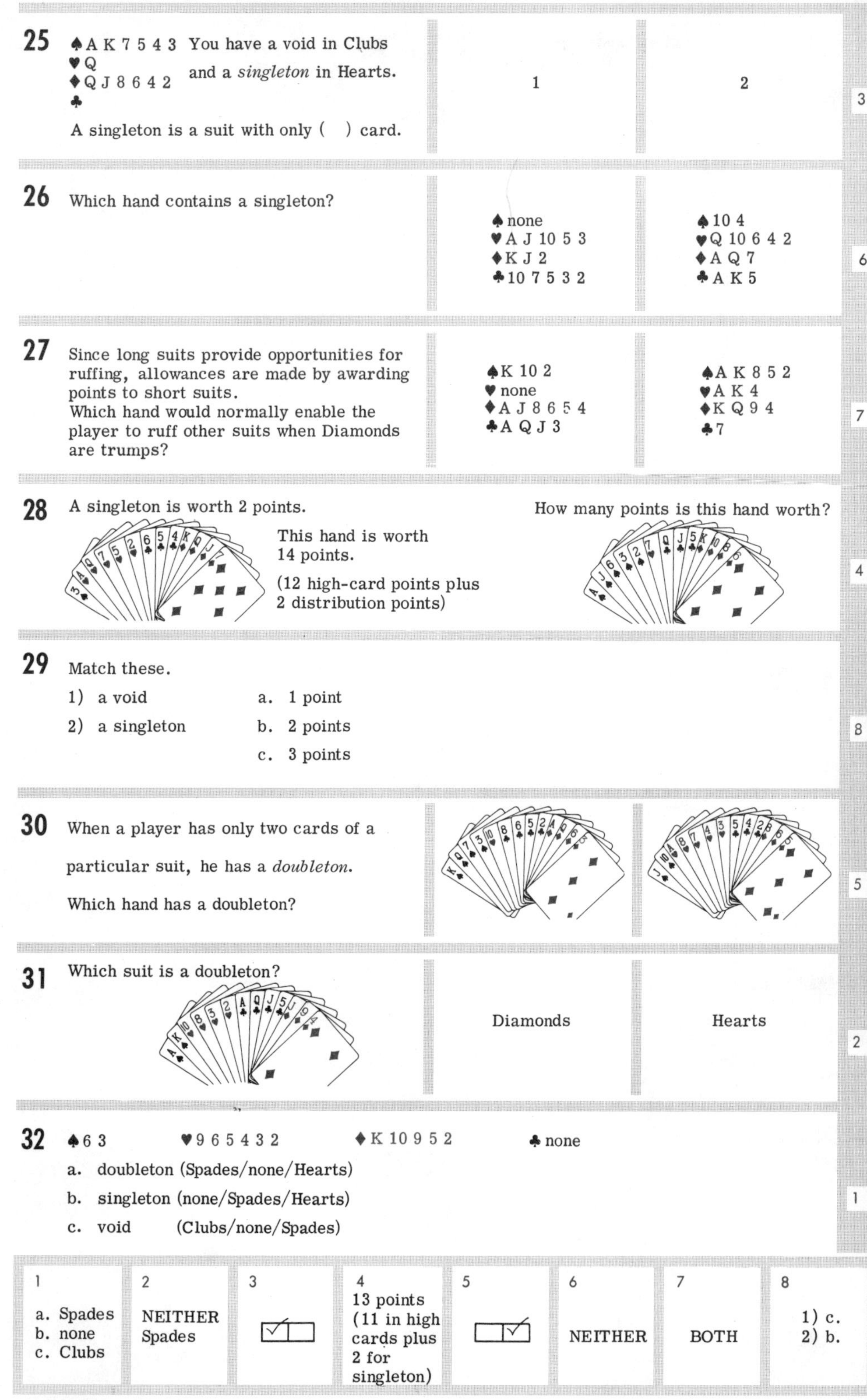

25 ♠A K 7 5 4 3 ♥Q ♦Q J 8 6 4 2 ♣ You have a void in Clubs and a *singleton* in Hearts.

A singleton is a suit with only (   ) card.

1	2

3

26 Which hand contains a singleton?

♠none ♥A J 10 5 3 ♦K J 2 ♣10 7 5 3 2	♠10 4 ♥Q 10 6 4 2 ♦A Q 7 ♣A K 5

6

27 Since long suits provide opportunities for ruffing, allowances are made by awarding points to short suits.
Which hand would normally enable the player to ruff other suits when Diamonds are trumps?

♠K 10 2 ♥ none ♦A J 8 6 5 4 ♣A Q J 3	♠A K 8 5 2 ♥A K 4 ♦K Q 9 4 ♣7

7

28 A singleton is worth 2 points.

This hand is worth 14 points.

(12 high-card points plus 2 distribution points)

How many points is this hand worth? 4

29 Match these.

1) a void   a. 1 point

2) a singleton   b. 2 points

c. 3 points

8

30 When a player has only two cards of a particular suit, he has a *doubleton*.

Which hand has a doubleton?

5

31 Which suit is a doubleton?

Diamonds	Hearts

2

32 ♠6 3   ♥9 6 5 4 3 2   ♦K 10 9 5 2   ♣none

a. doubleton (Spades/none/Hearts)

b. singleton (none/Spades/Hearts)

c. void (Clubs/none/Spades)

1

1	2	3	4	5	6	7	8
a. Spades b. none c. Clubs	NEITHER Spades	[✓][ ]	13 points (11 in high cards plus 2 for singleton)	[ ][✓]	NEITHER	BOTH	1) c. 2) b.

33 A suit with 2 cards is called a:

singleton.	void.

7

34 Answer the questions below with the proper suit or "none."

a. void ___________
b. singleton ___________
c. doubleton ___________

8

35 Match these.

1) Ace
2) King
3) Ten

a. 4 high-card points
b. 0 high-card points
c. 2 high-card points
d. 3 high-card points

1

36 Which suit is a doubleton?

6

37

void (no card) = 3 points
singleton (1 card) = 2 points
You might guess that
a doubleton (2 cards) = ( ) point(s).

3

38

void, 0 cards: 3 - 0 = 3 points
singleton, 1 card: 3 - 1 = ( ) points
doubleton, 2 cards: 3 - 2 = ( ) point(s)

2

39 If you subtract the number of cards in a suit from 3, you can arrive at the correct number of distribution points for that suit. Which is the correct expression for finding the number of points that a singleton is worth?

3 - 0 = 3	3 - 1 = 2

4

40 3 - (the number of cards in a suit) =

the distribution points of that suit.	the high-card points of that suit.

5

1	2	3	4	5	6	7	8
1) a. 2) d. 3) b.	2 1	1	[ ] [✓]	[✓] [ ]	Diamonds	NEITHER doubleton.	a. none b. Clubs c. Hearts

41 Match the items in the middle and right-hand columns with the descriptions in the left-hand column.

1) singleton	a. 3 points	I. a suit with only 2 cards
2) doubleton	b. 2 points	II. a suit with no cards
3) void	c. 1 point	III. a suit with only 1 card

3

42 Points for voids, singletons, and doubletons are called distribution points. How many distribution points are in this hand?

♠7 5 ♥A K Q 3 2 ♦none ♣K Q J 8 6 5

7

43 Which is worth 3 high-card points?

6

44 Name the suits that contain distribution points.

4

45 To get the correct number of distribution points for a suit, subtract the number of cards in that suit from:

3.	2.

5

46 How many distribution points in each suit?

2

47 Distribution points are given for:

a. singletons.
b. doubletons.
c. voids.
d. (all of these)
e. (none of these)

1

48 A singleton Ace would be worth:

a. ( ) high-card points.

b. ( ) distribution points.

8

1	2	3	4	5	6	7	8
d. (all of these)	♠ - 0 ♥ - 2 ♣ - 0 ♦ - 1	1) b. III 2) c. I 3) a. II	Spades doubleton Clubs singleton	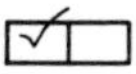 [✓] [ ]	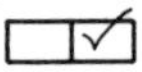 [ ] [✓]	4	a. 4 b. 2

49 Each A, K, Q, and J is awarded:	high-card points.	distribution points.	1

50 High-card points are deducted from face cards when they are not protected by small cards.
Points are subtracted because the unprotected face card may fall to a higher ranking card.
The small cards protecting the face card are called *guardians*.
The face cards protected by small cards are known as *stoppers*. GO TO NEXT FRAME 3

51
a. What is a *stopper*?
b. What are small cards called when they protect face cards? 8

52 All singleton high cards except the Ace lose 1 high-card point.
The King of Spades is worth 2 high-card points, not 3.
a. The Queen of Hearts is worth ( ) high-card points, not 2.
b. The Jack of Diamonds is worth ( ) high-card points, not 1. 4

53 The King of Spades gives you 2 distribution points, but it is only worth:	2 high-card points.	1 high-card point.	5
54 The Ace of Diamonds is worth 4 high-card points. How many high-card points is the Queen of Hearts worth?	2	3	2
55 Which shows the correct number of points to deduct from a singleton Ace?	0	1	6
56 Which of these cards do you deduct 1 high-card point from if it is the only card in that suit?	Ace	King	7

1	2	3	4	5	6	7	8
[✓][ ]	NEITHER only 1		a. 1 b. 0	[✓][ ]	[✓][ ]	[ ][✓]	a. a face card protected by small cards b. guardians

57 

The Queen of Hearts loses 1 high-card point but the King of Diamonds does *not* because:

it is a doubleton, not a singleton.	it is Diamonds, which receive a bonus.

3

---

58 

Would you deduct 1 high-card point for the singleton high card in Spades?

6

59

a. A singleton Queen is assigned ( ) high-card point(s).

b. A singleton Ace is worth only 3 high-card points. (True/False)

7

---

60 Which Queen is worth 3 high-card and distribution points?

singleton Queen	Queen with 4 small cards

4

---

61 When a Queen or a Jack is accompanied by only one small card, the Queen or Jack is reduced in value by 1 high-card point.

Using this principle, determine the high-card points in this hand.

8

---

62 How many total points is a singleton Queen worth?

(Remember, you get points for the Queen and points for the singleton.)

1	2

5

---

63 How many small cards must accompany the Jack or Queen in order to deduct 1 high-card point?

1	one

1

64

♠K 6
♥A J 10 9 7 5 3
♦A 5
♣Q 2

An Ace or King accompanied by one small card does not lose a point.
From which suit should a point be deducted?

Spades	Diamonds

2

1	2	3	4	5	6	7	8
BOTH	NEITHER Clubs		☑☐	NEITHER 3 points	No	a. 1 b. False	9 (You must deduct 1 point from the Queen of Hearts.)

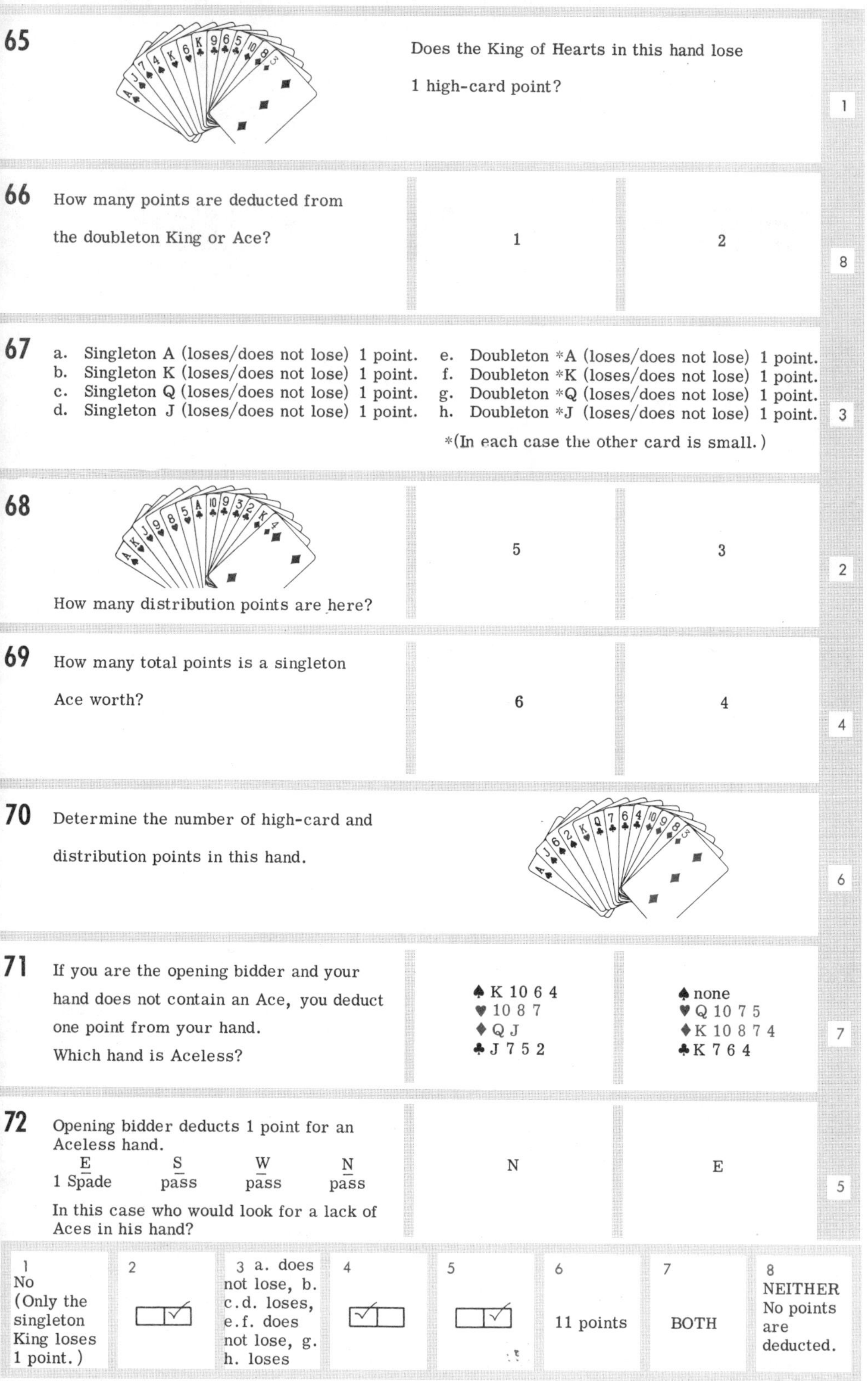

65 Does the King of Hearts in this hand lose 1 high-card point? — 1

66 How many points are deducted from the doubleton King or Ace?

1	2

— 8

67
a. Singleton A (loses/does not lose) 1 point.
b. Singleton K (loses/does not lose) 1 point.
c. Singleton Q (loses/does not lose) 1 point.
d. Singleton J (loses/does not lose) 1 point.
e. Doubleton *A (loses/does not lose) 1 point.
f. Doubleton *K (loses/does not lose) 1 point.
g. Doubleton *Q (loses/does not lose) 1 point.
h. Doubleton *J (loses/does not lose) 1 point.

*(In each case the other card is small.) — 3

68 How many distribution points are here?

5	3

— 2

69 How many total points is a singleton Ace worth?

6	4

— 4

70 Determine the number of high-card and distribution points in this hand. — 6

71 If you are the opening bidder and your hand does not contain an Ace, you deduct one point from your hand. Which hand is Aceless?

♠K 10 6 4 ♥10 8 7 ♦Q J ♣J 7 5 2	♠none ♥Q 10 7 5 ♦K 10 8 7 4 ♣K 7 6 4

— 7

72 Opening bidder deducts 1 point for an Aceless hand.

E	S	W	N
1 Spade	pass	pass	pass

In this case who would look for a lack of Aces in his hand?

N	E

— 5

1	2	3	4	5	6	7	8
No (Only the singleton King loses 1 point.)	☐☑	a. does not lose, b. c.d. loses, e.f. does not lose, g. h. loses	☑☐	☐☑	11 points	BOTH	NEITHER No points are deducted.

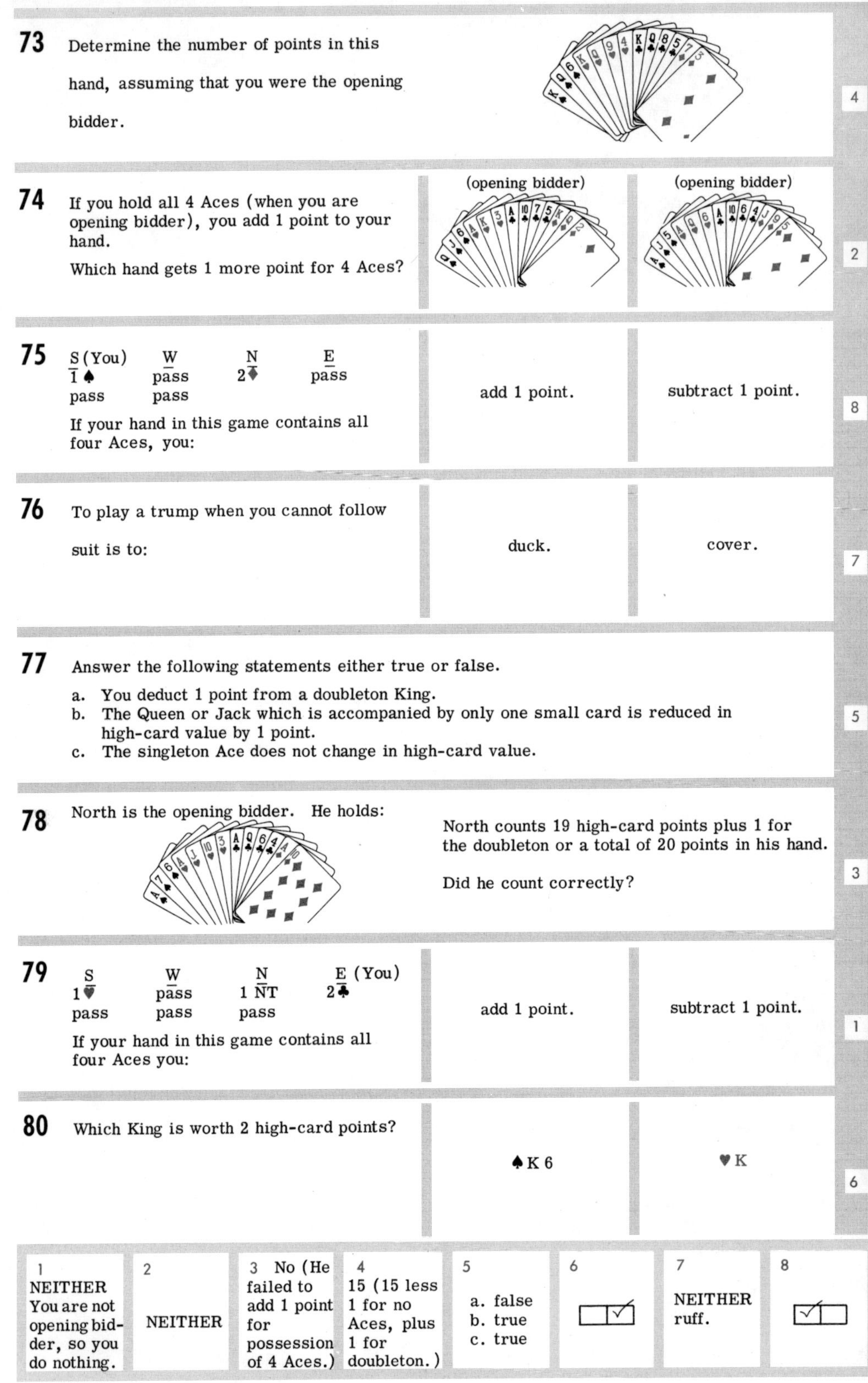

73 Determine the number of points in this hand, assuming that you were the opening bidder. — 4

74 If you hold all 4 Aces (when you are opening bidder), you add 1 point to your hand.
Which hand gets 1 more point for 4 Aces?

(opening bidder) | (opening bidder) — 2

75

S (You)	W	N	E
1 ♠	pass	2♦	pass
pass	pass		

If your hand in this game contains all four Aces, you:

add 1 point. | subtract 1 point. — 8

76 To play a trump when you cannot follow suit is to:

duck. | cover. — 7

77 Answer the following statements either true or false.

a. You deduct 1 point from a doubleton King.
b. The Queen or Jack which is accompanied by only one small card is reduced in high-card value by 1 point.
c. The singleton Ace does not change in high-card value.

— 5

78 North is the opening bidder. He holds:

North counts 19 high-card points plus 1 for the doubleton or a total of 20 points in his hand.

Did he count correctly? — 3

79

S	W	N	E (You)
1♥	pass	1 NT	2♣
pass	pass	pass	

If your hand in this game contains all four Aces you:

add 1 point. | subtract 1 point. — 1

80 Which King is worth 2 high-card points?

♠K 6 | ♥K — 6

1	2	3	4	5	6	7	8
NEITHER You are not opening bidder, so you do nothing.	NEITHER	No (He failed to add 1 point for possession of 4 Aces.)	15 (15 less 1 for no Aces, plus 1 for doubleton.)	a. false b. true c. true	☐ ☑	NEITHER ruff.	☑ ☐

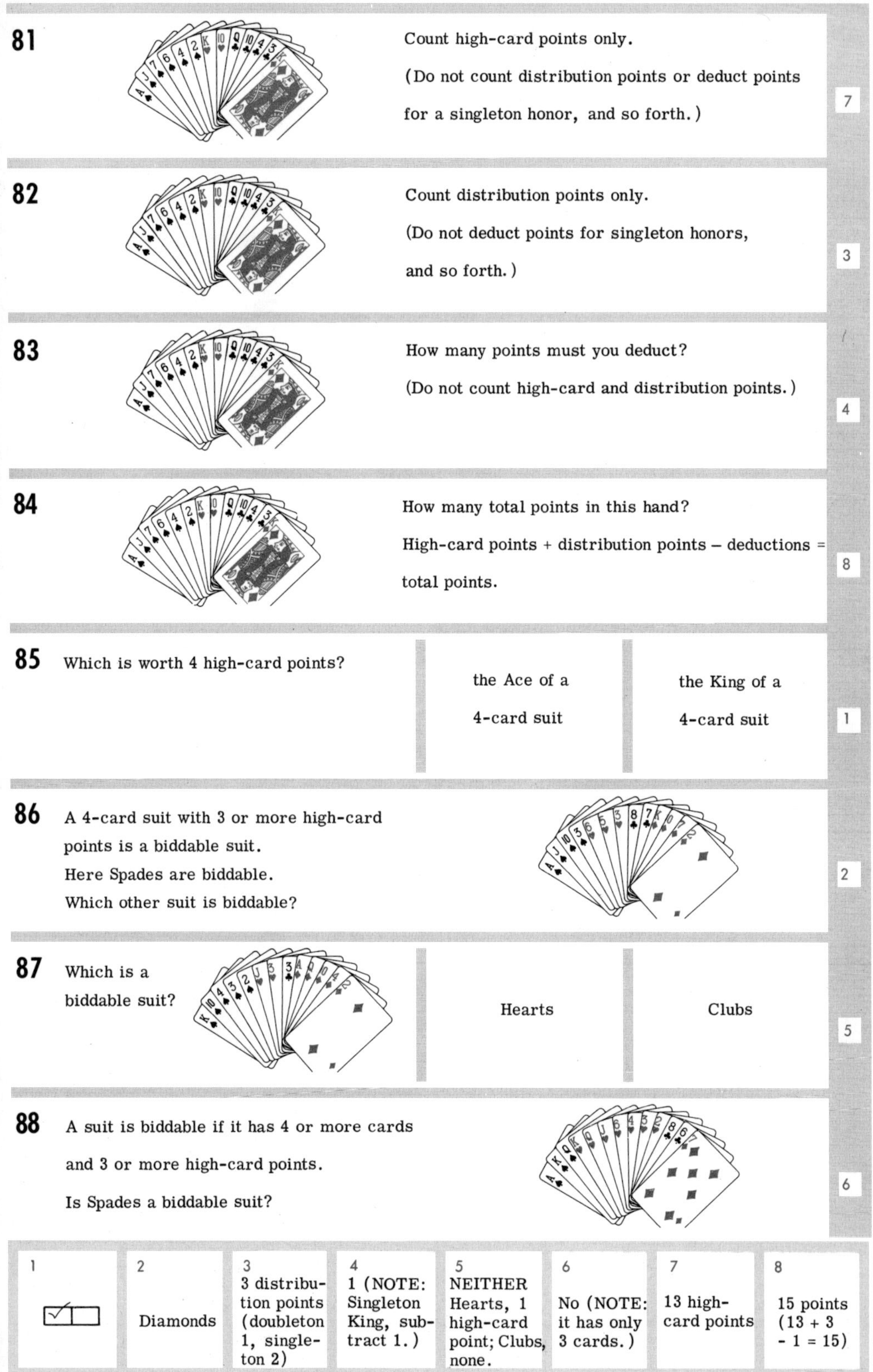

81 Count high-card points only.

(Do not count distribution points or deduct points for a singleton honor, and so forth.) 7

82 Count distribution points only.

(Do not deduct points for singleton honors, and so forth.) 3

83 How many points must you deduct?

(Do not count high-card and distribution points.) 4

84 How many total points in this hand?

High-card points + distribution points – deductions = total points. 8

85 Which is worth 4 high-card points?

the Ace of a 4-card suit	the King of a 4-card suit

1

86 A 4-card suit with 3 or more high-card points is a biddable suit.
Here Spades are biddable.
Which other suit is biddable? 2

87 Which is a biddable suit?

Hearts	Clubs

5

88 A suit is biddable if it has 4 or more cards and 3 or more high-card points.

Is Spades a biddable suit? 6

1	2	3	4	5	6	7	8
☑☐	Diamonds	3 distribution points (doubleton 1, singleton 2)	1 (NOTE: Singleton King, subtract 1.)	NEITHER Hearts, 1 high-card point; Clubs, none.	No (NOTE: it has only 3 cards.)	13 high-card points	15 points (13 + 3 - 1 = 15)

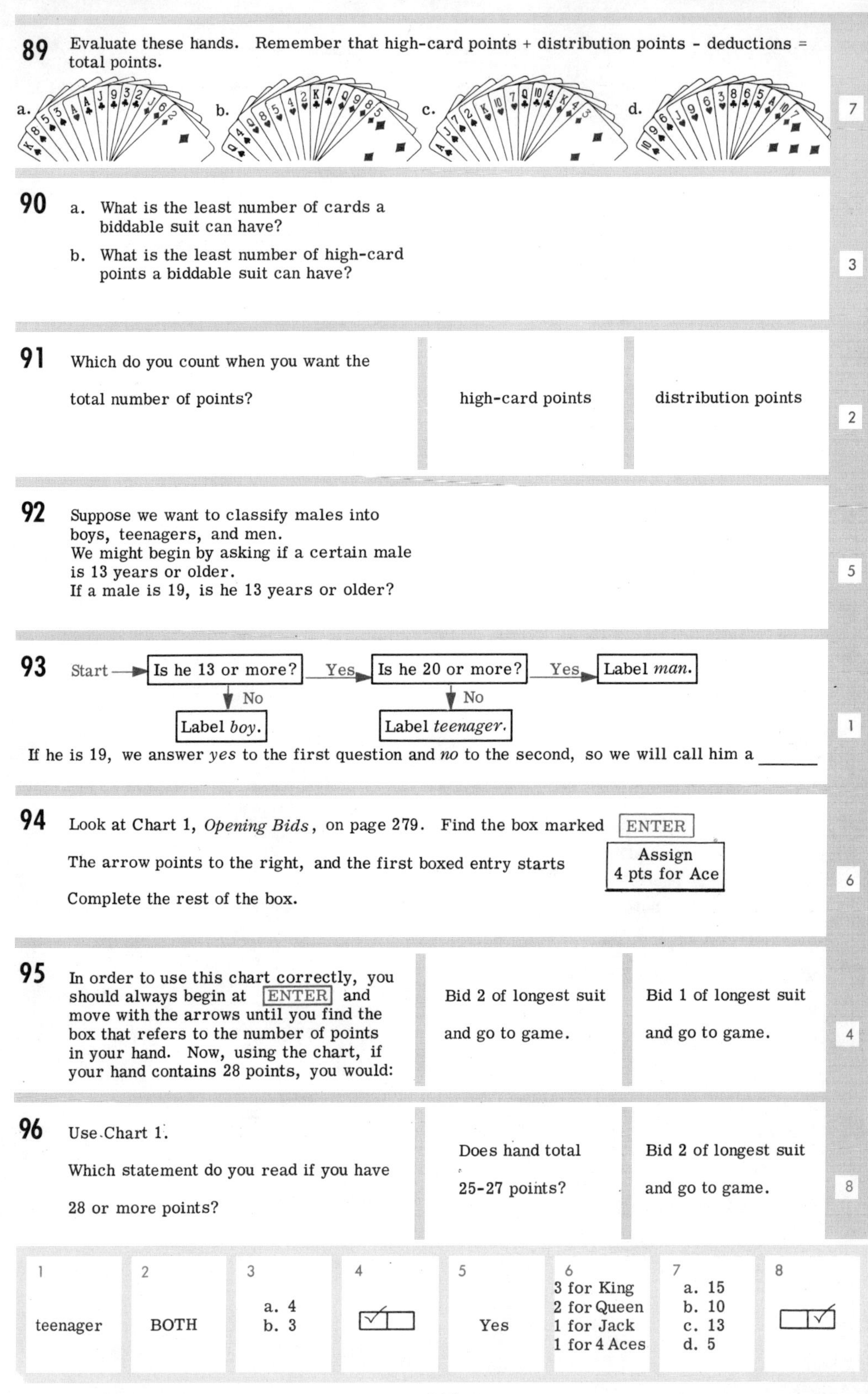

89 Evaluate these hands. Remember that high-card points + distribution points - deductions = total points.

a. b. c. d. 7

90 a. What is the least number of cards a biddable suit can have?

b. What is the least number of high-card points a biddable suit can have? 3

91 Which do you count when you want the total number of points?

high-card points	distribution points

2

92 Suppose we want to classify males into boys, teenagers, and men.
We might begin by asking if a certain male is 13 years or older.
If a male is 19, is he 13 years or older? 5

93 Start → Is he 13 or more? — Yes → Is he 20 or more? — Yes → Label *man.*
Is he 13 or more? — No → Label *boy.*
Is he 20 or more? — No → Label *teenager.*

If he is 19, we answer *yes* to the first question and *no* to the second, so we will call him a ______ 1

94 Look at Chart 1, *Opening Bids*, on page 279. Find the box marked ENTER

The arrow points to the right, and the first boxed entry starts

Assign
4 pts for Ace

Complete the rest of the box. 6

95 In order to use this chart correctly, you should always begin at ENTER and move with the arrows until you find the box that refers to the number of points in your hand. Now, using the chart, if your hand contains 28 points, you would:

Bid 2 of longest suit and go to game.	Bid 1 of longest suit and go to game.

4

96 Use Chart 1.

Which statement do you read if you have 28 or more points?

Does hand total 25-27 points?	Bid 2 of longest suit and go to game.

8

1	2	3	4	5	6	7	8
teenager	BOTH	a. 4 b. 3	[✓][ ]	Yes	3 for King 2 for Queen 1 for Jack 1 for 4 Aces	a. 15 b. 10 c. 13 d. 5	[ ][✓]

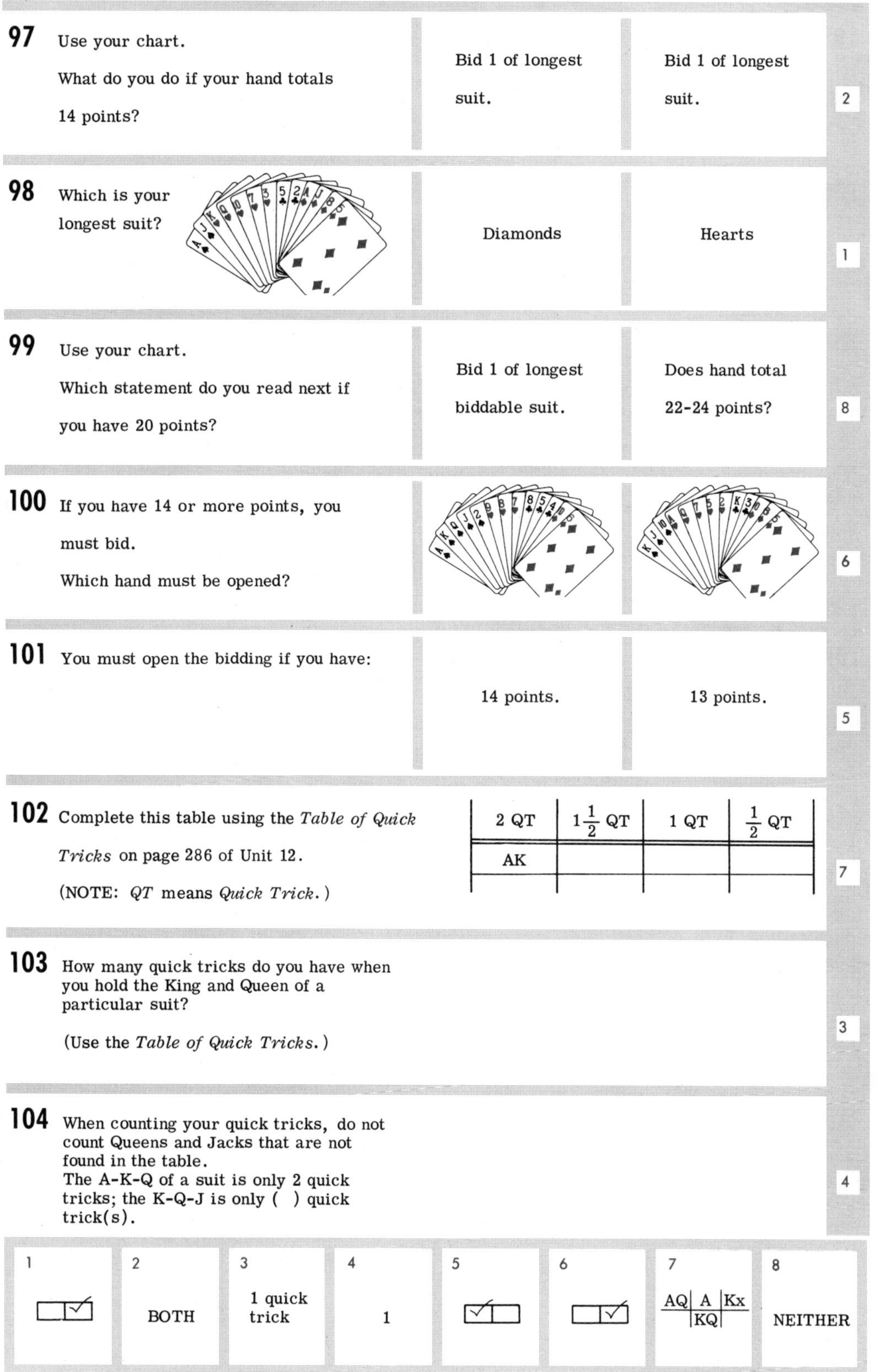

97 Use your chart.

What do you do if your hand totals 14 points?

Bid 1 of longest suit.	Bid 1 of longest suit.

2

98 Which is your longest suit?

Diamonds	Hearts

1

99 Use your chart.

Which statement do you read next if you have 20 points?

Bid 1 of longest biddable suit.	Does hand total 22-24 points?

8

100 If you have 14 or more points, you must bid.

Which hand must be opened?

6

101 You must open the bidding if you have:

14 points.	13 points.

5

102 Complete this table using the *Table of Quick Tricks* on page 286 of Unit 12.

(NOTE: *QT* means *Quick Trick.*)

2 QT	$1\frac{1}{2}$ QT	1 QT	$\frac{1}{2}$ QT
AK			

7

103 How many quick tricks do you have when you hold the King and Queen of a particular suit?

(Use the *Table of Quick Tricks.*)

3

104 When counting your quick tricks, do not count Queens and Jacks that are not found in the table.
The A-K-Q of a suit is only 2 quick tricks; the K-Q-J is only ( ) quick trick(s).

4

1	2	3	4	5	6	7	8
☐☑	BOTH	1 quick trick	1	☑☐	☐☑	AQ / A KQ / Kx	NEITHER

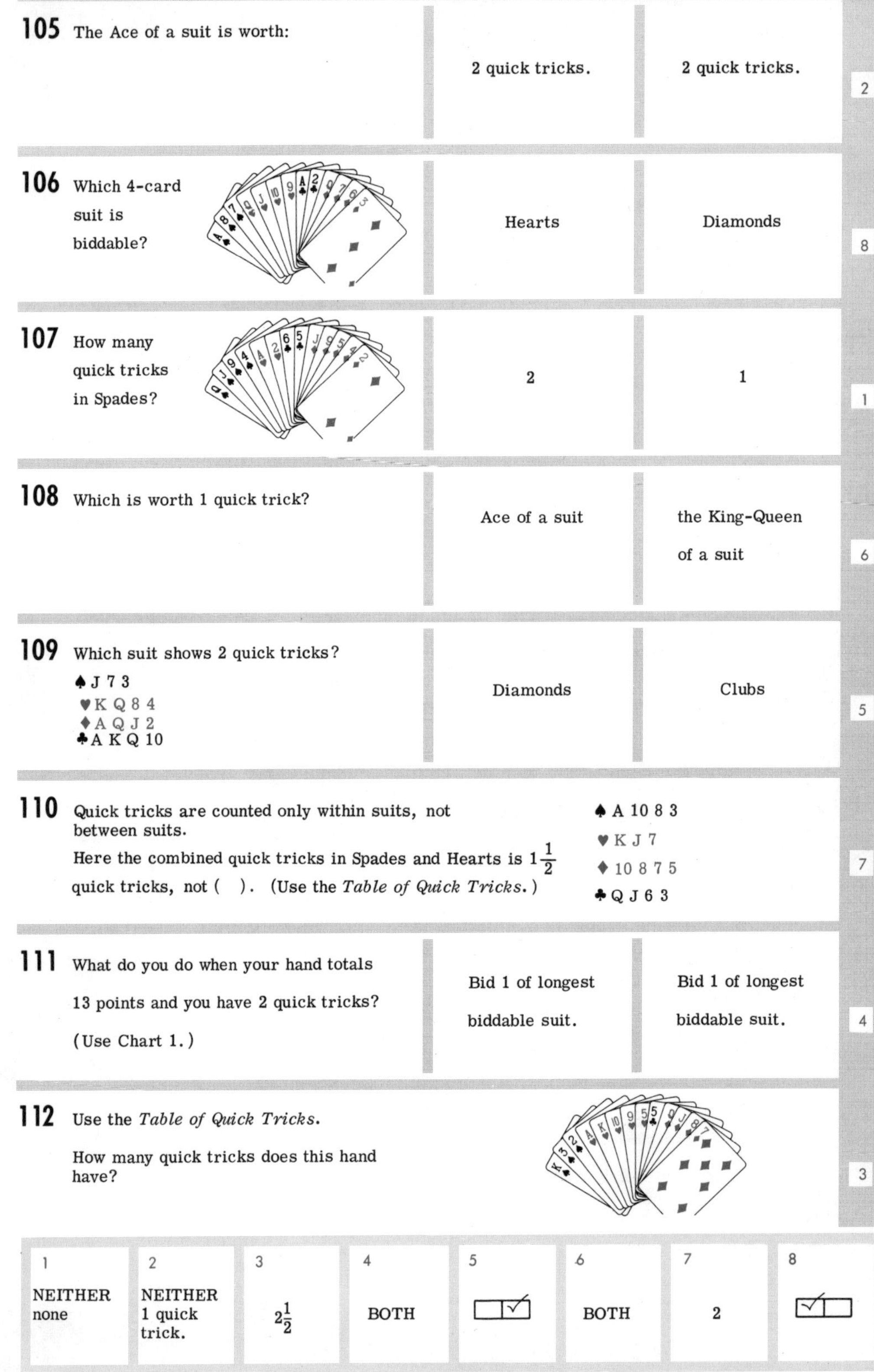

105 The Ace of a suit is worth:

2 quick tricks.	2 quick tricks.

2

106 Which 4-card suit is biddable?

Hearts	Diamonds

8

107 How many quick tricks in Spades?

2	1

1

108 Which is worth 1 quick trick?

Ace of a suit	the King-Queen of a suit

6

109 Which suit shows 2 quick tricks?

♠J 7 3
♥K Q 8 4
♦A Q J 2
♣A K Q 10

Diamonds	Clubs

5

110 Quick tricks are counted only within suits, not between suits.
Here the combined quick tricks in Spades and Hearts is $1\frac{1}{2}$ quick tricks, not ( ). (Use the *Table of Quick Tricks.*)

♠A 10 8 3
♥K J 7
♦10 8 7 5
♣Q J 6 3

7

111 What do you do when your hand totals 13 points and you have 2 quick tricks? (Use Chart 1.)

Bid 1 of longest biddable suit.	Bid 1 of longest biddable suit.

4

112 Use the *Table of Quick Tricks.*

How many quick tricks does this hand have?

3

1	2	3	4	5	6	7	8
NEITHER none	NEITHER 1 quick trick.	$2\frac{1}{2}$	BOTH	☐☑	BOTH	2	☑☐

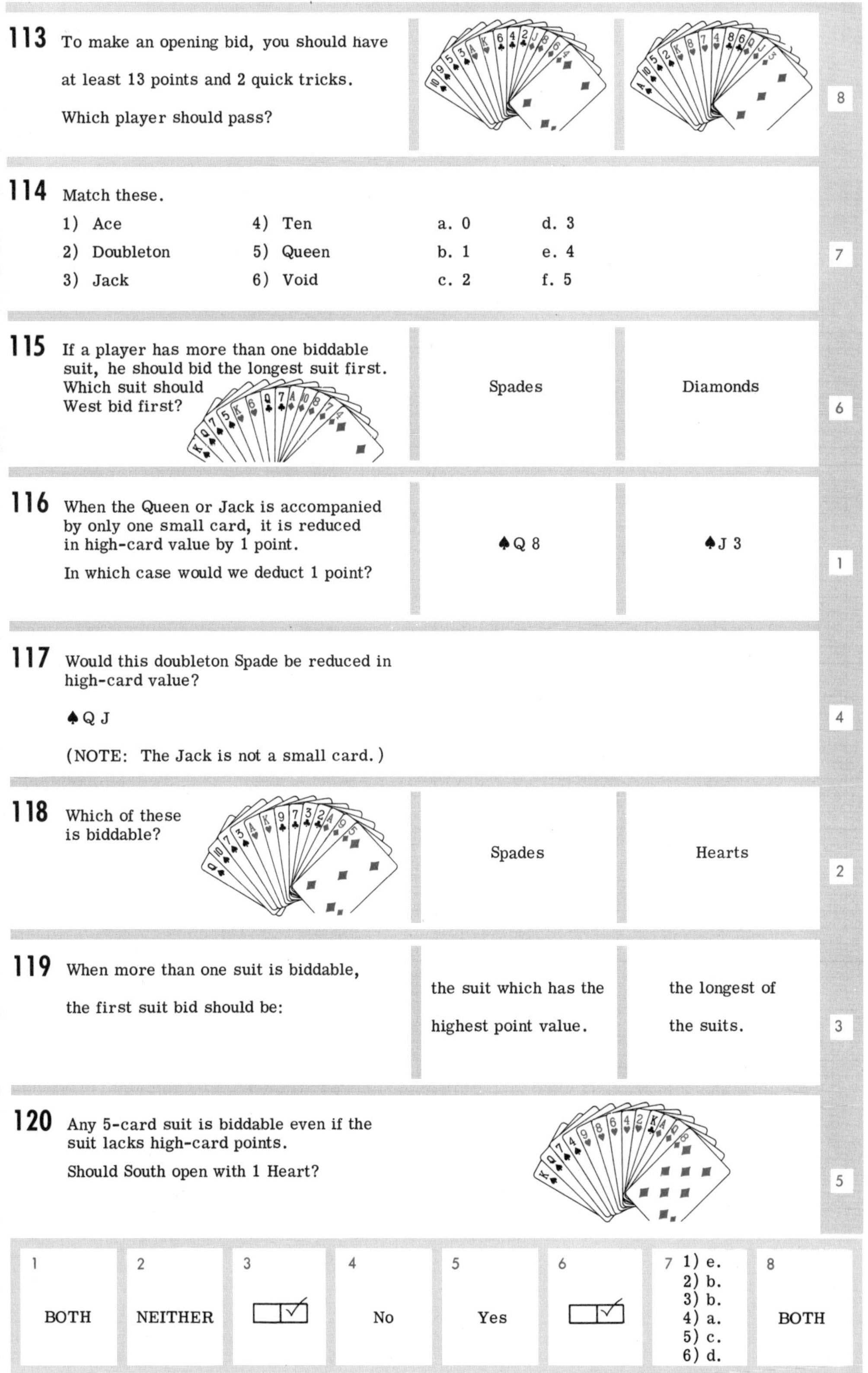

113 To make an opening bid, you should have at least 13 points and 2 quick tricks.

Which player should pass? 8

114 Match these.

1) Ace	4) Ten	a. 0	d. 3
2) Doubleton	5) Queen	b. 1	e. 4
3) Jack	6) Void	c. 2	f. 5

7

115 If a player has more than one biddable suit, he should bid the longest suit first. Which suit should West bid first?

Spades	Diamonds

6

116 When the Queen or Jack is accompanied by only one small card, it is reduced in high-card value by 1 point.

In which case would we deduct 1 point?

♠Q 8	♠J 3

1

117 Would this doubleton Spade be reduced in high-card value?

♠Q J

(NOTE: The Jack is not a small card.) 4

118 Which of these is biddable?

Spades	Hearts

2

119 When more than one suit is biddable, the first suit bid should be:

the suit which has the highest point value.	the longest of the suits.

3

120 Any 5-card suit is biddable even if the suit lacks high-card points.

Should South open with 1 Heart? 5

1	2	3	4	5	6	7	8
BOTH	NEITHER	☐☑	No	Yes	☐☑	1) e. 2) b. 3) b. 4) a. 5) c. 6) d.	BOTH

121 Which suit is higher ranking than Diamonds?

Spades	Hearts

8

122 If a hand contains two 5-card suits, the higher RANKING suit should be bid. Here Hearts have a higher point value than Spades, but the suit which is higher RANKING is __________.

6

123 Which Queen would be reduced in high-card value?

♣Q J	♦Q 6

3

124 When a player has two 5-card suits, he should bid the higher ranking suit first.

Should South bid Hearts or Diamonds first?

7

125 Which is a biddable suit?

4-card suit with 3 high-card points	6-card suit with no high-card points

1

126 Which suit would you bid first?

4-card suit with 3 high-card points	6-card suit with no high-card points

5

127 When a player has more than one 5-card suit, which should he bid first?

the one with the most high-card points	the one with the most face cards

2

128 How many total (high-card and distribution) points is a singleton Jack worth?

2	0

4

1	2	3	4	5	6	7	8
BOTH	NEITHER higher ranked	☐☑	☑☐	☐☑	Spades	Hearts	BOTH

129 A 5- or more-card suit does not need high-card points in order to be biddable.

With which suit should North open the bidding?

♠ K J 9 6 5
♥ 10 8 6 5 4 2
♦ A K
♣ none

4

130 Which suit should you bid?

♠ A 10 6 2
♥ 10 9 7 6 5 3
♦ A 9 5
♣ none

Diamonds	Spades

6

131 What is your best biddable suit?

the longest suit	Spades

2

132 A 6-card suit is biddable if it contains no high-card points. (True/False)

1

133 Which is the correct opening bid with this hand? (Use Chart 1.)

1 Heart	1 Club

3

134 Which is the correct opening bid for this hand?

1 Spade	1 Club

5

135 Subtracting the number of cards in a suit from 3 equals the number of:

high-card points.	distribution points.

8

136 Match a. and b. with the first statement, and c., d., and e. with the second statement.

A singleton Ace is worth: a. ( ) high-card point(s).
b. ( ) distribution point(s).

A singleton King is worth: c. ( ) high-card point(s).
d. ( ) distribution point(s).
e. ( ) deduction(s).

7

1	2	3	4	5	6	7	8
True	BOTH	☐ ☑	Hearts	NEITHER "Pass" is the correct bid.	NEITHER Hand contains only 11 points.	a. 4 b. 2 c. 3 d. 2 e. 1	☐ ☑

137 How many total points is a singleton King worth?	3	4	1
138 Which hand should you pass? (Use your chart.)			3
139 Your best biddable suit is:	the suit with the most high-card points.	the longest suit.	4
140 Any 5- or 6-card suit is biddable but a 4-card suit must have:	3 high-card points.	at least the Q-J of that suit.	7
141  Use your chart to determine which shows the correct opening bid.	1 Heart	1 Club	5
142 You are opening bidder. Which is true?	Add 1 point for Aceless hand. Subtract 1 point for all 4 Aces.	Add 1 point for all 4 Aces. Subtract 1 point for Aceless hand.	6
143 Which hand totals 15 points?			2
144 If your hand holds 13 points and 2 quick tricks, you:	may bid 1 of a suit.	must pass.	8

1	2	3	4	5	6	7	8
☐☑	BOTH	BOTH	☐☑	☐☑	☐☑	BOTH	☑☐

145 Which is a higher bid than 1 Spade?	1 No Trump	1 Heart	5
146 A 5-card suit requires at least ( ) face card(s) to be biddable.	1	2	6
147 Distribution points do *not* have any value in No Trump bidding. If you bid 1 No Trump, how many total points is a doubleton King worth?	4	1	1
148 In order to consider bidding 1 No Trump, the hand must have 16, 17, or 18 high-card points. With which hand might you check to see if you can bid 1 No Trump?			3
149 In order to bid 1 No Trump, the hand must be equally distributed. That is, it must be 4-3-3-3, 4-4-3-2, or 5-3-3-2 in distribution. Does this hand meet the requirements for a No Trump bid?			4
150 The distribution is *unbalanced* if the hand contains either a void, a singleton, or 2 doubletons. Which hand shows an unbalanced distribution?			8
151 Unbalanced hands have either a void, a singleton, or 2 doubletons. Which is unbalanced?	♠K Q 5 4 ♥A J 10 ♦A ♣K Q 4 3 2	♠9 8 7 ♥none ♦A Q 4 3 2 ♣A K Q J 10	7
152 If a hand contains 2 doubletons, it has a(n):	balanced distribution.	unbalanced distribution.	2

1	2	3	4	5	6	7	8
NEITHER 3 high-card points	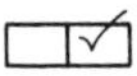 ☐☑	BOTH	No, a 5-4-3-1 hand is not balanced.	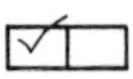 ☑☐	NEITHER No face cards are required.	BOTH	NEITHER

153 A hand has an unbalanced distribution when it contains a ________, ________, or ( ) ________. 8

154 Could you open with a No Trump bid when your hand contains 17 points and only 1 doubleton? 7

155 To open with 1 No Trump, the hand should be evenly distributed and contain from 16 to 18 high-card points.

Which hand should open with 1 No Trump? 4

156 Don't bid 1 No Trump when a hand contains a void, a singleton, or 2 doubletons.

Which player should bid No Trump?

(Remember, count high-card points.) 6

157 Which do you count to bid No Trump?

high-card points	distribution points

5

158 Use Chart 1 to answer this question.

To open with 1 No Trump, the hand must contain:

25-27 points.	33-37 points.

1

159 Holding 16-18 high-card points, a player can bid 1 No Trump even with a doubleton, provided that the doubleton contains an Ace, King, or Queen.
Which hand may be bid at 1 No Trump? 2

160 Which shows the high-card points needed for a 1 No Trump bid?

16	18

3

1	2	3	4	5	6	7	8
NEITHER 1 No Trump requires 16-18 points.	☑☐	BOTH	☑☐	☑☐	☑☐	Yes (With 2 doubletons you would bid longest suit.)	void singleton 2 doubletons

161 When bidding in a suit, you count:

distribution points.	high-card points.

2

162 An opening bid made at the level of 3 or higher to shut out competition is a *pre-emptive* bid.

Which of these would be pre-emptive if each were an opening bid?

4 Spades	3 Diamonds

5

163 A No Trump bid can be made when the hand contains a doubleton, provided that the 2-card suit contains a(n):

a. Ace.
b. King.
c. Queen.
d. (any of these)
e. (none of these)

6

164 Distribution points are counted when you open with a No Trump bid. (True/False)

4

165 When a small card of a suit protects a face card, the face card is called a *stopper*. An Ace does not require protection, but the King needs at least (1/2/3) small card(s) in order to be considered a stopper.

7

166 An opening bid made at the level of 3 or higher is:

an adverse bid.	a pre-emptive bid.

8

167 The Queen can be taken by 2 cards, either the Ace or the King.

In order to be a stopper, the Queen needs at least:

1 small card.	2 small cards.

1

168 In order to be a stopper:

a. The King requires ( ) small card(s).
b. The Queen requires ( ) small card(s).
c. The Jack requires ( ) small card(s).

3

1	2	3	4	5	6	7	8
☐☑	BOTH	a. 1 b. 2 c. 3	False	BOTH	d. (any of these)	1	☐☑

169 In order to bid 1 No Trump, you must have protection in at least three suits. This hand shows protection in Spades, Hearts, and __________. 8

170 To check for stoppers, look at the highest card in a suit, then see if it has the required number of small cards. King is the highest Spade. It has the required small cards. Which is true?

	In Hearts, the Jack is high. It has the required number of small cards.	In Diamonds, the Queen is high. It has the required number of small cards.

3

171 High cards which are protected by small cards are called __________. 5

172 To protect the Jack, you need at least ( ) small cards. 1

173 To determine if your suits are protected (contain the necessary number of small cards), you consider only the highest face card in that suit. Which card would you consider in Spades to determine if that suit is protected?

♠K J 7 ♥A K J 4 ♦K Q 2 ♣Q 9 4

King	Jack

6

174 To determine if this suit is adequately protected, you would consider only the _______, not the Jack. ♣Q J 7 7

175 Use Chart 1.

How many high-card points do you need to open with 2 No Trump?

22-24	25-27

2

176 How many stoppers are there in this hand?

(NOTE: Consider all stoppers in each suit.)

4	5

4

1	2	3	4	5	6	7	8
3	☑☐	NEITHER	☑☐	stoppers	☑☐	Queen	Clubs

177 (Use your chart.) To open with 1 No Trump, three suits must be protected. How many must be protected to open with 2 No Trump?	all of them	4	6
178 A bid of 6 No Trump means that declarer and dummy contract for a required total of ( ) trick(s).			8
179 Which is the best opening bid for this hand? (Use your chart.)	1 Heart	1 No Trump	4
180 You deduct 1 point from your Aceless hand only when you are:	responder.	opening bidder.	1
181 How many high-card points do you need to open with 3 No Trump? (Use your chart.)	16-18 high-card points	22-24 high-card points	3
182 You (add/subtract) one point from high-card points in your hand when a suit contains a doubleton Queen or Jack.			7
183 One doubleton is permitted when opening with 1 No Trump, provided that it contains a King, Ace, or Queen. (True/False)			2
184 a. How many total points in this hand? b. How many quick tricks here?			5

1	2	3	4	5	6	7	8
☐ ☑	True	NEITHER 25-27 high-card points	☐ ☑	a. 13 points b. $2\frac{1}{2}$	BOTH	subtract	12

185 Which hand shows 4 stoppers?

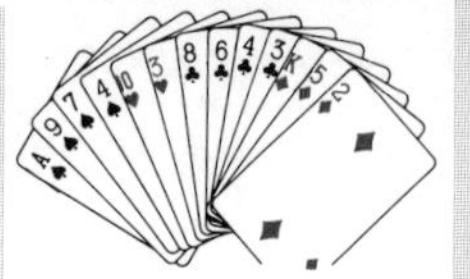

3

186 You have:

What is the total number of points?

1

187 E has:

a. There are ( ) high-card points in E's hand.
b. There is (are) ( ) distribution point(s) in E's hand.
c. E bid 1 No Trump. Is this the correct bid?

8

188 Which is the correct opening bid for this hand?

(Use the chart.)

1 No Trump	1 Heart

4

189 a. Which suit is the shortest (has the least number of cards)?

b. Which suit is directly below the shortest suit?

6

190 When you have two or more biddable 4-card suits, bid that suit which ranks immediately below the shortest suit. Which suit would you bid here?

Spades	Clubs

2

191 When you have two or more biddable 4-card suits, bid the suit below the:

stronger suit.	higher ranking suit.

5

192 If you have 14 to 20 total points and lack a No Trump distribution, bid your longest suit. Which suit should you bid here?

Diamonds	Clubs

7

1	2	3	4	5	6	7	8
7	NEITHER Diamonds	NEITHER Both hands have only two stoppers.	☑ ☐	NEITHER shortest suit.	a. Spades b. Hearts	NEITHER Hearts	a. 15 b. 1 c. No

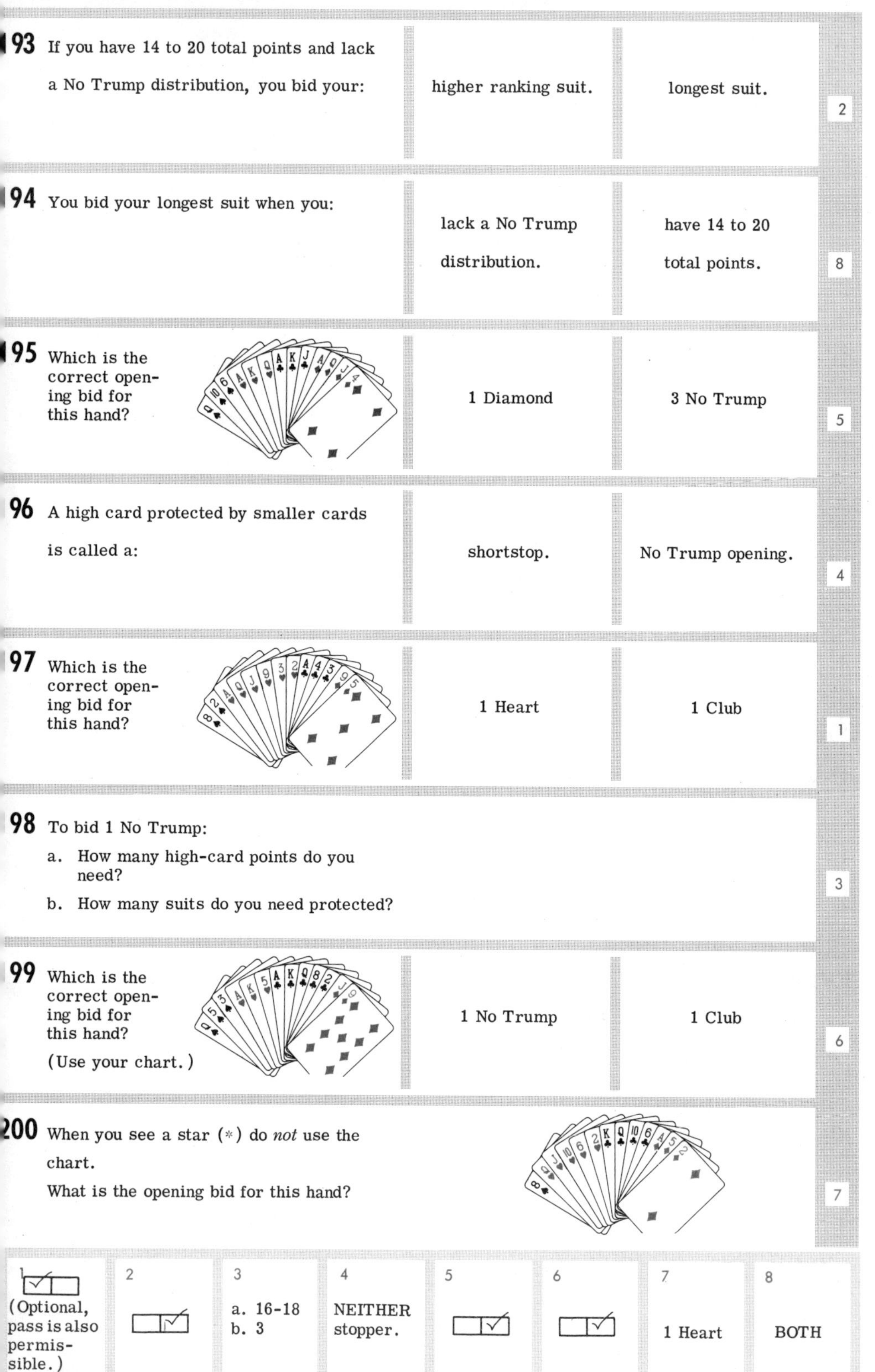

193 If you have 14 to 20 total points and lack a No Trump distribution, you bid your:

higher ranking suit.	longest suit.	2

194 You bid your longest suit when you:

lack a No Trump distribution.	have 14 to 20 total points.	8

195 Which is the correct opening bid for this hand?

1 Diamond	3 No Trump	5

196 A high card protected by smaller cards is called a:

shortstop.	No Trump opening.	4

197 Which is the correct opening bid for this hand?

1 Heart	1 Club	1

198 To bid 1 No Trump:

a. How many high-card points do you need?

b. How many suits do you need protected?

3

199 Which is the correct opening bid for this hand?

(Use your chart.)

1 No Trump	1 Club	6

200 When you see a star (*) do *not* use the chart.

What is the opening bid for this hand?

7

1	2	3	4	5	6	7	8
☑ ☐ (Optional, pass is also permissible.)	☐ ☑	a. 16-18 b. 3	NEITHER stopper.	☐ ☑	☐ ☑	1 Heart	BOTH

201 What is the opening bid for this hand?

(Since the * means not to use your chart, the absence of the * means to use your chart.)

4

202 Which hand should open with 2 Spades?

7

203 What is the opening bid for this hand?

3

204 Which is an optional opening bid? *

13 points and 2 quick tricks	2 quick tricks and 13 points

6

205 What is the opening bid for this hand? *

8

206 a. How many points here?

b. What is the correct opening bid?

2

207 Which is a correct description of this hand?

♠A K J 7 2
♥ none
♦8 3 2
♣K 10 8 4 3

12 points pass	11 points pass

1

208 a. How many points here?

b. What is the correct opening bid?

5

1	2	3	4	5	6	7	8
NEITHER 14 points, bid 1 Spade	a. 15 points b. 1 Heart	pass	1 Diamond	a. 15 points b. 1 Diamond	BOTH	NEITHER	1 Heart (If you got this correct, go to frame 208.)

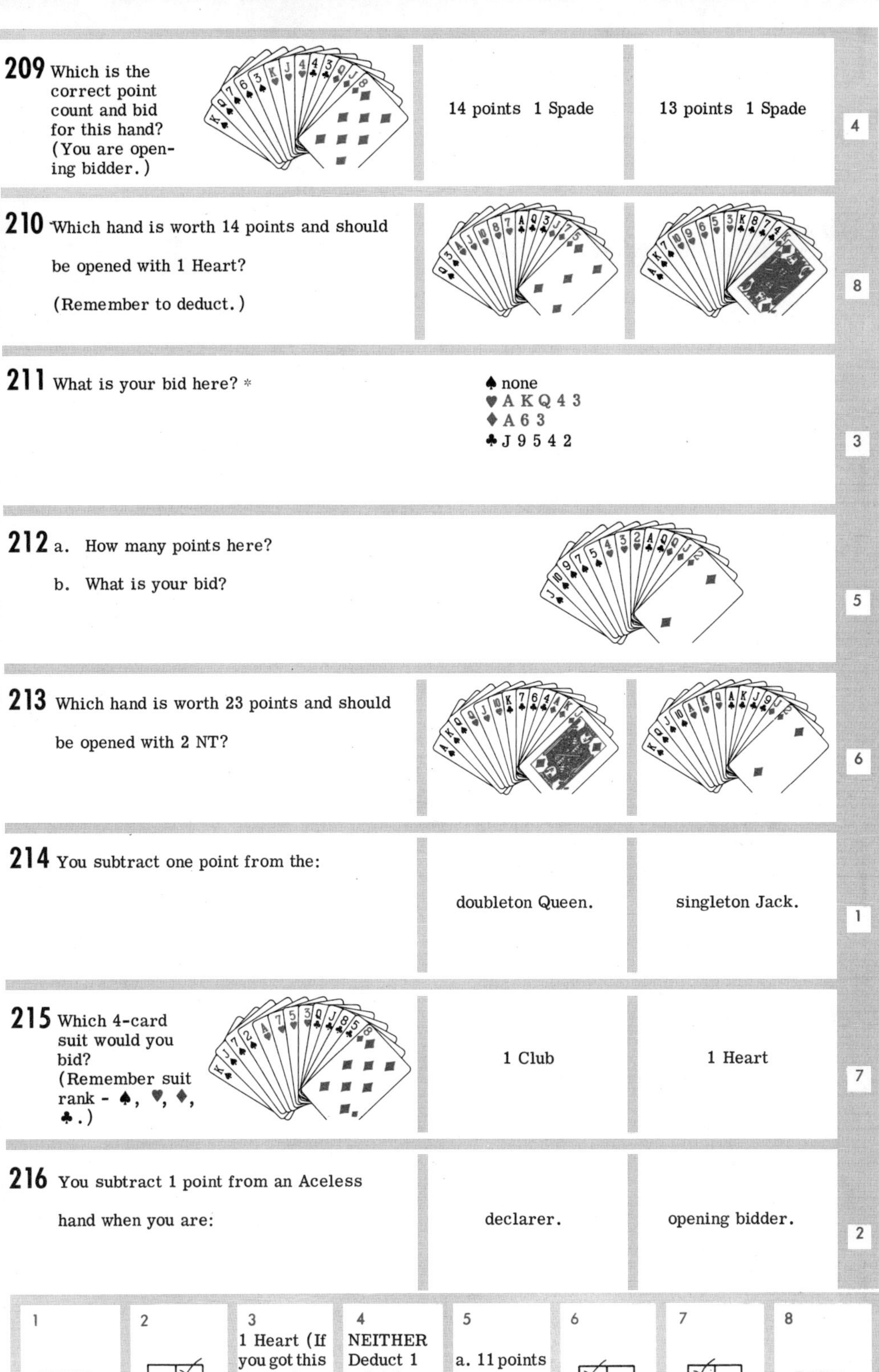

209 Which is the correct point count and bid for this hand? (You are opening bidder.)

14 points 1 Spade	13 points 1 Spade	4

210 Which hand is worth 14 points and should be opened with 1 Heart?

(Remember to deduct.) 8

211 What is your bid here? *

♠ none
♥ A K Q 4 3
♦ A 6 3
♣ J 9 5 4 2

3

212 a. How many points here?

b. What is your bid?

5

213 Which hand is worth 23 points and should be opened with 2 NT? 6

214 You subtract one point from the:

doubleton Queen.	singleton Jack.	1

215 Which 4-card suit would you bid? (Remember suit rank - ♠, ♥, ♦, ♣.)

1 Club	1 Heart	7

216 You subtract 1 point from an Aceless hand when you are:

declarer.	opening bidder.	2

1	2	3	4	5	6	7	8
BOTH	☐☑	1 Heart (If you got this correct, go to frame 217.)	NEITHER Deduct 1 point for no Aces.	a. 11 points b. pass	☑☐	☑☐	BOTH

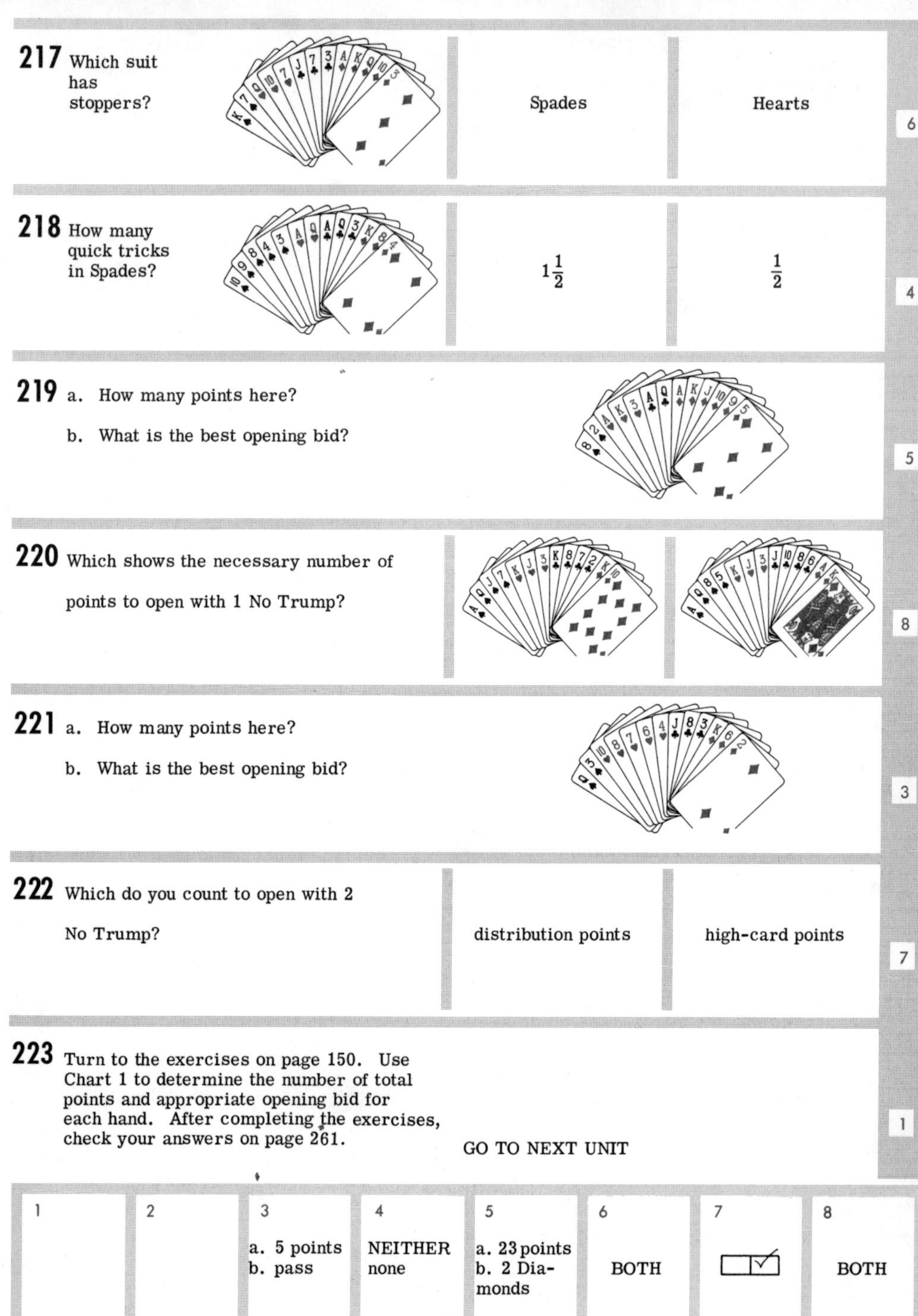

217 Which suit has stoppers?

Spades	Hearts

6

218 How many quick tricks in Spades?

$1\frac{1}{2}$	$\frac{1}{2}$

4

219 a. How many points here?

b. What is the best opening bid?

5

220 Which shows the necessary number of points to open with 1 No Trump?

8

221 a. How many points here?

b. What is the best opening bid?

3

222 Which do you count to open with 2 No Trump?

distribution points	high-card points

7

223 Turn to the exercises on page 150. Use Chart 1 to determine the number of total points and appropriate opening bid for each hand. After completing the exercises, check your answers on page 261.

GO TO NEXT UNIT

1

1	2	3	4	5	6	7	8
		a. 5 points b. pass	NEITHER none	a. 23 points b. 2 Diamonds	BOTH	☐☑	BOTH

TAKE UNIT 7 POST-TEST

UNIT 8

responses to the opening bid

Responses to both suit and No Trump openers are presented in this unit. The beginner is introduced to the concepts of trump support and honor promotion. Elementary concepts of the free bid are also presented.

PRE- AND POST-TEST

1. Your partner opens with 1 Heart. Your right-hand opponent passes.

   What would you do with each of the following?

a.

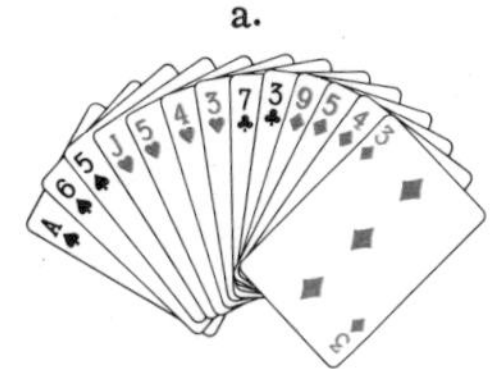

b.

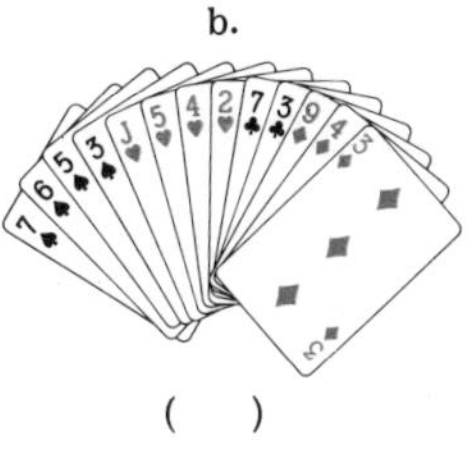

Number of points: ( ) ( )

You bid: __________ __________

c.

d.

Number of points: ( ) ( )

You bid: __________ __________

2. A singleton King is assigned a total of _____ points.

3. What is an honor?

4. Four small cards or 3 with the Queen or better in partner's bid suit is a(n) (surplus trump/complete sequence/trump support/honor sequence).

5. When do you promote honors in partner's suit?

6. How many tricks here?

7. When you respond to partner's 1 No Trump opener, you count [high-card points/distribution points/(both)/(neither)].

8. How many points are needed to respond in a suit that both partner and opponent have bid?

9. What is a response called when right-hand opponent passes?

10. What do we call a device designed to convey an artificial meaning to one's partner?

11. Assign the appropriate number of points to the following.

	Trump Support	No Trump Support
Void	______	______
Doubleton	______	______
Singleton	______	______

12. What are dummy points?

13. A point is deducted from your hand when you have [a 4-3-3-3 distribution/3 or less cards in the suit partner bid and respond in that suit/(both)/(neither)].

14. The Ace-Queen is worth [1/2/(both)/(neither)] quick tricks.

15. When both partner and opponent bid, your response is known as a [courtesy bid/free bid/(both)/(neither)].

16. What is the minimum number of pairs required for a courtesy bid?

17. You assign special distribution points [only in response to partner's bid/as opening bid/(both)/(neither)].

18. If you respond to partner's opening No Trump bid, you count [dummy points/high-card points/(both)/(neither)].

19. When partner pre-empts, you add the number of partner's bid to the number of [points in your hand/quick tricks/(both)/(neither)].

20. The ten is the only honor that is not promoted. (True/False)

21. Partner opened with 1 No Trump. Assume right-hand opponent passes. With which hand would you pass?

a. 

b. 

c. both

d. neither

22. Partner opened with 1 Diamond. Assume the right-hand opponent passed. With which hand would you raise partner's bid to 2 Diamonds?

a. 

b. 

c. both

d. neither

EXERCISES

You are South. North opens with 1 No Trump. You hold:

1.

This hand contains (   ) points.

You should respond with (   ) ________.

2.

This hand contains (   ) points.

You should respond with (   ) ________.

You are West. East opened with 2 No Trump and South passes. You hold:

3.

The hand contains (   ) points.

Your best response is (   ) ________.

4.

The hand contains (   ) points.

Your best response is (   ) ________.

You are East. The bidding has proceeded as follows: West -- 1 Heart, North -- pass.
You hold:

5.

The hand is worth (   ) points.

You should respond with (   ) ________.

6.

The hand is worth (   ) points.

You should respond with (   ) ________.

Partner opens with 2 Spades. Right-hand opponent passes. You hold:

7.

The hand contains (   ) points.

You should respond with (   ) _______.

8.

The hand contains (   ) points.

You should respond with (   ) _______.

You are South. North opens with 1 Club. East passes. You hold:

9.

The hand is worth (   ) points.

Your best response is (   ) _______.

10.

The hand is worth (   ) points.

Your best response is (   ) _______.

Partner opens with 1 Diamond. Right-hand opponent passes. You hold:

11.

This hand contains (   ) points.

You should respond with (   ) _______.

12.

This hand contains (   ) points.

You should respond with (   ) _______.

Partner opens with 1 Spade. Right-hand opponent passes. You hold:

13.

This hand contains (   ) points.

Your best response is (   ) ________.

14.

This hand contains (   ) points.

Your best response is (   ) ________.

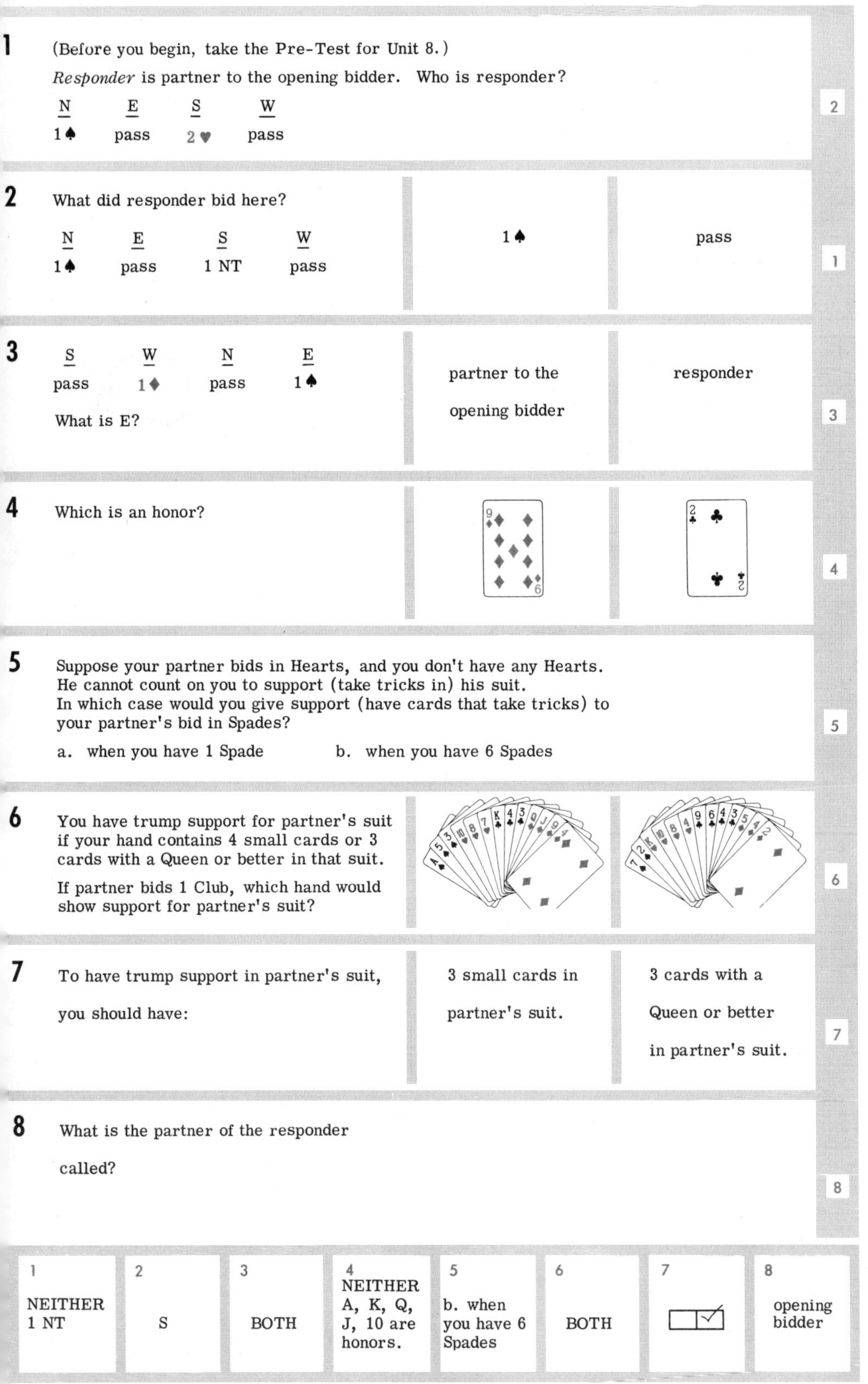

1 (Before you begin, take the Pre-Test for Unit 8.)

Responder is partner to the opening bidder. Who is responder?

N	E	S	W
1♠	pass	2♥	pass

2

2 What did responder bid here?

N	E	S	W
1♠	pass	1 NT	pass

1♠ | pass

1

3

S	W	N	E
pass	1♦	pass	1♠

What is E?

partner to the opening bidder | responder

3

4 Which is an honor?

4

5 Suppose your partner bids in Hearts, and you don't have any Hearts. He cannot count on you to support (take tricks in) his suit. In which case would you give support (have cards that take tricks) to your partner's bid in Spades?

a. when you have 1 Spade b. when you have 6 Spades

5

6 You have trump support for partner's suit if your hand contains 4 small cards or 3 cards with a Queen or better in that suit.

If partner bids 1 Club, which hand would show support for partner's suit?

6

7 To have trump support in partner's suit, you should have:

3 small cards in partner's suit. | 3 cards with a Queen or better in partner's suit.

7

8 What is the partner of the responder called?

8

1	2	3	4	5	6	7	8
NEITHER 1 NT	S	BOTH	NEITHER A, K, Q, J, 10 are honors.	b. when you have 6 Spades	BOTH	☐☑	opening bidder

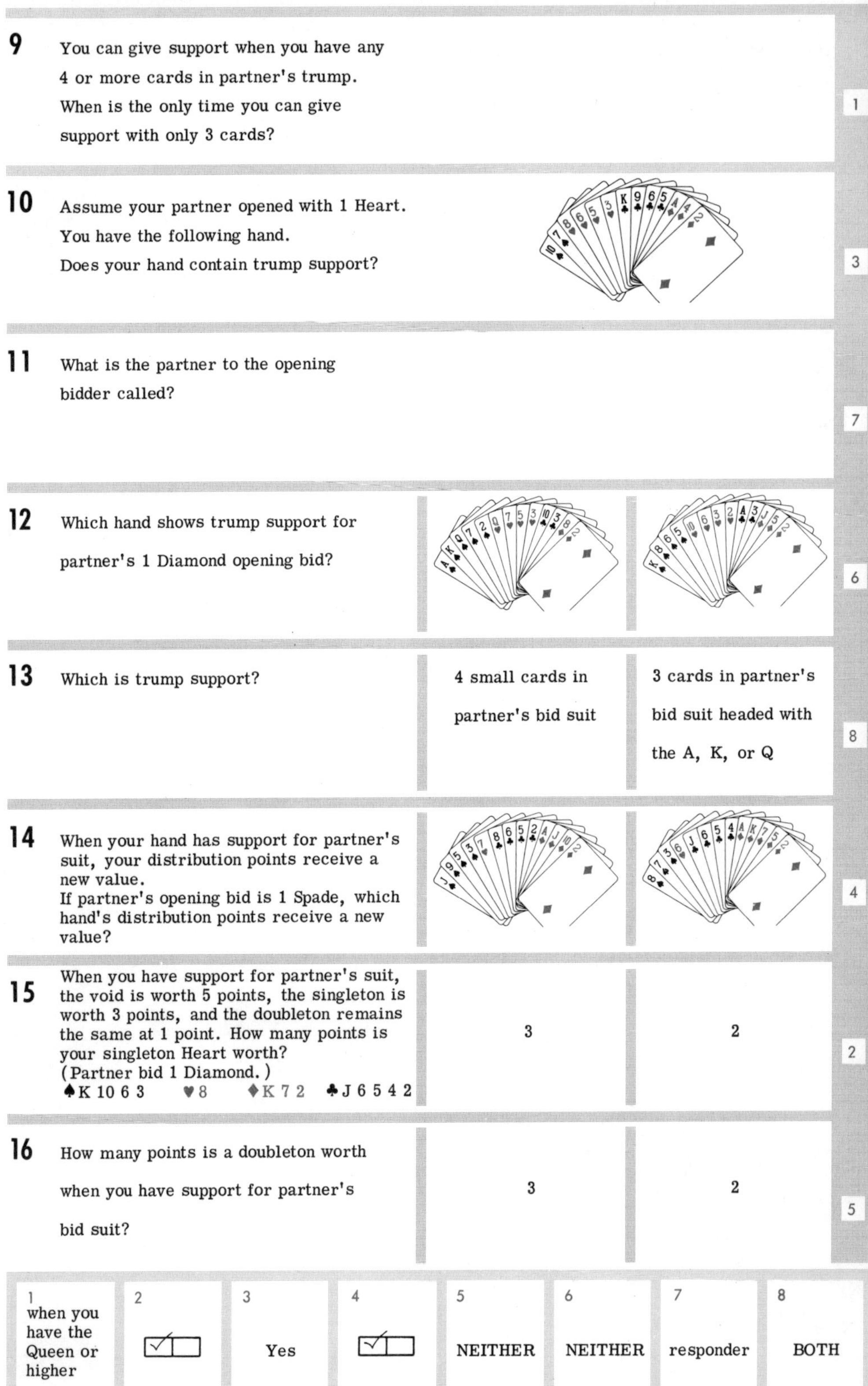

9 You can give support when you have any 4 or more cards in partner's trump. When is the only time you can give support with only 3 cards? 1

10 Assume your partner opened with 1 Heart. You have the following hand. Does your hand contain trump support? 3

11 What is the partner to the opening bidder called? 7

12 Which hand shows trump support for partner's 1 Diamond opening bid? 6

13 Which is trump support?

4 small cards in partner's bid suit	3 cards in partner's bid suit headed with the A, K, or Q

8

14 When your hand has support for partner's suit, your distribution points receive a new value. If partner's opening bid is 1 Spade, which hand's distribution points receive a new value? 4

15 When you have support for partner's suit, the void is worth 5 points, the singleton is worth 3 points, and the doubleton remains the same at 1 point. How many points is your singleton Heart worth? (Partner bid 1 Diamond.)
♠K 10 6 3 ♥8 ♦K 7 2 ♣J 6 5 4 2

3	2

2

16 How many points is a doubleton worth when you have support for partner's bid suit?

3	2

5

1	2	3	4	5	6	7	8
when you have the Queen or higher	☑☐	Yes	☑☐	NEITHER	NEITHER	responder	BOTH

17 Doubleton = 1 point
Singleton = 3 points
Void = 5 points
You have support for partner's suit.
[NOTE: The first 3 odd numbers (1, 3, 5) should help you remember the points.]

Add distribution points for this hand.

♠ none
♥ A K Q J 10 9 8 7 6 5 6
♦ J
♣ K J

---

18 Support for partner's suit requires:

	Queen or better with 2 small cards in partner's suit.	4 small cards in partner's suit.

1

---

19 How many points is a void worth if you have trump support?

	3	5

8

---

20 When you do *not* have support for partner's suit, the singleton is worth:

	3 points.	1 point.

3

---

21 Partner bid 1 Diamond. How many points is your void in Hearts worth here?

♠ A J 7 5
♥ none
♦ J 10 5 4
♣ Q J 6 5 3

	5	3

4

---

22 Match.
1) singleton with trump support — a. 1
2) void without trump support — b. 2
3) void with trump support — c. 3
4) doubleton with trump support — d. 4 2
5) singleton without trump support — e. 5
6) doubleton without trump support

---

23 In order to assign special distribution points to your void and singleton, you must have:

	4 small cards or 3 cards with the A, K, or Q in partner's bid suit.	trump support.

5

---

24 If you do *not* have trump support, then:

a. the void is worth ( ) points.
b. the singleton is worth ( ) points. 7
c. the doubleton is worth ( ) points.

1	2	3	4	5	6	7	8
BOTH	1) c. 4) a. 2) c. 5) b. 3) e. 6) a.	NEITHER 2 points.	☑ ☐	BOTH	♠ - 5 points ♥ - 0 points ♦ - 3 points ♣ - 1 point	a. 3 b. 2 c. 1	☐ ☑

25	Which is an honor?	Ten	King	4
26	When you do not have support, deduct 1 point if a raise in partner's suit is made. In which hand would you deduct 1 point if partner opens with 1 Heart and you wish to raise partner?			5
27	How many points do you deduct when you do not have support for partner's bid suit and wish to raise partner's suit?	2	0	6
28	In which hand would you assign 5 points for the void in Spades? Assume partner opened with 1 Diamond.	♠ none ♥ A K 10 5 4 ♦ Q 10 6 2 ♣ K Q 10 5	♠ none ♥ A K 10 5 4 ♦ J 6 2 ♣ K Q 10 5 3	7
29	You deduct a point if you do not have support in partner's bid suit:	only if you consider a raise in partner's suit.	even if you bid in a different suit.	8
30	*Special* distribution points are assigned when you have:	trump support.	4 small cards or 3 cards with the Queen or better in partner's bid suit.	1
31	Which is trump support?	4 small cards in partner's bid suit	3 cards with the Queen or better in partner's bid suit	3
32	You deduct 1 point when you have:	trump support.	3 or less trumps which are lower than the Queen and you wish to raise partner's bid suit.	2

1	2	3	4	5	6	7	8
BOTH	☐☑	BOTH	BOTH	☑☐	NEITHER 1	☑☐	☑☐

33 In which suit would you assign 3 points for the singleton? Partner opened with 1 Club.	Spades	Diamonds	4
34 In which instance would you deduct 1 point?	when you have 3 or less small trumps in partner's bid suit and want to bid that suit	when you have 4 small trumps in partner's bid suit	1
35 When you hold 4 cards of a suit and 3 cards in all other suits (3 in each), as responder you must deduct 1 point. In which hand would you deduct 1 point for a 4-3-3-3 distribution?			5
36 When you have trump support in partner's bid suit:	you assign 5 points to a void.	you assign 3 points to a singleton.	8
37 In order to have trump support for your partner's first opener, your hand must have: a. ( ) or more cards, or b. ( ) cards with a Queen or better.			7
38 Assume partner has opened with 1 Diamond. You hold: a. Do you have trump support? b. Does your hand have a biddable suit?			3
39 You deduct 1 point from your hand:	when you do not have support for partner's bid suit and you raise that suit.	when you have a 4-3-3-3 distribution.	2
40 The beginning of this unit assumes that partner N has always bid first and that right-hand opponent E has passed. N (opened), W, E, S Which is correct?	The beginning of this unit assumes that S's right-hand opponent bids after partner N.	The beginning of this unit assumes right-hand opponent E always passes first.	6

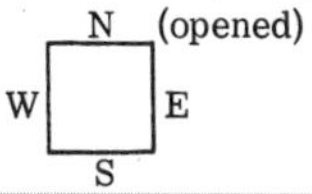

1	2	3	4	5	6	7	8
[✓][ ]	BOTH	a. No b. Yes (Spades)	BOTH	[ ][✓]	[ ][✓]	a. 4 b. 3	BOTH

41 Partner opens with 1 Heart. You hold:
♠ A 7 4 2
♥ none
♦ A K J 10 9
♣ K Q 7 4
How many points is your void worth?

5	3

2

42 Which of these is an honor card?

9♣	10♥

6

43 If you do not have trump support but have a biddable suit, do you assign special (*dummy*) distribution points to your hand? 7

44 In raising partner's opening bid of one of a suit, you assign special distribution (dummy) points when you have:

a biddable suit.	trump support.

8

45 If partner opens with one of a suit, you add 1 high-card point to *promote* the value of each high-card honor in partner's suit to a total of 4 high-card points.
The King becomes 4, the Queen becomes 3, and the Jack becomes ( ). 5

46 You promote only high-card (face-card) honors in partner's suit.
This means:

you do not promote the Ten.	you promote the Jack.

3

47 Partner bid 1 Spade.
If you hold ♠10 5 2, how many points is the Ten worth?

0	1

4

48 To promote honors in partner's suit and to assign dummy points, you must have ________ for partner's suit. 1

1	2	3	4	5	6	7	8
support	☐☑ (You had no support in Hearts.)	BOTH	☑☐	2	☐☑	No	☐☑

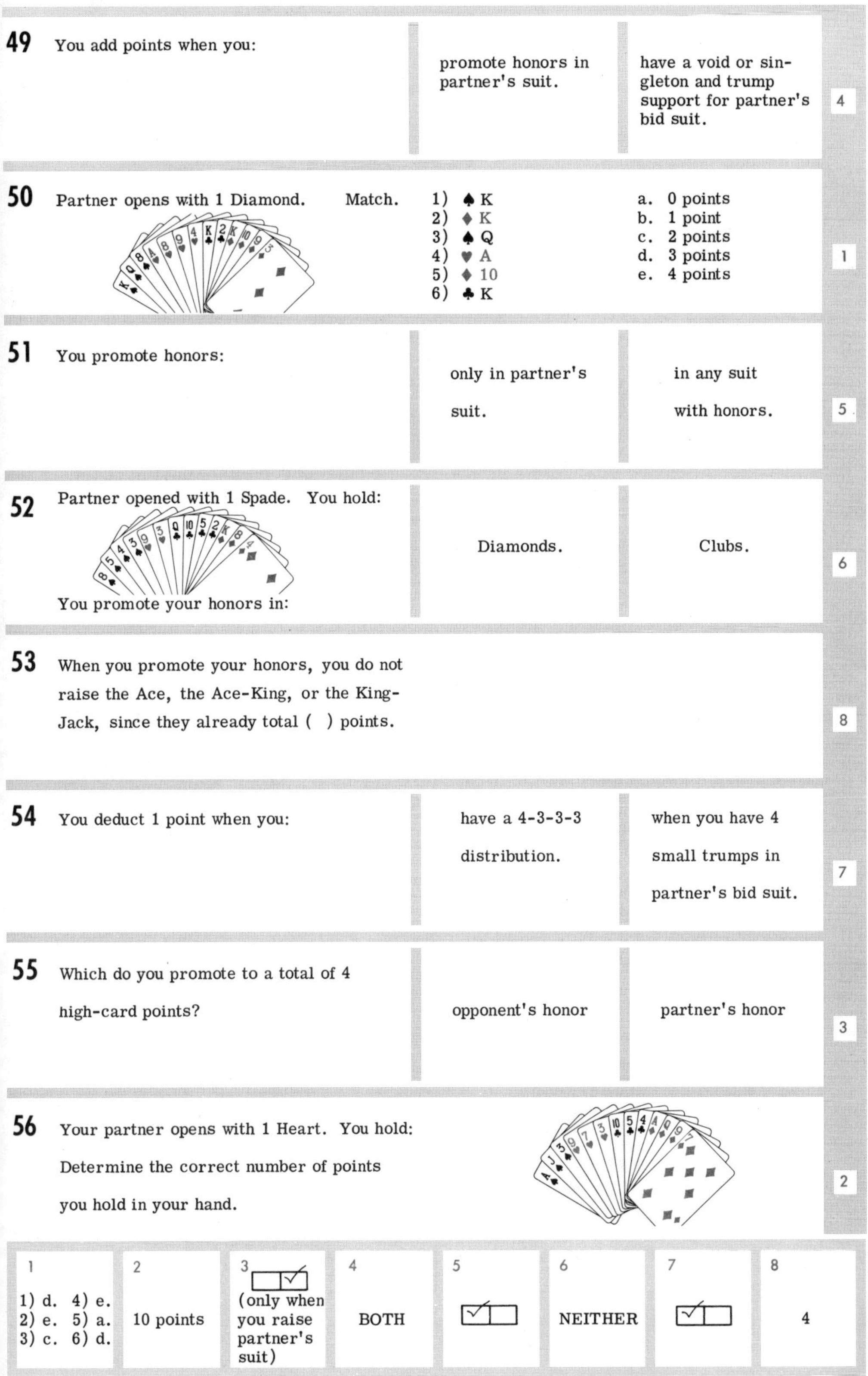

49 You add points when you:

promote honors in partner's suit.	have a void or singleton and trump support for partner's bid suit.

4

50 Partner opens with 1 Diamond. Match.

1) ♠ K	a. 0 points
2) ♦ K	b. 1 point
3) ♠ Q	c. 2 points
4) ♥ A	d. 3 points
5) ♦ 10	e. 4 points
6) ♣ K	

1

51 You promote honors:

only in partner's suit.	in any suit with honors.

5

52 Partner opened with 1 Spade. You hold:

You promote your honors in:

Diamonds.	Clubs.

6

53 When you promote your honors, you do not raise the Ace, the Ace-King, or the King-Jack, since they already total ( ) points.

8

54 You deduct 1 point when you:

have a 4-3-3-3 distribution.	when you have 4 small trumps in partner's bid suit.

7

55 Which do you promote to a total of 4 high-card points?

opponent's honor	partner's honor

3

56 Your partner opens with 1 Heart. You hold: Determine the correct number of points you hold in your hand.

2

1	2	3	4	5	6	7	8
1) d. 4) e. 2) e. 5) a. 3) c. 6) d.	10 points	☐☑ (only when you raise partner's suit)	BOTH	☑☐	NEITHER	☑☐	4

57	Which is correct?	You promote honors only when you raise partner's suit.	You promote honors even if you bid in a new suit.	7

58 If your partner opened with 1 of a suit and you have trump support, then a special value of 5 points is assigned to a 1) ________, 3 points to a 2) ________, and 1 point to a 3) ________. 4

59 When do you promote honors? 1

60	Turn to Chart 2, *Responses to Opening Suit Bids*. Which do you read if partner was not first opener?	Did partner open **1 of a suit**?	Support only if game is in sight.	8
61	Which do you read if partner opens with 1 of a suit?	Did partner open with **2 of a suit**?	Did partner open **3, 4, or 5 of a suit**?	2
62	When you have trump support in partner's suit, you:	promote honors in partner's suit.	count high-card points.	5
63	You add points to your high-card honors in:	every suit which has a high-card honor.	partner's bid suit.	6

64 Here are 4 steps in counting for response bid.

a. Look for support.
b. If you have support, count extra distribution points.
c. Count high-card points.
d. Promote honors in partner suit (4 points total).

GO TO NEXT FRAME 3

1	2	3	4	5	6	7	8
When you have trump support and raise partner's suit.	NEITHER		1) void 2) singleton 3) doubleton	[✓][ ]	[ ][✓]	[✓][ ]	[ ][✓]

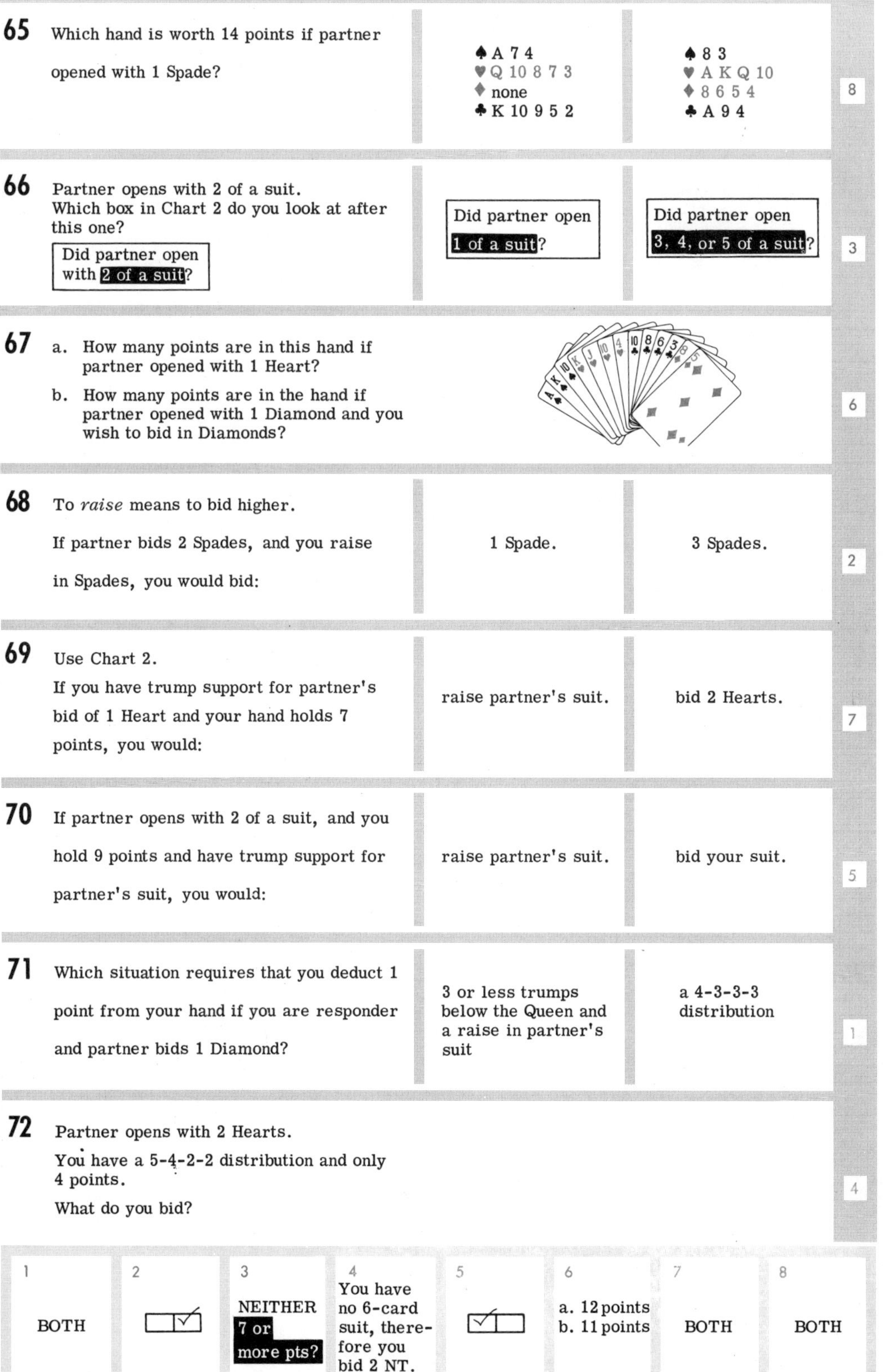

65	Which hand is worth 14 points if partner opened with 1 Spade?	♠A 7 4 ♥Q 10 8 7 3 ♦ none ♣K 10 9 5 2	♠8 3 ♥A K Q 10 ♦8 6 5 4 ♣A 9 4	8
66	Partner opens with 2 of a suit. Which box in Chart 2 do you look at after this one? Did partner open with **2 of a suit**?	Did partner open **1 of a suit**?	Did partner open **3, 4, or 5 of a suit**?	3
67	a. How many points are in this hand if partner opened with 1 Heart? b. How many points are in the hand if partner opened with 1 Diamond and you wish to bid in Diamonds?			6
68	To *raise* means to bid higher. If partner bids 2 Spades, and you raise in Spades, you would bid:	1 Spade.	3 Spades.	2
69	Use Chart 2. If you have trump support for partner's bid of 1 Heart and your hand holds 7 points, you would:	raise partner's suit.	bid 2 Hearts.	7
70	If partner opens with 2 of a suit, and you hold 9 points and have trump support for partner's suit, you would:	raise partner's suit.	bid your suit.	5
71	Which situation requires that you deduct 1 point from your hand if you are responder and partner bids 1 Diamond?	3 or less trumps below the Queen and a raise in partner's suit	a 4-3-3-3 distribution	1
72	Partner opens with 2 Hearts. You have a 5-4-2-2 distribution and only 4 points. What do you bid?			4

1	2	3	4	5	6	7	8
BOTH	☐☑	NEITHER **7 or more pts?**	You have no 6-card suit, therefore you bid 2 NT.	☑☐	a. 12 points b. 11 points	BOTH	BOTH

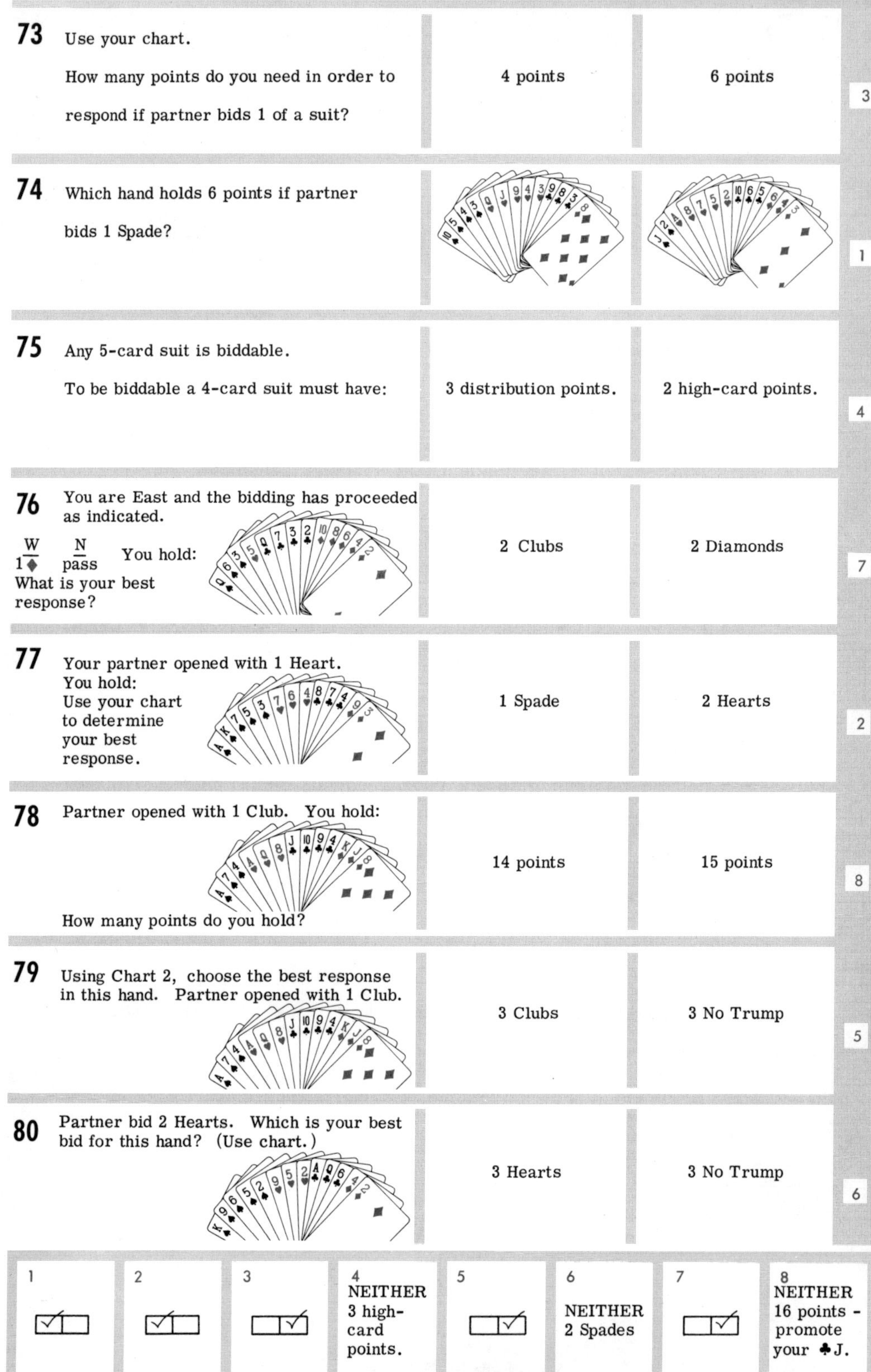

73	Use your chart. How many points do you need in order to respond if partner bids 1 of a suit?	4 points	6 points	3
74	Which hand holds 6 points if partner bids 1 Spade?			1
75	Any 5-card suit is biddable. To be biddable a 4-card suit must have:	3 distribution points.	2 high-card points.	4
76	You are East and the bidding has proceeded as indicated. W: 1♦ N: pass. You hold: What is your best response?	2 Clubs	2 Diamonds	7
77	Your partner opened with 1 Heart. You hold: Use your chart to determine your best response.	1 Spade	2 Hearts	2
78	Partner opened with 1 Club. You hold: How many points do you hold?	14 points	15 points	8
79	Using Chart 2, choose the best response in this hand. Partner opened with 1 Club.	3 Clubs	3 No Trump	5
80	Partner bid 2 Hearts. Which is your best bid for this hand? (Use chart.)	3 Hearts	3 No Trump	6

1	2	3	4	5	6	7	8
☑☐	☑☐	☐☑	NEITHER 3 high-card points.	☐☑	NEITHER 2 Spades	☐☑	NEITHER 16 points - promote your ♣J.

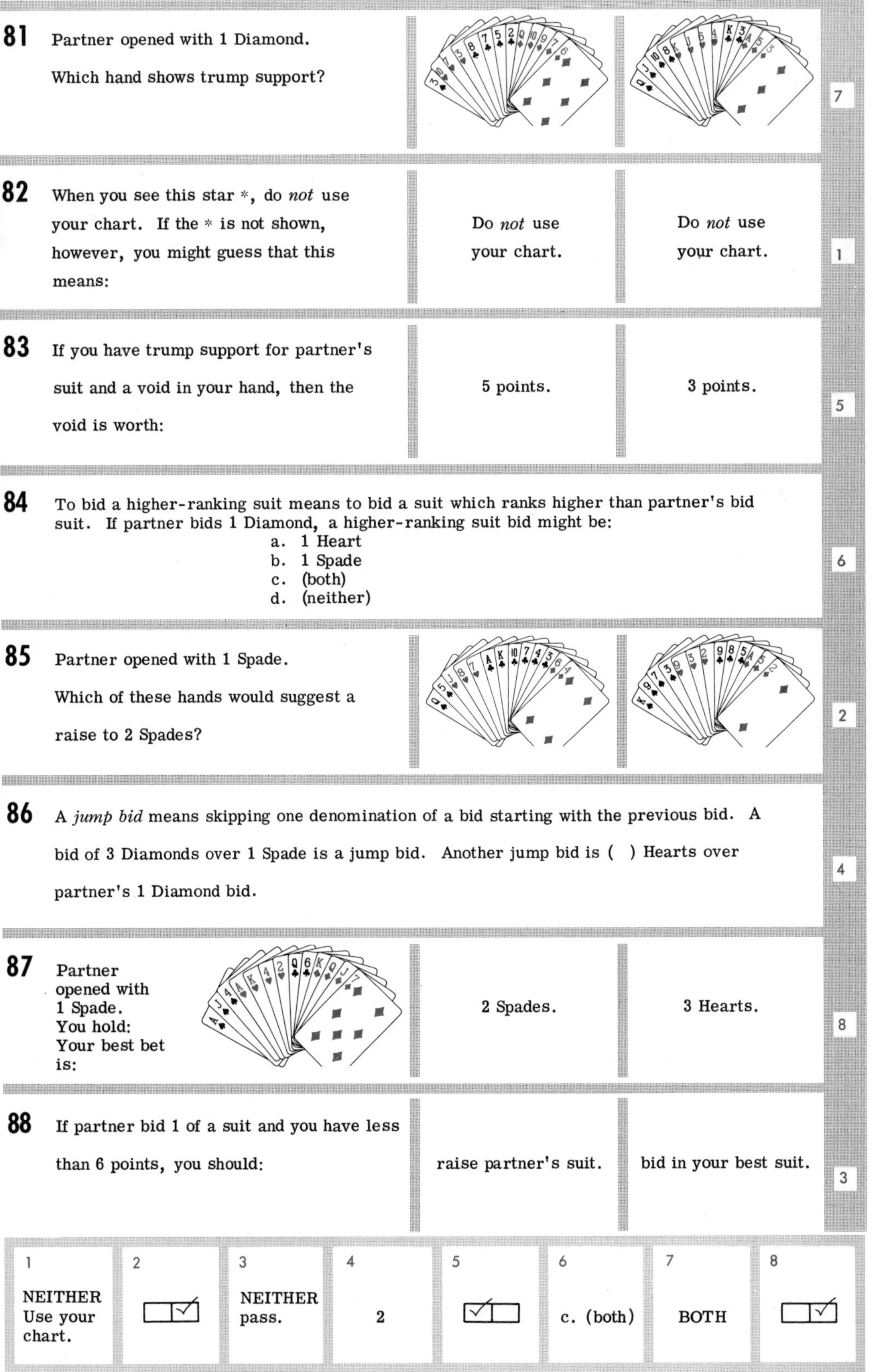

81 Partner opened with 1 Diamond. Which hand shows trump support?			7
82 When you see this star *, do *not* use your chart. If the * is not shown, however, you might guess that this means:	Do *not* use your chart.	Do *not* use your chart.	1
83 If you have trump support for partner's suit and a void in your hand, then the void is worth:	5 points.	3 points.	5

84 To bid a higher-ranking suit means to bid a suit which ranks higher than partner's bid suit. If partner bids 1 Diamond, a higher-ranking suit bid might be:

a. 1 Heart
b. 1 Spade
c. (both)
d. (neither)

6

85 Partner opened with 1 Spade. Which of these hands would suggest a raise to 2 Spades?			2

86 A *jump bid* means skipping one denomination of a bid starting with the previous bid. A bid of 3 Diamonds over 1 Spade is a jump bid. Another jump bid is ( ) Hearts over partner's 1 Diamond bid.

4

87 Partner opened with 1 Spade. You hold: Your best bet is:	2 Spades.	3 Hearts.	8
88 If partner bid 1 of a suit and you have less than 6 points, you should:	raise partner's suit.	bid in your best suit.	3

1	2	3	4	5	6	7	8
NEITHER Use your chart.	☐☑	NEITHER pass.	2	☑☐	c. (both)	BOTH	☐☑

89 Partner opened with 1 Diamond. You hold: Which is your best bid? *

pass	2 Diamonds	5

90 You deduct 1 point for a:

doubleton Jack.	4-3-3-3 distribution if you are responder.	7

91 How many points are in this hand?

2

92 You assign *special* distribution points when you have:

a void or singleton.	trump support for partner's bid suit.	1

93 Partner opened with 1 Heart.

a. How many points here?

b. What is your best bid?

4

94 Which honor would you promote 1 point if partner opened with 1 Diamond and you have support?

6

95 Partner opens with 1 Heart. You hold: Which statement describes your Heart suit?

trump support	5 trumps in partner's bid suit	3

96 Partner opened with 1 Diamond. You hold:

a. How many points are in your hand?

b. What is your best bid?

8

1	2	3	4	5	6	7	8
☐☑	3	BOTH	a. 4 points b. pass	☑☐ If you got this correct, go to frame 95.	☐☑	BOTH	a. 8 points b. 2 Diamonds

97 Partner opened with 1 Diamond. Which is the correct description of this hand?

10 points 1 Heart	11 points 1 Heart	5

98 When raising, you promote high-card honors in partner's suit if:

you have a 4-3-3-3 distribution.	you have 4 trumps or 3 trumps with the Queen or better.	2

99 Look at the second box on Chart 3, *Responses to Opening No Trump Bids*, on page 281. If partner opens with a No Trump, which do you count?

high-card points	distribution points	8

100 With a No Trump response, no honors are promoted and no distribution points are counted.
What is the total count for this hand? 7

101 Look at Chart 3. If partner opens with a No Trump, you:

promote your honors one point.	count your distribution points.	1

102 Which do you read if partner opens with 1 No Trump?

Did partner open with **2 NT**?	Does partner use Club Convention?	6

103 A convention is a device designed to convey an artificial meaning to one's partner.
Which is a convention in this sense?

Partner opened with 2 No Trump.	Partner uses the Club Convention.	3

104 If you respond with 2 Clubs to partner's opening 1 No Trump, then you and partner may be using:

a device designed to convey an artificial meaning to one's partner.	a Club Convention.	4

1	2	3	4	5	6	7	8
NEITHER	☐☑	☐☑	BOTH	☐☑	☐☑	16	☑☐

105 A response of 2 Clubs to opening bidder's 1 No Trump is a convention asking partner to respond in a biddable major suit. Which biddable suit might partner respond in?

Diamonds	Hearts	8

106 What do you do if partner opens with 2 NT

and you hold 17 high-card points? 5

107 Your partner opened with 1 No Trump. Use Chart 3 to determine which hand you should pass.
(NOTE: Partner does not use Club Convention.)

		6

108 Which statement describes this hand? Partner opens with a 3 NT.

10 points 4 Diamonds	12 points 7 No Trump	3

109 If partner opens with a suit bid,

which chart do you use?

Chart 3: *Responses to Opening No Trump Bids.*	Chart 2: *Responses to Opening Suit Bids.*	2

110 You are East, and West has opened the bidding with 1 Heart. You hold:

♠ A K Q 10 2 ♥ K 10 ♦ none ♣ 9 7 5 4 3 2

a. How many points do you hold?
b. What is your correct response? 7

111 Your partner bid 1 Diamond. You hold: Your correct response is:

2 Diamonds.	1 Club.	4

112 Your partner opens with 1 of a suit. You do not have trump support or a biddable suit, but your hand contains 14 points with protection in three unbid suits. What should your response be? 1

1	2	3	4	5	6	7	8
Jump bid to 2 No Trump.	☐☑	☐☑	NEITHER 1 Heart.	Bid 7 NT.	☑☐	a. 16 points b. 1 Spade	☐☑

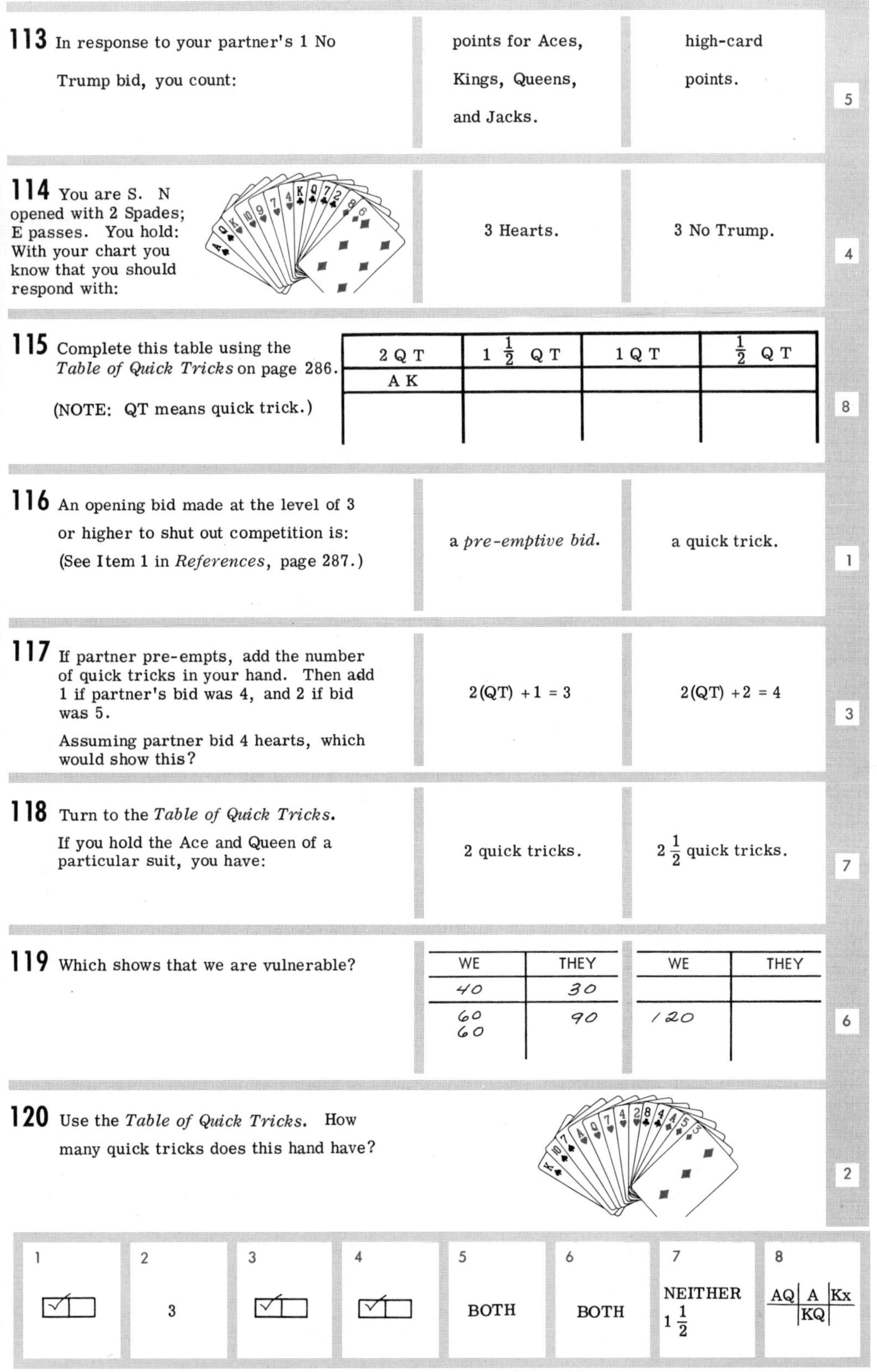

113 In response to your partner's 1 No Trump bid, you count:

points for Aces, Kings, Queens, and Jacks.

high-card points.

5

114 You are S. N opened with 2 Spades; E passes. You hold: With your chart you know that you should respond with:

3 Hearts.

3 No Trump.

4

115 Complete this table using the *Table of Quick Tricks* on page 286.

(NOTE: QT means quick trick.)

2 Q T	$1\frac{1}{2}$ Q T	1 Q T	$\frac{1}{2}$ Q T
A K			

8

116 An opening bid made at the level of 3 or higher to shut out competition is: (See Item 1 in *References*, page 287.)

a *pre-emptive bid.*

a quick trick.

1

117 If partner pre-empts, add the number of quick tricks in your hand. Then add 1 if partner's bid was 4, and 2 if bid was 5.

Assuming partner bid 4 hearts, which would show this?

2(QT) + 1 = 3

2(QT) + 2 = 4

3

118 Turn to the *Table of Quick Tricks.*

If you hold the Ace and Queen of a particular suit, you have:

2 quick tricks.

$2\frac{1}{2}$ quick tricks.

7

119 Which shows that we are vulnerable?

WE	THEY
40	30
60 60	90

WE	THEY
120	

6

120 Use the *Table of Quick Tricks.* How many quick tricks does this hand have?

2

1	2	3	4	5	6	7	8
☑☐	3	☑☐	☑☐	BOTH	BOTH	NEITHER $1\frac{1}{2}$	AQ | A | Kx / KQ

121 You are ________ when you and partner

win a game toward rubber. 1

---

122 Remember the A, K, Q, J, and 10 are honors. When you have support for partner's Diamonds and hold ♦J 10 5 2 which do you promote 1 point?

Jack	Ten

8

---

123 You hold:

If partner opened with 1 Club, you (would/would not) promote your honors in Clubs 1 point. 6

---

124 If you have trump support for partner's

Spade bid, the Ten of Spades is worth:

0 points.	1 point.

5

---

125 Match these. Assume trump support.

1) J-6-2	a. 4 points
2) J-10-3-2	b. 3 points
3) K-7-5	c. 2 points
4) J-9-5-3	d. 1 point
5) Q-J-8-4	

4

---

126 Assume No Trump support. Match.

a. 10-8-6-2	1) 4 points
b. J-10-3-2	2) 3 points
c. K-7-5	3) 2 points
d. J-9-5-3	4) 1 point
	5) 0 points

2

---

127 Which hand has 4 quick tricks? 3

---

128 Partner opens with a pre-emptive bid of 3 Clubs. You hold:
You are not vulnerable. Using the *Table of Quick Tricks* and Chart 2, determine your best response to partner's bid. 7

1	2	3	4	5	6	7	8
vulnerable	a. 5) b. 4) c. 2) d. 4)	NEITHER	1) d. 2) c. 3) a. 4) c. 5) a.	[✓] [ ]	would not (The K-Q is worth more than 4 points.)	pass	[✓] [ ]

129 If you have adequate trump support in partner's suit (Spades) and raise partner to the 2 level, which card would you promote one point?

	Q♠	10♠	8

130 In order to determine whether you should respond to partner's pre-emptive bid, you add the number of __________ __________ in your hand and the denomination of partner's hand. 1

131 Assume that neither you nor partner uses the Club Convention. Which is the correct response to partner's 1 NT with this hand?

♠A Q 10 6 3 ♥J 7 2 ♦K Q 10 ♣8 2

2 No Trump	4 No Trump	5

132 You respond with 7 No Trump to partner's opener of 2 No Trump when you hold:

12 or more points.	15 or more points.	4

133 You and partner are vulnerable. Partner opens with 3 Diamonds. You hold:
Use the *Table of Quick Tricks* and Chart 2 to arrive at your correct answering bid. 6

134 If you hold 15 or more points and partner opens with 2 No Trump, your correct response is: *

7 No Trump.	3 No Trump.	2

135 So far, we have considered that right-hand opponent has:

bid.	passed.	7

136 When opponent bids between opening bidder and responder, responder's bid is called a *free bid.*
Which situation illustrates a free bid? (N is opening bidder.)

N	E	N	E	3
1♦	1♥	1♠	1 NT	
S	W	S	W	
1 NT	pass	2♠	pass	

1	2	3	4	5	6	7	8
quick tricks	[✓][ ]	BOTH	[ ][✓]	NEITHER 3 No Trump	pass	[ ][✓]	[✓][ ] (The 10 is not a high-card honor.)

137 When opponent passes between opening bidder and responder, the responder's bid is called a *courtesy bid.*

Which illustrates a courtesy bid?

E	S
1♠	1 NT
W	**N**
1♥	pass

E	S
1♠	pass
W	**N**
2♥	pass

4

138 Charts 2 and 3 are to be used with the:

free bid.

courtesy bid.

5

139 In a courtesy bid:

Opponent bids between opening bidder and responder.

Opponent bids between opening bidder and responder.

7

140 Partner opened with 2 No Trump.

What is your response with this hand?

8

141 Match these.

a. free bid
b. opening bid
c. courtesy bid

1) a bid made by responder after opponent passes
2) the first bid made during the auction
3) a bid made by opening bidder after opponent passes
4) a bid made by responder after opponent bids

3

142 Partner bid 1 Spade.

a. How many points are there here?

b. What is your correct response?

1

143

N	E	S	W
pass	1♦	1♥	1 NT

West's bid is a:

courtesy bid.

free bid.

2

144 To make a free bid you must have at least 9 high-card and distribution points. If partner opened with 1 Heart and opponent bid 1 Spade, with which hand would you bid?

♠ 9 4 2
♥ K J 10 9 5 2
♦ J
♣ Q 7 5

♠ A Q J 6 3
♥ none
♦ 10 7 6 5
♣ 9 8 3 2

6

1	2	3	4	5	6	7	8
a. 18 points b. 2 Diamonds	☐☑	a. 4) b. 2) c. 1)	☐☑	☐☑	BOTH	NEITHER Opponent passes.	4 No Trump

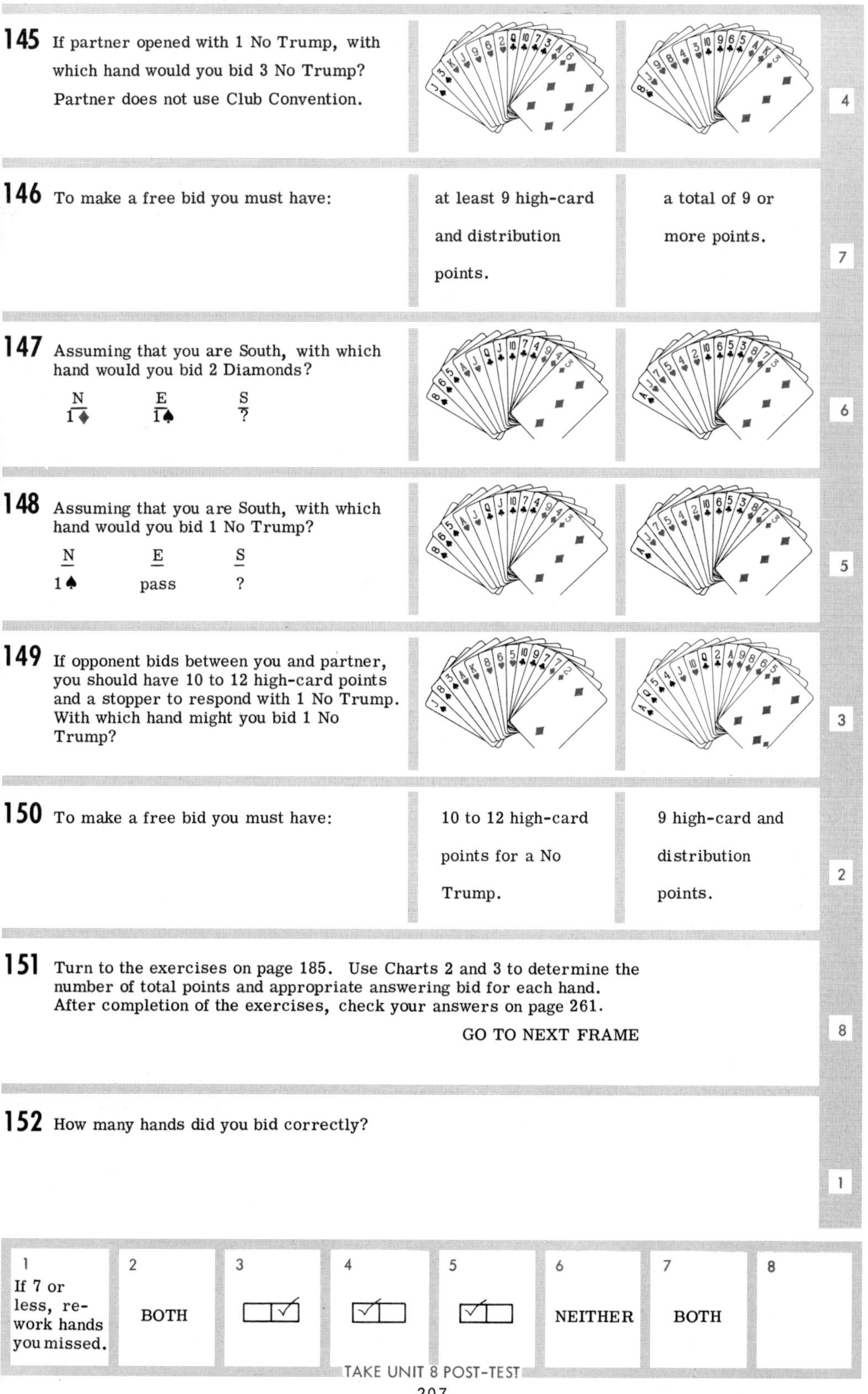

145 If partner opened with 1 No Trump, with which hand would you bid 3 No Trump? Partner does not use Club Convention. 4

146 To make a free bid you must have:

at least 9 high-card and distribution points.

a total of 9 or more points. 7

147 Assuming that you are South, with which hand would you bid 2 Diamonds?

N	E	S
1♦	1♠	?

6

148 Assuming that you are South, with which hand would you bid 1 No Trump?

N	E	S
1♠	pass	?

5

149 If opponent bids between you and partner, you should have 10 to 12 high-card points and a stopper to respond with 1 No Trump. With which hand might you bid 1 No Trump? 3

150 To make a free bid you must have:

10 to 12 high-card points for a No Trump.

9 high-card and distribution points. 2

151 Turn to the exercises on page 185. Use Charts 2 and 3 to determine the number of total points and appropriate answering bid for each hand. After completion of the exercises, check your answers on page 261.

GO TO NEXT FRAME 8

152 How many hands did you bid correctly? 1

1	2	3	4	5	6	7	8
If 7 or less, rework hands you missed.	BOTH	☐☑	☑☐	☑☐	NEITHER	BOTH	

TAKE UNIT 8 POST-TEST

COURTESY OF MARVIN KOHN

The tables are turned. The famous Sophie Tucker giving pointers to Mr. Goren — however, on gin rummy.

UNIT 9

rebids by either partner

This unit provides the student with a method for evaluating the combined point count of his partner's and his own hand. With a careful analysis of both the opening bid and response, the beginner is shown in which instance the partnership should "go for game" and in what circumstances it is more profitable to stop short of game.

PRE- AND POST-TEST

1. If you and your partner's combined point count is 26, you may make game in [No Trump/Spades/(both)/(neither)].

2. How many points are needed to make game in a minor suit?

3. A contract of 4 Hearts means that you and your partner should have a combined point count of (   ).

4. Which contract, if made, shows game in a minor suit?
   (4 Clubs/5 Spades/both/neither)

5. If you are the opening bidder and hold 16 points, how many points must your partner hold in order to make game in a major suit?

6. Match.

a.	10 tricks	I.	small slam	1)	7 Clubs
b.	11 tricks	II.	29 points	2)	4 Hearts
c.	12 tricks	III.	grand slam	3)	5 Diamonds
d.	13 tricks	IV.	26 points	4)	6 Spades

   a. (   )(   )   b. (   )(   )   c. (   )(   )   d. (   )(   )

7. If opponents hold [the Ace/the King/either the Ace or King/(neither of these)] in the trump suit, they will prevent a grand slam.

8. Which contract, if successful, will produce 100 points below the line?
   (3 No Trump/5 Clubs/both/neither)

9. a. How many points are needed in both hands for a grand slam?
   b. How many points are needed in both hands for a small slam?

10. How many points are needed in both hands to make a contract of 3 No Trump?

USE OF ***RESPONSES TO OPENING SUIT BIDS*** CHART

You opened with 2 hearts.

Partner responded with 2 No Trump.

Look at Chart 2 - *Responses to Opening Suit Bids*. Let's follow what your partner must have been thinking when he responded with 2 No Trump.

1. You opened with 2 of a suit, so he said *Yes* to that box. He is now on the right side of the chart.

2. He did not bid in your suit, so he cannot have either a biddable suit or a sufficient number of points. So we look down the column which has the *Did partner open 2 of a suit* box.

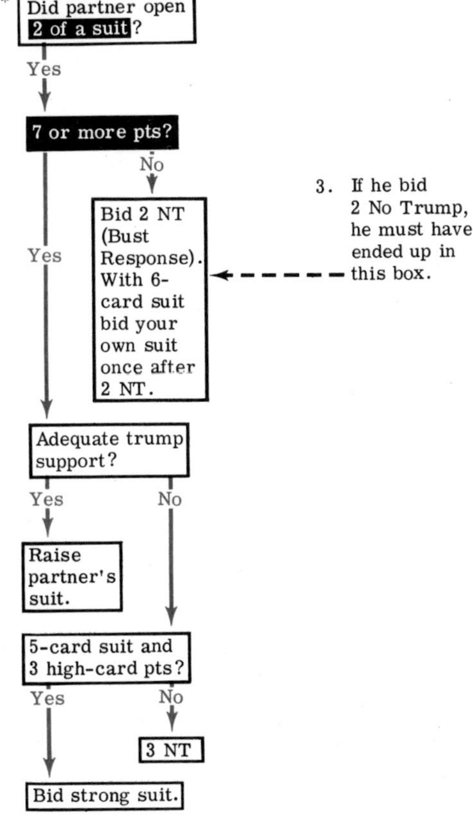

3. If he bid 2 No Trump, he must have ended up in this box.

4. So he may have no points at all, or he may have as many as 6 points.

GO ON TO FRAME 9.

EXERCISES *

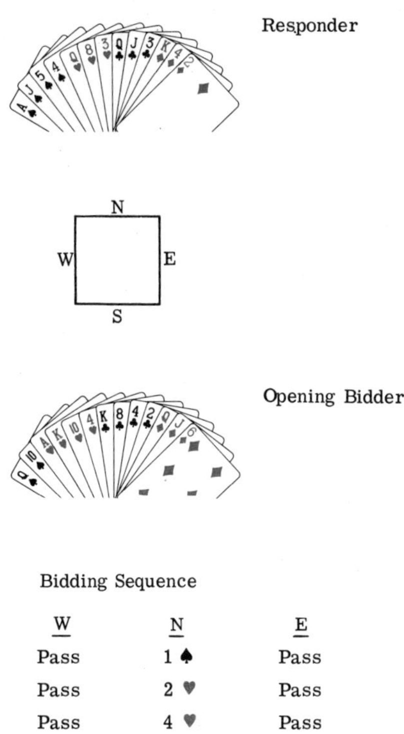

Bidding Sequence

S	W	N	E
1 ♥	Pass	1 ♠	Pass
2 ♣	Pass	2 ♥	Pass
3 ♥	Pass	4 ♥	Pass
Pass	Pass		

a. What is the contract?

b. How many tricks must contractors take to make their contract?

c. How many points will contractors score below the line if they make their contract?

d. Use Chart 2, *Responses to Opening Suit Bids,* to determine responder's maximum possible points. Hint: Look at responder's first bid.

e. Use Chart 2 to determine responder's minimum possible points. Use responder's first bid.

f. What is the actual point count in contractors' hands?

g. Is the combined point count sufficient to make game?

* These exercises are to be worked as directed in the text frames of Unit 9.

1 (Before you begin, take the Pre-Test for Unit 9.) The team which makes 100 or more points below the line makes game. Which team has made game?

WE	THEY
30	20
120	40
	100

WE | THEY 7

2 Which shows that THEY have made a rubber game?

WE	THEY
500	
20	
100	
	120
120	

WE	THEY
	30
	90
	60
120	70

3

3 Which contract, if made, will produce game?

4 Hearts | 5 Clubs 4

4 Usually, if the point count in the combined hands is 26, you can make game in either No Trump or a major suit.

If you hold 21 points, how many points must partner have to make game in Spades? 8

5 Usually, if the combined point count is 26, you can make game in either No Trump or a major suit.
If partner opens with 1 Spade and holds 20 points, which hand would make game? 6

6 If the combined point count is 26, you may have game in which of the following contracts?

3 No Trump | 5 Clubs 5

7 If you and partner have 29 points in your combined hands, you have a good chance to make game in a minor suit. In which suit might you make game with 29 points?

Diamonds | Clubs 1

8 Turn to Chart 2, *Responses to Opening Suit Bids*. Then read *Use of Responses to Opening Suit Bids Chart* on page 215.

GO TO NEXT FRAME 2

1	2	3	4	5	6	7	8
BOTH		NEITHER	BOTH	☑☐	☑☐	BOTH	5 points

9 You have to figure out what partner was thinking when he returned your bid.

You bid 1 Diamond; he passed.

You know he must have:

more than 6 points.	less than 6 points.	5

10 Use Chart 2. The bidding sequence:

N	E	S
1♠	pass	2♠

What is the maximum number of points South holds?

10 points	6 points	1

11 You have a good chance to make game if you have: (Match.)

1) ( ) points in a major suit.

2) ( ) points in a minor suit.

a. 26
b. 27
c. 28
d. 29

2

12 (Use the chart.) The bidding sequence:

S	W	N	E
pass	1♦	pass	2♦

Which is the minimum number of points East holds?

4 points	10 points	4

13 To make game in a minor suit, you and partner should have:

26 points.	29 points.	3

14 Which contract, if made, shows game in the minor suit?

4 Clubs	5 Spades	8

15 *Maximum* means the *most* points your partner can have.
You have decided partner ended up here.
Look at the preceding box.
What is the maximum points partner can have?

16—18 pts? and 4-3-3-3 distribution? — Yes → Jump to 3 NT. / No

16	18	7

16 26 points are needed in order to make game in:

a major suit.	No Trump.	6

1	2	3	4	5	6	7	8
☑☐	1) a. 2) d.	☐☑	NEITHER 6 points	☐☑	BOTH	☐☑	NEITHER 5 Clubs or Diamonds

17 (Use your chart.) Partner bids 1 Heart, right-hand opponent passes, and responder bids 2 Hearts. Opening bidder knows responder has:	6 to 10 points.	11 to 12 points.	1
18 *Minimum* means the *least* points your partner can have. You have decided partner ended up here. Look at the preceding box. What is the minimum points partner can have? [16—18 pts? and 4-3-3-3 distribution? Yes → Jump to 3 NT. / No]	16	18	4
19 Twenty-nine points are necessary to make game in:	Diamonds.	Clubs.	7
20 If partner raises your suit to the 2 level, you know that he has a minimum of 6 points. You bid 1 Spade and hold 20 points. If partner bids 2 Spades, should you go for game?			3
21 If you have 15 points and bid 1 Club, and partner raises you to 2 Clubs, you know that you and partner have a minimum of:	25 points.	21 points.	8
22 If you have 13 points and bid 1 Heart, and partner raises you to 2 Hearts, you know that you and partner have a minimum of:	23 points.	19 points.	2

23 a. To make game in a minor suit, partners need a total of ( ) points in their combined hands.

b. To make game in either No Trump or a major suit, the combined hands must have at least ( ) points. 5

24 You opened with 1 Club, and partner said 1 No Trump. You determined partner made this decision.

9—11 pts? Yes → 1 NT

a. What is his minimum number of points?

b. What is his maximum number of points? 6

1	2	3	4	5	6	7	8
☑☐	☐☑	Yes	☑☐	a. 29 b. 26	a. 9 b. 11	BOTH	☐☑

25	How many tricks are needed to make a contract of 4 Spades?	4 tricks and book	10 tricks	7
26	What is the minimum number of points the responder must have to raise partner's opening suit?			1
27	Opening bidder has 16 points and opens with 1 Spade. Responder bids 2 Spades. This means that responder has:	6 to 9 points.	6 to 10 points.	4
28	Opening bidder has 16 points and opens with 1 Diamond. Responder holds 9 points and bids 2 Diamonds. Should opening bidder and responder go to game with a contract of 5 Diamonds?			3
29	Which contract, if made, is enough for game?	4 Clubs	2 No Trump	5
30	Which contract, if made, will produce 12 tricks?	5 Spades	6 Diamonds	2
31	If contractors bid and make 12 tricks, they have made a small slam. Which is a small slam?	6 No Trump	4 Hearts	6
32	If responder raises the opening bid to the 2 level, responder has a maximum of 10 points. If opening bidder holds 15 points and bids 1 Club, and responder raises to 2 Clubs, should they go for game in a minor suit?			8

1	2	3	4	5	6	7	8
six (6 points)	☐ ☑	No	☐ ☑	NEITHER	☑ ☐	BOTH	No

33	If you have 15 points and bid 1 Diamond, and partner raises you to 2 Diamonds, you know that you and partner have a maximum of:	25 points.	30 points.	5
34	If opening bidder opens with 1 Spade and you bid 1 No Trump, opening bidder knows that you have:	trump support in his suit.	4 small cards in his suit.	4
35	If you bid and make 12 tricks, you have made a:	grand slam.	small slam.	6
36	Usually 33 points are necessary in order to make a small slam. How many points must you have to go for a small slam if partner holds 21 points and bids 2 Spades?	33 points	21 points	1
37	Which shows the combined point count necessary to make a small slam?	26 points	29 points	2
38	Partner bids 2 Hearts. If you have 6 points, you would bid:	2 No Trump.	3 Hearts.	3
39	If you and partner have 37 points in your combined hands, you can bid and usually take 13 tricks. Which contract, if made, would mean 13 tricks?	7 No Trump	7 Diamonds	7
40	A small slam is:	13 tricks.	12 tricks.	8

1	2	3	4	5	6	7	8
NEITHER 12 points (12 + 21 = 33)	NEITHER 33 points	[✓][ ]	NEITHER	[✓][ ]	[ ][✓]	BOTH	[ ][✓]

41	If you take 13 tricks, you have made a grand slam. Which contract, if made, would produce a grand slam?	4 Spades	6 Hearts	5
42	Match. a. grand slam b. minor suit game c. major suit or No Trump game d. small slam	1) 33 points 2) 26 points 3) 37 points 4) 29 points 5) 25 points		6
43	You bid in Clubs. Which card, if held by the opponents, would prevent a grand slam? (Remember: There are 40 high-card points in the deck.)	A ♣	K ♦	8
44	Look at Chart 6, *Rebids by Either Partner*, on page 284. Which box is directly below [Enter] ?	Analyze bidding to arrive at partner's **minimum** possible points.	Analyze bidding to arrive at partner's **maximum** possible points.	2
45	To arrive at partner's maximum possible points when you are the opening bidder, look at:	Chart 2 - *Responses to Opening Suit Bids.*	Chart 3 - *Responses to Opening No Trump Bids.*	1
46	Look at Chart 6. If combined hands total 23 points, which do you read?	Analyze bidding to arrive at partner's **minimum** possible points.	Stop short of game as soon as partner bids No Trump or fails to bid a new suit.	7
47	This bidding sequence shows that N-S has: N / E / S / W 1♦ / pass / 2♦ / pass 2 NT / pass / pass / pass	more than 25 points.	37 or more points.	3
48	Assume that you are the opening bidder. You bid 2 Spades and hold 23 points. Partner raises you to 3 Spades. What should you do?	Analyze bidding to arrive at partner's **minimum** possible points.	Stop short of game as soon as partner bids No Trump or fails to bid a new suit.	4

1	2	3	4	5	6	7	8
BOTH	[ ][✓]	NEITHER 25 or less points.	[✓][ ]	NEITHER 7 of a suit or No Trump	a. 3) b. 4) c. 2) d. 1)	[ ][✓]	[✓][ ]

49	Look at Chart 2. This bidding shows that partner has a minimum of: N E S W 1♠ pass 3♥ pass	19 points.	13 points.	3
50	Use Chart 6. If analysis reveals that you and partner hold 35 points, you would:	go for grand slam.	go for small slam.	5
51	Use Chart 3. If you bid 1 No Trump and responder bids 3 No Trump, you know that he has a maximum of:	14 points.	16 points.	2
52	You hold 16 points and bid 1 No Trump. If partner responds with 3 No Trump, you should:	bid 6 No Trump.	pass.	4
53	You open with 3 No Trump and have 25 points. Partner responds with 7 No Trump. You know that you have a combined minimum of:	26 points.	37 points.	8
54	Partner opens with 2 of a suit and you raise. Partner, who holds 21 points, knows that the combined maximum number of points is:	enough for game in a major suit.	at least 26 points.	6
55	Turn to the exercises on page 217. Answer questions a. and b.			7
56	Each trick bid and made over book in a major suit is worth 30 points. How many points are scored below the line if contractors bid and make 3 Hearts?			1

1	2	3	4	5	6	7	8
90 points	[✓][ ]	[✓][ ]	[ ][✓]	[ ][✓]	BOTH	a. 4 Hearts b. 10 tricks	[ ][✓]

57 If you and partner hold 26 points in your combined hands, you have enough for game in:

Clubs.	Diamonds.

4

58 Each trick over book that is bid and made in a minor suit is worth 20 points. How many points are scored below the line if contractors bid and make 2 Diamonds?

6

59 If successful, which contract would make 120 points below the line?

4 Spades	6 Clubs

1

60 Which score sheet shows the correct answer for question c. in exercises on page 217?

WE	THEY
80	

WE	THEY
120	

8

61 If you hold 19 points, what is the minimum point count that partner must have for you to make a small slam?

10 points	14 points

2

62 Turn to the exercises on page 217 and answer questions d. and e.

7

63 Answer questions f. and g. in the exercises on page 217.

5

1	2	3	4	5	6	7	8
BOTH	☐☑		NEITHER Spades, Hearts, or No Trump.	f. 28 points g. Yes	40 points	d. 18 points e. 10 points	☐☑

TAKE UNIT 9 POST-TEST

UNIT 10

the opening lead

After preliminary work with sequences, honor sequences, and complete sequences, the student is taught to observe the importance of the bidding in order to arrive at a proper opening lead. Toward the end of the unit, the beginner learns the appropriate leads to both suit and No Trump contracts.

PRE- AND POST-TEST

1. Which is a complete honor sequence?
   - a. two honor cards ranking next to each other in the same suit
   - b. three cards ranking next to each other in the same suit
   - c. (both)
   - d. (neither)

2. Which suit shows a sequence?

3.

N	E	S	W
1♥	pass	2♣	pass
2♦	pass	3♥	pass
4♥	pass	pass	pass

   - a. Who is declarer?
   - b. Which player makes the opening lead?
   - c. Did dummy bid a suit not supported by declarer?

4. Assume that you must make the opening lead.

S	W	N	E
1♦	1♥	2♦	pass
3♦	pass	4♦	pass
5♦	pass	pass	pass

   - a. Did partner bid?
   - b. Did you bid suit which was not supported by partner?

5. Assume that you make the opening lead.

The bidding:

N	E	S	W
1 ♦	pass	2 ♣	pass
3 ♦	pass	5 ♦	double
pass	pass	pass	

You hold:

a. Your best opening lead is the __________.

The bidding:

W	N	E	S
1 ♦	1 ♥	1 NT	pass
2 NT	pass	3 NT	pass
pass	pass		

You hold:

b. Your best opening lead is the __________.

EXERCISES

1.

N	E	S	W
1 ♣	1 ♠	pass	1 NT
pass	2 NT	pass	3 NT

N holds:

N's best opening lead is __________.

2.

W	N	E	S
1 ♠	1 NT	pass	2 NT
pass	3 NT	pass	pass
double			

E holds:

E's best opening lead is __________.

3.

S	W	N	E
1 ♥	pass	1 ♠	pass
1 NT	pass	2 NT	pass
3 NT	pass	pass	pass

W holds:

W's best opening lead is __________.

4.

E	S	W	N
1 ♦	pass	1 NT	pass
2 NT	pass	3 NT	pass
pass			

N holds:

N's best opening lead is __________.

5.

N	E	S	W
pass	1 NT	pass	6 NT
pass	pass	pass	

S holds:

S's best opening lead is __________.

6.

S	W	N	E
1 ♠	2 ♥	2 ♠	pass
3 ♦	3 ♥	3 ♠	pass
4 ♠	pass	pass	pass

W holds:

W's best opening lead is __________.

7.

W	N	E	S
1 ♦	1 ♥	pass	2 ♥
pass	3 ♥	pass	4 ♥

E holds:

E's best opening lead is __________.

8.

W	N	E	S
1♣	1♠	pass	2♠
pass	3♠	pass	4♠

E holds:

E's best opening lead is __________.

9.

N	E	S	W
1♦	pass	1♥	pass
2♦	pass	2♠	pass
3♥	pass	4♥	pass

W holds:

W's best opening lead is __________.

10.

E	S	W	N
2♣	pass	3♣	pass
4♣	pass	5♣	pass
pass	pass		

S holds:

S's best opening lead is __________.

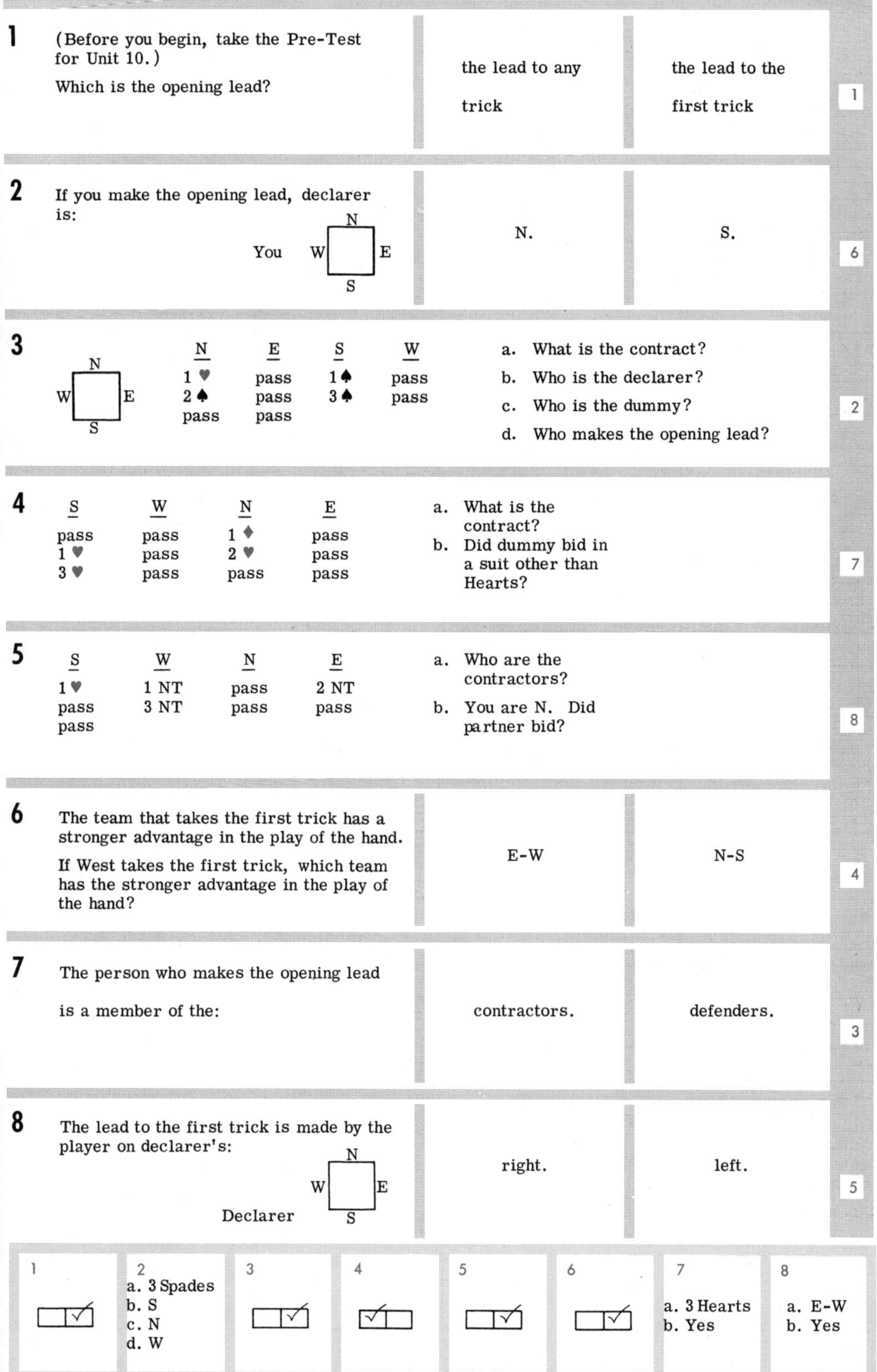

1	(Before you begin, take the Pre-Test for Unit 10.) Which is the opening lead?	the lead to any trick	the lead to the first trick	1
2	If you make the opening lead, declarer is: You W [N / E / S]	N.	S.	6
3	N / W E / S N: 1 ♥, 2 ♠, pass E: pass, pass, pass S: 1 ♠, 3 ♠ W: pass, pass	a. What is the contract? b. Who is the declarer? c. Who is the dummy? d. Who makes the opening lead?		2
4	S: pass, 1 ♥, 3 ♥ W: pass, pass, pass N: 1 ♦, 2 ♥, pass E: pass, pass, pass	a. What is the contract? b. Did dummy bid in a suit other than Hearts?		7
5	S: 1 ♥, pass, pass W: 1 NT, 3 NT N: pass, pass E: 2 NT, pass	a. Who are the contractors? b. You are N. Did partner bid?		8
6	The team that takes the first trick has a stronger advantage in the play of the hand. If West takes the first trick, which team has the stronger advantage in the play of the hand?	E-W	N-S	4
7	The person who makes the opening lead is a member of the:	contractors.	defenders.	3
8	The lead to the first trick is made by the player on declarer's: W [N / E / S] Declarer	right.	left.	5

1	2	3	4	5	6	7	8
☐ ☑	a. 3 Spades b. S c. N d. W	☐ ☑	☑ ☐	☐ ☑	☐ ☑	a. 3 Hearts b. Yes	a. E-W b. Yes

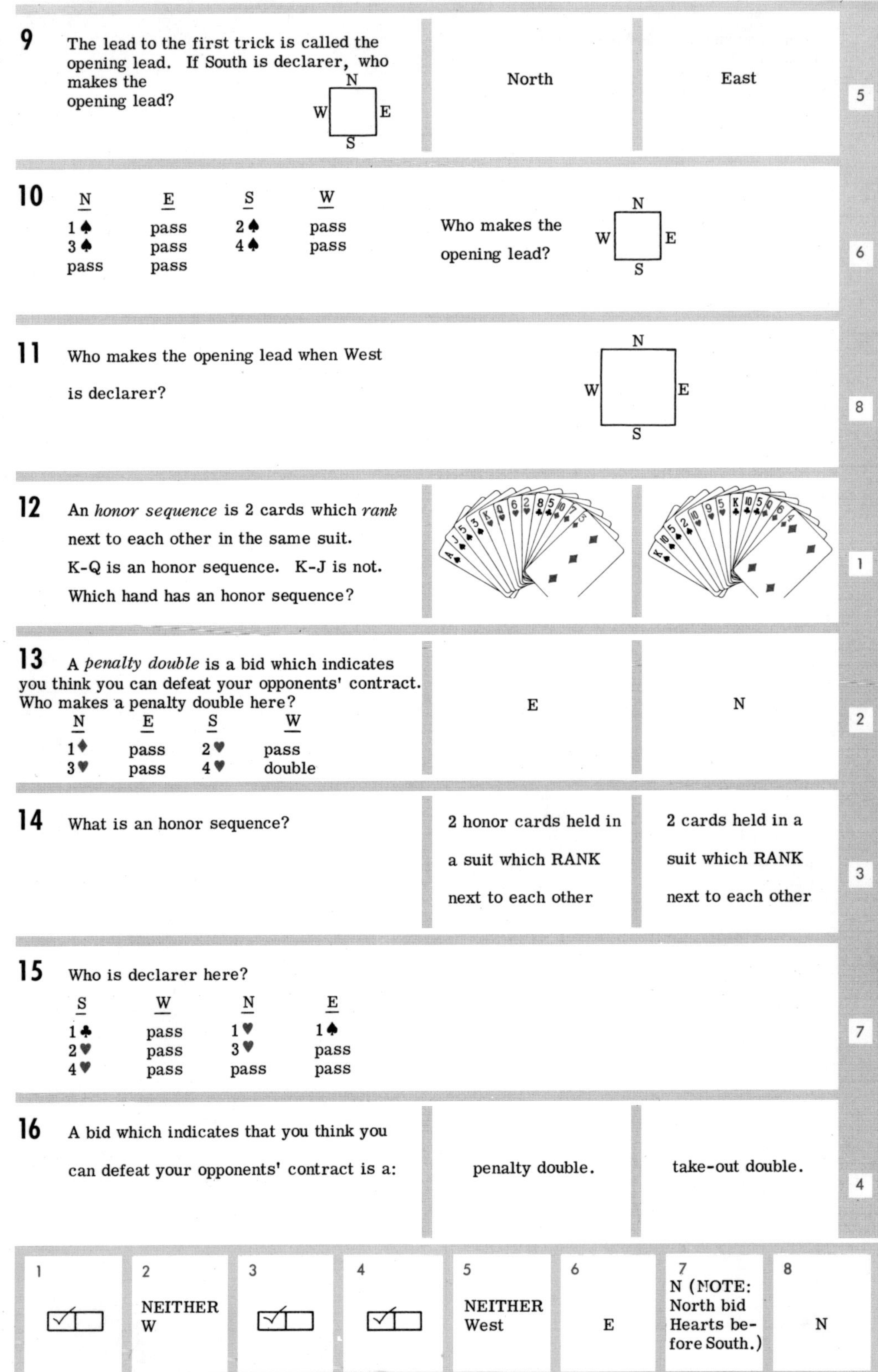

9 The lead to the first trick is called the opening lead. If South is declarer, who makes the opening lead?

N / W E / S

North	East	5

10

N	E	S	W
1♠	pass	2♠	pass
3♠	pass	4♠	pass
pass	pass		

Who makes the opening lead?

N / W E / S

6

11 Who makes the opening lead when West is declarer?

N / W E / S

8

12 An *honor sequence* is 2 cards which *rank* next to each other in the same suit. K-Q is an honor sequence. K-J is not. Which hand has an honor sequence?

1

13 A *penalty double* is a bid which indicates you think you can defeat your opponents' contract. Who makes a penalty double here?

N	E	S	W
1♦	pass	2♥	pass
3♥	pass	4♥	double

E	N	2

14 What is an honor sequence?

2 honor cards held in a suit which RANK next to each other	2 cards held in a suit which RANK next to each other	3

15 Who is declarer here?

S	W	N	E
1♣	pass	1♥	1♠
2♥	pass	3♥	pass
4♥	pass	pass	pass

7

16 A bid which indicates that you think you can defeat your opponents' contract is a:

penalty double.	take-out double.	4

1	2	3	4	5	6	7	8
☑☐	NEITHER W	☑☐	☑☐	NEITHER West	E	N (NOTE: North bid Hearts before South.)	N

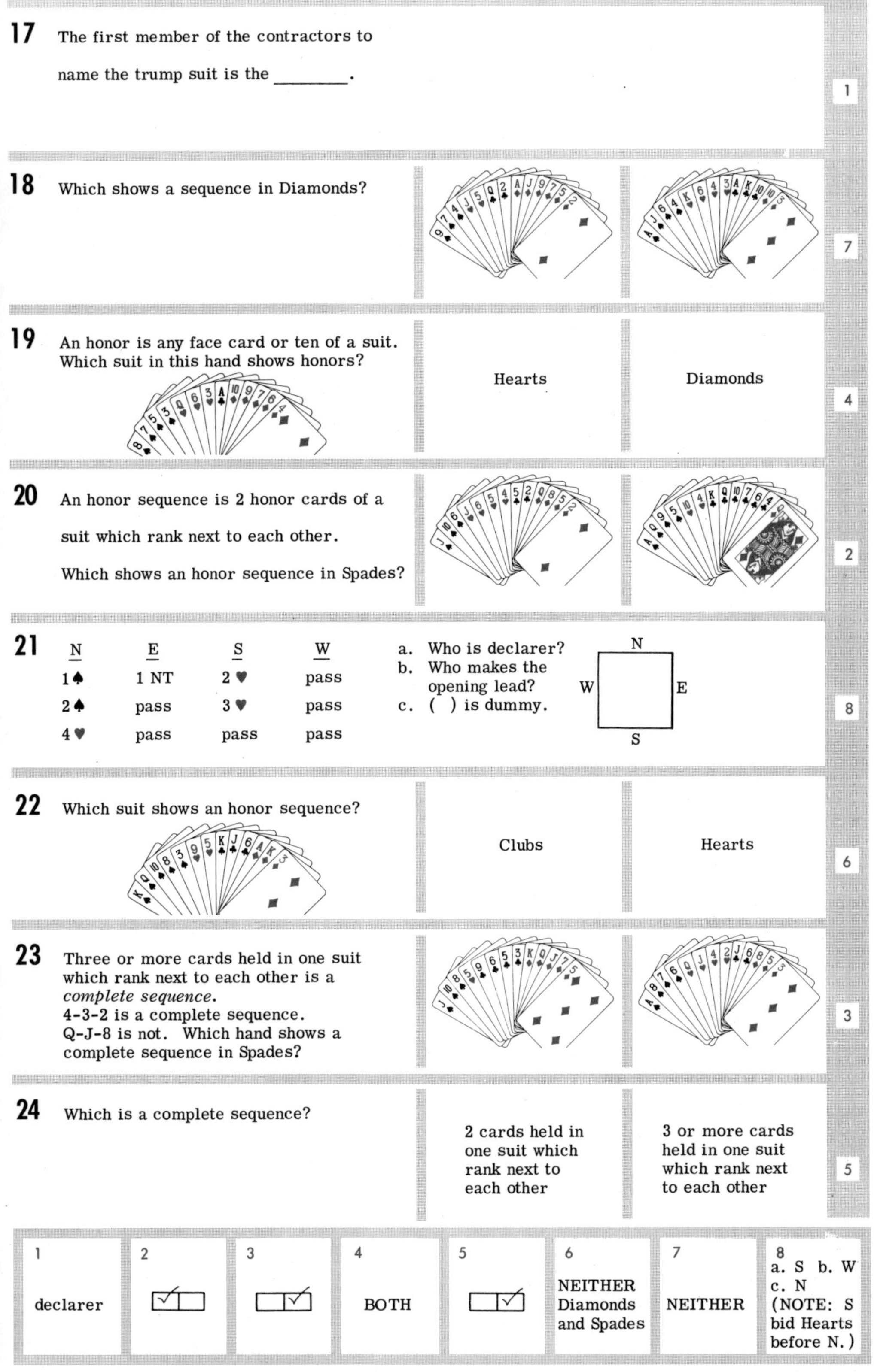

17 The first member of the contractors to name the trump suit is the ________. 1

18 Which shows a sequence in Diamonds? 7

19 An honor is any face card or ten of a suit. Which suit in this hand shows honors?

Hearts | Diamonds 4

20 An honor sequence is 2 honor cards of a suit which rank next to each other. Which shows an honor sequence in Spades? 2

21

N	E	S	W
1♠	1 NT	2♥	pass
2♠	pass	3♥	pass
4♥	pass	pass	pass

a. Who is declarer?
b. Who makes the opening lead?
c. ( ) is dummy.

8

22 Which suit shows an honor sequence?

Clubs | Hearts 6

23 Three or more cards held in one suit which rank next to each other is a *complete sequence*. 4-3-2 is a complete sequence. Q-J-8 is not. Which hand shows a complete sequence in Spades? 3

24 Which is a complete sequence?

2 cards held in one suit which rank next to each other | 3 or more cards held in one suit which rank next to each other 5

1	2	3	4	5	6	7	8
declarer	☑☐	☐☑	BOTH	☐☑	NEITHER Diamonds and Spades	NEITHER	a. S b. W c. N (NOTE: S bid Hearts before N.)

25 Which suit shows a complete sequence?

Spades	Diamonds

8

26 Match these.

a. honor sequence
b. complete sequence

1) 3 cards of a suit which rank next to each other
2) 2 honor cards of a suit which rank next to each other
3) an honor holding above and below an opponent's honor

7

27

N	E	S	W
1♦	pass	1♥	pass
2♦	pass	2♥	pass
3♠	pass	4♠	pass

Did dummy bid a suit not supported by declarer?

1

28 What do we call 2 honor cards ranking next to each other in the same suit?

4

29 Assume that you must make the opening lead.

S	W	N	E
1♠	1 NT	2♥	pass
3♥	pass	4♥	pass
pass	pass		

a. Who is declarer?

b. Did your partner bid?

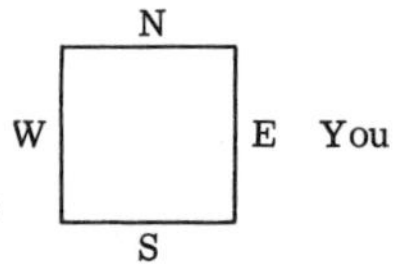

N
W E You
S

3

30 A *complete honor sequence* is 3 or more honor cards ranking next to each other in a suit.

Which hand shows a complete honor sequence?

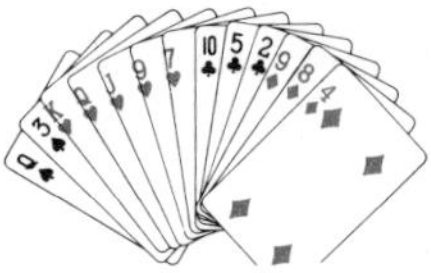

2

31 Assume that you (S) must make the opening lead.

W	N	E	S
1♣	pass	2♦	pass
3♦	pass	4♦	pass
5♦	double	pass	pass
pass			

Who doubled West?

partner	North

6

32 Which suit shows a complete honor sequence?

Spades	Clubs

5

1	2	3	4	5	6	7	8
Yes	☐☑	a. N b. Yes	honor sequence	☐☑	BOTH	a. 2) b. 1)	BOTH

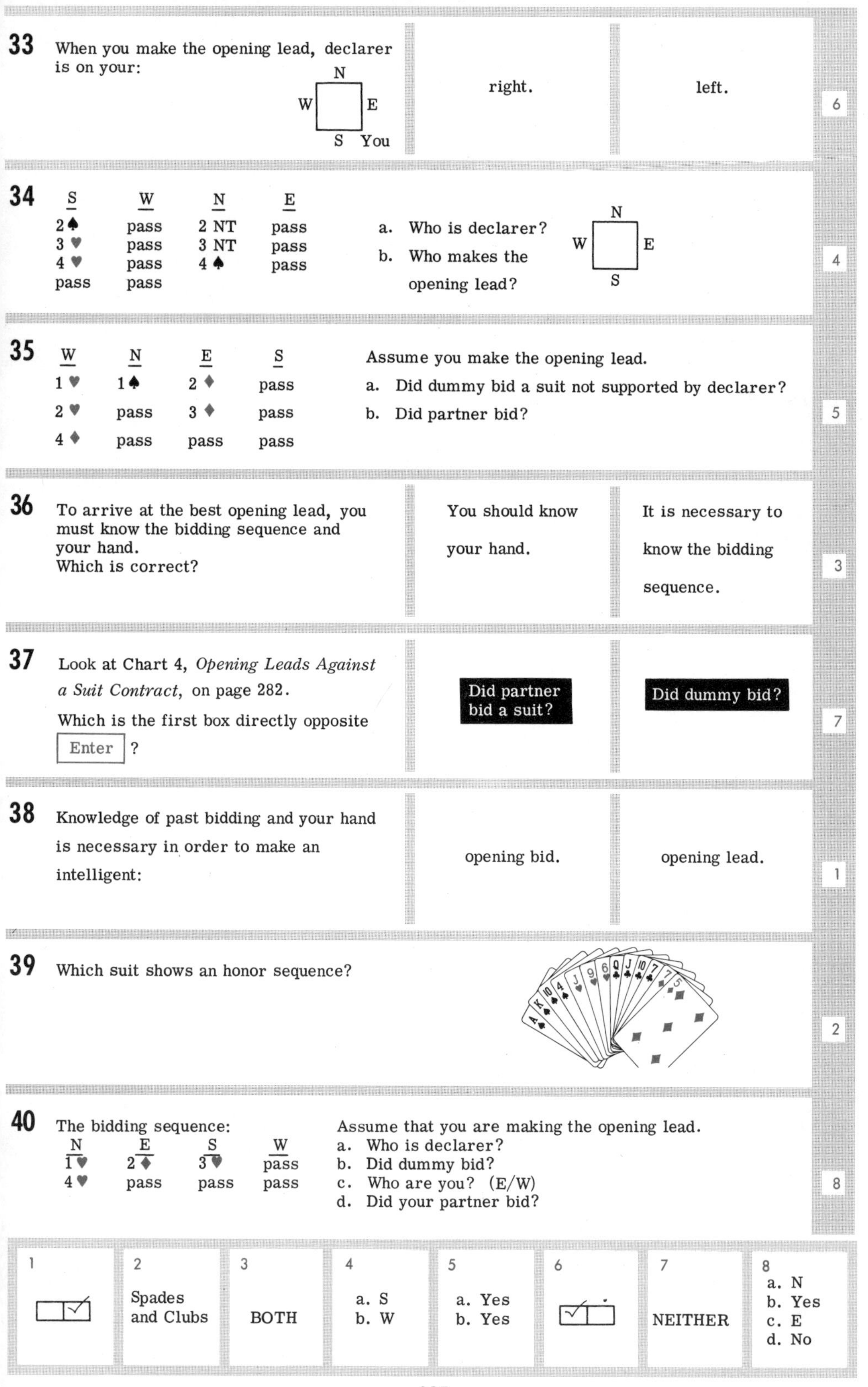

33 When you make the opening lead, declarer is on your:

right.	left.

6

34

S	W	N	E
2♠	pass	2 NT	pass
3♥	pass	3 NT	pass
4♥	pass	4♠	pass
pass	pass		

a. Who is declarer?
b. Who makes the opening lead?

4

35

W	N	E	S
1♥	1♠	2♦	pass
2♥	pass	3♦	pass
4♦	pass	pass	pass

Assume you make the opening lead.
a. Did dummy bid a suit not supported by declarer?
b. Did partner bid?

5

36 To arrive at the best opening lead, you must know the bidding sequence and your hand.
Which is correct?

You should know your hand.	It is necessary to know the bidding sequence.

3

37 Look at Chart 4, *Opening Leads Against a Suit Contract*, on page 282.
Which is the first box directly opposite [Enter] ?

Did partner bid a suit?	Did dummy bid?

7

38 Knowledge of past bidding and your hand is necessary in order to make an intelligent:

opening bid.	opening lead.

1

39 Which suit shows an honor sequence?

2

40 The bidding sequence:

N	E	S	W
1♥	2♦	3♥	pass
4♥	pass	pass	pass

Assume that you are making the opening lead.
a. Who is declarer?
b. Did dummy bid?
c. Who are you? (E/W)
d. Did your partner bid?

8

1	2	3	4	5	6	7	8
☐☑	Spades and Clubs	BOTH	a. S b. W	a. Yes b. Yes	☑☐	NEITHER	a. N b. Yes c. E d. No

41 Look at Chart 4. If partner bid a suit, which box would you look at next?

Do you have the Ace of partner's suit?	Did bidding indicate that dummy may have a short side suit?

7

42 Which is an honor sequence?

2 honor cards ranking next to each other in the same suit	3 or more honor cards ranking next to each other in the same suit

8

43 Which suit has a complete sequence?

Spades	Hearts

5

44 The bidding:

W	N	E	S
pass	pass	pass	1♥
pass	2♣	2♠	3♣
3♠	4♣	pass	pass
pass			

a. Who makes the opening lead?
b. Who is dummy?
c. Did dummy bid a suit not supported by declarer?

6

45 Look at Chart 4.

Which do you do if partner bids a suit of which you have the Ace?

Lead lowest card.	Lead Ace.

4

46 Which suit has a complete honor sequence?

1

47 Which do you do if partner did not bid a suit and you have a suit with a sequence of 3 or more honors?

Lead highest, except with A-K, lead K.	Lead highest, except with A-K, lead K.

2

48 Follow Chart 4.
The bidding sequence:

N	E	S	W
1♥	2♦	3♥	pass
4♥	pass	pass	pass

a. Who is declarer? E holds hand at right.
b. What is E's best opening lead?

3

1	2	3	4	5	6	7	8
Clubs	BOTH	a. N b. ♦K	[ ] [✓]	NEITHER	a. E b. S c. Yes	[✓] [ ]	[✓] [ ]

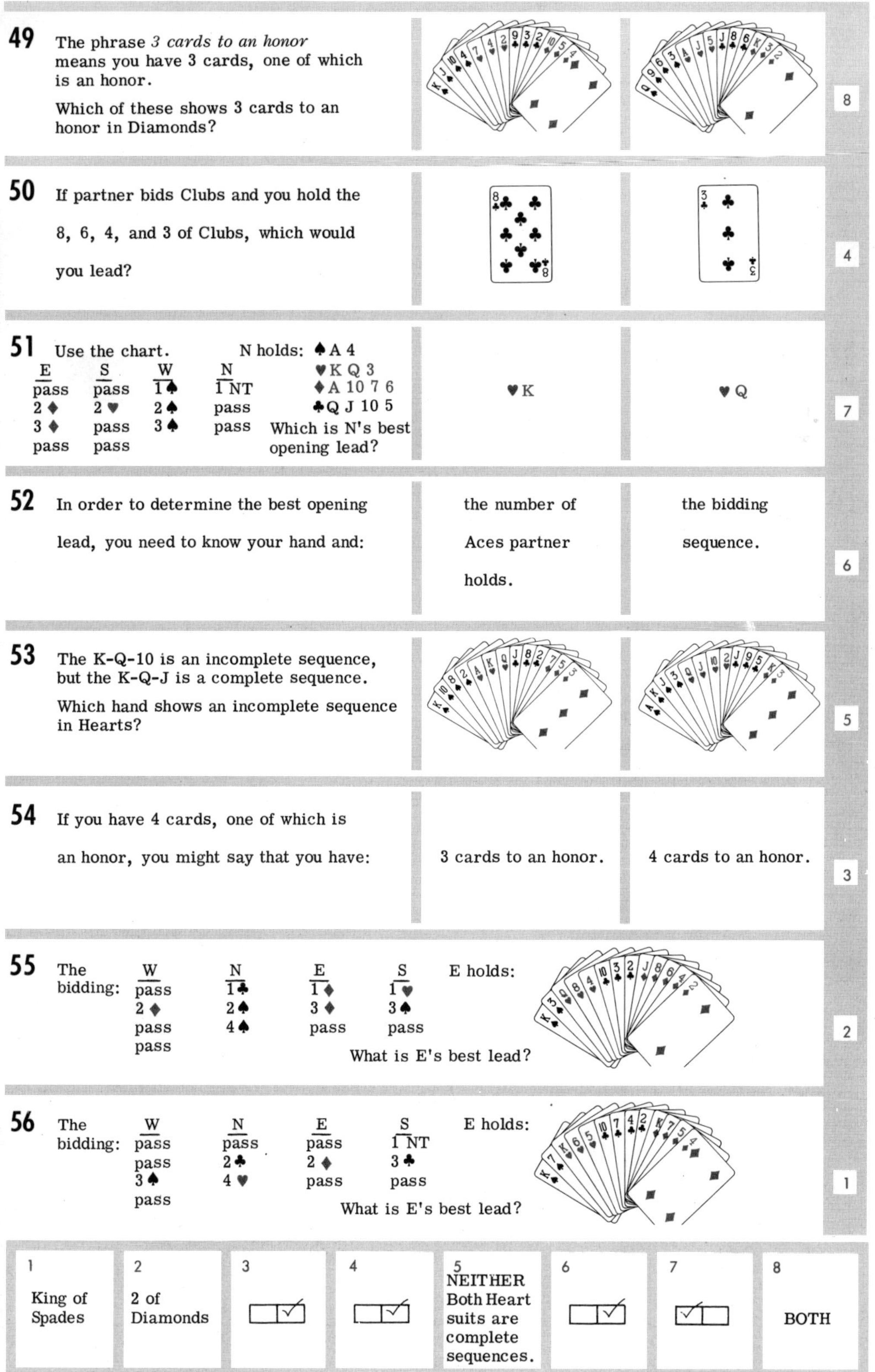

49 The phrase *3 cards to an honor* means you have 3 cards, one of which is an honor.

Which of these shows 3 cards to an honor in Diamonds?

8

50 If partner bids Clubs and you hold the 8, 6, 4, and 3 of Clubs, which would you lead?

4

51 Use the chart.

E	S	W	N
pass	pass	1♠	1 NT
2♦	2♥	2♠	pass
3♦	pass	3♠	pass
pass	pass		

N holds: ♠A 4 ♥K Q 3 ♦A 10 7 6 ♣Q J 10 5

Which is N's best opening lead?

♥K | ♥Q

7

52 In order to determine the best opening lead, you need to know your hand and:

the number of Aces partner holds. | the bidding sequence.

6

53 The K-Q-10 is an incomplete sequence, but the K-Q-J is a complete sequence.

Which hand shows an incomplete sequence in Hearts?

5

54 If you have 4 cards, one of which is an honor, you might say that you have:

3 cards to an honor. | 4 cards to an honor.

3

55 The bidding:

W	N	E	S
pass	1♣	1♦	1♥
2♦	2♠	3♦	3♠
pass	4♠	pass	pass
pass			

E holds:

What is E's best lead?

2

56 The bidding:

W	N	E	S
pass	pass	pass	1 NT
pass	2♣	2♦	3♣
3♠	4♥	pass	pass
pass			

E holds:

What is E's best lead?

1

1	2	3	4	5	6	7	8
King of Spades	2 of Diamonds	☐☑	☐☑	NEITHER Both Heart suits are complete sequences.	☐☑	☑☐	BOTH

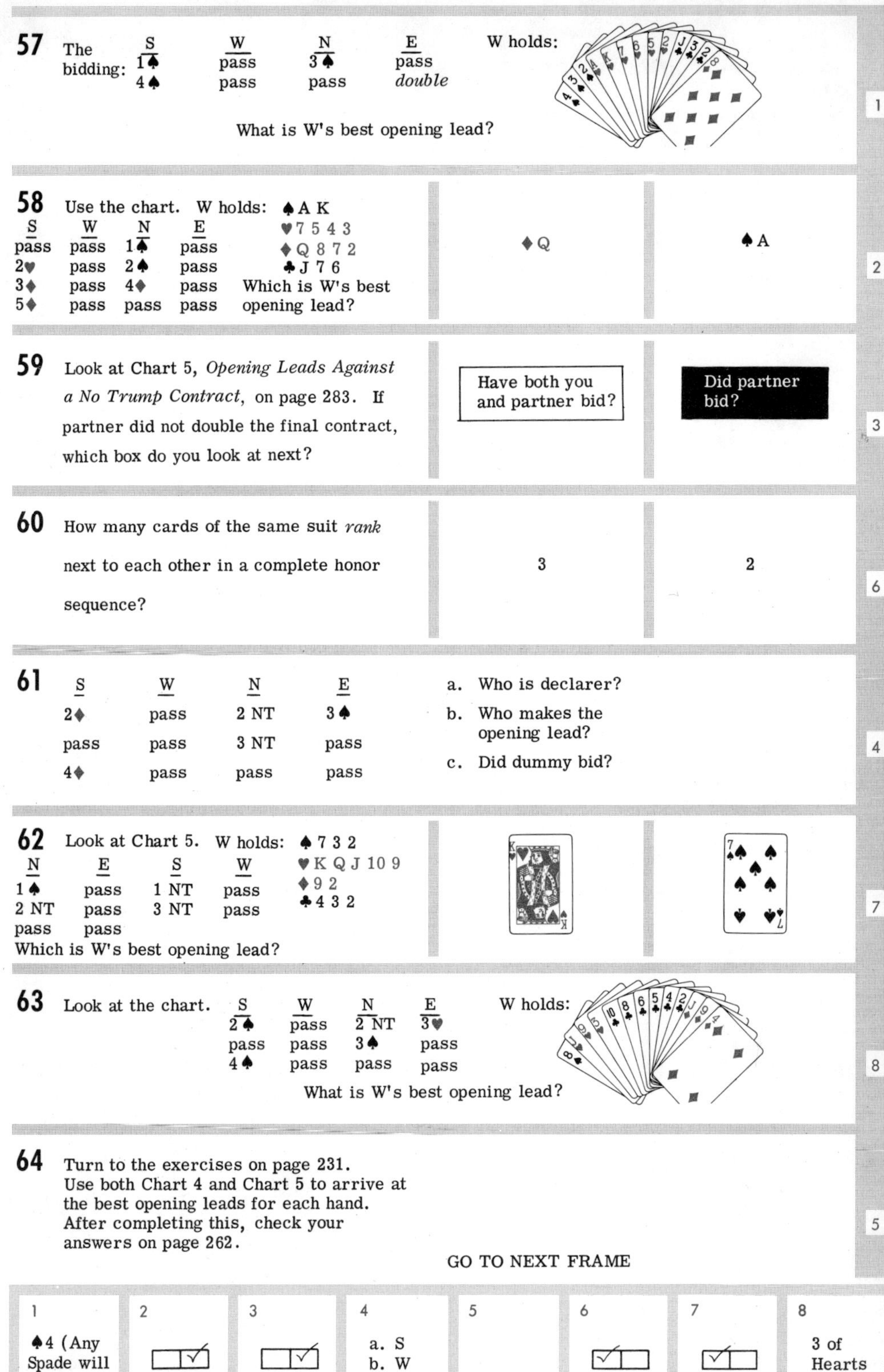

57 The bidding:

S	W	N	E
1♠	pass	3♠	pass
4♠	pass	pass	*double*

W holds:

What is W's best opening lead? — 1

---

58 Use the chart. W holds: ♠A K ♥7 5 4 3 ♦Q 8 7 2 ♣J 7 6

S	W	N	E
pass	pass	1♠	pass
2♥	pass	2♠	pass
3♦	pass	4♦	pass
5♦	pass	pass	pass

Which is W's best opening lead?

♦Q | ♠A — 2

---

59 Look at Chart 5, *Opening Leads Against a No Trump Contract*, on page 283. If partner did not double the final contract, which box do you look at next?

Have both you and partner bid? | Did partner bid? — 3

---

60 How many cards of the same suit *rank* next to each other in a complete honor sequence?

3 | 2 — 6

61

S	W	N	E
2♦	pass	2 NT	3♠
pass	pass	3 NT	pass
4♦	pass	pass	pass

a. Who is declarer?
b. Who makes the opening lead?
c. Did dummy bid? — 4

---

62 Look at Chart 5. W holds: ♠7 3 2 ♥K Q J 10 9 ♦9 2 ♣4 3 2

N	E	S	W
1♠	pass	1 NT	pass
2 NT	pass	3 NT	pass
pass	pass		

Which is W's best opening lead?

[King of Hearts] | [7 of Spades] — 7

---

63 Look at the chart.

S	W	N	E
2♠	pass	2 NT	3♥
pass	pass	3♠	pass
4♠	pass	pass	pass

W holds:

What is W's best opening lead? — 8

---

64 Turn to the exercises on page 231. Use both Chart 4 and Chart 5 to arrive at the best opening leads for each hand. After completing this, check your answers on page 262. — 5

GO TO NEXT FRAME

1	2	3	4	5	6	7	8
♠4 (Any Spade will do.)	☐☑	☐☑	a. S b. W c. Yes		☑☐	☑☐	3 of Hearts

65 How many opening leads did you miss?

2

1	2	3	4	5	6	7	8
	3 or more, work hands again.						

TAKE UNIT 10 POST-TEST

UNIT 11

proprieties

Rules governing frequent bridge irregularities are presented. The beginning player learns the penalties invoked for playing out of turn, making an insufficient bid, and revoking. The student is also instructed in good bridge manners.

PRE- AND POST-TEST

1. If you are displeased with your partner's bid, may you tell him so during the bidding?

2. Who determines the penalty when a defender plays out of turn?

3. If you have revoked, must you admit it when you have discovered your error?

4. The penalty for offenders who take six tricks after an established revoke is __________.

5. When is a revoke established?

6. E bids insufficiently. If he changes his bid to a higher denomination in the same suit without any other intervening insufficient bid, his partner must pass. (True/False)

7. If a player makes an insufficient bid good by bidding in another suit, the penalty assigned is:
   a. defenders must lead with the suit specified by declarer.
   b. left-hand opponent must pass.
   c. (both)
   d. (neither)

8. If defender plays out of turn, which penalty may be invoked?
   (declarer may take lead/declarer may treat offending card as penalty card/both/neither)

9. Penalties for revokes are assigned for the first ( ) tricks.

10. If offenders take only one trick after a revoke is established, the nonoffenders receive ( ) trick(s).

11. In which situation would W be barred from entering the auction?

a.

N	E	S	W
	1♥		

b.

N	E	S	W
pass			1 NT

c. (both)

d. (neither)

BRIDGE PROPRIETIES

I. Do not pick up your cards before dealer finishes dealing and picks up his own cards.

II. Do not look at either opponent's hand or ask to see partner's hand when you are dummy.

III. Do not put down trumps before the opening lead is made when you are dummy.

IV. Do not engage in conversation, exclusive of proper bidding, which conveys information about a player's hand.

V. Do not vary the language used in bidding.

VI. Do not indicate the strength of your hand by a special inflection or intonation of your voice or by passing or doubling with exceptional haste or delay.

VII. Do not gather a trick before all hands have played to it.

VIII. Do not arrange tricks in an order inconsistent with the order of tricks taken.

BRIDGE LAWS *

The Lead Penalty: When declarer has the right to impose a lead penalty, he may either 1) require the offender's partner to lead a specified suit or 2) prohibit the offender's partner from leading a specified suit. This prohibition continues for as long as the offender's partner retains the lead.

The Revoke: A revoke is a failure to follow suit when able to do so.

A revoke becomes *established* when the offending side leads or plays to the next trick.

Penalties: The penalty for an established revoke is two tricks, provided that at least two tricks are taken by offenders after a revoke. This includes the trick which is taken during the revoke.

Revokes become established only on the first eleven tricks. There is no penalty for a revoke on the twelfth trick, but it must be corrected if discovered before the cards have been mixed together. Declarer or either defender, as the case may be, may then require the offender's partner to play to the twelfth trick either of the two cards he could legally have played to that trick.

* IN ACCORDANCE WITH 1963 RULES

Call Out of Turn: A call out of turn (rotation) covers passes, doubles, and redoubles, as well as bids. Unless the offender's left-hand opponent calls over the call out of turn, any call out of rotation is void. (If the left-hand opponent overcalls the offender, the penalty is waived and the auction proceeds as though no irregularity had occurred.)

Pass Out of Turn: 1) If a player passes out of turn before any player has bid, or when it is the turn of the offender's right-hand opponent, the offender must pass when his regular turn comes. 2) If a player passes out of turn after there has been a bid, and when it is the turn of offender's partner, the offender is barred from bidding throughout the auction. The offender's partner may not double or redouble at that turn, and if the offender's partner passes and the opponents play the hand, declarer may impose a lead penalty.

Bid Out of Turn: 1) If a player bids out of turn before any player has called, the offender's partner is barred from bidding throughout the auction. 2) If a player bids out of turn after any player has called, and when it is the turn of the offender's partner, the offender's partner is barred from bidding throughout the auction and is subject to a lead penalty if he has the opening lead. 3) If a player bids out of turn after any player has called, and when it is the turn of the offender's right-hand opponent, the offender must repeat his bid without penalty if his right-hand opponent passes. However, if his right-hand opponent bids, the offender may take any call and his partner is barred from bidding at his next turn.

Double or Redouble Out of Turn: 1) If a player doubles or redoubles out of turn when it is the turn of offender's partner, the partner is barred from bidding throughout the auction and is subject to a lead penalty if he has the opening lead. The offender may not double or redouble the same bid. 2) If a player doubles or redoubles out of turn when it is the turn of the offender's right-hand opponent, the offender must repeat his double or redouble without penalty if his right-hand opponent passes. However, he may make any legal call if that opponent bids, in which case the offender's partner is barred from bidding at his next turn.

Insufficient Bid: A bid which is not high enough to overcall the last previous bid.

A player making an insufficient bid must substitute a sufficient bid or a pass.

Penalties:

a. When a player makes an insufficient bid in a suit and changes to a sufficient bid in a different suit, the offender's partner must pass when it is his turn to bid.

b. When a player substitutes a pass for an insufficient bid, the offender's partner must pass. If the offending side becomes the defending side, the declarer may require or forbid the opening lead of a specified suit.

c. When a player makes an insufficient bid and changes to a sufficient bid in the same suit, no penalty is assessed against the player or his partner, provided that no unauthorized information is given by change of call.

Here are two examples of Penalty c.

1)

S	W	N	E
1♠	pass	3♠	3♥
			4♥

In this instance no penalty is assessed against East or his partner, since no unauthorized information was exchanged in East's change of call.

2)

S	W	N	E
1♠	pass	3♠	3♥
			3♣
			4♥

In this instance, however, South is permitted, should he become declarer, to apply a lead penalty against West to lead Clubs or prohibit West from leading Clubs. If East's second insufficient bid had been in No Trump, South could have required West to lead in any suit named by South.

Playing Out of Turn: If declarer leads from the wrong hand, defenders may require him to play from the correct hand.

Penalty: The incorrect lead is placed back in the hand, but declarer must lead from the same suit in the correct hand unless, of course, he has a void in that suit. In this case, he may lead any suit.

If defender plays out of turn, several penalties may be invoked.

Penalties:

a. Declarer may treat the offending card as a penalty card. In this instance, the card is placed to the side and played at the first legal opportunity.

b. Declarer may take the lead.

c. Declarer may forbid the correct leader to lead in the suit played by offender.

d. Declarer may require a lead of the suit led out of turn.

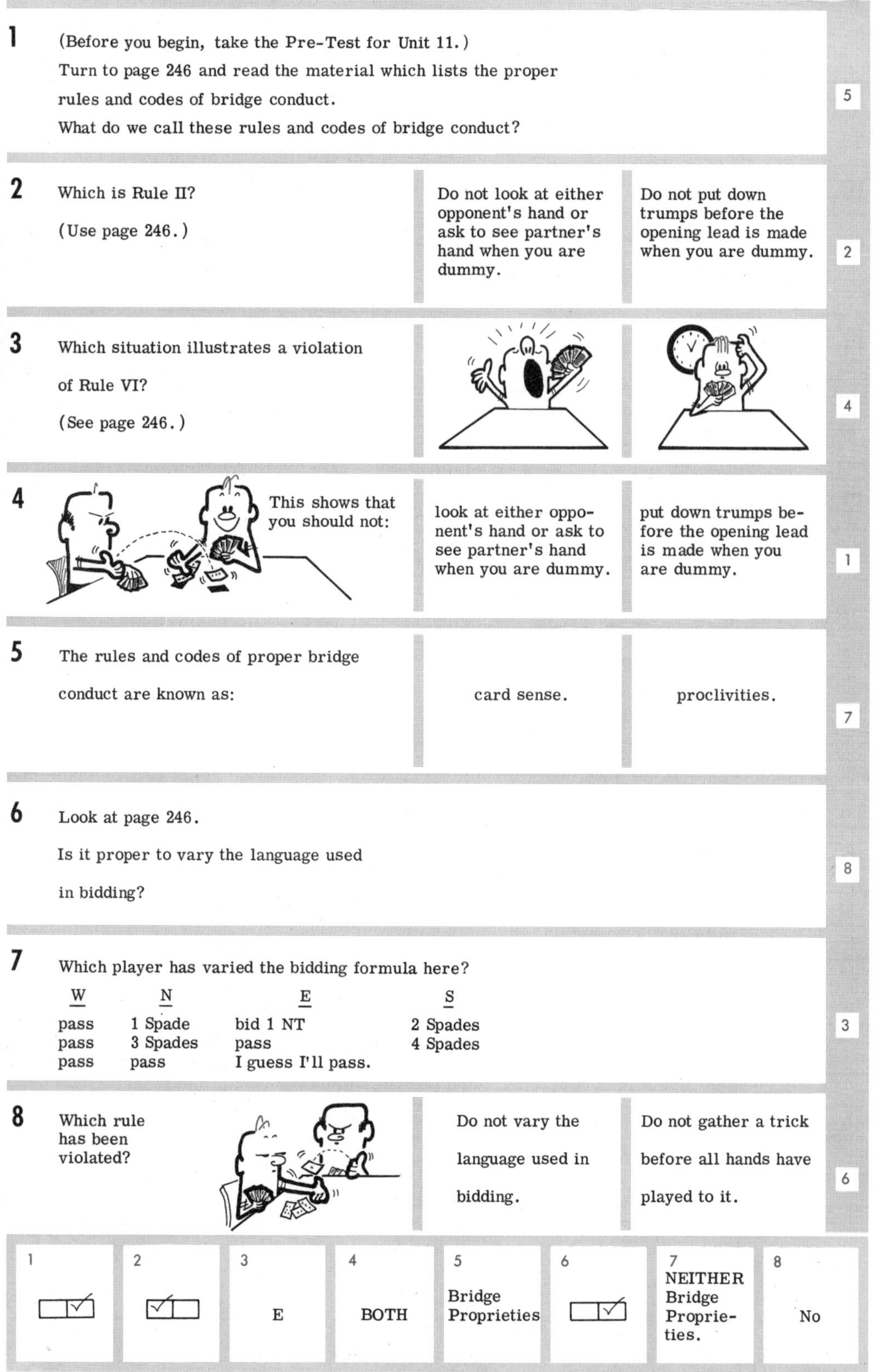

1 (Before you begin, take the Pre-Test for Unit 11.)
Turn to page 246 and read the material which lists the proper rules and codes of bridge conduct.
What do we call these rules and codes of bridge conduct? 5

2 Which is Rule II?
(Use page 246.)

Do not look at either opponent's hand or ask to see partner's hand when you are dummy.	Do not put down trumps before the opening lead is made when you are dummy.

2

3 Which situation illustrates a violation of Rule VI?
(See page 246.)

4

4 This shows that you should not:

look at either opponent's hand or ask to see partner's hand when you are dummy.	put down trumps before the opening lead is made when you are dummy.

1

5 The rules and codes of proper bridge conduct are known as:

card sense.	proclivities.

7

6 Look at page 246.
Is it proper to vary the language used in bidding? 8

7 Which player has varied the bidding formula here?

W	N	E	S
pass	1 Spade	bid 1 NT	2 Spades
pass	3 Spades	pass	4 Spades
pass	pass	I guess I'll pass.	

3

8 Which rule has been violated?

Do not vary the language used in bidding.	Do not gather a trick before all hands have played to it.

6

1	2	3	4	5	6	7	8
[ ] [✓]	[✓] [ ]	E	BOTH	Bridge Proprieties	[ ] [✓]	NEITHER Bridge Proprieties.	No

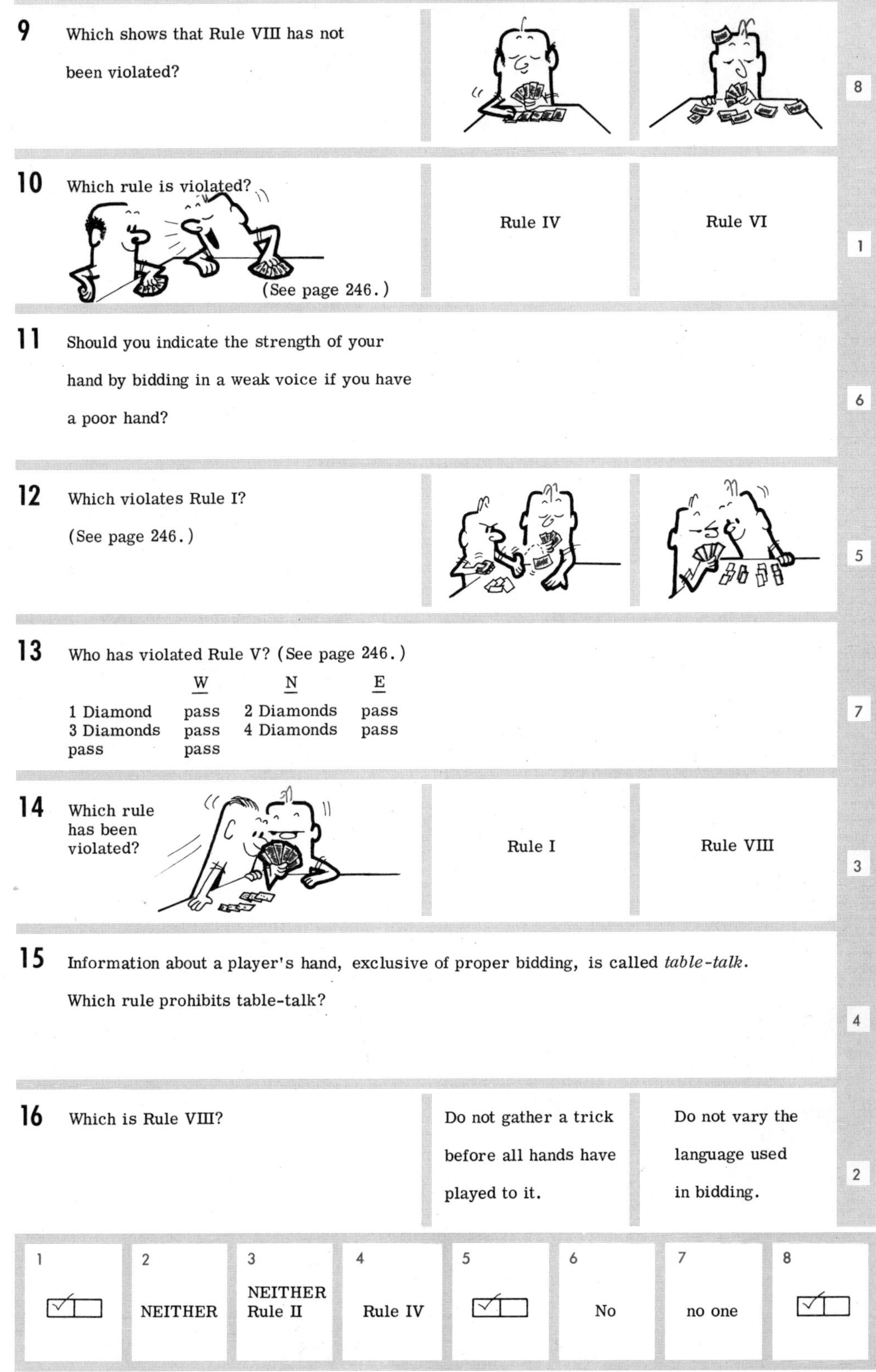

9 Which shows that Rule VIII has not been violated? 8

10 Which rule is violated? (See page 246.)

Rule IV	Rule VI

1

11 Should you indicate the strength of your hand by bidding in a weak voice if you have a poor hand? 6

12 Which violates Rule I?

(See page 246.) 5

13 Who has violated Rule V? (See page 246.) 7

	W	N	E
1 Diamond	pass	2 Diamonds	pass
3 Diamonds	pass	4 Diamonds	pass
pass	pass		

14 Which rule has been violated?

Rule I	Rule VIII

3

15 Information about a player's hand, exclusive of proper bidding, is called *table-talk*.

Which rule prohibits table-talk? 4

16 Which is Rule VIII?

Do not gather a trick before all hands have played to it.	Do not vary the language used in bidding.

2

1	2	3	4	5	6	7	8
☑☐	NEITHER	NEITHER Rule II	Rule IV	☑☐	No	no one	☑☐

17	Which is Rule VI?	Do not indicate the strength of your hand by special inflection of your voice.	Do not indicate the strength of your hand by passing or doub-ling in haste or delay.	7
18	Anything, exclusive of proper bidding, that conveys information about a player's hand is ________-________.			4
19	Which rule is being violated?	Rule VIII	Rule VII	3
20	Which of these violates Rule IV?			6
21	Look at *Bridge Laws* beginning on page 246. Which is a *revoke*?	playing out of turn	not following suit when able to do so	2
22	Which rule is violated?	Rule II	Rule VIII	8
23	Diamonds are trumps. W leads the ♥10. Which card must N play to revoke?	5♥	3♣	5
24	What is wrong here? S: 1♣ W: pass N: 1 NT E: 1♠ (Use page 247.)	revoke	insufficient bid	1

1	2	3	4	5	6	7	8
☐☑	☐☑	☐☑	table-talk	☐☑	☑☐	BOTH	NEITHER

25 Look at page 247.
Which of these indicates a bid which is not high enough to overcall the last previous bid?

insufficient bid	bid out of turn

6

26 Which is revoking?
(Clubs are trumps.)

7

27 Which is the lead penalty?
(See page 246.)

Declarer has the right to require the offender's partner to lead a specified suit.	Declarer has the right to prohibit the offender's partner from leading a specified suit.

1

28 Is there a penalty for revoking?
(See page 246.)

3

29 Which law has been violated?
See page 247.

Insufficient Bid	Bid Out of Turn

2

30 How many tricks must offenders turn over to nonoffenders if offenders revoke?
(Use page 246.)

1	3

5

31 A call refers to any bid, pass, double, or redouble.
In which situation has S called?

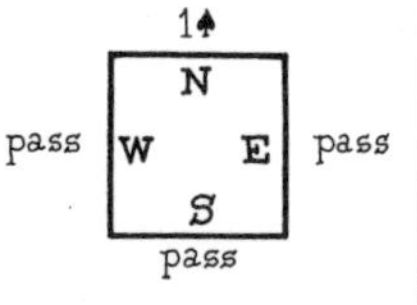

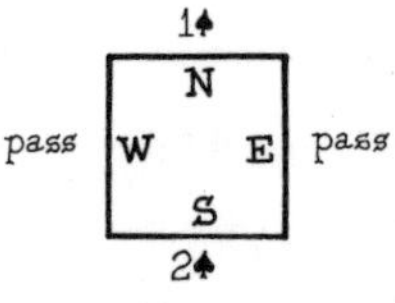

8

32 Any call out of rotation is void unless the offender's left-hand opponent calls over it before attention is drawn to the irregularity.
Which call out of rotation is cancelled?
(North opened in each case.)

4

1	2	3	4	5	6	7	8
BOTH	BOTH	Yes	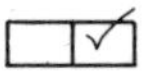	NEITHER		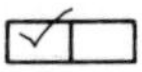	BOTH

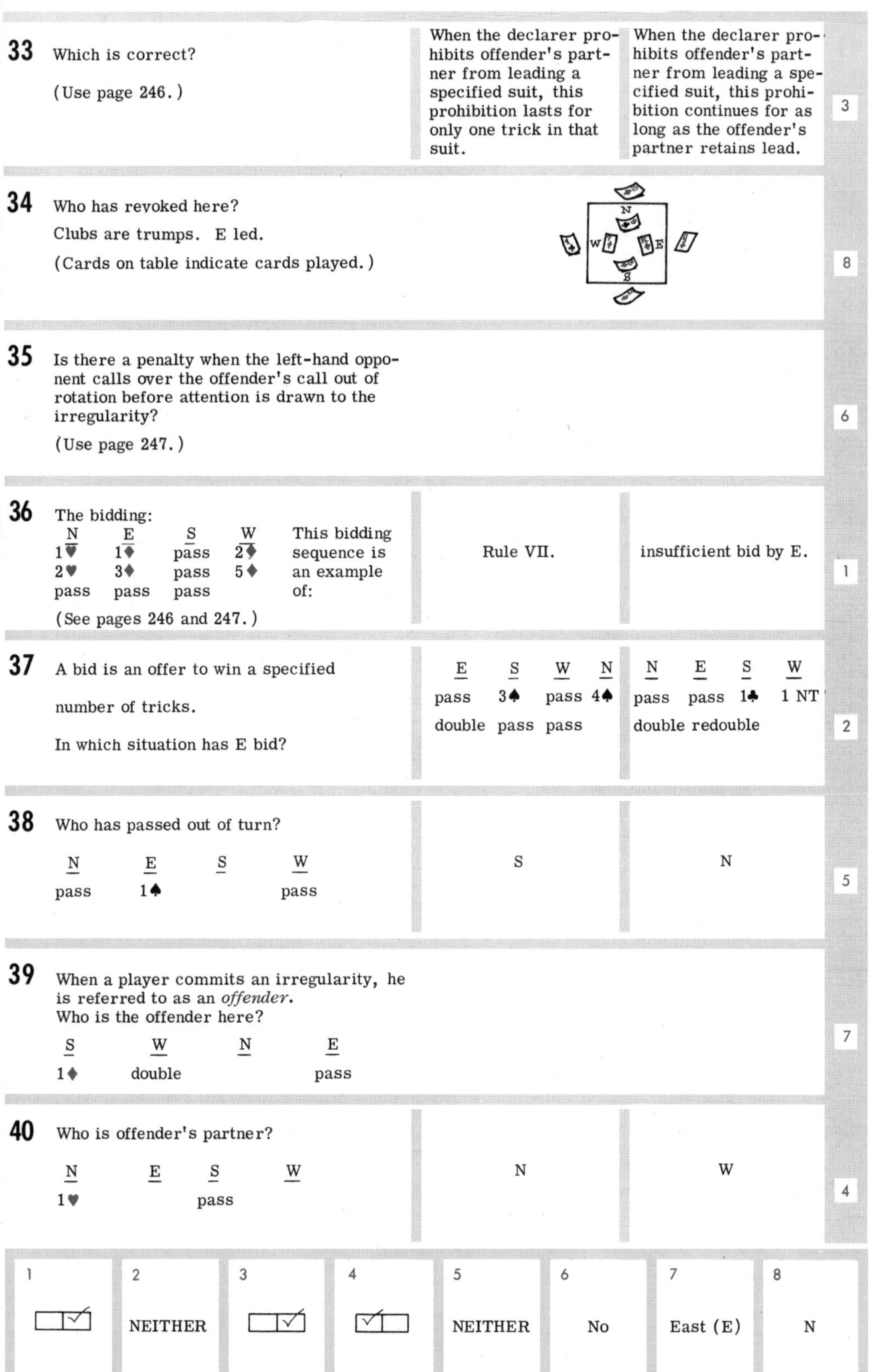

33 Which is correct?

(Use page 246.)

When the declarer prohibits offender's partner from leading a specified suit, this prohibition lasts for only one trick in that suit.	When the declarer prohibits offender's partner from leading a specified suit, this prohibition continues for as long as the offender's partner retains lead.

3

34 Who has revoked here?

Clubs are trumps. E led.

(Cards on table indicate cards played.)

8

35 Is there a penalty when the left-hand opponent calls over the offender's call out of rotation before attention is drawn to the irregularity?

(Use page 247.)

6

36 The bidding:

N	E	S	W
1♥	1♦	pass	2♦
2♥	3♦	pass	5♦
pass	pass	pass	

This bidding sequence is an example of:

(See pages 246 and 247.)

Rule VII.	insufficient bid by E.

1

37 A bid is an offer to win a specified number of tricks.

In which situation has E bid?

E	S	W	N
pass	3♠	pass	4♠
double	pass	pass	

N	E	S	W
pass	pass	1♣	1 NT
double	redouble		

2

38 Who has passed out of turn?

N	E	S	W
pass	1♠		pass

S	N

5

39 When a player commits an irregularity, he is referred to as an *offender*. Who is the offender here?

S	W	N	E
1♦	double		pass

7

40 Who is offender's partner?

N	E	S	W
1♥		pass	

N	W

4

1	2	3	4	5	6	7	8
☐☑	NEITHER	☐☑	☑☐	NEITHER	No	East (E)	N

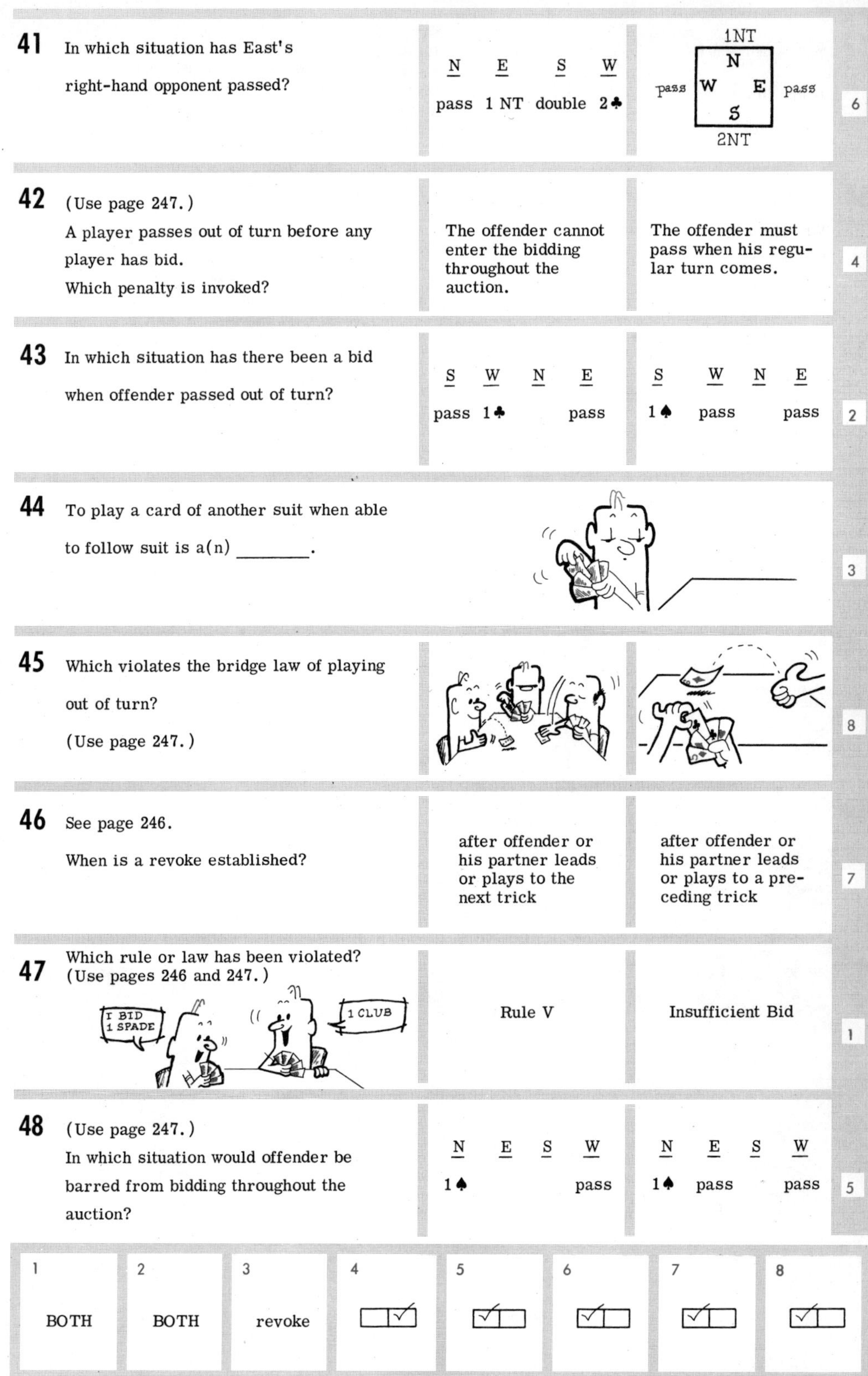

41 In which situation has East's right-hand opponent passed?

N	E	S	W
pass	1 NT	double	2♣

1NT (N); pass (W); pass (E); 2NT (S)

6

42 (Use page 247.)
A player passes out of turn before any player has bid.
Which penalty is invoked?

The offender cannot enter the bidding throughout the auction.

The offender must pass when his regular turn comes.

4

43 In which situation has there been a bid when offender passed out of turn?

S	W	N	E
pass	1♣		pass

S	W	N	E
1♠	pass		pass

2

44 To play a card of another suit when able to follow suit is a(n) ________.

3

45 Which violates the bridge law of playing out of turn?
(Use page 247.)

8

46 See page 246.
When is a revoke established?

after offender or his partner leads or plays to the next trick

after offender or his partner leads or plays to a preceding trick

7

47 Which rule or law has been violated?
(Use pages 246 and 247.)

Rule V

Insufficient Bid

1

48 (Use page 247.)
In which situation would offender be barred from bidding throughout the auction?

N	E	S	W
1♠			pass

N	E	S	W
1♠	pass		pass

5

1	2	3	4	5	6	7	8
BOTH	BOTH	revoke	☐☑	☑☐	☑☐	☑☐	☑☐

49 Which penalty would be invoked?

N	E	S	W
1♠	pass		pass

(Use page 247.)

W must pass when it is his regular turn.	W is barred from the bidding throughout the auction.

1

---

50 What is a bid called which is not high enough to overcall the last previous bid?

4

---

51 (Use page 247.)

When a player bids out of turn:

the offender's partner cannot enter the auction if offender bid *before* any player called.	the offender's partner cannot enter the auction if offender bid *after* any player called and when it was the turn of offender's partner.

2

52

This situation shows that:

the declarer is invoking the lead penalty.	a defender is telling declarer he cannot lead Spades.

7

---

53 Which is a revoke?

(Hearts are trumps.)

8

---

54 Which is a possible penalty if declarer leads from the wrong hand?

(See page 248.)

Declarer may treat offending card as a penalty card.	Declarer may take the lead.

3

---

55 Which law has been violated?

S	W	N	E
1♥	pass	2♠	2♦
3♥	pass	pass	pass

6

---

56 Which is correct?

(Use page 246.)

Revokes become established only on the first eleven tricks.	No penalty is assessed for a revoke on the twelfth trick.

5

1	2	3	4	5	6	7	8
☑☐	BOTH	NEITHER	insufficient bid	BOTH	insufficient bid	☑☐	BOTH

57 Read Sentence c. of the insufficient bid on page 247.

In which situation might the lead penalty be imposed?

3

58 Which violates Rule VI of the bridge proprieties?

5

59 Who would be prevented from entering the auction?

S	W	N	E
pass			1♥

(Use page 247.)

8

60

S	W	N	E
pass	1♦		1♦

1) Who is offender?
2) Who is offender's right-hand opponent?
3) Who is offender's partner?

4

61 In which situation is a penalty assessed for an insufficient bid?

1

62 If a player bids out of turn before any player has called, or after any player has called when it is the turn of the offender's partner, which penalty is appropriate?

(Use page 247.)

There is no penalty if right-hand opponent passes.

Offender cannot enter the auction.

2

63 Spades are trumps. Which rule or law has been violated?

Rule V

revoking

7

64 Which is the penalty here?

S	W	N	E
pass	1♠		1 NT

(Use page 247.)

There is no penalty if N decides to pass.

If N bids, then W cannot bid on the second round.

6

1	2	3	4	5	6	7	8
☐ ☑	NEITHER	☑ ☐	1) E 2) N 3) W	☑ ☐	BOTH	☐ ☑	W

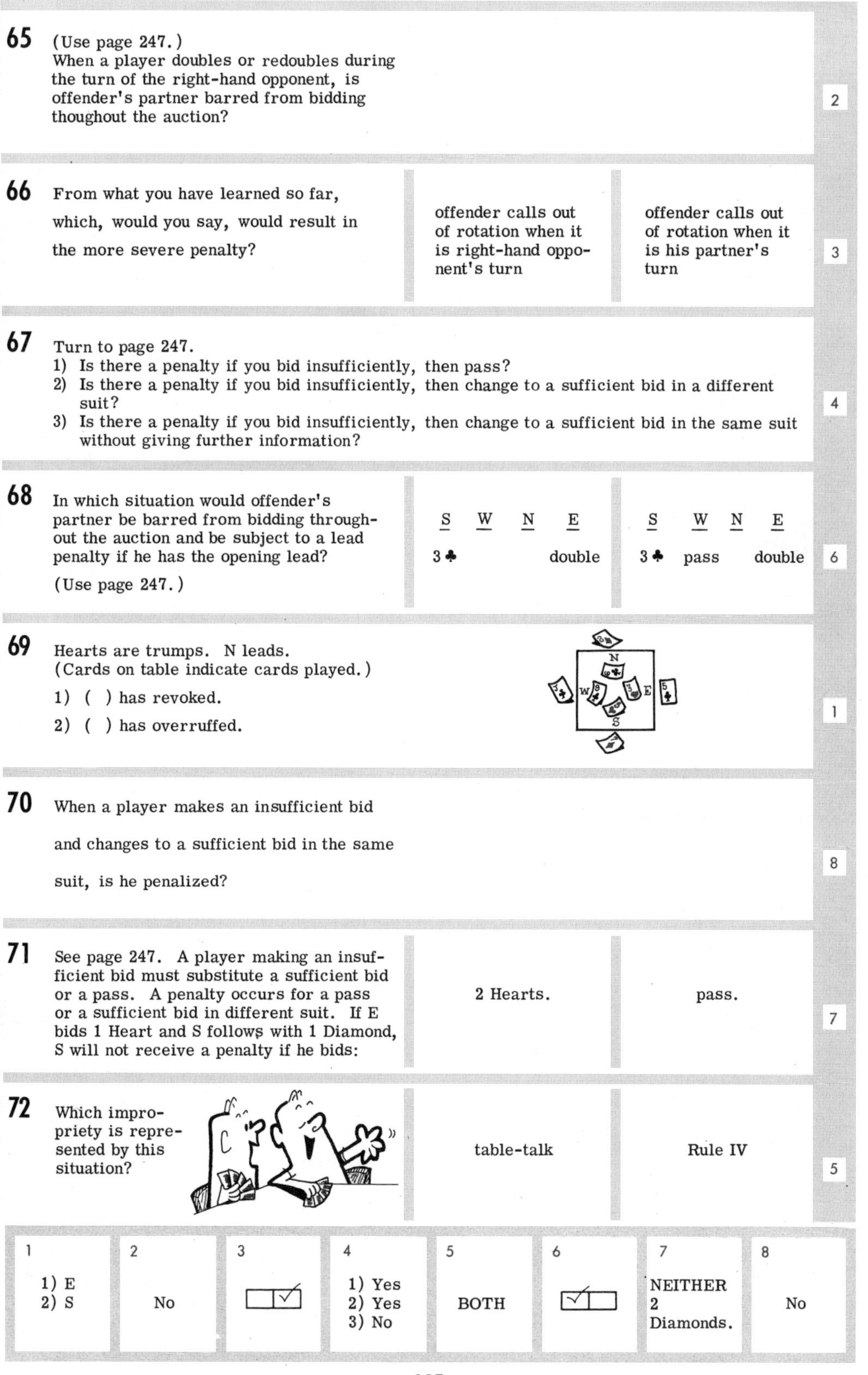

65 (Use page 247.)
When a player doubles or redoubles during the turn of the right-hand opponent, is offender's partner barred from bidding thoughout the auction? 2

66 From what you have learned so far, which, would you say, would result in the more severe penalty?

offender calls out of rotation when it is right-hand opponent's turn	offender calls out of rotation when it is his partner's turn

3

67 Turn to page 247.
1) Is there a penalty if you bid insufficiently, then pass?
2) Is there a penalty if you bid insufficiently, then change to a sufficient bid in a different suit?
3) Is there a penalty if you bid insufficiently, then change to a sufficient bid in the same suit without giving further information? 4

68 In which situation would offender's partner be barred from bidding throughout the auction and be subject to a lead penalty if he has the opening lead?
(Use page 247.)

S	W	N	E
3 ♣			double

S	W	N	E
3 ♣	pass		double

6

69 Hearts are trumps. N leads.
(Cards on table indicate cards played.)
1) ( ) has revoked.
2) ( ) has overruffed. 1

70 When a player makes an insufficient bid and changes to a sufficient bid in the same suit, is he penalized? 8

71 See page 247. A player making an insufficient bid must substitute a sufficient bid or a pass. A penalty occurs for a pass or a sufficient bid in different suit. If E bids 1 Heart and S follows with 1 Diamond, S will not receive a penalty if he bids:

2 Hearts.	pass.

7

72 Which impropriety is represented by this situation?

table-talk	Rule IV

5

1	2	3	4	5	6	7	8
1) E 2) S	No	☐☑	1) Yes 2) Yes 3) No	BOTH	☑☐	NEITHER 2 Diamonds.	No

73 If only one trick is taken by the offenders after a revoke, then one trick is transferred to the ________. 7

74 (Use page 247.)
In which bidding situation is E subject to the lead penalty if he makes the opening lead?

N	E	S	W
3♣			double

N	E	S	W
3♣	pass		double

6

75

N	E	S	W
	1♥		

Which penalty is invoked for this irregularity? (Use page 247.)

East's partner is barred throughout the bidding.

If East makes the opening lead, he is subject to a lead penalty.

8

76 Which is a call?

pass or double

bid

1

77 Offenders take 6 tricks after establishing a revoke. How many tricks must they transfer to opponents?
(See page 246.)

3

1

4

78 If a player commits a revoke on the twelfth trick and the revoke is discovered before the cards are mixed together, may opponents require offender's partner to play either of the two cards he could legally have played to the twelfth trick?
(Use page 246.) 5

79 Read page 248.
A penalty card is a card which:

is placed to the side and played at the first legal opportunity.

cannot be played at all.

2

80 A player revokes on the twelfth trick.
This means that:

he must give opponents two tricks.

he must give opponents one trick.

3

1	2	3	4	5	6	7	8
BOTH	[✓][ ]	NEITHER There is no penalty for a revoke here.	NEITHER 2	Yes	[ ][✓]	nonoffenders (their opponents)	[✓][ ]

81 Who determines the penalty when a defender plays out of turn?	declarer	the player who first bid the suit the contract is played in	5
82 When offender's left-hand opponent calls over the call out of turn:	the call out of rotation is void.	the call out of rotation is cancelled.	8
83 When you have revoked, you are under no obligation to tell opponents. This means:	It will become obvious that a revoke has been committed during subsequent play of the hand.	You do not have to admit committing a revoke.	3

1	2	3	4	5	6	7	8
		BOTH		BOTH			NEITHER The call is allowed to stand.

TAKE UNIT 11 POST-TEST

EXERCISE ANSWERS

UNIT FIVE

1. Yes

2. Yes. In order to establish the suit, play the high card in the short hand first. In this instance play the Ace. On the second round of play you may lead toward either the King or Queen because they are in sequence.

3. The opponents have 7 cards in Spades. Since the most probable split is 4-3, the probability is high that the Queen of Spades will be the highest card in the opponent's hand which holds the 4 cards. Therefore, the Queen will not fall to either the King or Ace.

4. do not play for a drop

5. 6

UNIT SEVEN

1. 9 points - pass

   (Your hand does not have an adequate number of points to open the bidding.)

2. 12 points - pass

   (You must deduct 1 point for the doubleton Jack.)

3. 14 points - 1 Club

   (You contain sufficient points for a mandatory bid. Your best bid is 1 Club.)

4. 8 points - pass

   (Deduct 1 point for aceless hand.)

5. 15 points - 1 Diamond

   (You have enough points for a mandatory bid. Follow the rule of bidding the longest suit.)

6. 23 points - 2 No Trump

   (You have a 4-3-3-3 distribution with protection in all 4 suits.)

7. 12 points - pass

   (You must deduct 1 point for the doubleton Queen.)

UNIT SEVEN (Continued)

8. 16 points - 1 Club

   (Bid the suit below the shortest suit.)

9. 15 points - 1 Spade

   (You hold 10 high cards and 5 distribution points. Your biddable suit below the shortest suit is Spades.)

10. 21 points - 2 Spades

    (You have a strong 7-card suit in Spades and 21 points. Your best opener is Spades.)

11. 16 points - 1 Diamond

    (Remember, bid the suit below the shortest suit, in this case Diamonds.)

12. 26 points - 2 Hearts

    (Your hand contains a strong 5-card suit and 26 points; therefore, a bid of 2 of that suit is desirable.)

UNIT EIGHT

1. 7 points - 2 Hearts

   (The hand has a long 7-card suit in Hearts. The unequal distribution of the hand does not permit a No Trump response.)

2. 9 points - 2 No Trump

   (Since partner's opener is 1 No Trump, you count only high-card points. The hand contains 2 Aces. A 2 No Trump bid is your response.)

3. 10 points - 3 Spades

   (Your hand has a strong Spade suit with 10 high-card points. The 3 Spade response will allow partner to rebid and you to follow with a 4 No Trump on the next round.)

4. 9 points - 4 No Trump

   (Since all suits are equally distributed and you hold 9 high-card points, your best response is 4 No Trump asking partner to bid 6 NT if he has the maximum 24 pts.)

UNIT EIGHT (Continued)

5. 16 points - 2 Diamonds

   (Since you do not have trump support for partner's suit, your best response is 2 of a lower-RANKING suit.)

6. 12 points - 2 Diamonds

   (Don't discourage partner with a single raise in his suit. Bid outside and raise next round.)

7. 4 points - 2 No Trump

   (Your response of 2 No Trump indicates to partner that you have a very poor hand. 1 point was deducted for 4-3-3-3 distribution.)

8. 12 points - 3 Diamonds

   (Your 5-card suit with 5 high-card points places your response at the 3-Diamond level.)

9. 24 points - 3 Diamonds

   (Your answering bid tells partner that you possess 19 or more points.)

10. 8 points - 1 Heart

    (You hold only 7 points after deductions. In order to keep the bidding open, respond 1 Heart.)

11. 7 points - 1 Heart

    (Your singleton is worth 3 dummy points. This value and the Ace of Spades permits a courtesy bid.)

12. 14 points - 1 Heart

    (You have 13 high-card points and 2 points for the two doubletons. But you must deduct from the doubleton Jack since it does not have sufficient protection.)

13. 17 points - 3 Spades

    (Since you have excellent support for partner's bid suit, raise partner from 1 to 3.)

14. 15 points - 2 Diamonds

    (Your two singletons are worth 6 dummy points. This added to your high-card value gives you a sufficient number of points to respond with 2 Diamonds.)

UNIT TEN

1. 5 of Spades (♠5) - Since partner did not bid, your best lead is in the suit with 4 or more cards.

2. 3 of Spades (♠3) - Partner's double may be interpreted as a call for a lead in his suit. Since you hold four cards in partner's suit, lead the fourth highest card.

3. 6 of Diamonds (♦6) - Declarer bid a suit which dummy did not support. Your best suit is not the same as declarer's; therefore, lead from the suit with at least 4 cards to the Queen.

4. Queen of Diamonds (♦Q) - Since dummy had a suit not supported by declarer and you hold an honor sequence in that suit, lead the top of the sequence.

5. Queen of Hearts (♥Q) - Your best bet is to open from the top of your complete honor sequence in Hearts.

6. King of Hearts (♥K) - Since you hold an honor sequence, lead the top of that sequence.

7. 3 of Diamonds (♦3) - Your best lead is the lowest from the suit which partner bid.

8. Queen of Clubs (♣Q) - Since your partner bid in a Club suit and you have an honor sequence in that suit, your best lead is the top of that sequence.

9. Ace of Clubs (♣A) - Due to your holding of surplus trumps and the A-K doubleton, your best lead is from the top of the honor sequence.

10. King of Diamonds (♦K) - Your complete honor sequence in Diamonds necessitates the lead of the King.

PRE- AND POST-TEST ANSWERS

UNIT ONE

1. two
2. 52
3. Clubs, Diamonds, Hearts, Spades
4. Yes
5. ♠K ♦10 ♠6 ♥10
6. ♦J
7. E
8. opponents
9. E
10. a.
11. S E
12. E shuffles the other deck and places it to the right.
13. S
14. left

UNIT TWO

1. E
2. W
3. S
4. must play ♠K
5. may play either the ♥2 or the ♣3
6. may play either the ♦A or the ♦3
7. W (♠9)
8. N (♦2)

UNIT TWO (Continued)

9. E (♦Q)
10. N (♥2)
11. E (♣10)
12. 4
13. ducking
14. to lead
15. N

UNIT THREE

1. d. 10 tricks
2. b. 5 tricks
3. E
4. E bid out of turn.
5. 1 Club is an insufficient bid.
6. The bidding is over when N passes.
7. Yes
8. a. 4 Spades
   b. S
   c. S
   d. N
9. a. 2 Hearts
   b. N
   c. E
10. a. S
    b. W
11. 3

UNIT FOUR

1. rubber
2. part-score
3. a. 5 d. 5
   b. 3 e. 4
   c. 4
4. Yes
5. 500
6. 100
7. grand slam
8. True
9. a. above e. above
   b. above f. above
   c. below g. above
   d. below
10. slam
11. c.
12. vulnerable
13. 700
14.

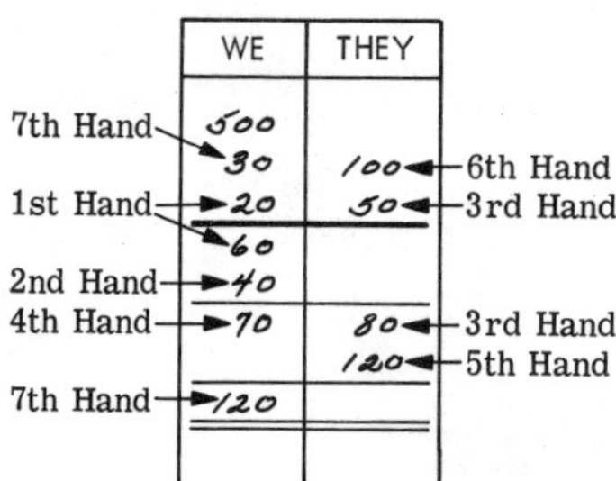

15. WE
16. WE - 490 points

UNIT FIVE

1. 4-2
2. 3
3. b
4. 1) a.
   2) b.
5. 2
6. (both)
7. 3-1; 2-2
8. 3
9. (both)
10. c. both
11. a. tenace
    b. sequence
12. d. neither
13. only one hand
14. play for a drop
15. a. 3
    b. 6
    c. greater than
    d. Yes

UNIT SIX

1. (neither)
2. finesse
3. a. E
   b. N"
   c. toward
4. Jack, Queen

UNIT SIX (Continued)

5. a.

♦ A K 3

Dummy
Declarer

♦ J 10 4

6. lead an honor

7. ruffing

8. Yes

UNIT SEVEN

1. 40

2. a.

3. a. 3 b. 3 c. 1 d. 4 e. 2

4. Queen

5. 14

6. (both)

7. opening bidder

8. a. 2 b. 4 c. 2 d. 6 e. 4

9. Diamonds (♦K 2)

10. $\frac{1}{2}$

11. $4\frac{1}{2}$

12. a. 23 points
1 Diamond

e. 18 points
1 No Trump

b. 9 points
pass

f. 15 points
1 Heart

c. 16 points
1 Club

g. 23 points
2 Hearts

d. 12 points
pass

UNIT EIGHT

1. a. 6 points 2 Hearts
b. 2 points pass
c. 8 points 1 Spade
d. 12 points 2 Diamonds

2. 4

3. any face card or the ten of a suit

4. trump support

5. Promotion of honors in partner's suit occurs when you have trump support in partner's suit and raise in partner's suit.

6. $2\frac{1}{2}$

7. high-card points

8. 9 points

9. courtesy response

10. convention

11.

	Trump Support	No Trump Support
Void	5	3
Doubleton	1	1
Singleton	3	2

12. Dummy points are special points assigned to voids and singletons when you have trump support for partner's bid suit.

13. (both)

14. (neither)

15. free bid

16. 6 points

17. only in response to partner's bid

18. high-card points

19. quick tricks

20. True

21. a.

22. d. neither

UNIT NINE

1. (both)
2. 29 points
3. 26
4. neither
5. 10 points
6. a. IV. 2)
   b. II. 3)
   c. I. 4)
   d. III. 1)
7. Ace
8. both
9. a. 37 points
   b. 33 points
10. 26 points

UNIT TEN

1. d. (neither)
2. Clubs
3. a. N
   b. E
   c. Yes
4. a. No
   b. Yes
5. a. 5 of Diamonds (♦5)
   b. 8 of Hearts (♥8)

UNIT ELEVEN

1. No
2. declarer
3. No
4. two tricks
5. A revoke becomes established when the offending side leads or plays to the next trick.
6. False
7. (neither)
8. both
9. 11
10. 1
11. a.

GLOSSARY

ABOVE THE LINE: The place on the score sheet where premiums and penalties are scored.

AUCTION: The period when the bidding takes place.

BELOW THE LINE: The place on the score sheet where the game score is entered.

BID: An offer to win a specified number of tricks in play.

BIDDABLE SUIT: A suit that contains at least four cards and three points.

BOOK: The first six tricks taken by declarer.

CALL: Any bid - a bid, double, redouble, or pass.

CLUBS: The minor suit denoted by the symbol ♣.

CONTRACT: The last bid during the auction.

CONTRACTORS: The team which makes the final bid.

CONVENTION: A bid which conveys an arbitrary meaning.

COURTESY BID: An answering bid required of responder to partner's opener if opponent passes and responder has a minimum of 6 points in his hand.

COVER: To play a higher card than has already been played in the suit led.

DEAL: To distribute the cards, one at a time to the four players, in clockwise rotation.

DEALER: The player who deals. Also the opening caller.

DECK: The 52 bridge cards.

DECLARER: The first member of the contractors to name the trump suit.

DEFEAT THE CONTRACT: To prevent the declarer from winning the number of tricks bid. Also SET THE CONTRACT.

DEFENDERS: Opponents of the contractors.

DIAMONDS: A minor suit denoted by the symbol ♦.

DISTRIBUTION: Division of cards among the hands, especially the number of each suit held by each hand. In No Trump bidding, the suits should be distributed into one of the following patterns: 4-3-3-3, 4-4-3-2, 5-3-3-2.

DOUBLE: 1. Penalty Double - a bid which indicates that you think you can defeat opponents. Also BUSINESS DOUBLE.

2. Take-Out Double - a convention bid that requires your partner to bid.

DOUBLETON: A holding of two cards of a suit.

DOWN: Failure to make contract. A player is *down one* if he fails by one trick, *down two* if he fails by two tricks, and so on.

DRAW TRUMPS: To lead trumps until opponents have none left. Also PULL TRUMPS.

DUCK: To play a card lower than has already been played in the suit led.

DUMMY: Declarer's partner. His hand is placed on the board and played by declarer.

ENTRY: A trick-taking card that enables you to enter the hand from which you wish to lead.

FINESSE: An attempt to win a trick with a card which is lower than an outstanding card.

FREE BID: A bid by responder when opponent bids between opening bidder and responder. Responder needs at least 9 points in order to answer partner.

GAME: A score of 100 or more points below the line.

GRAND SLAM: The winning of all thirteen tricks.

GUARDIAN: Small cards used to protect lower honors until they are good. See "PROTECTION."

HEARTS: A major suit denoted by the symbol ♥.

HONOR: The Ace, King, Queen, Jack, or Ten of a suit.

HONOR WINNER: An honor backed by sufficient guardians to assure that it will take a trick.

INSUFFICIENT BID: A bid that is not high enough to overcall the previous bid.

LONG-CARD WINNERS: The extra small cards in a long suit which may become winners after the honors are played.

NO TRUMP: A bid for play without trumps. The value of the cards is established by their face, and the suit led cannot be superseded.

OPENER: The player who makes the first bid.

OPENING BID: The first bid.

OPENING LEAD: The lead to the first trick made by left-hand opponent of declarer.

OVERRUFF: To play a higher trump than one already played to the same trick.

OVERTRICK: Each trick won in excess of those contracted.

PART SCORE: A score for tricks bid and made which is less than game.

PASS: A bid which expresses the wish of a player not to enter the auction at that point.

PENALTIES: Points scored above the line for setting a contract.

PRE-EMPTIVE BID: A bid made at the level of three or higher to shut out competition.

PREMIUMS: Scores awarded overtricks, grand and small slams, and so forth.

PROTECTION: Small cards which guard honors. If higher honors are led, you can play the guardians rather than an honor. (For example: The King needs 1 card in order to be protected, a Queen, 2 cards, and so on.)

PUNT: Leading the top of worthless 3-card suit, doubleton, or singleton, preferably in a major suit, when no good offensive or defensive lead is available.

QUICK TRICK: An honor that can take a trick within the first two rounds. (See page 286.)

RANK: The ordinal position of a card within a suit (e.g., the 6 is higher than the 5) or the ordinal position of the suits themselves (e.g., Clubs are lower than Diamonds).

RESPONDER: The partner of an opening bidder.

RESPONSE: Answering bid.

REVOKE: The failure to follow suit when able to do so.

RUBBER: The winning of the first two-out-of-three games by one side.

RUFF: To play a trump when another suit is led.

SCORE: The total number of points won by a side.

SEQUENCE: Two cards, ranking next to each other, held in one suit.
1. Honor Sequence: Two honors, ranking next to each other, in one suit.
2. Complete Sequence: Three or more cards, ranking next to each other, in one suit.
3. Complete Honor Sequence: Three or more honors, ranking next to each other, in one suit.

SET: To defeat, as in DEFEAT THE CONTRACT.

SINGLETON: An original holding of one card of a suit.

SMALL SLAM: The winning of twelve tricks by one side.

SPADES: A major suit denoted by the symbol ♠.

SPLIT: Refers to the distribution of the cards. "Opponents' Clubs were split 5-1."

STOPPER: A high honor which can stop an opponent from running a suit. (e.g., the King protected with one small card is a stopper.)

SUFFICIENT BID: A bid high enough to supersede the previous bid.

SURPLUS TRUMP: A small trump which is not needed to protect an honor holding.

TENACE: An honor holding directly above and below some honor held by an opponent.

TRICK: The four cards led and contributed by the four players in a round of play.

TRUMP SUIT: One of the four suits which has greater trick-taking power than any of the other three suits.

VOID: No cards of a particular suit.

VULNERABLE: Refers to increased penalties for failure to make contract after completing first game of a rubber.

INDEX

Parenthesized numbers refer to frames. This index references only the first frame in which each item is mentioned in the course.

UNIT 12

charts

HOW TO USE THE CHARTS

Each chart starts with an *ENTER* box. Follow the arrow to the next box or boxes which show how to count your hand for the best use of the chart. Following the arrow down into the chart itself, you first come to a box with white type in a black background. This box will ask if your hand totals a certain number of points. If the answer is *No,* follow the *No* arrow until you reach a box where the required point count agrees with the count in your hand. Then follow the *Yes* and *No* arrows through the other question boxes until you come to the last box of that sequence. That box tells you the best way to bid or play your hand.

Suppose you are the opening bidder and this is your hand:

Refer to Chart 1: *OPENING BIDS.* Following the arrow from the *ENTER* box, you first assign honor-winner points as listed in the first box. You have 23 honor-winner points. The arrow then leads to a box listing distribution points. You have 2 distribution points. The next arrow leads to a box which shows what combinations should deduct points from your hand (x denotes any small card). The deduction from this hand is 0 points. 23 + 2 - 0 = 25 total points.

Now follow the arrow down into the main part of the chart. The first box with white on a black background asks *28 or more pts?* You do not have 28 or more points, so you follow the *No* arrow to the next black box to read *25-27 pts?* You have 25 points, so you follow the *Yes* arrow down to the box which asks *Are suits equally protected and distributed, containing 25-27 high-card pts?* ① The symbol ① means you should turn to the *REFERENCES* on page 287. Check number 1 to assure correct appraisal of your hand. Only 23 of your points are high-card points, so you follow the *No* arrow to the next box to read *Does hand have strong 5-card suit and 25 pts, and lack only 1 trick of game?* Your hand agrees with this, so you follow the *Yes* arrow to the last box, which tells you to *Bid 2 of that suit and go to game*. Your opening bid is "2 Hearts."

This is how you worked through the chart:

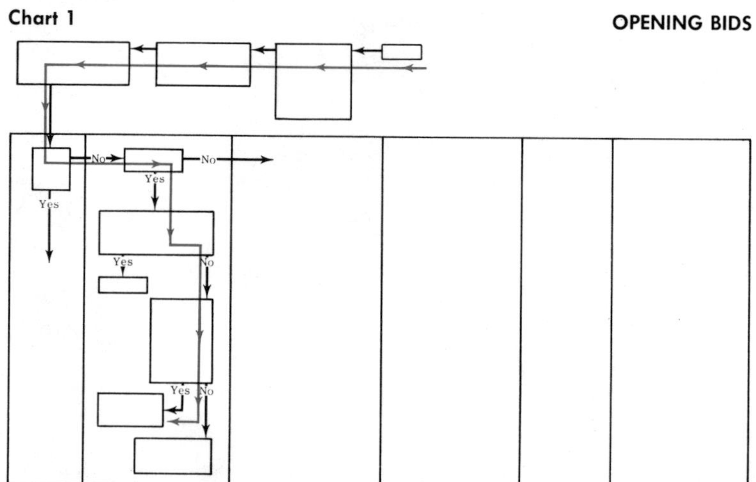

Suppose that you are the responding partner to the opening bid of 2 Hearts. This is your hand:

Refer to Chart 2: *RESPONSES TO OPENING SUIT BIDS.* Following the arrow from the *ENTER* box you are asked to *Count high-card pts and special distribution (dummy) pts, and promote honors.*[4] Your hand totals 8 points. The arrow then leads to the box asking *Is partner first opener?* Your partner was the opening bidder so you follow the *Yes* arrow down into the main chart to the first black box. This asks *Did partner open 1 of a suit?* He did not, so you follow the *No* arrow to the next box which asks *Did partner open 2 of a suit?* He did, so you follow the *Yes* arrow down to the box that asks *7 or more pts?* You have 8 points so you follow the *Yes* arrow to the next box which asks if you have *Adequate trump support?* Your Hearts are inadequate so you follow the *No* arrow to the box which asks *5-card suit and 3 high-card pts?* Your Clubs are a 5-card suit and you have 6 high-card points so you follow the *Yes* arrow to the last box which tells you to *Bid strong suit.* You bid "3 Clubs."

This is how you worked through the chart:

Chart 2 **RESPONSES TO OPENING SUIT BIDS**

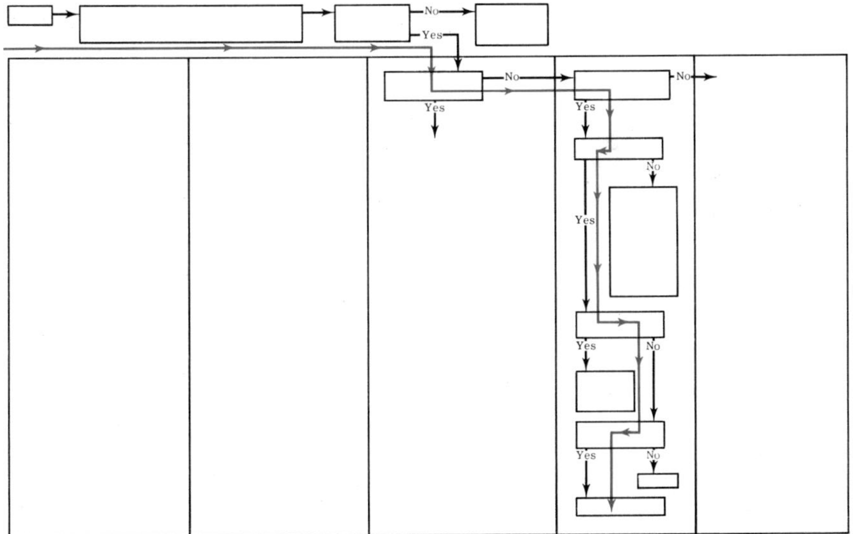

Chart 1

OPENING BIDS

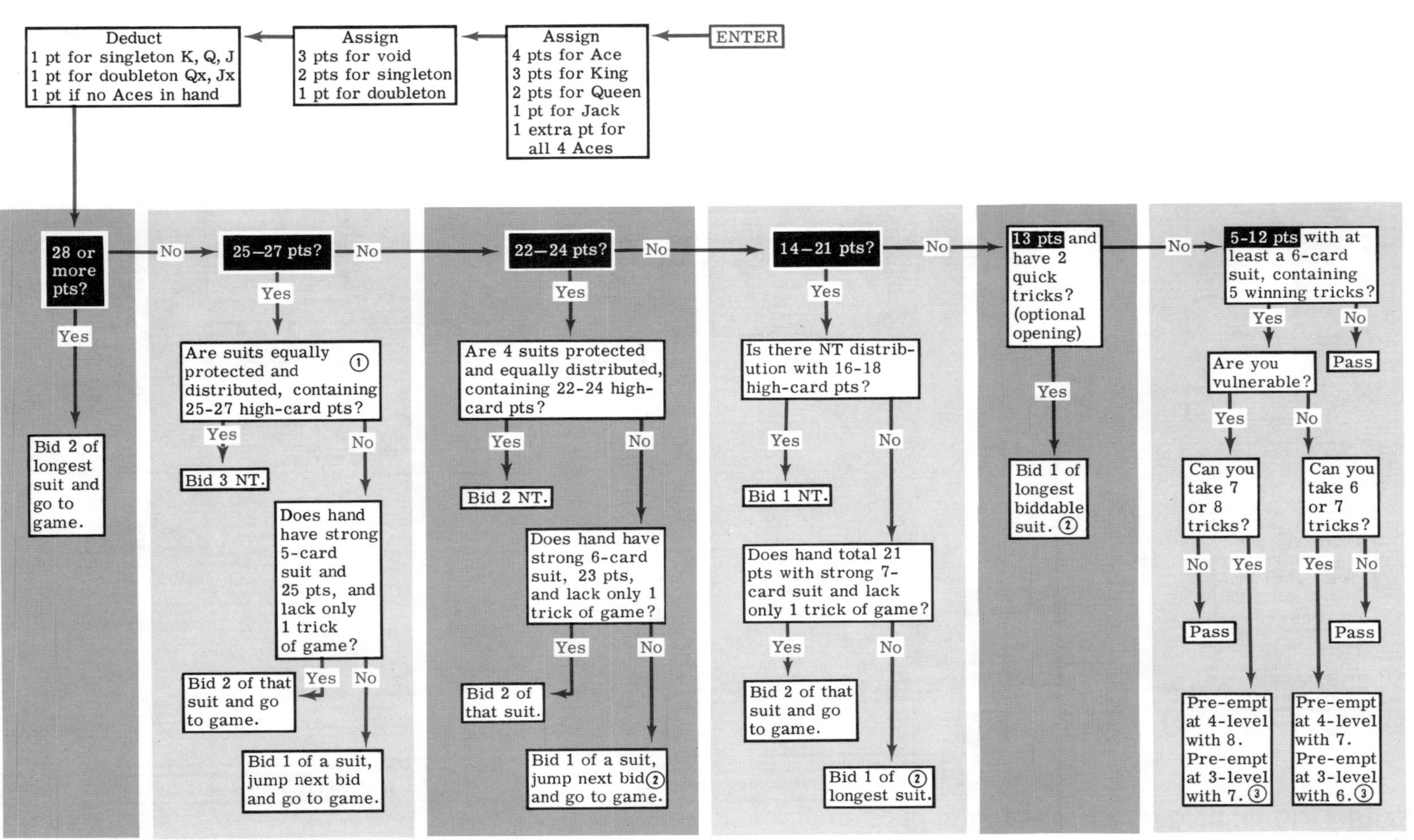

Chart 2

RESPONSES TO OPENING SUIT BIDS

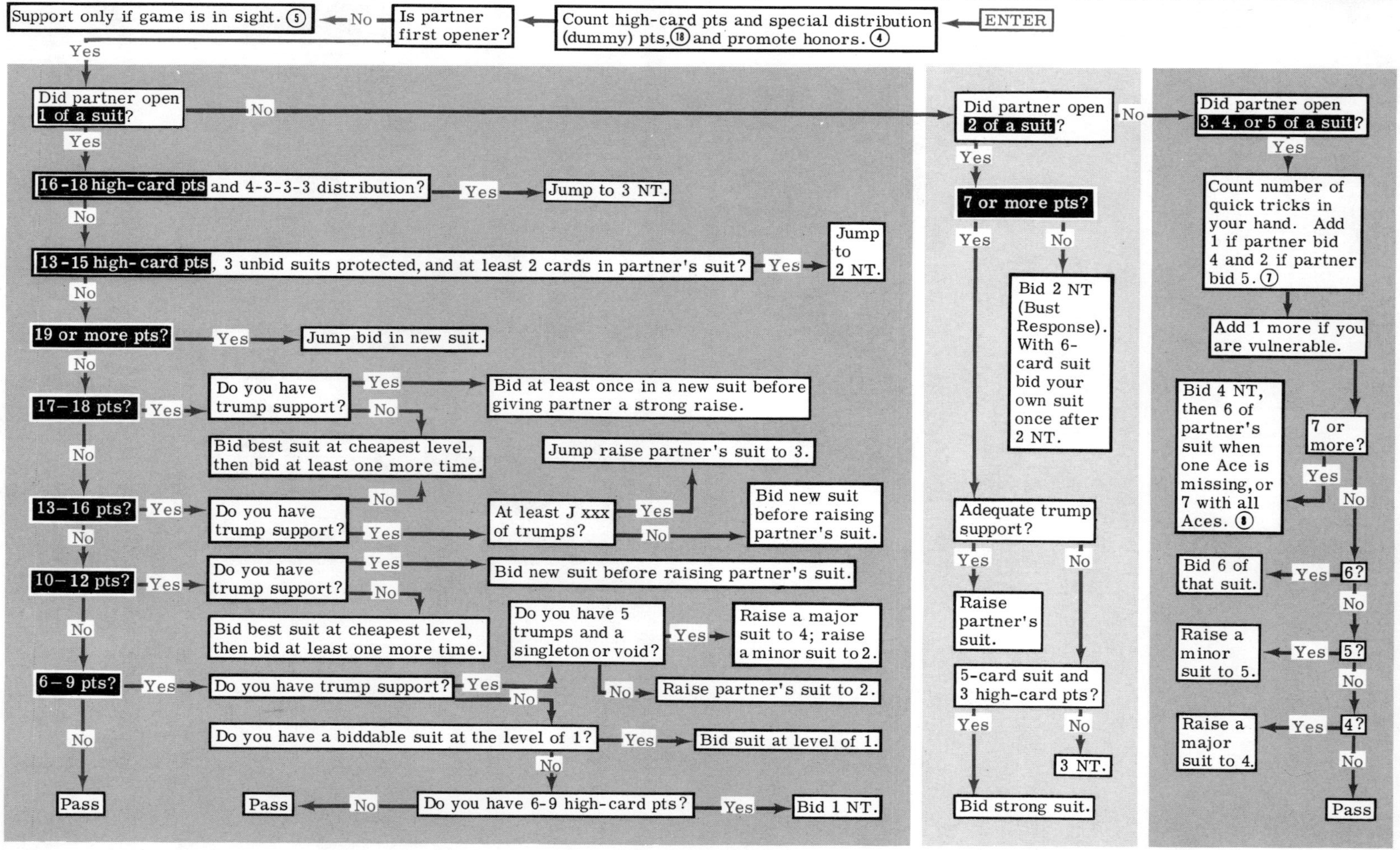

ENTER → Count high-card pts and special distribution (dummy) pts, (18) and promote honors. (4)

→ Is partner first opener?
- No → Support only if game is in sight. (5)
- Yes → Did partner open **1 of a suit**?

Did partner open 1 of a suit?
- No → Did partner open 2 of a suit?
- Yes → **16-18 high-card pts** and 4-3-3-3 distribution?
  - Yes → Jump to 3 NT.
  - No → **13-15 high-card pts**, 3 unbid suits protected, and at least 2 cards in partner's suit?
    - Yes → Jump to 2 NT.
    - No → **19 or more pts?**
      - Yes → Jump bid in new suit.
      - No → **17–18 pts?**
        - Yes → Do you have trump support?
          - Yes → Bid at least once in a new suit before giving partner a strong raise.
          - No → Bid best suit at cheapest level, then bid at least one more time.
        - No → **13–16 pts?**
          - Yes → Do you have trump support?
            - No → Bid best suit at cheapest level, then bid at least one more time.
            - Yes → At least J xxx of trumps?
              - Yes → Jump raise partner's suit to 3.
              - No → Bid new suit before raising partner's suit.
          - No → **10–12 pts?**
            - Yes → Do you have trump support?
              - Yes → Bid new suit before raising partner's suit.
              - No → Bid best suit at cheapest level, then bid at least one more time.
            - No → **6–9 pts?**
              - Yes → Do you have trump support?
                - Yes → Do you have 5 trumps and a singleton or void?
                  - Yes → Raise a major suit to 4; raise a minor suit to 2.
                  - No → Raise partner's suit to 2.
                - No → Do you have a biddable suit at the level of 1?
                  - Yes → Bid suit at level of 1.
                  - No → Do you have 6-9 high-card pts?
                    - Yes → Bid 1 NT.
                    - No → Pass
              - No → Pass

Did partner open 2 of a suit?
- No → Did partner open 3, 4, or 5 of a suit?
- Yes → **7 or more pts?**
  - No → Bid 2 NT (Bust Response). With 6-card suit bid your own suit once after 2 NT.
  - Yes → Adequate trump support?
    - Yes → Raise partner's suit.
    - No → 5-card suit and 3 high-card pts?
      - Yes → Bid strong suit.
      - No → 3 NT.

Did partner open 3, 4, or 5 of a suit?
- Yes → Count number of quick tricks in your hand. Add 1 if partner bid 4 and 2 if partner bid 5. (7)
  → Add 1 more if you are vulnerable.
  → 7 or more?
  - Yes → Bid 4 NT, then 6 of partner's suit when one Ace is missing, or 7 with all Aces. (8)
  - No → 6?
    - Yes → Bid 6 of that suit.
    - No → 5?
      - Yes → Raise a minor suit to 5.
      - No → 4?
        - Yes → Raise a major suit to 4.
        - No → Pass

Chart 3

RESPONSES TO OPENING NO TRUMP BIDS

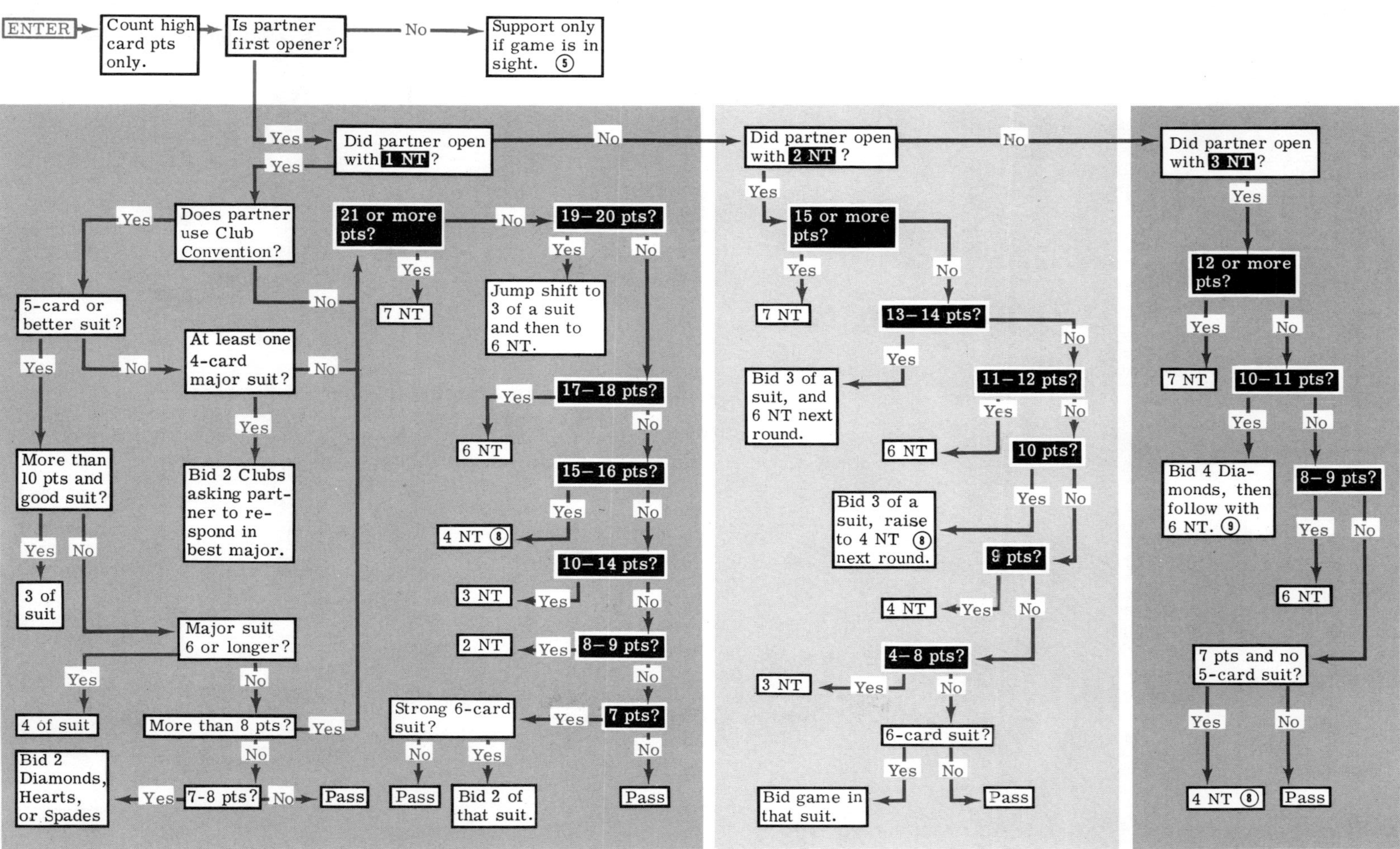

Chart 4

OPENING LEADS AGAINST A SUIT CONTRACT

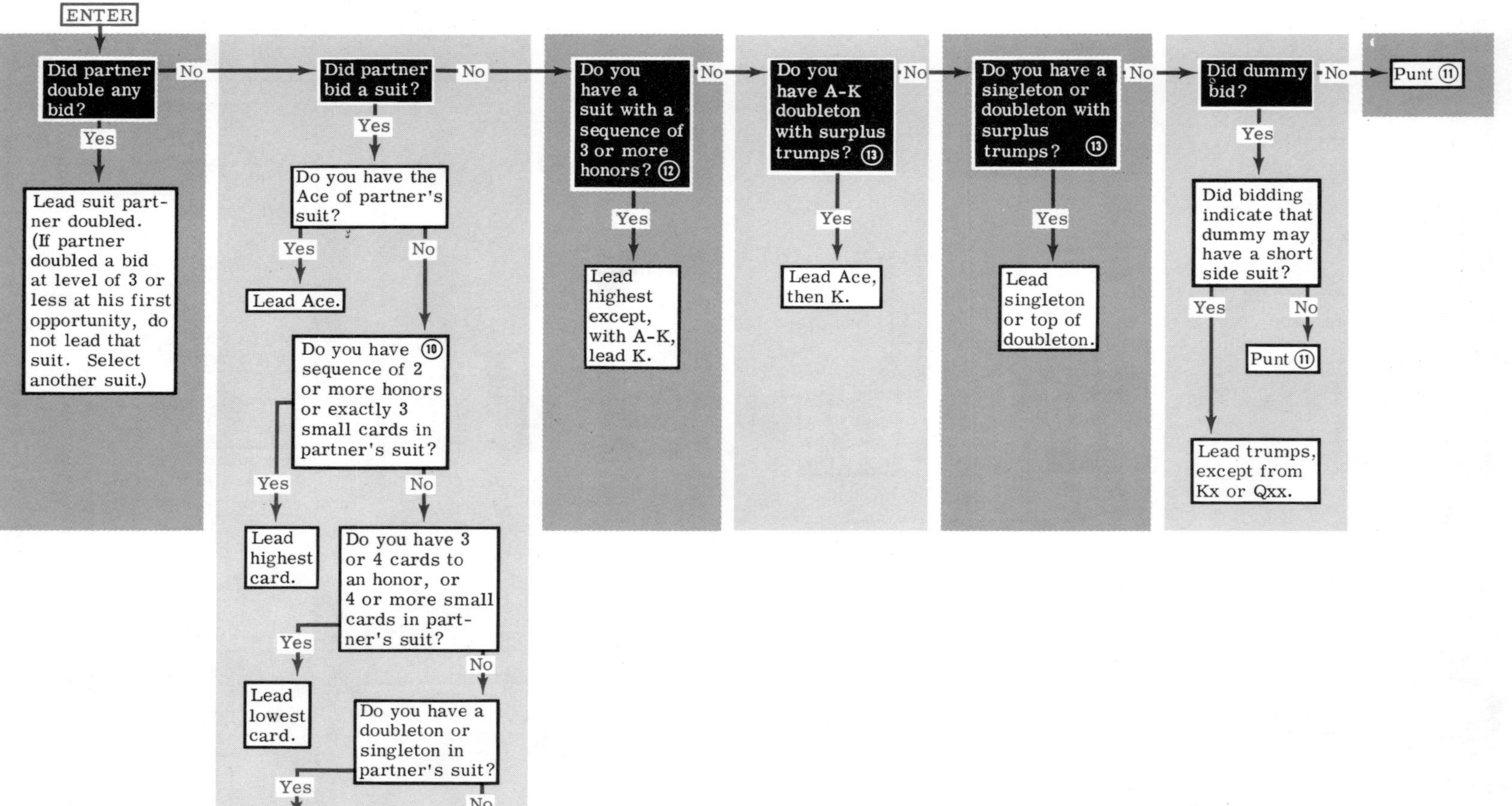
ENTER
Did partner double any bid?
Yes
Lead suit partner doubled. (If partner doubled a bid at level of 3 or less at his first opportunity, do not lead that suit. Select another suit.)
No
Did partner bid a suit?
Yes
Do you have the Ace of partner's suit?
Yes
Lead Ace.
No
Do you have sequence of 2 or more honors or exactly 3 small cards in partner's suit? (10)
Yes
Lead highest card.
No
Do you have 3 or 4 cards to an honor, or 4 or more small cards in partner's suit?
Yes
Lead lowest card.
No
Do you have a doubleton or singleton in partner's suit?
Yes
Lead singleton or top of doubleton.
No
Punt (11)
No
Do you have a suit with a sequence of 3 or more honors? (12)
Yes
Lead highest except, with A-K, lead K.
No
Do you have A-K doubleton with surplus trumps? (13)
Yes
Lead Ace, then K.
No
Do you have a singleton or doubleton with surplus trumps? (13)
Yes
Lead singleton or top of doubleton.
No
Did dummy bid?
Yes
Did bidding indicate that dummy may have a short side suit?
Yes
Lead trumps, except from Kx or Qxx.
No
Punt (11)
No
Punt (11)

CAUTION- PANELS ACROSS TOP OF THIS CHART DO NOT NECESSARILY INDICATE ORDER OF PRIORITY. ANY ONE OF THESE MAY BE THE BEST SELECTION IN A GIVEN SITUATION.

Chart 5

OPENING LEADS AGAINST A NO TRUMP CONTRACT

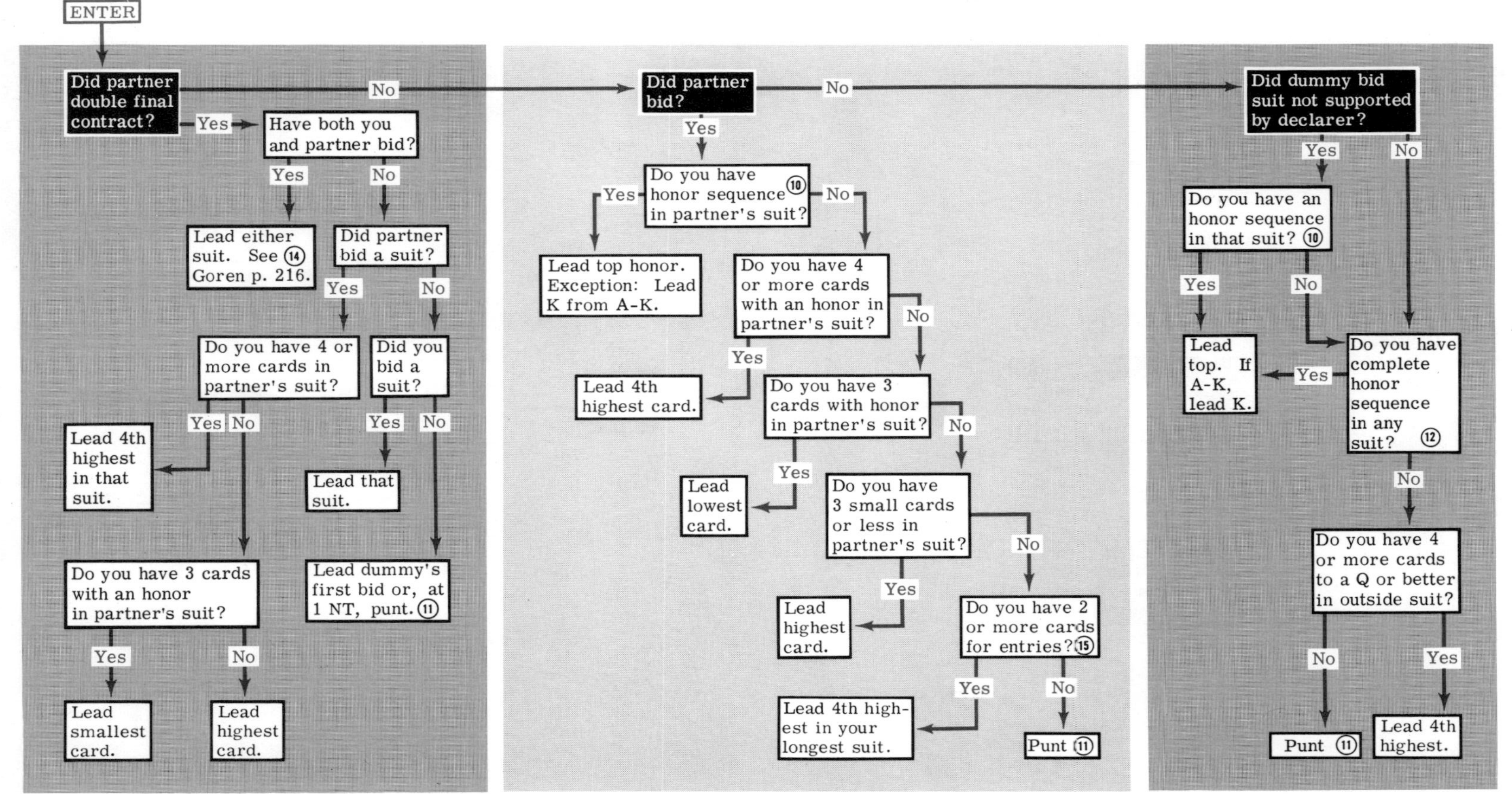

CAUTION- ORDER OF LEADS SHOWN HERE MAY NOT ALWAYS BE BEST. AS YOU GAIN EXPERIENCE YOU WILL BE ABLE TO DETERMINE WHICH IS BETTER FOR ANY GIVEN SITUATION.

Chart 6

REBIDS BY EITHER PARTNER

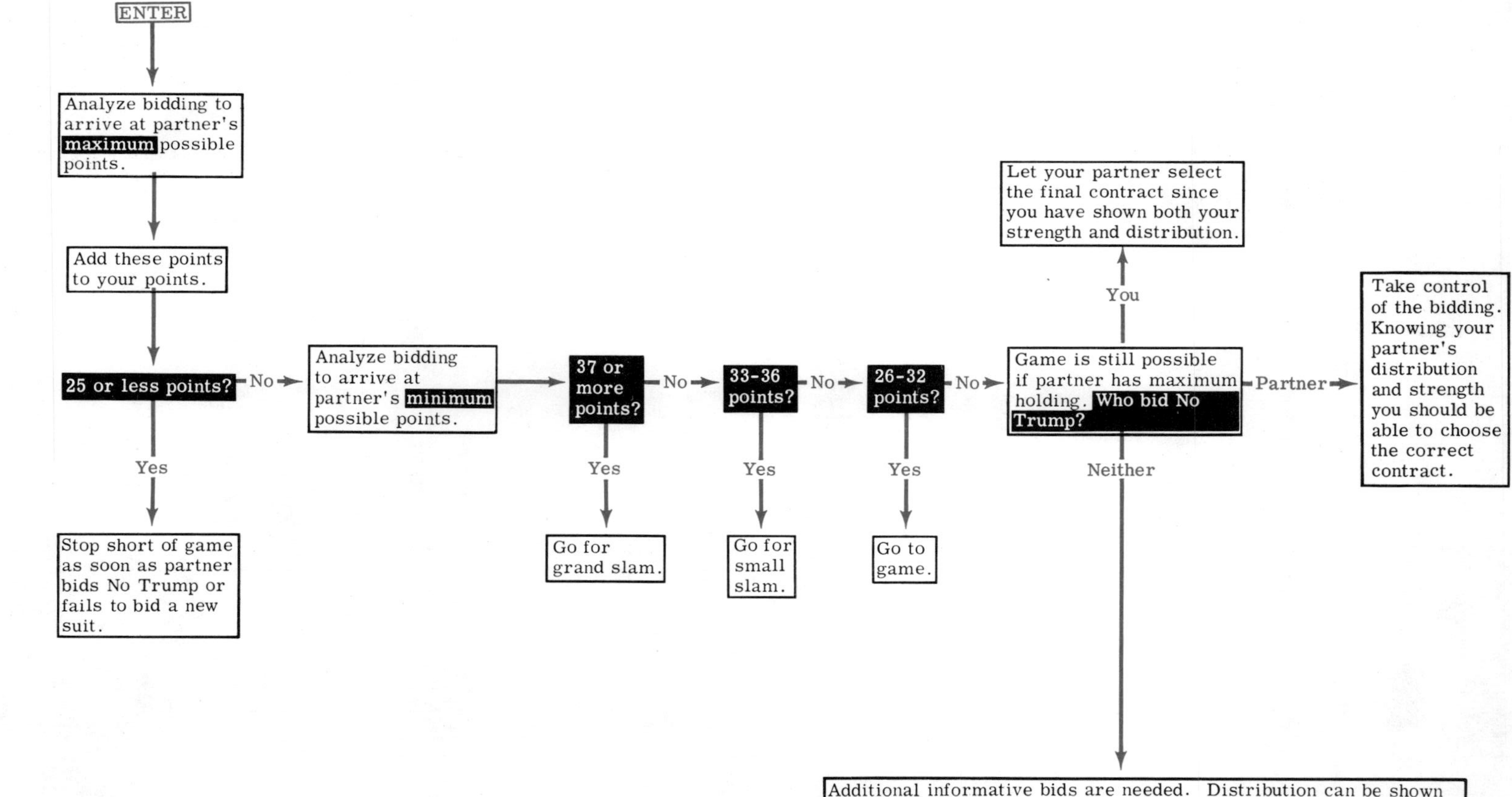

ENTER
Analyze bidding to arrive at partner's maximum possible points.
Add these points to your points.
25 or less points?
No
Yes
Stop short of game as soon as partner bids No Trump or fails to bid a new suit.
Analyze bidding to arrive at partner's minimum possible points.
37 or more points?
No
Yes
Go for grand slam.
33-36 points?
No
Yes
Go for small slam.
26-32 points?
No
Yes
Go to game.
Game is still possible if partner has maximum holding. Who bid No Trump?
You
Let your partner select the final contract since you have shown both your strength and distribution.
Partner
Take control of the bidding. Knowing your partner's distribution and strength you should be able to choose the correct contract.
Neither
Additional informative bids are needed. Distribution can be shown by supporting partner's suit, bidding a new suit, rebidding your suit, or bidding No Trump. Additional strength may be shown by jump shifts, jump raises, or bidding a new suit.

Chart 7

PLAY OF A SUIT CONTAINING AT LEAST ONE HONOR

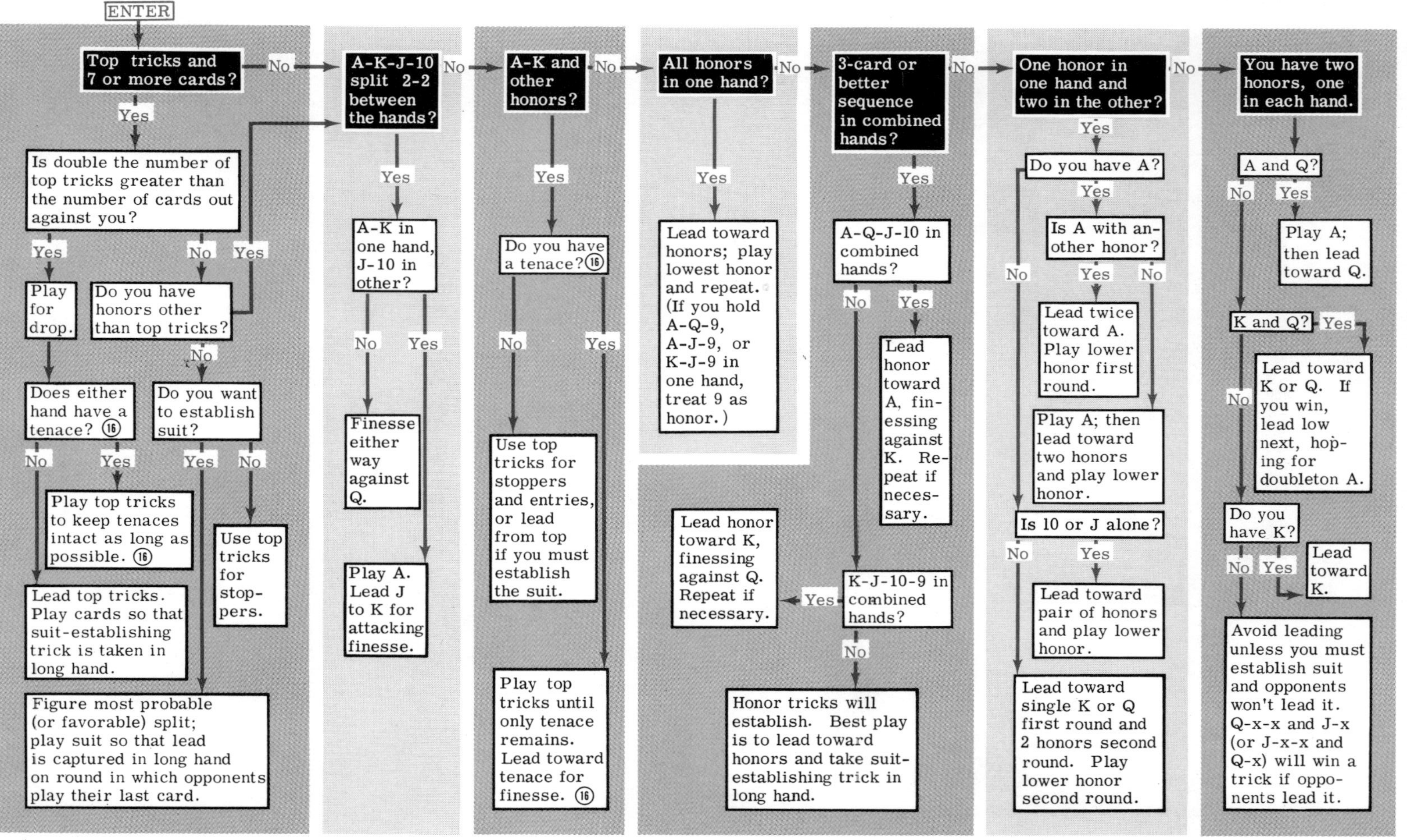

ENTER
Top tricks and 7 or more cards?
Yes
No
Is double the number of top tricks greater than the number of cards out against you?
Yes
No
Yes
Play for drop.
Do you have honors other than top tricks?
No
Does either hand have a tenace? (16)
No
Yes
Play top tricks to keep tenaces intact as long as possible. (16)
Lead top tricks. Play cards so that suit-establishing trick is taken in long hand.
Do you want to establish suit?
Yes
No
Use top tricks for stoppers.
Figure most probable (or favorable) split; play suit so that lead is captured in long hand on round in which opponents play their last card.
A-K-J-10 split 2-2 between the hands?
Yes
No
A-K in one hand, J-10 in other?
No
Yes
Finesse either way against Q.
Play A. Lead J to K for attacking finesse.
A-K and other honors?
Yes
No
Do you have a tenace? (16)
No
Yes
Use top tricks for stoppers and entries, or lead from top if you must establish the suit.
Play top tricks until only tenace remains. Lead toward tenace for finesse. (16)
All honors in one hand?
Yes
No
Lead toward honors; play lowest honor and repeat. (If you hold A-Q-9, A-J-9, or K-J-9 in one hand, treat 9 as honor.)
3-card or better sequence in combined hands?
Yes
No
A-Q-J-10 in combined hands?
No
Yes
Lead honor toward A, finessing against K. Repeat if necessary.
K-J-10-9 in combined hands?
Yes
No
Lead honor toward K, finessing against Q. Repeat if necessary.
Honor tricks will establish. Best play is to lead toward honors and take suit-establishing trick in long hand.
One honor in one hand and two in the other?
Yes
No
Do you have A?
No
Yes
Is A with another honor?
Yes
No
Lead twice toward A. Play lower honor first round.
Play A; then lead toward two honors and play lower honor.
Is 10 or J alone?
No
Yes
Lead toward pair of honors and play lower honor.
Lead toward single K or Q first round and 2 honors second round. Play lower honor second round.
You have two honors, one in each hand.
A and Q?
No
Yes
Play A; then lead toward Q.
K and Q?
Yes
No
Lead toward K or Q. If you win, lead low next, hoping for doubleton A.
Do you have K?
No
Yes
Lead toward K.
Avoid leading unless you must establish suit and opponents won't lead it. Q-x-x and J-x (or J-x-x and Q-x) will win a trick if opponents lead it.

Chart 8 ESTABLISHING TRICKS BY RUFFING ⑰

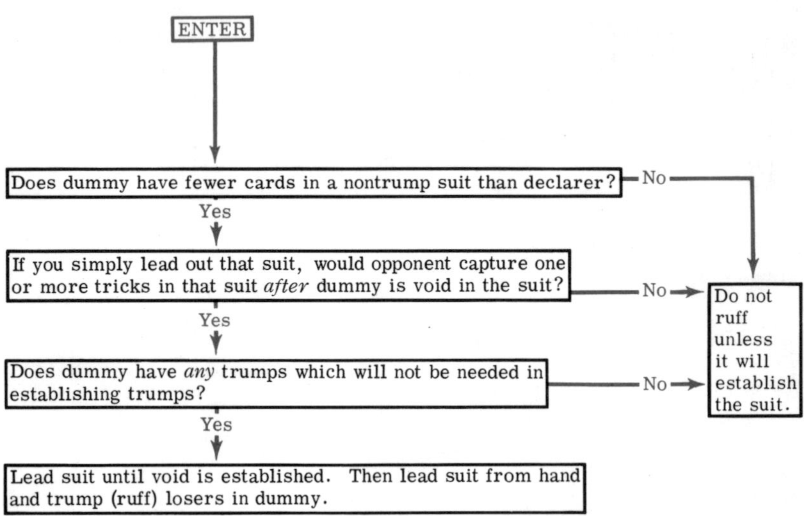

TABLE OF QUICK TRICKS ⑦

2 Quick Tricks	$1\frac{1}{2}$ Quick Tricks	1 Quick Trick	$\frac{1}{2}$ Quick Trick
AK	AQ	A	Kx
—	—	KQ	—

REFERENCES

1. PROTECTION - Cards which are guarded by others: e.g., a King needs 1 card to protect it, a Queen 2 cards, and so on.

2. If hand contains two 5- or 6-card suits, bid higher ranking suit. For exception, see Goren p. 11 and 12.[14] If hand contains two or three 4-card biddable suits, bid the suit that ranks below shortest suit in hand. For exception, see Goren p. 11.[14]

3. PRE-EMPTIVE BID - A bid made at level of 3 or higher to shut out competition. Must be able to take within 2 tricks of bid if vulnerable and 3 tricks if nonvulnerable.

4. HONOR PROMOTION - Add 1 high-card point to the value of each honor in partner's suit to a total of 4 high-card points: e.g., the King becomes 4, the Queen becomes 3, and so forth. Do not raise Ace, A-K, or K-J, since they already total 4 points.

5. You may support as a defensive measure when not vulnerable against vulnerable opponents even if game is not in sight.

6. If your biddable suit is lower ranking than partner's, and you have adequate trump support with only 6-10 points, raise partner.

7. QUICK TRICK - In order for a trick to qualify as *quick,* it must be able to win on the first two rounds. (See Table of Quick Tricks on page 286.)

8. BLACKWOOD - A system of Ace- and King-showing to reach slams. For explanation of this convention see Goren p. 127.[14]

9. For players using Gerber's 4-Club Convention, bid 4 Diamonds on first response. For explanation of the convention see Goren p. 134.[14]

10. SEQUENCE - Two cards held in one suit, ranking next to each other.

11. PUNT - Lead top of worthless 3-card suit, a doubleton, or a singleton, preferably in a major suit.

12. COMPLETE SEQUENCE - Three or more cards held in one suit which rank next to each other.

13. SURPLUS TRUMP - A small trump which is useless as a guardian.

14. Goren, Charles H. *Goren's New Contract Bridge Complete,* New York: Doubleday, 1957.

15. ENTRY - A trick-taking card that enables you to enter the hand from which you wish to lead.

16. TENACE - Having an honor holding directly above and below some honor held by an opponent. (Both honors must be held in the same hand.)

17. RUFFING - Playing a trump when you cannot follow suit.

18. SPECIAL DUMMY POINTS - If you have 4 high-card points in *trump suit,* add 1 point. Add 1 point for each doubleton, 3 points for each singleton, and 5 points for each void. Take away 1 point for only 3 trumps, 1 point for 4-3-3-3 distribution, and 1 point for unguarded honor.